State Legislatures: An Evaluation of Their Effectiveness

The Citizens Conference on State Legislatures

The Praeger Special Studies program—utilizing the most modern and efficient book production techniques and a selective worldwide distribution network—makes available to the academic, government, and business communities significant, timely research in U.S. and international economic, social, and political development.

State Legislatures: An Evaluation of Their Effectiveness

The Complete Report by the Citizens Conference on State Legislatures

PRAEGER SPECIAL STUDIES IN U.S. ECONOMIC AND SOCIAL DEVELOPMENT

734526

Praeger Publishers New York Washington London

PRAEGER PUBLISHERS
111 Fourth Avenue, New York, N.Y. 10003, U.S.A.
5, Cromwell Place, London S.W.7, England

Published in the United States of America in 1971
by Praeger Publishers, Inc.

Library of Congress Catalog Card Number: 72-170026

Printed in the United States of America

This report is the third in a series of publications resulting from the Legislative Evaluation Study by the Citizens Conference on State Legislatures (CCSL).

The first, titled Summary Report: An Evaluation of the Fifty State Legislatures, provides an overview of the major portions of the study. The second publication, a paperback book issued by Bantam Books, Inc., and titled The Sometime Governments, describes the study and contains its 1,300 recommendations. This volume was written by John Burns, with a Foreword by John Gardner, Chairman of Common Cause. Recommendations were developed and written by Larry Margolis, Executive Director, and the staff of the Citizens Conference on State Legislatures. The Sometime Governments, written in layman's language, is for all citizens, public affairs groups, business and trade associations and other organizations concerned with the improvement of state legislatures.

This publication, State Legislatures: An Evaluation of Their Effectiveness, The Complete Report by the Citizens Conference on State Legislatures, is the document on which the first two publications were based. It contains information on:

. the background and purposes of the study

. what the study does and does not do

. the design and conduct of the study

. the evaluation apparatus

. the results and their interpretation

. a detailed series of technical appendixes
  for each major segment of the project

In addition, it contains a complete set of suggested state-by-state recommendations for legislative improvement.

This report is directed primarily toward members of the academic community, research organizations, civic associations and other scholars who wish to delve more deeply into the Legislative Evaluation Study--its methodology and conclusions.

The Legislative Evaluation Study was not designed as an academic project but as a practical working tool to assist organizations engaged in the reform and modernization of the fifty state legislatures.

While the Legislative Evaluation Study was to be a working instrument, the CCSL was always aware of the valuable and unique information which would be gathered through this undertaking. Because of the prior paucity of comparative information, the Conference believes that the data from the field work and research of this project will provide a valuable and unique resource for scholarship and to practical efforts at reform.

In carrying out the Legislative Evaluation Study, the CCSL used the best available techniques to make it reasonable, accurate and honest, and to connect it with the real problems of the structure, processes and operations of the state legislatures as functioning institutions of government.

In addition to the three publications resulting from the Legislative Evaluation Study, two data banks have been established. A data book on each of the states is maintained by the Citizens Conference at its headquarters in Kansas City. The fifty-two-page books contain the questions which were evaluated, the preferred answer(s) to each question and the answers for each state legislature.

A second legislative data resource base has been established at the Institute of Government Studies, University of California at Berkeley, under the guidance and supervision of Professor William Bicker, Director. A machine readable code book will cover the entire range of study data. The data will be available to all qualified academicians, researchers and civic organizations.

Certain acknowledgements must be made, not out of duty, but because so many people helped so valuably in this ground-breaking study.

Without the support of the Ford Foundation, this study would not have been possible. A grant from that institution for basic research on state legislatures enabled the CCSL to undertake the massive collection of information and analysis which comprise the bulk of the project.

Serving as technical consultants to the project, the firm of Baxter, McDonald and Company rendered invaluable assistance. The contribution of Alfred W. Baxter, Jr., was most notable in this regard. Other personnel staff members were: Angus N. McDonald, Elaine T. Hussey, William R. Zion, Richard DeLeon and Grant Bornzin; in data processing: Gregory T. Small, Gary M. Swee, William L. Kent, Andrea Heikkinen and Duane Anderson. The supporting staff consisted of: Patricia A. Gerdes, David F. Hussy, Marilyn Madsen and Gerold Stone.

CCSL staff members who contributed most directly to the project include Larry Margolis, Executive Director; Karsten Vieg, Director of Research and Program Development; Donald Quinn, Director of Communications; Jesse W. Whitley, Director of Operations; Donald Glickman, Deputy Director of Research and Program Development and Project Director of the Legislative Evaluation Study; Zale Glauberman, Associate in Research and Program Development; Albert de Zutter, CCSL Publications Editor; Linda Brown, Research Assistant; Rosemary Moeykens, Research Assistant; Justin P. Orr, Communications Assistant; and Scott Smith, Assistant in Operations. Their efforts were supported by the CCSL's Board of Trustees and Program Development Committee and augmented by the talent and energies of the entire staff--clerical, professional, administrative, and executive--to the extent that the study is a product of the entire Citizens Conference on State Legislatures.

CONTENTS

LIST OF TABLES

LIST OF FIGURES

PART

I

**THE
STUDY
AND
ITS RESULTS**

1

GOALS,
LIMITATIONS,
AND ACCOMPLISHMENTS
OF THE STUDY

GOALS

In February, 1969, the Citizens Conference on State Legislatures (CCSL) began the process of assembling and applying comparative information on the technical capabilities of the fifty state legislatures in the United States. "Technical" as used throughout this report refers to the legislatures' capability for decision-making, i.e., how decisions are made, rather than which decisions are made. The Legislative Evaluation Study (LES) involved two major tasks:

1. The development of specific criteria for the evaluation of the technical capabilities of the legislatures.

2. The collection of data and the subsequent ranking of state legislatures according to the specific criteria, to significant groupings of criteria, and to total composite scores.

The study was designed to achieve four important goals:

1. To focus the attention and concern of members of the public and legislators on many of the significant disabilities which limit the effective performance of some state legislatures.

2. To furnish diagnostic indicators of particular deficiencies in particular states and thus to give guidance to lay and legislative efforts toward legislative improvement.

3. To provide benchmark documentation as a yardstick for measuring progress over time in improving legislative capability. (Legislative capability in the context of this report denotes such abilities as the collection, analysis, and application of information, the ability to represent effectively the various interests and values held by a state's citizens, the ability independently to contribute to

the formulation and review of state policies, the ability to conduct
the basic activities necessary to function as a legislative body, and
the ability of constituents to hold legislators and legislatures accountable for their actions.)

4. To generate discussion on what constitutes effective legislative organization and procedure, and why.

The firm of Baxter, McDonald and Company, of Berkeley,
California, served as prime consultant on the study and carried out
some of the basic research.

LIMITATIONS

If the results are to serve the study's intended purposes, they
must be viewed within the self-imposed limitations of the study.
Accordingly, it is important to stress at the outset what the study
does and does not undertake to do.

Limitations on Political Evaluation

As a nonprofit organization, the Citizens Conference is not
concerned in the present study with the advocacy of particular substantive programs. Its interest is focused upon the technical improvements of legislative organization, structure, and procedures which
are largely independent of specific governmental programs. Nor
does the study deal with the structure or quality of political party
organization at the local and state levels. Under recently revised
federal tax laws, the Conference may not and does not advocate
particular programs or support particular items of substantive
legislation. Neither does the Conference take any part in political
campaigns, nor does it campaign for or against specific legislative
measures.

Several members of the national panel which advised the Conference staff on the design of the evaluation study argued that in
focusing concern on procedures and forms of organization, the study
neglected issues of great social and political importance. In the
views of these critics, reform must be sought in case-by-case battles
for particular legislation; crucial victories are decided in political
arenas and not in research libraries or computer rooms. These
views have a good measure of justice. There is no question that there
are major areas of substantive legislation which call urgently for
attention and action in most states. But these areas must necessarily
lie beyond the scope of this study.

The Citizens Conference and its consultants are convinced, however, that not least among state problems are those dealing with the arena and the apparatus for making policy and designing programs. The forms, organizational structures, and procedures used by state legislatures are vital to the quality of general government. While poorly organized, understaffed, and underpaid legislatures may occasionally pass enlightened and technically sophisticated laws and exercise competent review over executive programs and public expenditures, the odds are low. Neither can we claim that the better legislatures (in terms defined below) are not capable of sorry results on specific bills and issues. Sound organization and procedures do not compel satisfactory performance (however this be judged), but they increase the probability of such performance.

We believe that if one is to educate wisely, revise outworn institutions to fit current circumstances, and balance the pressures from executive branches of government (state and national), then one must begin at a minimum with structural and procedural reform. Such attention is only a beginning, but it seems to us a necessary one for any programs to improve the quality, style, and responsiveness of state governments.

Limitations on Applicability

In formulating broadly applicable standards, we realize that such standards may not apply in particular instances. Thus, we believe, for example, that the powers of legislative leadership should be somewhat diffused and suitably constrained. These standards carry the implicit qualification "on balance," or "in the main," for there are specific states where a strong and centralized structure may be a necessary precondition for important reforms in other areas of organization and procedure.

This point must be made quite plainly. We are not offering a set of specific recommendations uniformly applicable to all state legislatures at all times. Responsible diagnosis depends upon full awareness of the details of individual institutional circumstances. We do suggest, however, that as general rules some useful things can be said about desirable features of legislative operation.

Limitations on Completeness and Finality

The evaluative apparatus had to make use of information which could be collected for all states within the time and budget constraints of the study. Some obviously relevant subjects had to be omitted because of the lack of adequate data. One such omission concerns the quality of professional legislative staffs. Although we considered the possibility of using numerical indicators as proxies for direct and subjective qualitative appraisals, this approach proved neither plausible nor practical. Years of college, years of experience, age distributions of staff members, and similar substitutes for qualitative evaluations were so shaky and so difficult to obtain in comparable detail that, although an extensive effort was made, this important area of evaluation had to be omitted from the study.

Furthermore, the evaluative apparatus concentrates primarily on those aspects of legislative organization and procedure which are subject to influence through current programs of the Citizens Conference. Criteria relating to the quality of individual legislators or to the specific characteristics of legislative turnover, for example, while relevant to legislative capability, are not directly affected by current CCSL programs, and consequently are deemphasized in the present study.

Finally, the merit and plausibility of the present evaluations depend directly upon the reasonableness and acceptability of the underlying criteria. For this reason, we give substantial space to the various doctrinal assumptions made in the evaluative work. But we make no claim to either completeness or finality in the assignment of these criteria. As in many other matters concerning mechanisms for the political resolution of conflicting values, there are wide ranges of informed and honest disagreement in the area of legislative norms. Many such differences emerged among members of the staffs which were responsible for the present report. Further differences will surely be recorded by those who review the work. It is for these reasons that we say the study produces "answers" and not "the answers" in the difficult and comparatively undeveloped field of normative political science applied to state legislative organization and procedure. Clearly, much more work remains to be done to build a body of widely applicable standards against which the capabilities of legislatures in general, and features of specific legislatures, may be judged and compared.

ACCOMPLISHMENTS

Having stressed what the study does not attempt to do, we can now indicate what we think are its accomplishments.

First Overall Evaluation of
State Legislatures

The study makes available the results of a comparative survey
and analysis of the technical capabilities of all fifty state legislatures.
It provides uniform information for every legislature on a long list
of topics, including committee structure, compensation, staffing,
length of sessions, rules and procedures, work scheduling devices,
interim activities, and the treatment of minorities. Further, the
study relates these specific pieces of information to broader objectives: each legislature's independence, accountability, uses of information, aspects of its capacity to be representative, and the degree
to which it is functionally organized.

General Rankings of the
State Legislatures

The study produces general rankings of all the state legislatures in terms of both specific and composite criteria of technical
capability. We emphasize that the rankings are general. It will
seldom be warranted to conclude that the seventh-ranked state is
considerably "better" than the ninth-ranked state, or that the fortieth
state is clearly "worse" than the thirty-seventh. But one can certainly
conclude that the states ranked, say, 6 through 10 are substantially
"better" than those ranked 36 through 40. "Better" is used always
and only in relation to the available elements of comparative data
and to the body of evaluative doctrine. Changes in data or in preferences would change the operational meaning of "better."

The rankings clearly indicate the stronger and weaker legislatures across the nation, and the stronger and weaker features of
specific legislatures, in terms of their structural and procedural
capabilities. This is new and important information, and we believe
that the system of criteria itself is a valuable contribution to the
development of evaluative doctrines and techniques.

In the course of our legislative visits and from special questionnaires distributed nationally to over 2,000 legislative and civic leaders,
we found that even the most well-informed laymen and the most con-
scientious and experienced legislators seldom had detailed information
about legislatures other than their own. The new data will provide
a valuable yardstick to supplement local experience and intuition in
the comparative evaluation of the fifty diverse legislatures.

2

DESIGN
AND CONDUCT
OF
THE STUDY

This chapter presents a general description of the design of the evaluative structure and the way in which information was assembled and utilized for ranking purposes. Full technical details are given in the technical appendixes.

SUMMARY

The brief summary of the major steps in the study provided in the following paragraphs will help to establish a context for the fuller descriptions which follow.

The initial task was the formulation of broad objectives which state legislatures must meet in order to fulfill minimum requirements of organizational and procedural capability. Various indicators of these several objectives were then identified, and specific items of fact were listed as measures of each of these indicators. Following review and revision of these candidate items by a national panel of technical advisers, the approved items were incorporated into a checklist of data to be collected in field visits.

Field interviewers then visited all fifty state legislatures and completed the fact sheets for each state, using published documents to supplement information from extensive interviews with legislative personnel. In no state did interviewers meet with fewer than six legislators and members of legislative staffs. Care was taken to insure that majority and minority leaders were included in the interview schedule as well as junior and more senior members of the legislature from each party. Where legislatures were served by more than one staff group, interviews were held with senior members of each staff agency: clerks' offices, fiscal review staffs, legal services groups, etc.

After the data had been compiled from field visits, the completed questionnaires were sent to legislative leaders and senior legislative staff members in each state for review and comment. Replies from these officials revealed occasional errors of fact and interpretation which were corrected before the data were processed for machine accessibility.

Concurrently with the processing of data, a set of preference rules was established for each of the evaluative criteria. It was decided, for example, that states which distributed notices of committee meetings and agendas well in advance of the meeting dates were to be preferred to states wherein no such notice was given. In questions which asked for the breadth of available staff services, preferences were given to legislatures which had more types of staff services available.

Rank orders of states were then generated for each of the evaluative questions. These rank orders were combined to reflect the comparative positions of the several states on clusters of related questions. Finally, weights were assigned to each of seventy-three subcriteria to reflect the staffs' best judgment of the relative importance of various organizational and procedural features. On the basis of the data, the preference rules, and the subcriteria weightings, final state rank orders were generated.

The ranking procedures were tested for their sensitivity to hypothetical changes in the facts used in the evaluation and to changes in such elements as the preference rules and weighting assignments, in order to assure that minor alterations did not produce large or undamped changes in resultant rank-order positions. By design, the evaluative system is quite insensitive to minor changes but does reflect proportionately greater responses to major alterations in the data base for any state or to major changes in the rules and weights used in the evaluation.

THE FAIIR EVALUATION SYSTEM

The literature and practice of legislative improvement repeatedly exhibit a small set of goals and objectives. More adequate time for deliberations, improved professional staff services, additional compensation, more explicit and complete rules of procedure, streamlined committee structures, and better facilities have been cited, among other similar features, as objectives of legislative improvement. We share with other students and practitioners of legislative reform the belief that such objectives are valid. We do not believe that they are ends in themselves.

Because of this belief, we have formulated five objectives of legislative improvement which are appropriate as ends in themselves. We believe that, at a minimum, citizens should expect their legislatures to be functional, accountable, informed, independent, and representative. The intermediate objectives of legislative improvement cited above are all appropriate as means to one or more of these final objectives. There is no merit in large legislative staffs, per se. Large staffs can serve merely as vehicles for comparatively unobstrusive individual and party patronage. Staffs have value to the extent that they heighten the ability of legislatures to learn, remember, analyze, and evaluate large volumes of complicated information. In this sense, staffs have value as elements of an information-processing capability. Information-processing capabilities are to be valued in themselves. Who would prefer ignorant to informed representatives as a matter of principle?

Analogously, modern office space and well-designed and well-equipped committee rooms have value because they encourage thoughtful work to be done by individuals and groups and facilitate access to the legislative process by citizens and interest groups who wish to lobby for their views or to seek guidance from an individual legislator. It is hard to lobby a man one can't find or to show mass support for a bill before a committee which meets in a room with no chairs for the public. Facilities are important because they serve the functionality and the accountability of state legislatures.

In addition to claiming that the five proposed characteristics are ends in themselves and not merely way stations to further objectives, we believe that the five objectives are collectively exhaustive or are capable of such an interpretation. By this, we mean that there are no objectives missing from the list which are neither variants nor components of one or more of the five characteristics proposed. In claiming exhaustiveness for our list, we do not claim that other terms might not be selected to designate these objectives.

We also believe that the general objectives are so related as not to permit trade-off equivalencies among them. State legislatures ought to exhibit substantial attainment in each of the five fields; more of one characteristic does not make up for shortage or weakness in another. Serious deficiencies in one particular characteristic reduce the general benefits of attainment in other fields. It makes no sense to value independence at the price of ignorance or to see merit in the most functional and informed legislatures if they are neither representative of nor accountable to their constituencies.

In summary, we claim that the major elements of our evaluative system are appropriate as final objectives of organizational and procedural improvements to legislatures, that they are collectively exhaustive of such objectives, and that none are substitutes for the others

In the FAIIR (functional, accountable, informed, independent, representative) evaluation system each of the five major characteristics is defined in terms of subordinate criteria and subcriteria which are ultimately related to specific questions of fact covered in the questionnaire filled out for each legislature. For example, one of the five major criteria for the evaluation of a legislature's independence is its degree of freedom from domination by the executive branch of state government. This criterion is composed of a number of subcriteria, one of which concerns veto relationships. And this particular subcriterion is related to specific questions of fact about veto procedures. Thus the evaluative apparatus of the study relates the factual information in the questionnaire and the major characteristics of legislative capability through the treelike structure diagramed in Figure 1.

FIGURE 1

Illustration of the FAIIR Structure

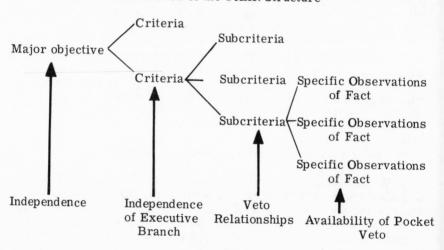

In Figure 1, we indicate how the general objective of legislative independence is defined in terms of various criteria. One of these criteria, independence of the executive branch of government, is indicated. (The complete schedule of criteria for independence, and for the other four objectives, is shown in Appendix B.) Among the several measures used to evaluate the degree of legislative independence from domination by the executive branch, we show those related to veto relationships and provisions. Does the legislature have the power to override a veto? If so, by what kind of majority vote? Are special sessions to consider possible override actions available automatically (as in California), at the option of the legislature itself, or not at all? Does the governor have the specific ability to withhold his signature from a bill and prevent its going into effect despite its passage by the legislature? In Figure 1, we consider the specific availability of the pocket veto as one of the indicators of the relative power position of the legislature in respect to the governor.

A significant feature of the evaluative apparatus is that the definitional elements used for the five major objectives are not mutually exclusive. Factors which, for example, contribute to the information-collecting ability of a legislature may also improve its accountability. It follows that certain items of fact collected in the questionnaire are used in more than one context. The availability of well-designed and well-equipped committee rooms encourages the scheduling of legislative hearings on various issues and thus contributes to a better-informed legislature. The same facilities also make legislative activities more accessible to public view and thus contribute to a more accountable legislature. Professional staff, a key component of technical capability; relates to several of the major objectives, as do the amount and distribution of time available for various phases of legislative work.

While certain factual items were used more than once during the evaluation, they were not necessarily assigned the same weight each time, since they may be of major significance to one aspect of legislative capability but of only moderate or minor significance to another aspect.

Table 1 recapitulates the major features of the FAIIR mechanism down to the subcriteria level, and the rest of this chapter summarizes the doctrinal rationale behind the major features of the evaluative structure.

TABLE 1

Outline of FAIIR Components

Functionality Criteria/Subcriteria	Accountability Criteria/Subcriteria	Information-Handling Capability Criteria/Subcriteria	Independence Criteria/Subcriteria	Representativeness Criteria/Subcriteria
I Time and Its Utilization	I Comprehensibility in Principle	I Enough Time	I Legislative Autonomy Regarding Legislative Procedures	I Identification of Members and Constituents
1. Amount and Distribution of Time Resources	1. Districting	1. Session Time	1. Time for Deliberation	1. Identification
2. Techniques for the Management of Time Resources	2. Selection of Leaders	2. Pre-Session Activities	2. Expenditure Control & Compensation-Reimbursement Powers	II Diversity
3. Uses of Pre-Session Time	3. General Complexity	II Standing Committees (as Information-Processing and -Applying Units)	3. Reapportionment	2. Qualifications
II General-Purpose Staff	4. Explicit Rules & Procedures	3. Number of Committees	II Legislative Independence of Executive Branch	3. Compensation
4. Personal Aides and Assistants to Leaders and Members	5. Anti-Limbo Provisions	4. Testimony	4. Access to Information and Analysis	4. Voting Requirements
III Facilities	6. Planning, Scheduling, Coordination, and Budgeting	5. Facilities	5. Veto Relationships	III Member Effectiveness
5. Chambers	II Adequacy of Information and Public Access to It (Comprehensibility in Practice)	III Interim Activities	6. Lt. Gov. Problem	5. Size and Complexity of Legislative Body
6. Leaders' Offices	7. Public Access to Legislative Activities	6. Interim Activities	7. Budget Powers	6. Diffusion and Constraints on Leadership
7. Committee Facilities	8. Records of Voting and Deliberation	7. Structure & Staffing	8. Miscellaneous	7. Access to Resources
8. Facilities for Service Agencies	9. Character and Quality of Bill Documents	8. Reporting and Records	III Capability for Effective Oversight of Executive Operations	8. Treatment of Minority
9. Members' Offices	10. Conditions of Access by Press and Media	IV Form and Character of Bills	9. Oversight Capabilities	9. Known Rules
IV Structural Characteristics Related to Manageability	11. Information on Legislature's Interests	9. Bill Status and History	10. Audit Capability	10. Bill Reading
10. Size of Houses	12. Information on Lobbyists	10. Bill Content and Summaries	IV Interest Groups	
11. Standing Cte. Structure	III Internal Accountability	11. Quantity and Distribution	11. Lobbyists	
V Organization & Procedures to Expedite Flow of Work	13. Diffusion and Constraints on Leadership	12. Timeliness and Quality	V Conflicts & Dilutions of Interest	
12. Origin & Sponsorship of Bills	14. Treatment of Minority	V Professional Staff Resources	12. Dilution of Interest	
13. Joint Committee Usage		13. General Research Coverage		
14. Treatment of Cte. Rpts.		14. Legal		
15. Anti-Limbo Provisions		VI Fiscal Review Capabilities		
16. Emergency Procedures		15. Fiscal Responsibility		
17. Bill Carry-over		16. Staff Support for Fiscal Analysis and Review		
VI Provisions for Management and Coordination		17. Fiscal Notes		
18. Continuity & Powers of Leadership				
19. Inter-House Coordination				
VII Order and Dignity of Office				

THE FUNCTIONAL LEGISLATURE

Under the general heading "functional legislature," we consider evidence of the capability of legislatures to conduct the several types of activities basic to legislative performance: deliberation, program design and drafting, review and evaluation, compromise, public education, policy formulation, etc. We maintain that each and every one of these component types of legislative activity is facilitated by the following seven components:

Time

Adequate time and flexibility in its use, including adequate devices for scheduling and management of work flow, are minimum requirements for functionality both during and between sessions. While we do not argue that longer sessions are better, per se, than shorter ones, we do argue that state legislatures ought to be able to determine for themselves the amount and distribution of time needed for adequate deliberation and research. Accordingly, states wherein severe limitations are imposed on the frequency, duration, or possible agenda of sessions are rated lower than states in which the legislature determines the magnitude and uses of time and resources. For any given level of available time, we also argue that those states are superior technically which have provided systematic ways to monitor the flow of work, in order to reduce the very critical bottleneck problems which frequently occur at the ends of legislative sessions. The impossibility of giving considered attention to a flood of 500 bills in the last forty-eight hours of a session can hardly be questioned, and the likelihood of inadvertent errors resulting from conditions of frantic speed is well known.

Staff

Multi-purpose staff support to leaders and to individual members, distinguished from more institutionalized and special-purpose staffs, such as found in research offices, clerks' departments, and other bureaus, also seems to be an important source of functional capability. At this point, our argument is that several different types of staff services are required for an adequately functional legislature and that, by and large, these various types cannot be substituted for one another. In particular, staff aides to individual members can provide a variety of support and assistance in constituent relations, writing, agency liaison, etc., which are generally too specific for coverage by members of an auditor's office, a clerk's staff, or a fiscal review agency.

Facilities

Adequate facilities, ranging from chambers and committee rooms
to individual offices for legislators and their staffs, are necessary.
In ranking states, we have placed highest those legislatures which
provide individual offices for legislators and have committee rooms
of adequate size and quality in numbers proportional to the size and
complexity of the state and the volume of its legislative work load.
It is hard for us to see how any work can be done without adequate
places in which to do it. Desks on the floor of legislative chambers
are wholly inadequate, as are crowded, remote, or semi-public working spaces for legislative staffs.

Structure

Structural characteristics related to manageability include
neither too few nor too many standing committees, legislative bodies
of reasonable size, and a moderate number of committee assignments
per member.

Procedures

Organizational and procedural features are essential to expedite
the flow of work. Under this criterion we consider the ways in which
bills may be originated and sponsored, provisions for at least the
occasional use of joint committees, provisions for extraordinary or
emergency treatment of urgent items, the variety of ways for treating
committee reports, and anti-limbo provisions. (Anti-limbo provisions are those which prevent bills or legislative proposals from
disappearing anywhere within the system, especially those proposals
which have been passed by committees or approved in substance by
one house or the other).

Management

While advocating diffused and constrained leadership, we also
urge the importance of continuity of leadership and the possibility and
value of bipartisan participation in the various management aspects
of legislative operations: scheduling, space assignment, inter-house
coordination, personnel management, etc.

Decorum

Finally, and in part because members of the national panel of
advisers urged the importance of these matters, we have included

indicators of order, decorum, and dignity of office.

In summary, we argue that the resources and organizational features listed above are necessary for any legislative body to perform any of its major functions with minimum competence. Without time and the ability to plan its use, a place to work, professional and clerical assistance, rules and procedures to facilitate and manage work flow, and suitable organizational provisions, little can be done and little should be expected.

THE ACCOUNTABLE LEGISLATURE

The structure and doctrines embodied in the evaluations of legislative accountability have three principal elements.

Comprehensible Forms

The organizational structure, forms, and procedures of the legislature must be subject to public understanding--they must be comprehensible in principle. Under this major criterion we identify six subcriteria or indicators:

Single-member districting.

Selection of leaders by election by the full house or, at a minimum, by the majority caucus.

Explicit, published rules and procedures which are uniform and stable.

Anti-limbo provisions.

The availability of explicit institutions, devices, and documents for planning, budgeting, scheduling, and coordinating the work of individual houses and of the full legislature.

The general size and complexity of legislative houses and of standing committee structures.

Public Access

In addition to comprehensibility in principle, there must be actual public access to and understanding of legislative operations. Devices which facilitate public access include advance notices of committee meetings and agendas, open meetings, and adequate facilities.

Other indicators of public access to legislative activities are regular provisions for the compilation and publication of records of discussion, debate, and voting. The quantity, quality, and timeliness of documents form a third cluster of criteria of the openness and accessibility of legislative procedures to interested parties. Physical facilities and other aids to media coverage of legislative activities form another such cluster. The final measures of public access are related to the availability of specific information about legislators' private interests and about the nature, character, and extent of professional lobbyists' activities.

Internal Influence of Individual Members

We define legislative accountability in internal as well as external terms. If, for example, the actual power of the legislature is centered in some small oligarchy--say, a majority of the members of a majority caucus--or if the speakership is an office of strongly centralized and relatively unconstrained powers, then it is almost pointless to speak of the accountability of individual members. What actions individual members do or do not take can have relatively little influence on the fate of bills in committee, or on whether they ever reach committee, or on whether bills passed by committees ever reach the floor of one house for debate.

Accordingly, we utilize indicators of the degree to which individual members have established modes of influencing leadership elites and the decisions of these groups. The modes of influence may range from the basic methods for selecting leaders to rules and traditions which set the powers of members in relation to committee chairmen, minority leadership, and management agencies. Many of the same specific indicators of internal accountability also occur among the measures of representativeness, since they concern the effectiveness of individual members in both contexts.

In summary, to meet minimum standards of accountability, a legislature must score high on the indicators of intelligibility or comprehensibility in principle, high on indicators of the adequacy of information about the legislature and of the press and public's access to it, and high on the several indicators of individual member effectiveness in relation to internal leadership elites.

A citizen cannot exercise responsible judgment regarding an institution which is incomprehensible to him or which, while comprehensible in theory, fails to provide the ingredients essential for actual understanding. Finally, we believe that a legislature is less than accountable when the views and votes of a majority of its members do not really count. It does little good, for example, for a disapproving citizenry to vote their representative out of office if his views and those of most of his colleagues have little to do with the actions and positions taken, nominally, by the full legislature.

THE INFORMED LEGISLATURE

State legislatures function as institutions for the collection, analysis, and application of information. They are more than this, to be sure, but their information-processing functions are of great importance directly and of comparable importance indirectly, since information-handling capabilities affect many of the other legislative functions. These other functions include policy formulation and review, negotiation and compromise, oversight of government operations, and provision of a forum for minority viewpoints. A legislature dependent for information solely on interest group or executive agency representatives, for example, has compromised its vitality as an independent branch of government for purposes of review and oversight.

We use the notion of information handling quite broadly to comprehend the following types of activities:

Initiation of information collection and analysis.

Supervision of these activities by legislative agencies.

Design and maintenance of continuing systems for the stimulation of testimony from diverse sources.

Use of standing and interim committees as devices for the specialized use and analysis of information bearing upon particular classes of related problems.

Careful design of legislative documents to heighten their information-transmitting powers--summaries, fiscal notes, typographic devices to indicate amendments and deletions, etc.

Capability for rapid editing, printing, and distribution of bills during passage through committees and houses.

In keeping with this deliberately broad usage, we have identified six principal aspects of information collection, analysis, and use, and have organized the specific evaluative criteria under appropriate major headings.

Adequate Time

In addition to measures of adequacy of session time, we have developed indicators of the use of pre-session activities which we believe to be essential to facilitate organizational work and to channel the results of interim studies directly and efficiently into productive deliberations early in the session. The more stringent the limitations on session length or session frequency, the more important become the uses of the post-election, pre-session period.

Standing Committees

The structure and use of standing committees as devices for specialization in information application are of considerable relevance. There can be too few as well as too many committees, and there can be excessive numbers of committee assignments per member. Lapses on the low side of number of committees are infrequent and often are remedied by compensating subcommittee structures. Lapses on the high side are more frequent, since committee chairmanships are often political rewards. High-side variation is also more serious because too many committees unduly fracture the comprehensiveness and span of legislative concern. In addition, where resources of talent, time, experience, and responsibility are short, large numbers of working committees aggravate the shortages.

Under the general rubric of standing committee structures, we also consider the procedures used to solicit testimony, including the advance publication of meeting notices and agendas, the requiring of written testimony in advance from organized groups, etc. Finally, we evaluate the quantitative and qualitative adequacy of committee rooms.

Interim Activities

Interim activities represent a powerful and widely neglected opportunity for specialized information collection and analysis removed from the in-session pressure of immediate deliberation, bargaining, and political compromise. Limitations on the scale of interim activities and imperfections in the mechanisms for linking the planned output of interim work to the deliberative work of legislative sessions are therefore particularly serious. Unfortunately, it was not possible to obtain reliable data on the levels or amounts of interim work conducted in each state. Had it been possible, we would have used committee meeting days, for example, as a further indicator of actual effort spent in legislative work outside of formal legislative sessions.

Bill Documents

The form and character of bill documents and the timeliness with which amendments can be made available in printed form are central features of the information system in any legislature. Related to these features are the adequacy of indexing systems and the apparatus for maintaining current records on the location, status, and form of pending legislation.

Some states do not print bills after amendment. Others do so, but with long time lags between the amendment and its availability to legislators and members of the public. On the other hand, states with good information-handling capabilities have immediate or overnight printing capability and typically distinguish typographically between old material, deletions, and new or amended materials. These devices, simple to use and understand, facilitate the tracking of successive actions during the progress of a bill through a legislature.

Professional Staff

A professional staff of adequate size and embodying a reasonable diversity of skills and areas of technical expertise is the fifth major criterion by which the adequacy of legislative information processing is evaluated. Without specialists in the collection, analysis, and organization of data (including opinions as well as hard facts), the most dedicated legislature is seriously handicapped as an informed body, however adequate it may be from other standpoints.

Fiscal Information

Because so much legislative policy formulation is embodied in state budgets, the capability of a legislature to handle fiscal information deserves separate evaluation. Under this criterion we comprehend not only specialized staff resources but also the basic posture and role of the legislature in the budget development and review process and the legislative use of specific technical devices, such as short-term and long-term fiscal notes, to identify the financial implication of proposed laws.

THE INDEPENDENT LEGISLATURE

We have defined and measured the independence of legislatures with reference to five major criteria.

Legislative Activities

Autonomy in legislative activities reflects measures of legislative control (or lack of control) over the frequency, duration, and agendas of legislative sessions, the degree to which legislatures determine for themselves their districting and apportionment plans, and the extent to which the legislature alone determines the size and allocation of budgets for the support of exclusively legislative activities. In many instances, basic conflicts are not between legislative and executive interests and prerogatives, but between legislative autonomy and overly restrictive constitutional provisions concerning legislative matters.

Independence from the Executive Branch

Independence from the executive branch reflects more detailed measures of the legislature's independent access to information and analysis, veto relationships, budget powers, and the role of lieutenant governors (as constitutional officers) in the details of legislative affairs. We argue that it is inappropriate for elected constitutional officers, such as the lieutenant governor in most states, to have any but ceremonial powers and responsibilities regarding the legislature. In keeping with this doctrine, we have classified states on the basis of the degree of actual legislative power enjoyed by the lieutenant governor. Three gradations of involvement were distinguished and states ranked accordingly.

Legislative Oversight Capabilities

Legislative independence is also evaluated in terms of legislative capabilities for program review, governmental oversight, and audits of expenditures and of program results measured in other than fiscal terms. If these vital legislative responsibilities are not met, many of the reasons for an independent legislative branch of government are not served.

We take as indicators of these important functional features of independence such matters as the existence of a legislatively oriented audit staff, a capability for systematic program review and evaluation (possessed and employed by all too few states), and the existence of interim programs specifically aimed at periodic reviews of the adequacy and economy of existing statutes and administrative arrangements.

Registration of Lobbyists

The fourth of our criteria of legislative independence relates to
the form and quantity of information regarding lobbyists and to the
degree to which registration-based information is available to legislators, to the press, and to the public. While the indicators used fall
far short of complete coverage of the intricate relationships between
interest group representatives and legislators, they do reflect generally desirable minimum levels of regulation and registration procedure.

Conflicts of Interest

Finally, we consider legislative independence as exemplified
by freedom from conflicts and dilutions of legislative interest. Here
again, our indicators reflect minimum rules regarding conflicts of
interest, the holding of multiple public offices, employment of rela-
tives, and the possibilities of compensated professional practice or
other commercial transactions between legislators and state and local
governmental agencies.

In summary, we favor a high degree of legislative autonomy
over legislative affairs. The frequency and duration of legislative
sessions and the amount and diversity of interim activities ought not
to be limited by rigid constitutional provisions. Legislators should
set their own salaries and expense reimbursement procedures by
statute, and should also determine districting and apportionment provisions. The legislature should be independent of the executive in its
resources for the collection and analysis of information and should
possess reasonable opportunities for the overturn of vetoes. Legislatures should have and exercise powers for the general review and
oversight of governmental activities and for the audit of expenditures
and program results.

Finally, to be fully independent in the broad sense of the term,
our legislatures and the public should have adequate and accurate
information on organized lobbying activities and should have care-
fully drawn and enforced regulations regarding conflicts and dilutions
of interest.

THE REPRESENTATIVE LEGISLATURE

We have defined out usage of "representativeness" with reference to three principal headings.

Identification of Members and Constituents

Does each legislator have a unique constituency and does each citizen have a representative who is his legislator? Are there clear lines of responsibility and accountability?

We argue that representativeness increases as the identification of member and district approaches 1:1. Accordingly, we have measured this aspect of representativeness in terms of the ratios of legislative districts in each house to the number of legislative seats. A perfect score is attained only by states which have single-member districts for each house.

Because district offices enhance the possibility of communication between a member and his constituents, credit is given to states which make at least some contribution to the establishment and maintenance of district offices in addition to those provided in the state capital.

Diversity

The mix of characteristics among members of the legislature should, to some degree, reflect important clusters of interest of citizens in the state. An adequately diverse legislature will display a wide rather than narrow distribution of ages among its members; it will have representatives from various commercial and professional backgrounds; it will have members with particular ties with and commitments to particular social, racial, or other groups within the state. It is likely that the more drastic the restrictions on who may run and who may serve, the less diverse will be the resulting legislative bodies.

We examine first the stringency of age, residence, and citizenship requirements for office seekers. In general, we take the position that slight or modest restrictions are preferable to severe ones.

Second, we consider that compensation rates, including provisions for the reimbursement of necessary expenses and provisions for retirement, are factors which affect the number of people who may consider running for legislative offices. Other things being equal, the diversity of legislatures will increase as it is economically possible for larger numbers of people to consider running for office.

We acknowledge that little is known about the combined effects of variations in compensation rates and total time demands. Both conditions will alter the size and composition of the pool of potential office seekers. Because of the lack of information on these combined effects, we have used compensation rates only, and acknowledge the limitations of this factor as an indicator of potential diversity.

The final aspect of diversity treated in the study relates to the size and voting requirements of various types of legislative bodies. We argue that it is important not only to have diversity in the full house but also to prevent small groups of legislators from wielding disproportionate influence. It is possible for a legislature to exhibit considerable diversity among its members and yet be so structured internally that the voices and influence of a few members are over-whelming. In other words, diversity may be present but inoperative because of extraordinary concentrations of power in the hands of small leadership elites.

Quorum requirements for standing committees are used as one indicator of the possibility of disproportionate influence, as are the minimum sizes required for conference committees. Similar con-siderations are reflected in our treatment of the dispersion of leader-ship powers.

Membership Effectiveness

After election, the ability of an individual legislator to represent his constituency is affected by his access to technical resources, by the stability and predictability of legislative procedures, and by the general treatment accorded to various minority interests. Given ideal districting and conditions maximizing diversity, there remain major questions regarding the actual ability of individual legislators to do their jobs. We are concerned here only with institutional prac-tices and not with individual talents.

We believe that the effectiveness of individual members declines as the size of legislative houses increases.

Furthermore, the stronger and more concentrated the powers of leadership and management, the lower will be the limits of the con-tributions of individual members. As is shown in detail in the tech-nical appendixes, several indicators of the relationships between individual members and various kinds of leadership devices have been developed. These indicators cover relationships between mem-bers and, respectively, leaders, committee chairmen, scheduling and calendaring officers, and conference committee members.

The third factor affecting members' effectiveness lies in the stability and coverage of rules of procedure and practice and the

availability of documents and special briefings regarding such procedures. A game without rules or with shifting or unpublished rules
is particularly hard for novices to play effectively.

The treatment afforded to minority members by the majority
and within the minority caucus is the fourth factor reflected.

The fifth factor comprises the terms of access by members to
facilities, staff assistance and other resources. Of particular importance among the potentially available resources are those which
facilitate two-way communication between members and constituents:
offices, legislative aides, assistance with press and media relations,
etc.

3

THE STUDY

AND

ITS PROCEDURES

COLLECTION, VERIFICATION, STORAGE, AND AVAILABILITY OF DATA

The basic schedule of data to be gathered about the organizational and procedural features of the fifty state legislatures was developed by the Citizens Conference with substantial aid from a national advisory panel.

Upon completion of the master questionnaire or checklist of information, each state legislature was visited for a period of days by a senior staff member of the Citizens Conference or of its consultants. During the visits to the capitals, information was assembled from published documents and from extensive interviews with legislators, experienced staff members, press representatives, and others. The completed information schedules were then reviewed by the Citizens Conference staff and checked for completeness and consistency with major published sources of information.

Following this first round of review, over 360 verified questionnaires were mailed to legislators and legislative staff members in all fifty states for final review and comment on accuracy and reliability. The Citizens Conference is indebted to those busy legislators and staff members who identified inaccuracies of fact and who suggested corrections of interpretations and judgments.

When the basic questionnaires had been completed and verified by state officials, the data and the annotations necessary to interpret them were processed for machine accessibility. Because of the large number of special circumstances from state to state, the bare bones of an answer were often inadequate for an understanding of, say, the precise role of the Senate Majority Caucus in Arizona or the functioning

of the Rules Committee of the Washington Senate. Appropriate annotations were carried forward into the computer printout so that the process of evaluation could be conducted in the light of the bare facts
supplemented by applicable qualifications. The data storage format is
indicated in Table 2 for one of the typical questions in the checklist
dealing with fiscal notes. (The full list of such questions and the rules
adopted for preferring one answer to another are given in Appendix A.)

The resources of the data collected and used in the LES are on
file. Copies of printouts containing annotated answers to each question by each state will be placed in selected aniversity libraries, and
the same information is available stored on magnetic tape. Documentation is available that explains the basic data file structure. (Appendix D documents the computer programs used in the study.)

PREFERENCE RULES AND WEIGHTING

The order in which possible answers to questions were to be
preferred was determined by a staff committee of the Citizens
Conference and their consultants and certain of the Conference's
advisers. This determination often involved exercise of considerable
discretion and judgment. For example, it seems reasonably clear
that too few standing committees may hamper legislative operations
and concentrate power unduly, while too many committees may be
cumbersome and may occasion numerous disputes over jurisdiction.
What, then, is the optimum number or optimum range of numbers of
committees? Or, again, it may be obvious that the total absence of
restrictions on lobbying will lead to abuses by special interest groups,
whereas too many restrictions will cripple the legitimate expression
of views of constituent groups. What kinds of answers should be
given top preference in the scoring of questions concerning lobbying?
Should too little restriction be preferred to too much?

Another complex subject is the relative significance or weight
assigned to different components of a composite ranking. For example,
in the ranking of facilities, should equal weight be attached to the importance of offices for the leadership and offices for individual members? Should different weights be assigned to facilities for committees and for caucuses? Since the various criteria are of different
degrees of importance, it was necessary to assign weights. Not assigning weights is equivalent to assigning equal weights to all subcriteria.
This is a weighting decision like any other and much worse than most.

The assignment of preference rules and weighting was done as
conscientiously as possible, and on the basis of experience and informed judgment. It would not be suprising, however, to learn that

TABLE 2

Format for Data Storage:
Question 096, Are Fiscal Notes Prepared by a Legislative Service Agency?

State No.	2-Letter State Abbrev.	Annotation Code	Answer	Annotation	Continuation Code for Computer Program Only
01	AL		1		
02	AK		1		
03	AZ		5		
04	AR		–		
05	CA	1	5	Refers to Leg. Analyst	
06	CO	1	–	Reviewed by Joint Budget Comm.	
07	CT		1		
08	DE		–		
09	FL	1	5	In House Only	
10	GA		5		
11	HI		1		
12	ID		1		
13	IL	1	1	The Rules Do not Fix Responsibility For Prepar. of Fiscal Notes	A
	*	1			B
14	IN		5		
15	IA		5		
16	KS		1		
17	KY	1	1	Only on Request of Leg. Res. Comm. Chairman	
18	LA		5		
19	ME	1	1	Legislative Fiscal Officer	
20	MD		5		
21	MA	3	5	Usually by Com. Staff	
22	MI		5		
23	MN		–		
24	MS		1		
25	MO		1		
26	MT		1		
27	NB		5		
28	NV		5		
29	NH		1		
30	NJ		5		
31	NM		–		
32	NY		5		
33	NC		1		
34	ND	1	1	By Exec. Agency	
35	OH		–		
36	OK		1		
37	OR	3	1	When Occasional Summaries Are Provided, They	A
	*	3		Are Done by a Legis. Agency	B
38	PA		–		
39	RI		1		
40	SC		1		
41	SD	1	1		
42	TN	1	1	But Commsr. of Fin. and Ad. Prepares a Cumulative Fiscal Note Each Week (TCA SEC. 3-207)	A
	*				B
43	TX		5		
44	UT		5		
45	VT		1		
46	VA		5		
47	WA	1	5	By Bdgt. Office and LBC.	
48	WV		1		
49	WI	1	1	Leg. Ref. Bur. Makes Initial Determination That Bill Needs a Fiscal Note	A
	*	1			B
50	WY		1		

some readers would disagree with various details of these decisions. If issue is to be taken with any of these decisions, the alternative decision must be at least as justifiable as the decision made and must make significant differences in the overall resultant rank order. (The preference rules which were applied to particular answers are in Appendix A; the weightings assigned to component subcriteria are shown in Appendix C.)

TREATMENT OF STATES OF DIFFERENT SIZES

With each of the component questions, we asked whether a given answer could be adequate for a small state and inadequate for a large one. To what extent is it reasonable to apply sliding scales related to state population, state expenditures, or other measures of size and complexity? In general, we believe that in only a few cases are such sliding scales appropriate.

What constitutes an adequate number of auditorium hearing rooms with space for visitors clearly depends upon the volume of potentially controversial legislation and upon the probable sizes of groups of citizens wishing to observe or take part in hearings and committee meetings. These values go up with state populations and were so treated in the ranking system.

The numerical size of technical and professional staffs is also to be judged in relation to indexes of state size and complexity. We do not argue that Wyoming should have professional staffs of the same size as New York and California. We do believe that all states will benefit substantially from some professional staff and that the distribution of specialized services available to the legislature should not be much less in small than in large states. Attorneys assigned to a bill drafting office are not substitutes for auditors, just as audit staffs are not substitutes for research teams expert in particular subject matter and program areas. None of these types of staff services replaces secretarial help or adequately organized and staffed clerks' offices.

Adequate notice of the times, places, and agendas of committee meetings should not depend upon state size; neither should the availability of explicit rules of house and committee procedure. A popularly elected lieutenant governor with genuine as well as ceremonial powers in the legislature is as disadvantageous in small as in large states because of the resulting impairment of internal and external legislative accountability and independence.

We believe that the rate of legislative compensation should approximate that of professional people with comparable responsibilities

Given this doctrine of rates of effective compensation, the total compensation should vary in some way with the total time demands placed upon legislators both during and between formal legislative sessions. The notion that legislative work is accomplished only during sessions is wrong and seriously weakening to the capabilities of state legislatures. Accordingly, total time demand for constituent meetings, interim research, deliberation, and other types of legislative activity should be reflected in total compensation levels.

Because the total amount of time given to legislative business will vary among legislators and over time with individual legislatures, total compensation levels should strike an average. We believe strongly that it is far better to overcompensate those who work the least than it is to undercompensate those who contribute more generously of their time and talents. Actual and necessary expenses should be reimbursed to avoid the murky and unsatisfactory practices of using reimbursements as covert compensation or of attenuating effective compensation by inadequate reimbursement provisions.

On the difficult question of how much time is enough time for adequate legislative work, we have taken two positions:

That the nature and stringency of limitations on the ability of legislatures to set their own session frequencies and session lengths and agendas provides a relatively clear basis for judgment. States which are limited by constitution to short, biennial sessions are in a worse position than states wherein legislatures can set the frequency and duration of session lengths without impairment of compensation, reimbursement, or other provisions.

That the actual time needed for formal sessions depends in part on the frequency of sessions--shorter sessions are more tolerable if they are annual and not biennial--and in part upon the legislature's own perception of the scope of policy problems and its ability to deal with this work load under the applicable conditions of political and policy compromise.

We do not presume to judge questions of the latter sort, nor do we believe that small states can uniformly "get by" with shorter sessions than larger states. Alaska has a small population. This circumstance, by itself, does not mean that the policy problems of Alaska are fewer, smaller, or more tractable than those of other states. If consideration is given to the position of Alaska legislators as trustees for 1.1 percent of the world's land area and major fractions of many of its important resources, it seems clear that state population and adequate deliberative time have no stable and necessary relationship.

Nor do we believe that the size of legislatures should increase with the size of state populations. Once a legislative body is large enough to have the potential to reflect various localities and various types of interest and policy preferences (these capabilities are dependent upon far more than mere numbers), questions of manage-ability, comprehensibility, and individual member effectiveness become predominant. We believe that the considerations argue that as individual houses grow much larger than 100, their effectiveness declines with increasing steepness. In accordance with this doctrine, we have not scored the sizes of senates, all of which are within a tolerable range, and have given low scores only to those houses which have memberships in excess of 100.

In summary, we have treated only a few criteria in the light of measures of state population. With the exceptions noted above, we believe that minimum standards of public accessibility, subject matter coverage of professional staffs, compensation rates, facilities, and published rules of procedure, etc., should be independent of state size. The dollar costs of adequate clerical support to send out timely notice of committee meetings, to maintain current records of bill status, and to reprint bills after each amendment are small in rela-tion to the contributions that these and related services make to the overall capability of state legislatures.

COMBINATION RULES

A rank order of states was generated for each individual evaluative element in the data checklist. (A schedule of these elements and the preference rules applied to particular answers is provided in Appendix A.) Where the fact in question was reflected by a yes or no answer for a whole state legislature, the rank order would have only two components.

To move from rank orders based upon individual questions of fact, we employed various standard procedures or rules to generate one combined ranking from two or more individual rankings. Several of the more common combination rules used in this process are described below.

Ordered Eight-Way Rule

In cases where three questions, each with a yes-no answer, can be ordered in importance or degree of significance, the eight possible answers to each question were considered as shown below.

| | Answers to Questions in Order of Importance | | |
	Most Important	Next	Least Important
Group 1 (best)	Yes	Yes	Yes
Group 2	Yes	Yes	No
Group 3	Yes	No	Yes
Group 4	Yes	No	No
Group 5	No	Yes	Yes
Group 6	No	Yes	No
Group 7	No	No	Yes
Group 8 (worst)	No	No	No

The Measure of Distance

In cases where two questions were of roughly equal importance, and where the answers could be scaled from 0 to 100 percent, a simple geometric representation was used to compute the distance of any pair of answers from the "perfect" value of (100, 100). This scheme is diagrammed below.

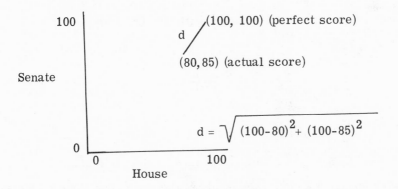

This method is generally used to combine house and senate scores for questions for which scales could be devised.

It should be noted that this method, in contrast with averaging the two score values, penalizes states where, for example, one house is quite bad and the other quite good. In many of these cases, we believe that the net effect of two disparate scores is a poorer performance indicator, overall, than would be obtained by two houses with more balanced development. A poor partner sets the limits on the quality of the combined performance.

Sum of Yes Answers

In many cases where questions within a set were judged to be
of equal value or where no basis for differentiation could be identified,
states were ranked on the basis of the total number of yes answers
received on the set of questions. This format for combination was
used frequently in measuring the extent of the coverage of professional
staff services as indicated by the number of different types of analyses
and services available to legislators. The "sum of yes answers"
rule was also used to combine ranks for the houses and senates of
individual states on yes-no questions.

Matrix Combinations

In many cases, states could be ordered in a few groups on each
of two sets of questions. If the two groups were of approximately
equal weight and importance and if the groupings happened to be, say,
four in number in each case, a combined ten-way grouping was
generated by the matrix shown below.

State Rank Position on Question A

		I	II	III	IV
State Rank Position on Question B	I	1	2	4	7
	II	2	3	5	8
	III	4	5	6	9
	IV	7	8	9	10

Entries are the state rank position in the new, combined rank order.

Edge-Dominant Matrices

In cases where a composite rank order was to be generated
from questions of substantially dissimilar importance, a matrix form
was utilized which gave "dominance" to one or the other of the
questions. A composite rank ordering generated by a three-by-five
matrix is shown below; the question generating the threefold grouping
is the more important, and each element in the first row is better
than any element of succeeding rows.

	I	II	III	IV	V
I	1	2	3	4	5
II	6	7	8	9	10
III	11	12	13	14	15

Special-Form Matrices

In some cases of combining two rank orders, we could perceive neither clear dominance, i.e., a great disparity in significance between the two evaluative criteria, nor rough comparability between the two. In such cases, a special-form matrix was generated to reflect informed judgments upon the proper order in which to prefer various combinations of ranks. An example of such a special-form matrix is shown below.

	I	II	III	IV	V	VI	VII	VIII
I	1	2	3	4	13	14	19	19
II	5	6	7	8	15	16	20	20
III	9	10	11	12	17	18	21	21

Weighted Normalized Combinations

In many cases, particularly those where the ranks to be combined were themselves combinations, it was appropriate to generate a composite ranking from more than two component rankings at the same time. The rule which produced the composite ranking for the information schedule from the six major criteria rankings is a case in point. In this instance, we normalized the rank positions of each state on each of six criteria to a scale from 0 to 100. If a ranking had four groups, states in the first group would be assigned 25, states in the second group 50, states in the third 75, etc. In this way, we could combine, in a uniform and intuitively satisfactory way, rank orders with different numbers of internal divisions or gradations.

Where the component criteria were of unequal importance, the position of a state on the composite ranking corresponds to the sum of its weighted positions in the normalized scales. Where marked

similarities in importance were found to obtain among the criteria,
equal numerical weights were assigned as a rough way of reflecting
the judgments on differences in criteria importance.

Aggregations and Consolidations

In many cases, preference rules and combined rank orders
would indicate a high degree of discrimination between states; the
extreme of this case is a rank order with fifty different positions,
such as those of the final FAIIR rank orders and the overall composite ranking. We do not pretend that the evaluative system is
capable of such fine-grained discriminations at high levels of aggregation. Accordingly, when we found a rank order with, say, twenty-
eight groups, we would ask whether such fine gradations were discernible to the judgment of informed and expert students of legislative operations. In many cases, the decision was made that the me-
chanics of the system produced finer gradations than could be discern-
ed in actual practice. In these cases, we then looked for reasonable
ways of aggregating many rank groups to fewer, broader classifications. It was often the case that the data indicated a clear top, middle,
and bottom group but only slight differentiation within these gross
groupings. In such cases, the composite rank order would be aggre-
gated to three groups.

With respect to the interpretation of the final rank orders, we
must emphasize here (as we do at greater length in Chapter 4), that
the effective differences in overall legislative capability between states
only a few positions apart are discernible by the methodology employed
but the net differences are in many instances quite small.

Treatment of "Not Applicable" Answers

In one-party states, questions about the powers of minority
leaders were generally inapplicable because no such officers exist.
In other circumstances, questions about the relationship between standing committees and interim committees were inapplicable because of
the complete lack of interim committees. These problems produced
by application of a standard checklist of questions to a highly diverse
collection of state legislatures were anticipated.

Treatment of "not applicable" answers took one of the following
forms. First, we would consult the notes of interviewers and of the
state respondents who reviewed the data. Often the annotations indicated the basic facts of a particular state's circumstances or practice
and these facts were sufficient to justify the assignment of a standard

answer to the state in question. If the question was not "convertible" in
the sense described into one of the standard form answers, case-by-
case judgments were made to insure equitable treatment. For example,
in unicameral Nebraska, questions regarding House procedures were
always inapplicable. Accordingly, we double-weighted the answers
given for the Nebraska Senate. Looking at an individual question, a
state that does not have any noncalculable benefits (automobiles, credit
cards, and the like) would be scored "not applicable" for the question
"How are noncalculable benefits regulated?" States not having these
benefits were thus not penalized for not having adequate procedures
regulating their use. We were not judging the merit of these benefits,
merely the presence of adequate procedures regulating them if they
existed. (Appendix C documents in detail the procedures used for
coding of the subcriteria in the FAIIR study.)

SYSTEM SENSITIVITY

A class of important questions must be asked of any ranking
system such as the one described here. If one of the answers to one
of the questions were changed for one of the states, what would happen
to the rank-order position of that state? If we were to impose a different preference order upon the possible answers to a given question--
for example, if more stringent limitations on session length were
preferred to less stringent ones--what would happen to the resulting
rank orders of states? If we were to impose weights different from
the ones selected in generating combined rank orders, or if we aggre-
gated rank group in different ways, what would be the results in terms
of the positions of various states?

These are all questions relating to the sensitivity of the rank
orders to hypothetical changes of fact or of ranking policy and procedure. One of the technical features of the evaluation system used
here is that the sensitivities are proportional, i.e., little or no change
in composite rank orders occurs when comparatively small changes
are made in matters of fact or in preference rules. As the magnitude
of changes increases, for example, as a criterion weight is doubled
or tripled, the effects on rank ordering are of commensurate magnitude.

The sensitivity test of reasonableness is met in the sense that
minor changes made early and in matters of detail have relatively
little consequence in the final or highly composite rankings. Con-
versely, major changes made in basic features of the system as it
moves to the highly aggregate criteria have substantial effects. Put
another way, there is no single change nor any small set of changes
which could be made to the data or to the evaluative apparatus which
would make Wyoming outrank New York.

4

**THE RESULTS,
THEIR INTERPRETATION,
AND THE IMPLICATIONS
FOR
LEGISLATIVE IMPROVEMENT**

THE COMPOSITE RANKINGS

Table 3 shows the rank order of the fifty state legislatures on each of the five major objectives and their overall ranking as produced by the methods previously described. It will be noted that many states rank rather high on some schedules and comparatively low on others. The final or composite rank order of states depends upon an aggregation of their rank orders on each of the component schedules. As noted above, we believe that all of the five major objectives are of equal importance and necessity; therefore, no weights were used in obtaining the composite rank ordering from the orderings on each of the FAIIR component schedules.

Because the evaluation procedure depends upon discriminations of "better" or "worse," it is not possible to say how much better or worse one state is than another. The rank order of states is an ordinal listing and is to be understood in the sense of first, second, third, and not in the cardinal usage of 1, 2, and 3, wherein the second state is twice as bad as the first. The system does not permit such comparisons.

We have made no attempt to characterize a perfect state legislature, because even if one were to invent such a legislature by listing all of the characteristics which would lead to a preferred answer on each question, the results would still reflect a very limited view of perfection. Notwithstanding the known limitations of the evaluative apparatus, it is instructive for diagnostic purposes to identify the changes in particular low-ranking state legislatures which would rank them with the leaders. Several examples of this procedure are provided below.

TABLE 3

Rank Order by State for the FAIIR Criteria

Final Rank	State	Rank-Order Position on FAIIR Component Schedules				
		Funct.	Account	Inform.	Ind.	Rep
1	California	1	3	2	3	2
2	New York	4	13	1	8	1
3	Illinois	17	4	6	2	13
4	Florida	5	8	4	1	30
5	Wisconsin	7	21	3	4	10
6	Iowa	6	6	5	11	25
7	Hawaii	2	11	20	7	16
8	Michigan	15	22	9	12	3
9	Nebraska	35	1	16	30	18
10	Minnesota	27	7	13	23	12
11	New Mexico	3	16	28	39	4
12	Alaska	8	29	12	6	40
13	Nevada	13	10	19	14	32
14	Oklahoma	9	27	24	22	8
15	Utah	38	5	8	29	24
16	Ohio	18	24	7	40	9
17	South Dakota	23	12	15	16	37
18	Idaho	20	9	29	27	21
19	Washington	12	17	25	19	39
20	Maryland	16	31	10	15	45
21	Pennsylvania	37	23	23	5	36
22	North Dakota	22	18	17	37	31
23	Kansas	31	15	14	32	34
24	Connecticut	39	26	26	25	6
25	West Virginia	10	32	37	24	15
26	Tennessee	30	44	11	9	26
27	Oregon	28	14	35	35	19
28	Colorado	21	25	21	28	27
29	Massachusetts	32	35	22	21	23
30	Maine	29	34	32	18	22
31	Kentucky	49	2	48	44	7
32	New Jersey	14	42	18	31	35
33	Louisiana	47	39	33	13	14
34	Virginia	25	19	27	26	48
35	Missouri	36	30	40	49	5
36	Rhode Island	33	46	30	41	11
37	Vermont	19	20	34	42	47
38	Texas	45	36	43	45	17
39	New Hampshire	34	33	42	36	43
40	Indiana	44	38	41	43	20
41	Montana	26	28	31	46	49
42	Mississippi	46	43	45	20	28
43	Arizona	11	47	38	17	50
44	South Carolina	50	45	39	10	46
45	Georgia	40	49	36	33	38
46	Arkansas	41	40	46	34	33
47	North Carolina	24	37	44	47	44
48	Delaware	43	48	47	38	29
49	Wyoming	42	41	50	48	42
50	Alabama	48	50	49	50	41

Note: Final rank order derived from an aggregation of component rank-order scores and not by addition of positions on individual rank orders, which would produce ties.

A second point of interpretation relates to the consequences of using weights as a device for discriminating among degrees of relative importance of the seventy-three subcriteria. These weights represent the best judgment of the CCSL staff. This judgment reflects a view not only of the intrinsic importance of the subcriteria but also of the adequacy of the data selected as a measure of the presence or absence of the subcriteria factors. It is quite possible for other sets of weights to be proposed and defended. Any significant change in weights, for example, on the order of plus or minus 10 percent, would produce a change in the component and final rank orders. These changes generally would be of the order of a one- or two-place change in the rank-order sequence. Quite large changes in the weights are required to cause substantial changes in the rank order. We could find no sets of weights which would lower the top states below the tenth or twelfth position, and none which would raise the bottom states materially.

A third critical point of interpretation relates to the relative degree of discrimination among states. Because of the arithmetic of the system, composite rank positions are dependent upon an aggregation of the component rank orders, and not upon the sum of the rank positions. This allows for finer discrimination when states are clustered around a value. Using this system allows states to have adjacent final rank positions while having divergent positions on the individual component rankings, as illustrated below.

Final Rank	State	Func- tional	Account- able	In- formed	Inde- pendent	Repre- sentative
25	West Virginia	10	32	37	24	15
26	Tennessee	30	44	11	9	26

No account is taken nor interpretation made of factors associated with divergent rank positions despite a general feeling among the participating staffs that balanced development is to be preferred to widely divergent rank position distributions. The dragging or negating effects of very poor capability in one or two objectives more than offsets the effects of the relative superiority indicated by high-rank positions on other component schedules. It must be emphasized that such opinions are highly judgmental and subjective and are not supported by any known empirical studies.

A final point which must be emphasized regarding the interpretation of the resultant rank order is that the differences between adjacent states are net differences. These net differences are derived from rank orders combined, at a fairly high level of aggregation, with weightings. Further, even on the numerical scale derived from the sum of unweighted rank positions on each of the five objective schedules, there is not much net difference among the states in the middle of the fifty-state list. There are distinguishable differences between adjacent states, and the comparative inferiority of one adjacent state to another can be identified and the grounds for the inferiority explained and defended. In many cases, however, the net differences are quite slight. To illustrate these differences, Figure 2 shows the distribution of the fifty states on the composite rank order. While there is considerable difference between California and Alabama, there is comparatively little differentiation (given the apparatus employed) between states ranked 21 and 30, even though these states are nine positions apart and vary less than 4 percent of the spread. In summary, we believe that there are identifiable and explainable differences in technical capability between and among the fifty states; we also believe that the net difference is in many cases quite small.

REASONS FOR THE
VARIATION AMONG THE STATES

What makes Alabama last and California first? From the vantage point of the evaluative apparatus used in this study, the answer is that California has characteristics which generally put that state in the preferred answer category for most questions; for Alabama the reverse is true. What are some of the specific differences between states which rank high and those which rank low? What are some of the things that contribute to the distinctions between adjacent states? Much of the rest of this chapter deals with each of the five component schedules, taking as sources of examples widely divergent states (usually from the top ten and the bottom ten) and states which are adjacent in the individual schedule rankings. As will be shown, states near the top of the list generally exhibit most or all of the desired characteristics, while states near the bottom possess few or none of the requisites.

States having adjacent positions on one of the five major schedules usually have similar answers and hence similar positions on the overall schedule rank order, and on the most heavily weighted subcriteria. When this similarity does not exist and the states diverge, most often there is another subcriterion, also heavily weighted, in which the states in question diverge in the opposite direction. As a result of balancing, these states occupy adjacent positions on the overall schedule rank.

FIGURE 2

Final Rank Distrubution
of the States

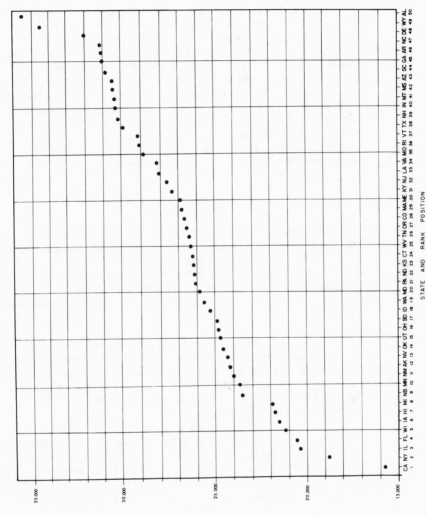

43

THE FUNCTIONAL SCHEDULE

The most heavily weighted subcriterion in the functional schedule was Committee Structure -- subcriterion no. 11, which had a weight
of 9. As with each of the other four schedules, the sum of the subcriteria weights on each schedule was made equal to 100. Table 4
compares widely divergent Oklahoma and South Carolina and closely
ranked Indiana and Texas (nos. 9, 50, 44, and 45, respectively, on
the functional schedule) on this most heavily weighted subcriterion.
Indiana and Texas score similarly on the questions in this subcriterion,
with Indiana scoring slightly better on committee assignments per
member. Oklahoma scored consistently better than South Carolina,
with the single exception of question 45. For the three most heavily
weighted subcriteria on the functional schedule, Table 5 summarizes
the respective positions of the states analyzed above.

THE ACCOUNTABLE SCHEDULE

The two most heavily weighted subcriteria in the accountable
schedule were those dealing with explicit rules and procedures, and
records of voting and deliberation, with weights of 10 and 11, respectively. Table 6 summarizes the responses to these subcriteria of
Nebraska and Rhode Island, overall nos. 1 and 46 on the accountable
rank order, as well as Utah and Iowa, two medium-small states
ranking no. 5 and no. 6 on the schedule.

As Table 6 shows, Rhode Island could easily improve its position
by having uniform committee rules, joint operating rules, and various
procedures which allow the public to identify a legislator's actions,
such as required roll call votes, public committee voting records,
and the like. Changes of this type can be made with little or no expenditure of funds.

Discernible differences between adjacent states Utah and Iowa
include Iowa's having electric roll call recorders available only in
the House, and Utah's not having roll call votes regularly taken and
published on final committee action. Otherwise, their responses
were the preferred responses, as reflected in their high rankings.

THE INFORMATION SCHEDULE

The two most heavily weighted subcriteria on the information
schedule deal with session time and fiscal responsibility, having
weights of 9 and 11, respectively. Table 7 summarizes the questions

Comparison of Oklahoma, South Carolina, Indiana, and Texas
on the Most Heavily Weighted Subcriterion on the Functional Schedule

Question No. and Title		Widely Divergent			Closely Ranked	Preferred
		Oklahoma	South Carolina	Indiana	Texas	
38 Number of Standing Committees (percent score)	House	99% (15 ctes.)	0% (8 /7 ctes.)*	24% (28 ctes.)	0% (45/37 ctes.)*	(16-17 ctes.)
	Senate	99% (15 ctes.)	0% (26/18 ctes.)*	0% (26 ctes.)	0% (27/23 ctes.)*	(12-14 ctes.)
45 (185) Standing Committee with Interim Status	House	None	None	--	0.02	1.0
	Senate			--	0.07	1.0
	Joint			1.0	--	1.0 (all)
42a Standing Committee Assignments per Member						
Percent House Members with > 3 Cte. Assignments		3%	0%	75%	99%	0%
Percent Senate Members with > 4 Cte. Assignments		0%	100%	34%	100%	0%

*The larger number is the total number of committees. The smaller number, on which the rankings were based, is the number of policy or substantive committees, arrived at by subtracting the administrative or nonpolicy committees from the total.

TABLE 5

Comparison of Rank Positions of Oklahoma, South Carolina,
Indiana, and Texas on the Three Most Heavily Weighted
Subcriterion on the Functional Schedule

Subcriteria		No. of Rank Positions	Rank Position			
No. and Title	Weight		Oklahoma	South Carolina	Indiana	Texas
			(9)	(50)	(44)	(45)
2 Management of Time Resources	8	33	9	30	13	23
11 Committee Structure	9	50	5	49	40	46
18 Leadership Power and Continuity	8	6	1	4	1	1

*Number in parentheses is each state's ranking under the criteria of functional.

TABLE 6

Comparison of Nebraska, Rhode Island, Utah, and Iowa
on the Two Most Heavily Weighted Subcriteria on the Accountable Schedule

	Widely Divergent		Closely Ranked		
	Nebraska	Rhode Island	Utah	Iowa	Preferred Response
Subcriterion No. 4: Explicit Rules and Procedures					
Rank Position Out of a Possible 20	6	20	6	6	
Questions					
52 Are There Uniform Committee Rules?	Yes	No	Yes	Yes	Yes
128 Are There Joint Rules?	Unicameral Legislature	No	Yes	Yes	Yes
127 Are There Back-up Rules?	Yes	Only in Senate	Yes	Yes	Yes
Subcriterion No. 8: Records of Voting and Deliberation					
Rank Position out of a Possible 48	4	48	5	6	
Questions					
123a,b Is Roll Call Required on Final Passage?	Yes	No	Yes	Yes	Yes
48a Are Committee Votes Regularly Taken?	Yes	No	Yes	Yes	Yes
48b Are Committee Votes Regularly Recorded?	Yes	No	Yes	Yes	Yes
48c Are Roll Calls Regularly Taken and Published on Final Committee Actions?	No	No	No	Yes	Yes
30a,b Row 11 Are Electric Roll Call Recorders Available?	Available	Not Available	Available	Available in House Only	Available
50a Is a Record of Committee Deliberation Taken and Available to the Public?	Yes	No	Yes	Yes	Yes
50b Are the Minutes and Transcript Taken and Publicly Available?	Transcript Only	Not Applicable	Minutes Only	Minutes Only	Yes
70a,b Are Interim Committee Reports Required and Are They Submitted?	Yes Always	Yes Always	Yes Always	Yes Always	Yes Always
Are The Results of Interim Committee Activities Recorded and Made Public	Yes	Yes	Yes	Yes	Yes

contained within these subcriteria, using New York and Kentucky, which ranked first and forty-eighth as divergent examples, and New Mexico and Idaho, which ranked twenty-eighth and twenty-ninth, respectively, as examples of the differences between states in adjacent positions on the information schedule rank order.

Session length restrictions, as evaluated in question 178, occur in several schedules. Those states having no limitations and/or few session restrictions benefit overall from this. Kentucky and other states doing poorly on this subcriterion (and also on subcriterion no. 1 on the functional schedule) would improve considerably if they had annual sessions and fewer and less stringent restrictions on available time.

With regard to fiscal responsibility, we believe that the governor should develop the budget, as is done in New York, and not that there should be an independently developed legislative budget, as in New Mexico. We distinguish between the legitimate legislative responsibility for budget review and the executive responsibility for budget preparation and execution.

Additionally, where significant sums are involved, dual committee consideration should be required. Dual consideration exists when one committee looks at the policy question, such as the education committee, and the other committee evaluates financial feasibility and overall priorities, such as the ways and means committee. Thus, New Mexico ranks slightly higher than Idaho overall, partly because New Mexico requires dual committee consideration of bills involving significant sums.

THE INDEPENDENCE SCHEDULE

The most heavily weighted subcriteria on the independence schedule were time available for deliberations (no. 1) and legislative access to information and analysis (no. 4), having weights of 16 and 14, respectively. As on the information and functional schedules, session patterns and available time play an important part in the independence ranking. Table 8 summarizes the questions contained in subcriteria nos. 1 and 4, and looks at the responses of California and Alabama (nos. 3 and 50, respectively) as well as Alaska and Hawaii, two small states, which rank 6 and 7, respectively, on the independence schedule.

California has unlimited session time available, while Alabama is restricted both by being limited to biennial sessions and by maximum time limitations on those sessions. Alaska also has unlimited

TABLE 7

Comparison of New York, Kentucky, New Mexico, and Idaho
on the Two Most Heavily Weighted Subcriteria on the Information Schedule

| | Widely Divergent | | Closely Ranked | | Preferred |
	New York	Kentucky	New Mexico	Idaho	Response
Subcriterion No. 1: Session Time					
Rank Position out of a Possible 4	1	4	2	2	
Questions					
3 (178) What Is the Maximum Time Available to the Legislators and How Is Time Limited?	Unlimited Sessions	Biennial Sessions, Limited by Number of Days	Annual Sessions, Limited by Topic	Unlimited Sessions, but Pay Ceases After a Specified Number of days	Unlimited Sessions
4 What Is the Actual Time Available?	Greater Than 120 Days Annually	Less Than 120 Days Biennially	Less Than 120 Days Annually	Less Than 120 Days Annually	Greater Than 120 Days Annually
Subcriterion No. 15: Fiscal Responsibility					
Rank Position out of a Possible 6	1	6	4	6	
Questions					
89 Who Develops the Budget?	Governor	Governor and Legislature Jointly	Governor and Legislature Jointly	Governor and Legislature Jointly	Governor
62 Is Dual Committee consideration Re-Quired Where Significant Sums Are Involved?	Yes	No	Yes	No	Yes

TABLE 8

Comparison of California, Alabama, Alaska, and Hawaii
on Subcriteria 1 and 4 of the Independence Schedule

	Widely Divergent		Closely Related		Preferred Response
	California	Alabama	Alaska	Hawaii	
Subcriterion No. 1: Time Available for Deliberation					
Rank Position out of a Possible 24	8	20	5	4	
Questions					
3 (178) What Is The Limit of Session Length?	Unlimited sessions	Biennial sessions limited by time	Unlimited sessions	Annual sessions limited by time	Unlimited sessions
6a, b Does Legislature Have Power to Call Special Sessions?	No	No	Yes	Yes	Yes
15a, b Can the Legislature Expand the Agenda of a Special Session?	No	Yes	No	Yes	Yes
17 (186) Are There Interim Program Limitations?	No	No	No	No	No
Subcriterion No. 4: Legislative Access to Information and Analysis					
Rank Position out of a Possible 48	3	48	8	10	
Questions					
21a What Types of Distribution Coverage Are There of Available Staff Services? (possible 21 services each for House and Senate)	38	16	34	22	42
96 Are Independent Legislative Fiscal Notes Required?	Yes	No	No	No	Yes
24 Is There a Liaison or Research Office in Washington D.C.?	Yes	No	No	No	Yes
22a,b,c What is the Professional Staff Size per 1,000 Population?	Few (.02/1000)	Very Few (.003/1000)	Some (.163/1000)	Some (.113/1000)	
194 Legislative Expenditure/Capita in Legislative Activities	$.97	$.31	$4.05	$2.36	
194 Legislative Expenditure/State Budget	.22%	.09%	.42%	.39%	
61a,b What Kind of Subpoena Power Do Standing Committees Have?	All Committees Have Power	No Power	In House	In House	All Committees Have Power
71a,b What Kind of Subpoena Power Do the Interim Committees Have?	All Committees Have Power	In House	No Power	In House	All Committees Have Power

sessions, and Hawaii's annual sessions are limited by time restrictions. California has more than twice the staff coverage per capita that Alabama has, and Alaska has slightly more than Hawaii. Alaska and Hawaii are identical in all respects on subcriterion 4, with the exception of staff coverage noted above. California is significantly better than Alabama throughout the subcriteria evaluated here. All low rankings, with respect to session time, could be remedied with little or no expenditure, as could the requirements for subpoena power, a contingency included in subcriterion 4.

THE REPRESENTATIVE SCHEDULE

Identification of a legislator with his constituency was the most heavily weighted subcriterion on the representative schedule, with a weight of 18. This subcriterion considered both the provision for district offices and, more seriously, an index equal to legislative districts divided by the number of legislative seats available. Table 9 summarizes subcriterion no. 1, identification, for the top (New York) and the bottom (Arizona) of the representative rank order, as well as New Hampshire and North Carolina, two states adjacent in rank position near the bottom of the rank order.

In order for a legislature to be representative, the individual citizen must be able to identify his legislator, to vote him out of office when the citizen is displeased, and to retain him when the citizen is pleased. This cannot be easily done in multi-member districts.

TABLE 9
Comparison of New York, Arizona,
New Hampshire, and North Carolina on the Most Heavily
Weighted subcriteria on the Representative Schedule

| | | | Answers | | |
Question	New York	Ari- zona	New Hamp- shire	North Caro- lina	Preferred Response
83. What is the ratio of legislative districts to legislative seats? (House and Senate)	70/70 57/57	8/60 8/30	193/400 24/24	49/120 33/50	Same no. districts as seats
32b. Is there provision made for district offices?	Some	No	No	No	Office provided

Running at large also reduces the possibility of a geographically coherent minority getting a voice in the legislature, thereby reducing potential legislative diversity. Neither Arizona, New Hampshire, nor North Carolina makes provisions for members' district offices. Arizona has a very low ratio for districts per seat in both the House and Senate.

It is significant that improvement in most of the heavily weighted subcriteria could come with little or no expenditure. Changes in the rules, to provide for things such as regular voting procedures, and joint rules need no expenditure at all. Additional discussion of these points will be found below.

IMPLICATIONS FOR LEGISLATIVE IMPROVEMENT

What Can Be Done

In states whose legislators and concerned citizens find that our lists of indicators of legislative capability are pertinent and persuasive, and whose rank order is below what the legislators and citizens would like, what can be done? The hope of raising such a question was and is a central motive for the evaluation study.

The first thing that can be done is to compare the state answers with the "ideal" answers for each of the individual questions. Such an item-by-item comparison will indicate where a particular state is deficient from the proposed, generally applicable norms. To the extent that our "ideal" answers are thought to be applicable, the comparative list will provide a schedule of changes which, if made, would result in an improved position in some subsequent ranking.

Following this item-by-item comparison, it would be possible to review the weightings assigned to the subcriteria. To the extent that a state is defective (in the senses described) on subcriteria which we and many state officials agree are important, the result would be a kind of rough priority order of deficiencies to be removed. The priority order thus generated depends upon judgments of comparative importance and not on comparative ease or convenience in removing the deficiency.

A third round of analysis might be undertaken which would identify the types of changes necessary to reduce or eliminate a deficiency which all concerned agree is a deficiency and is of major importance. In many cases, improvements will require constitutional

revisions: to eliminate a lieutenant governor from a position of
effective leadership in a senate, or to change the size of a house, or
to eliminate pocket veto capabilities of a governor. Items in the
"constitutional revision" group could serve as the starting agenda
for groups within and outside the legislature concerned with constitutional reform and revision.

A second large class of deficiencies might be related to the
number and types of staffing availability. Here the basic remedies
involve legislative decisions to provide more adequate staff, to
appropriate the required money, and to make legislative provisions
for recruitment, assignment, supervision, and use of expanded staff
capabilities. For many legislatures, we believe that a small percentage
increase of the legislative budget, in proportion to the state budget,
plus the time and effort necessary for supervision and use of staff
work, would make a remarkable difference in the capability and
standing of a state legislature.

A third large group of deficiencies can be removed without
changing the constitution and without spending money. Improved
rules and better procedures can be drafted and put into effect where
there is the will to do so. Vastly improved procedures for the planning
and conduct of interim activities in most states can be effected almost
by a decision to require committee chairmen to present plans of
action and budgets and by the establishment of a central bipartisan
body to review these proposals and weld them into a coherent and
balanced overall program.

Large improvements in the accessibility of legislative operations
to public involvement and scrutiny can be obtained by requiring that
meetings be open and that transcripts be made and published, and by
providing for early and widely distributed notices of committee meetings and agendas. Such changes as these require the commitment of
legislators to make the necessary changes, reinforced or stimulated
by a concerned press and public.

In summary, we believe that there is a four-phase program
available to any state seriously concerned about the quality of its
legislature:

1. Compare state answers with hypothetical "ideal"answers
and decide if the ideal is applicable to that particular state.

2. For evaluative elements which survive this test of fact and
judgment, list the disabilities in a priority order of importance.

3. Classify the disabilities by the types of actions necessary to remove them, i.e., constitutional revision, budget changes, internal managerial decisions.

4. Establish appropriate internal and external bodies to undertake the work of specific constitutional draftsmanship, specific staffing programs and budgets, specific revisions of standing rules, or specific changes in internal managerial procedures.

In each and all of these procedures, a substantial body of experience may be drawn from states which have already gone through such programs of self-improvement. There is no need for each state to invent the wheel independently. There is need for each state to evaluate its own capabilities in a systematic program of review and to initiate appropriate programs of improvement where there is consensus that improvement is needed and available.

The Costs and Benefits of Improvement

To the extent that our proposed evaluation apparatus is persuasive in its form and coverage, it provides an index to major interrelationships among the bases for capability in various fields. Increases in the breadth of discretion available to a legislature in setting the frequency and duration of sessions will have effects not only upon the information-processing capability of a legislature but also upon its independence and its general functional abilities.

This and other examples of interdependencies suggest that programs of improvement should be mounted on broad rather than on narrow fronts. Additions of professional staff, for example, may be seriously limited in their contribution unless legislators and legislative leaders have the time and energy to provide direction, supervision, and application of the products of good staff work. To obtain the maximum advantages of particular improvements, it may often be necessary to make sets of related changes.

If this perception is valid--if coherent, multifacted reform is the appropriate tactic, rather than narrow, single-purpose change--it follows that citizens and legislators must be prepared to account for the costs of reform under several headings. Money will generally be a minor factor. Political willpower and conviction must also be reckoned among the costs of internal change. Finally, trouble, effort, and political risk must be identified as the main costs of programs seeking constitutional change. It is no light task to reduce the size of an overly large legislature, to put the legislature in the position of master of its own house with respect to time spent, compensation paid, reimbursement available, and staff help deployed. It will take secure legislators to open their deliberations to public view and to record the substance and results of their actions.

Against these several categories of cost--time, effort, and will for constitutional change; money and the managerial skills to spend it well; political risk to advocate and associate with marked change in practice--must be reckoned the several categories of benefits. We see the following to be chief among the potential harvest of legislative reform:

Better and more responsive state government.

Heightened satisfaction for individual legislators and legislative leaders, derived from being on a competent and productive team.

An invigoration of the state legislature as an active and capable element in the federal system.

We argue that the benefits of reform are individual as well as governmental and that the governmental benefits will have consequences for the quality of national affairs as well as at the state and local levels. For this reason, efforts toward improving state legislatures along the lines advocated in this study (or along other lines identified by analogous methods of analysis) are worthy of national as well as local concern and support.

5

CORRELATES
OF
LEGISLATIVE
CAPABILITY

Are there discernible relationships between the rank-order positions of states as evaluated by the LES procedure and other state characteristics, such as wealth, government expenditures, population size, geographic location? Is high technical capability associated with certain types of political systems but not others? Is there a tendency for states which are innovative in the area of legislative structures and procedures to be innovative in other policy areas as well? How comparable are our measures of technical capability with other measures which have been employed in comparative legislative research? In short, what are some of the correlates of technical capability in American state legislatures? And, given a set of correlates, what kinds of inferences might be drawn from them to guide governmental reform and inform political research? These and related questions are explored in this chapter.

The results of our investigation, which are reported and discussed below, should be of particular interest to those who wish to improve the quality and capabilities of American state legislatures. A knowledge of why legislatures are the way they are--for better or for worse--should help them to identify those factors which must be altered or manipulated in order to achieve more fully the results of positive institutional reform. Apart from practical applications, the findings of our study are offered as a contribution to the growing literature of comparative state policy research.[1] Reciprocally, many of the socioeconomic, cultural, political, and policy indicators considered in this study, and many of the hypotheses which we examine, are drawn from that same literature.

SOME PROPOSITIONS TO GUIDE RESEARCH

The primary objectives of comparative state policy research are to characterize and explain interstate variation across a wide range of public policies operating in varied circumstances. The first step in "explaining" variation, methodologically speaking, is a preliminary search for predictor variables which will help to account for a state's position on some normative ranking or on some scale which orders public policy outputs. This search may be guided by a set of assumptions of theoretical expectations as to which predictor variables will possess the greatest explanatory power. Lacking a theoretical framework, such a search becomes a "fishing expedition." This section reports suggestive results from both kinds of search. The second step in explaining variation is to correlate the selected predictor variables with the policy variables being examined. If our final aim is to specify causal linkages among variables, then a necessary condition for a cause-effect relationship to exist is that they co-vary. Finally, the third step in explaining variation is causal analysis, which involves (1) making causal inferences from observed relationships among variables and (2) assessing the weight of each causal factor.[2]

Given the practical aims of the study and given also the limitations on time and resources, the analysis presented here cannot venture beyond steps one and two: developing hypotheses and correlating variables. But these are necessary first steps in any effort to describe networks of cause and effect, and the findings which we report here will enable us (1) to reject certain hypotheses which one might offer to account for differences in legislative capabilities, and (2) to make educated guesses as to which factors do seem to account for (or at least march together with) such differences.

The fifty state legislatures exhibit considerable variation on each of our scales of functionality, accountability, information-handling capability, independence, and representativeness. On the final composite ranking by the FAIIR criteria, California's state legislature does best, Alabama's worst. Why? For the sake of convenience, let us sort out the roster of possible explanatory factors into the following categories: (1) regional/geographical factors, (2) demographic/socio-economic factors, (3) historical/cultural factors, and (4) political factors. These categories are by no means exhaustive or mutually exclusive, but they have proved useful in other research for organizing data and reporting findings.[3]

Regional/Geographical Factors

In comparative analyses of state public policies, clear regional patterns in such areas as government spending, taxation, and public service have been discovered. States in the western regions, for example, generally spend at levels above the national average, while those in the Northwest tend to spend at below average levels.[4] Even after controlling for the influence of other factors, such as a state's wealth, regional affiliations explain much of the interstate variation in public policy-making.[5] Norms of government action are often regionally determined through processes of emulation, imitation, and competition. Assuming that similar processes are at work in the area of structural/technical policies affecting legislative capability, we expect to find regionally affiliated states clustering together on each of the FAIIR scales and on the final ranking.

Demographic/Socioeconomic Factors

Most studies in comparative policy research have found that demographic and socioeconomic variables constitute the single most important set of factors explaining differences in state government policies.[6] On the basis of this generalization, we hypothesize that levels of urbanization, industrialization, income, and related aspects of socioeconomic development will be strongly associated with state position on the FAIIR rank orders.

Historical/Cultural Factors

A recent study by Ira Sharkansky, which extends the earlier work of Daniel Elazar, suggests the importance of political cultural patterns in the American states for explaining differences in policy-making processes and policy outcomes.[7] Elazar conceives of political culture as "the particular pattern of orientation to political action in which each political system is embedded."[8] This orientation, Sharkansky explains, "may be found among politicians and the general public, and it may affect their understanding of what politics is and what can be expected from government, influence the types of people who become active in politics, and influence the ways in which they practice politics and formulate public policy."[9]

In Elazar's analysis, historical migration and settlement patterns of various ethnic and religious groups influenced the regional and subregional distribution of distinctive political cultures throughout the American states. The three basic types of political culture which he identifies are moralistic, individualistic, and traditionalistic, which form a continuum on each cultural dimension from moralistic to traditionalistic.

The various cultural dimensions include the following:

1. Orientations toward political participation: moralist

cultures emphasize participation as the duty of all citizens;
traditional cultures limit participant roles to elites.

2. Orientations toward bureaucracy: moralist cultures
stress the values of extensive, well-paid professional administrative corps at all levels of government; traditional cultures
oppose the growth of bureaucracy as a restraint on the political
elite.

3. Orientations toward the government's intervention in
the community: moralist cultures welcome intervention for the
good of the commonwealth; traditional cultures oppose all government interventions except those necessary for maintaining elites
in power.

4. Orientations toward the initiation of new programs:
moralist cultures welcome innovation; traditional cultures re-
sist it.

No single culture can be said to dominate a given state completely, although Minnesota, Nevada, and Mississippi, respectively,
represent the purest strains of moralist, individualist, and traditionalist cultures.

Sharkansky's measure of political culture (0 for moralist states,
9 for traditionalist states, intermediate values assigned to individualist
states and the various culture mixtures) will enable us to test the
proposition that a state's political culture strongly influences the
character of legislative institutions and will be highly associated with
positions on the FAIIR rank orders.

Political Factors

Keeping in mind the danger of making spurious causal connections,
we expect the following political variables to be strongly and positively
associated with legislative capability: competitive political parties
(indicated by small majorities or frequent power shifts from party to
party), high citizen participation in elections, strong governors, and
legislative professionalism. An extensive body of theoretical and
empirical literature relates all of these factors to liberalism and
innovation across a wide range of public policies.[10] We therefore
assume that the influence of these same factors will extend to policies
governing legislative institutions and procedures.

Other political system characteristics which might be associated,
positively or negatively, with high legislative capability include the

equity of apportionment systems, the degree of centralization in legislative policy-making, the magnitude of political conflict within state
legislatures, the controllability of state government budgets, and the
extent to which legislative seats are mandatory base offices for political
careers.

Other Factors

The population size and population density of states may influence
the character and scale of legislative capabilities. In order to test
this possibility, we have included population size and density figures
in the correlational analysis.

Policy Consequences

Given the assumptions underlying many of our propositions, and
given the extensive literature supporting those assumptions, we an-
ticipate strong relationships between legislative capability and various
measures of state policy outputs. Thus, we expect highly capable
legislatures to spend more on public services, to tax more, to respond
more rapidly in adopting innovative programs, and in general to
"intervene" more extensively in the public life of their communities.
This is a straightforward deduction from propositions which we advanced earlier. For example, if legislatures in wealthy states spend
more, and if legislative capability is high in wealthy states, we deduce
that legislative capability will be associated with higher levels of
spending.

OPERATIONALIZING THE KEY VARIABLES

If our objective is to make statements of the form "The more
X, the higher the legislative capability," then it is necessary for us
to construct valid and reliable measures of X. This can be a most
difficult task, particularly where X stands for extremely complex
phenomena, such as urbanization and political culture. Although our
understanding of these phenomena is often imperfect at best, considerable work has been done in comparative state research to lend greater
precision to our concepts as well as to increase the validity and reliability of the measures we construct for them. "Operationalization"
is the broad term used to describe this effort. The various factors
which are discussed above are operationalized below as scales and
indexes for measuring the political and socioeconomic forces shaping
legislative capability. In Table 10 and in the following text, each
measure is described briefly.

TABLE 10

State Rank Orders from the Studies Used for Correlation with the FAIIR Study
(values in parentheses indicate score for cited study)

(1) Sharkansky-Elazar		(2) Francis		(3) Schlesinger		(4) Grumm		(5) Sharkansky-Hofferbert		(6) Sharkansky-Hofferbert		(7) Lockhard	
Political Culture Scale*		Centralization Index		Combined Index of Governor's Formal Powers*		Professionalism Index		Professionalism Local-Reliance Factor Scores*		Competition-Turnout Factor Scores*		Party Integration Index	
Minn.	(1.00)	Ala.	(.86)	N.Y.	(19)	Calif.	(2.294)	N.Y.	(4.230)	Utah	(1.629)	Conn.	(1)
Wash.	(1.66)	N.J.	(.82)	Ill.	(18)	Mass.	(2.185)	Calif.	(2.140)	Nebr.	(1.494)	Mass.	(1)
Colo.	(1.80)	Tenn.	(.79)	N.J.	(18)	N.Y.	(2.145)	Mass.	(1.651)	Minn.	(1.339)	Mich.	(1)
Iowa	(2.00)	Ga.	(.75)	Penn.	(17)	Penn.	(1.715)	Penn.	(1.648)	Idaho	(1.266)	N.J.	(1)
Mich.	(2.00)	Ark.	(.74)	Va.	(17)	Mich.	(1.538)	Mich.	(1.354)	Mont.	(1.235)	N.Y.	(1)
N. Dak.	(2.00)	Conn.	(.69)	Wash.	(17)	N.J.	(1.455)	Ill.	(1.154)	Ind.	(1.152)	Del.	(2)
Oreg.	(2.00)	La.	(.65)	Calif.	(17)	Ill.	(1.043)	N.J.	(1.010)	Ill.	(1.034)	Ind.	(2)
Utah	(2.00)	Haw.	(.64)	Md.	(16)	Haw.	(1.010)	Ohio	(.619)	Wis.	(.949)	Ohio	(2)
Wis.	(2.00)	Penn.	(.60)	Mo.	(16)	Wis.	(.837)	Wis.	(.558)	Oreg.	(.913)	Penn.	(2)
Maine	(2.33)	Wis.	(.60)	Oreg.	(16)	Tex.	(.795)	Md.	(.500)	N.J.	(.843)	R.I.	(2)
N.H.	(2.33)	N.Y.	(.60)	Utah	(16)	Ohio	(.599)	Minn.	(.417)	N.Dak.	(.780)	Colo.	(3)
Vt.	(2.33)	Ariz.	(.58)	Wyo.	(16)	Oreg.	(.396)	Tex.	(.289)	Wash.	(.694)	Haw.	(3)
Idaho	(2.50)	Ky.	(.56)	Mont.	(16)	S.C.	(.325)	Fla.	(.260)	Colo.	(.679)	Ill.	(3)
Conn.	(3.00)	R.I.	(.54)	Ala.	(15)	Del.	(.317)	Conn.	(.200)	Mich.	(.627)	Mont.	(3)
Mont.	(3.00)	Del.	(.50)	Conn.	(15)	Fla.	(.279)	Mo.	(.126)	Conn.	(.431)	Wis.	(3)
R.I.	(3.00)	Ind.	(.50)	Ohio	(15)	La.	(.273)	Del.	(.116)	Wyo.	(.413)	Alaska	(4)
S. Dak.	(3.00)	Calif.	(.50)	Tenn.	(14)	Ga.	(.248)	Ga.	(.087)	Calif.	(.363)	Calif.	(4)
Calif.	(3.55)	W. Va.	(.50)	Ky.	(14)	Conn.	(.226)	Ind.	(.036)	Kans.	(.359)	Md.	(4)
N.Y.	(3.62)	Maine	(.50)	Mich.	(14)	Md.	(.219)	La.	(.031)	Iowa	(.326)	Minn.	(4)
Kans.	(3.66)	Va.	(.47)	Minn.	(14)	Minn.	(.203)	Alaska	(0)	Mo.	(.305)	Wash.	(4)
Mass.	(3.66)	Ill.	(.46)	Nev.	(14)	Mo.	(.202)	Haw.	(0)	W.Va.	(.281)	Ariz.	(5)
Nebr.	(3.66)	Utah	(.45)	Colo.	(14)	Wash.	(.142)	Ariz.	(-.005)	Ohio	(.226)	Nev.	(5)
N. J.	(4.00)	Mich.	(.44)	Idaho	(14)	Ala.	(.104)	S. C.	(-.013)	Del.	(.192)	N.Mex.	(5)
Wyo.	(4.00)	Md.	(.44)	Alaska	(13)	R.I.	(-.065)	Kans.	(-.159)	Penn.	(.192)	Oreg.	(5)
Penn.	(4.28)	Alaska	(.42)	Haw.	(13)	N.C.	(-.096)	Wash.	(-.160)	N.H.	(.191)	Wyo.	(5)
Ill.	(4.72)	Ohio	(.42)	La.	(13)	Ariz.	(-.100)	N. C.	(-.161)	R.I.	(.166)	Idaho	(6)
Alaska	(5.00)	Wash.	(.40)	Okla.	(13)	Okla.	(-.101)	Iowa	(-.163)	Mass.	(.071)	Ky.	(6)
Haw	(5.00)	Colo.	(.38)	Iowa	(12)	Nebr.	(-.107)	Oreg.	(-.207)	Maine	(.045)	Mo.	(6)
Nev.	(5.00)	Okla.	(.38)	Nebr.	(12)	Maine	(-.114)	Miss.	(-.210)	Alaska	(0)	Utah	(6)
Ohio	(5.16)	Kans.	(.37)	Wis.	(12)	Miss.	(-.122)	Nev.	(-.221)	Haw.	(0)	W.Va.	(6)
Ariz.	(5.66)	Mont.	(.36)	Ga.	(12)	Ind.	(-.150)	Va.	(-.243)	S. Dak.	(-.138)	Iowa	(7)
Ind.	(6.33)	Mass.	(.34)	Mass.	(12)	Colo.	(-.173)	Colo.	(-.255)	Ariz.	(-.141)	Kans.	(7)
Del.	(7.00)	Mo.	(.32)	Ind.	(12)	Alaska	(-.188)	Nebr.	(-.297)	Nev.	(-.170)	Maine	(7)
Md.	(7.00)	Minn.	(.31)	Ark.	(11)	Ky.	(-.218)	R. I.	(-.328)	N. C.	(-.198)	Okla.	(7)
N. Mex.	(7.00)	N.Dak.	(.31)	S.Dak.	(11)	Kans.	(-.260)	Ala.	(-.399)	Okla.	(-.293)	N.H.	(7)
Tex.	(7.11)	Wyo.	(.28)	N.Mex.	(11)	W.Va.	(-.366)	Tenn.	(-.582)	Ky.	(-.351)	Nebr.	(8)
W.Va.	(7.33)	Miss.	(.25)	Kans.	(11)	Iowa	(-.382)	Maine	(-.619)	Md.	(-.377)	N.Dak.	(8)
Ky.	(7.40)	S.Dak.	(.23)	Maine	(11)	Va.	(-.613)	Ky.	(-.661)	Vt.	(-.483)	S.Dak.	(8)
Mo.	(7.66)	Tex.	(.20)	N.H.	(10)	Nev.	(-.697)	N.Mex.	(-.734)	Tenn.	(-.556)	Tenn.	(8)
Fla.	(7.80)	Idaho	(.19)	R.I.	(10)	Ark.	(-.765)	W.Va.	(-.739)	Fla.	(-.560)	Vt.	(8)
Va.	(7.86)	N.C.	(.19)	N.C.	(10)	S.Dak.	(-.821)	N.H.	(-.752)	Tex.	(-.566)	Ga.	(9)
La.	(8.00)	N. Mex.	(.18)	Vt.	(10)	N.Mex.	(-1.006)	Okla.	(-.799)	N.Mex.	(-.615)	La.	(9)
Okla.	(8.25)	Iowa	(.18)	Ariz.	(10)	Tenn.	(-1.190)	Ark.	(-.827)	N.Y.	(-.643)	N.C.	(9)
N.C.	(8.50)	Vt.	(.13)	Del.	(10)	Vt.	(-1.203)	N.Dak.	(-.869)	Va.	(-.964)	S.C.	(9)
Tenn.	(8.50)	Oreg.	(.11)	W.Va.	(8)	N.H.	(-1.357)	S.Dak.	(-.976)	La.	(-1.152)	Va.	(9)
Ala.	(8.57)	N.H.	(.09)	Fla.	(8)	N.Dak.	(-1.364)	Utah	(-1.032)	Ark.	(-1.360)	Ala.	(10)
S.C.	(8.75)	Nebr.	(.08)	Miss.	(7)	Utah	(-1.366)	Idaho	(-1.052)	Miss.	(-1.770)	Ark.	(10)
Ga.	(8.80)	S.C.	(.06)	S.C.	(7)	Idaho	(-1.545)	Mont.	(-1.095)	Ala.	(-2.504)	Fla.	(10)
Ark.	(9.00)	Nev.	(.04)	Tex.	(7)	Mont.	(-1.827)	Wyo.	(-1.421)	Ga.	(-2.516)	Miss.	(10)
Miss.	(9.00)	Fla.	(.00)	N.Dak.	(7)	Wyo.	(-2.355)	Vt.	(-1.546)	S.C.	(-2.838)	Tex.	(10)

*Data not included for Alaska and Hawaii in the original study. In these instances, Alaska and Hawaii were given the mean value for correlation purposes.

TABLE 10 (cont'd)

(values in parentheses indicate score for cited study)

Deleon		(9) Ranney		(10) Crittenden		(11) Crittenden		(12) Hofferbert		(13) Hofferbert		(14) Gini	
uid Resources ale*		Partisanship Index		Metro-Urbanism Factor Scores*		Integrative Message Exchange Factor Scores*		Industrialization Factor Scores*		Cultural Enrichment Factor Scores*		Index of State Income Inequality	
J.	(98)	S.C.	(1.000)	N.Y.	(87)	Conn.	(63)	N.J.	(1)	Nev.	(1)	Miss.	(.510)
1.	(97)	Ga.	(.9915)	Calif.	(70)	Iowa	(61)	Conn.	(2)	Calif.	(2)	Ark.	(.486)
1.	(96)	La.	(.9867)	Ill.	(68)	Kans.	(60)	N.Y.	(3)	Wyo.	(3)	Ala.	(.478)
Y.	(90)	Miss.	(.9805)	N.J.	(65)	Mass.	(60)	Mass.	(4)	Colo.	(4)	Tenn.	(.478)
.	(78)	Tex.	(.9590)	Mass.	(62)	Nebr.	(60)	Ill.	(5)	Oreg.	(5)	La.	(.477)
nn.	(77)	Ala.	(.9565)	Tex.	(62)	N.H.	(59)	Penn.	(6)	Wash.	(6)	S.C.	(.474)
lif.	(72)	Ark.	(.9427)	Penn.	(61)	Utah	(59)	R.I.	(7)	Mont.	(7)	Ky.	(.474)
.	(71)	Fla.	(.9220)	Ohio	(60)	Wis.	(59)	Del.	(8)	Nebr.	(8)	Ga.	(.469)
ash.	(70)	Va.	(.8795)	Fla.	(59)	Ind.	(58)	Ohio.	(9)	Kans.	(9)	Okla.	(.465)
C.	(70)	N.C.	(.8793)	Md.	(57)	Minn.	(58)	Calif.	(10)	Utah	(10)	N.C.	(.465)
Mex.	(69)	Tenn.	(.8715)	Mo.	(57)	N.J.	(58)	Mich.	(11)	Conn.	(11)	Tex.	(.464)
.	(68)	Okla.	(.8193)	Mich.	(56)	R.I.	(58)	Md.	(12)	Del.	(12)	Fla.	(.462)
v.	(65)	Ky.	(.7650)	Colo.	(54)	S.Dak.	(58)	Ind.	(13)	Idaho	(13)	Va.	(.461)
eg.	(64)	Ariz.	(.7490)	Conn.	(53)	Idaho	(57)	Wis.	(14)	Fla.	(14)	Mo.	(.459)
k.	(64)	W.Va.	(.7223)	Ga.	(52)	Ohio	(57)	Mo.	(15)	Iowa	(15)	S.Dak.	(.456)
ss.	(63)	Md.	(.7137)	La.	(52)	N.Dak.	(56)	N.H.	(16)	Ariz.	(16)	Alaska	(.456)
Va.	(61)	N.Mex.	(.7023)	Wis.	(52)	Oreg.	(56)	Wash.	(17)	Minn.	(17)	W.Va.	(.451)
.	(61)	Alaska	(.6767)	Wash.	(52)	Vt.	(56)	N.C.	(18)	N.Y.	(18)	Haw.	(.446)
aine	(61)	Mo.	(.6603)	Minn.	(51)	Colo.	(56)	Va.	(19)	N.J.	(19)	Ariz.	(.445)
1.	(61)	R.I.	(.6327)	Va.	(51)	Del.	(56)	Tenn.	(20)	Mass.	(20)	N.Mex.	(.440)
a.	(61)	Wash.	(.5647)	Tenn.	(50)	Mich.	(56)	Minn.	(21)	Ill.	(21)	Nebr.	(.440)
).	(60)	Del.	(.5420)	Okla.	(50)	Mont.	(56)	Ga.	(22)	Ohio.	(22)	Kans.	(.439)
i.	(60)	Nev.	(.5263)	Nev.	(49)	Ill.	(55)	S.C.	(23)	Mich.	(23)	Iowa	(.439)
Dak.	(57)	Mass.	(.5227)	Ind.	(49)	Penn.	(55)	Alaska	(24)	Alaska	(24)	Del.	(.434)
va	(57)	Haw.	(.4897)	Kans.	(48)	Wyo.	(55)	Haw.	(24)	Haw.	(24)	Vt.	(.434)
.	(57)	Colo.	(.4827)	Ariz.	(48)	Alaska	(55)	La.	(24)	N.Mex.	(24)	Minn.	(.431)
w.	(57)	Mont.	(.4695)	Ala.	(48)	Haw.	(55)	Iowa	(25)	S.Dak.	(25)	N.Dak.	(.430)
aska	(57)	Minn.	(.4610)	Alaska	(48)	Maine	(54)	Maine	(26)	Okla.	(26)	N.Y.	(.429)
ho	(56)	Utah	(.4605)	Haw.	(48)	Wash.	(54)	W.Va.	(27)	Tex.	(27)	Calif.	(.427)
io	(52)	Conn.	(.4420)	R.I.	(47)	Calif.	(52)	Oreg.	(28)	Ind.	(28)	Colo.	(.425)
olo.	(49)	Penn.	(.4050)	Nebr.	(47)	Md.	(51)	Tex.	(29)	Md.	(29)	Md.	(.424)
iz.	(49)	Calif.	(.3930)	Oreg.	(47)	Mo.	(51)	Vt.	(30)	N.H.	(30)	Ill.	(.423)
br.	(47)	Nebr.	(.3875)	Iowa	(45)	Nev.	(50)	Ala.	(31)	N.Dak.	(31)	R.I.	(.418)
Dak.	(46)	Ill.	(.3847)	Miss.	(45)	W.Va.	(46)	Fla.	(32)	Wis.	(32)	Mont.	(.415)
H.	(46)	Idaho	(.3780)	Utah	(44)	Okla.	(46)	Ky.	(33)	Penn.	(33)	Ind.	(.414)
nt.	(46)	Mich.	(.3770)	N.Mex.	(43)	N.Y.	(46)	Kans.	(34)	Mo.	(34)	Nev.	(.414)
ass.	(46)	N.J.	(.3605)	Mont.	(43)	Va.	(43)	Colo.	(35)	Vt.	(35)	Mass.	(.414)
ich.	(43)	Ind.	(.3545)	Ky.	(43)	Ariz.	(43)	Utah	(36)	R.I.	(36)	Wash.	(.413)
la.	(41)	Oreg.	(.3545)	N.C.	(43)	Ky.	(43)	Nebr.	(37)	Maine	(37)	Penn.	(.412)
is.	(39)	Ohio	(.3523)	Ark.	(42)	N.Mex.	(42)	Okla.	(38)	Va.	(38)	Wis.	(.412)
ah	(38)	Wyo.	(.3470)	Del.	(42)	Tenn.	(39)	Miss.	(39)	Ky.	(39)	Maine	(.412)
.	(38)	N.Y.	(.3173)	S.C.	(42)	Tex.	(39)	Ark.	(40)	W.Va.	(40)	Oreg.	(.411)
nn.	(37)	Wis.	(.2997)	Wyo.	(42)	N.C.	(37)	Ariz.	(41)	Ga.	(41)	Mich.	(.409)
ro.	(36)	N.H.	(.2680)	W.Va.	(41)	Fla.	(37)	Nev.	(42)	Tenn.	(42)	Ohio	(.408)
ex.	(34)	Iowa	(.2495)	N.H.	(40)	Ga.	(34)	Idaho	(43)	La.	(43)	N.H.	(.407)
ns.	(34)	Kans.	(.2415)	Maine	(38)	Ala.	(33)	Mont.	(44)	Ark.	(44)	Conn.	(.404)
nn.	(26)	Maine	(.2405)	S.Dak.	(37)	Ark.	(32)	N.Mex.	(45)	Ala.	(45)	N.J.	(.403)
nn.	(23)	S.Dak.	(.2320)	N.Dak.	(36)	S.C.	(32)	S.Dak.	(46)	N.C.	(46)	Idaho	(.402)
.	(13)	N.Dak.	(.1860)	Idaho	(35)	La.	(30)	Wyo.	(47)	S.C.	(47)	Wyo.	(.399)
a.	(13)	Vt.	(.1760)	Vt.	(35)	Miss.	(24)	N.Dak.	(48)	Miss.	(48)	Utah	(.394)

*Data not included for Alaska and Hawaii in the original study. In these instances, Alaska and Hawaii were given the mean value for correlation purposes.

(cont'd)

TABLE 10 (cont'd)

(values in parentheses indicate score for cited study)

(15) State Population (thousands)		(16) Population Density		(17) Expenditures per pupil in ADA, 1968-69		(18) Sharkansky-Hofferbert Welfare-Education Factor Scores*		(19) Per Capita General Revenue, State and Local		(20) Crittenden Scope of Government Factor Scores*		(21) Walker Innovation Index	
Calif.	(18,990)	N.J.	(949.0)	N.Y.	(1140)	Calif.	(1.849)	Alaska	(1085)	N.Y.	(76)	N.Y.	(.65
N.Y.	(18,022)	R.I.	(868.4)	Alaska	(987)	Mass.	(1.446)	Wyo.	(784)	Wyo.	(73)	Mass.	(.62
Penn.	(11,671)	Mass.	(679.9)	N.J.	(913)	Wis.	(1.445)	Calif.	(712)	La.	(71)	Calif.	(.60
Ill.	(10,887)	Conn.	(616.0)	Conn.	(826)	Minn.	(1.316)	Nev.	(699)	N.Dak.	(66)	N.J.	(.58
Tex.	(10,857)	N.Y.	(382.7)	Oreg.	(793)	Ill.	(1.258)	N.Y.	(680)	Colo.	(63)	Mich.	(.57
Ohio	(10,488)	Md.	(380.6)	Md.	(775)	N.Y.	(1.152)	Haw.	(656)	Vt.	(61)	Conn.	(.56
Mich.	(8608)	Del.	(272.5)	Wis.	(787)	N.J.	(1.035)	N.Dak.	(601)	Oreg.	(61)	Penn.	(.56
N.J.	(6981)	Penn.	(262.1)	R.I.	(756)	N.Dak.	(.901)	Minn.	(599)	Nev.	(61)	Oreg.	(.54
Fla.	(6035)	Ohio	(261.8)	Del.	(745)	Kans.	(.852)	Wash.	(595)	Calif.	(60)	Colo.	(.53
Mass.	(5434)	Ill.	(197.7)	Penn.	(743)	Conn.	(.846)	N.Mex.	(588)	Mont.	(60)	Wis.	(.53
N.C.	(5059)	Mich.	(154.3)	Ill.	(742)	Iowa	(.845)	Vt.	(578)	Wash.	(59)	Ohio	(.52
Ind.	(5012)	Ind.	(141.4)	Wyo.	(715)	Wash.	(.789)	Del.	(573)	Minn.	(58)	Minn.	(.52
Mo.	(4587)	Calif.	(124.2)	Iowa	(707)	Okla.	(.785)	Mont.	(564)	S.Dak.	(58)	Ill.	(.52
Va.	(4541)	Haw.	(123.6)	Ariz.	(698)	Mich.	(.761)	Colo.	(558)	Miss.	(57)	Wash.	(.51
Ga.	(4490)	Fla.	(117.4)	Calif.	(697)	Oreg.	(.735)	S.Dak.	(545)	N.Mex.	(56)	R.I.	(.50
Wis.	(4194)	Va.	(117.2)	Mont.	(696)	Colo.	(.711)	Oreg.	(542)	Okla.	(53)	Md.	(.48
Tenn.	(3936)	N.C.	(106.5)	Nev.	(685)	Nebr.	(.705)	Wis.	(539)	Utah	(52)	N.H.	(.48
Md.	(3680)	Tenn.	(96.3)	Minn.	(684)	R.I.	(.640)	Mass.	(534.48)	Mass.	(51)	Ind.	(.46
La.	(3663)	S.C.	(88.9)	Haw.	(677)	Ohio	(.284)	Ariz.	(534.39)	Idaho	(51)	La.	(.45
Minn.	(3625)	La.	(82.9)	Mass.	(673)	Wyo.	(.220)	Mich.	(533)	Iowa	(50)	Maine	(.45
Ala.	(3533)	Ky.	(81.1)	Wash.	(673)	N.Mex.	(.184)	Utah	(532)	Kans.	(50)	Va.	(.45
Wash.	(3208)	Ga.	(79.7)	Mich.	(665)	Ind.	(.155)	Iowa	(531)	Ark.	(50)	Utah	(.44
Ky.	(3201)	N.H.	(79.4)	Vt.	(660)	Utah	(.124)	Md.	(508)	Ariz.	(48)	N.Dak.	(.44
Conn.	(2918)	Wis.	(77.7)	Fla.	(647)	Penn.	(.085)	Okla.	(505)	Alaska	(47)	N.C.	(.42
Iowa	(2722)	W.Va.	(75.5)	Kans.	(647)	S.Dak.	(.072)	Conn.	(502)	Haw.	(47)	Alaska	(.42
S.C.	(2638)	Ala.	(69.4)	Ind.	(640)	Haw.	(0)	Idaho	(500)	Maine	(47)	Haw.	(.42
Okla.	(2516)	Mo.	(67.4)	Colo.	(636)	Alaska	(0)	Nebr.	(498)	Nebr.	(47)	Kans.	(.42
Miss.	(2344)	Wash.	(51.0)	Ohio	(634)	Idaho	(-.045)	R.I.	(491)	W.Va.	(46)	Nebr.	(.42
Kans.	(2281)	Miss.	(49.8)	La.	(632)	Mont.	(-.063)	La.	(480)	Wis.	(46)	Ky.	(.41
Colo.	(2012)	Iowa	(49.6)	N.H.	(624)	S.Dak.	(-.072)	Kans.	(479)	Fla.	(46)	Vt.	(.41
Oreg.	(1981)	Vt.	(47.3)	Mo.	(619)	Md.	(-.155)	N.J.	(471)	Ga.	(46)	Iowa	(.41
Ark.	(1972)	Minn.	(46.7)	N.Mex.	(611)	Ariz.	(-.266)	Ill.	(468)	Mich.	(45)	Ala.	(.40
W.Va.	(1807)	Tex.	(42.5)	Va.	(600)	Mo.	(-.378)	Fla.	(447)	Del.	(45)	Fla.	(.39
Ariz.	(1637)	Ark.	(38.2)	N.Dak.	(585)	Del.	(-.390)	Ind.	(445)	N.H.	(43)	Ark.	(.39
Nebr.	(1443)	Okla.	(37.2)	S.Dak.	(582)	Maine	(-.465)	W.Va.	(429)	S.C.	(43)	Idaho	(.39
Utah	(1022)	Maine	(31.6)	Maine	(547)	Nev.	(-.535)	Penn.	(427)	Tex.	(43)	Tenn.	(.38
N.Mex.	(1002)	Kans.	(28.3)	Idaho	(545)	Vt.	(-.615)	Ga.	(417)	Ill.	(42)	W.Va.	(.38
Maine	(982)	Oreg.	(21.1)	Ky.	(535)	La.	(-.729)	Ohio	(413)	N.C.	(42)	Ariz.	(.38
R.I.	(901)	Colo.	(20.2)	Ga.	(530)	Tex.	(-.798)	Mo.	(412.77)	Ala.	(42)	Ga.	(.38
Haw.	(762)	Nebr.	(18.9)	Utah	(527)	Fla.	(-.875)	Ky.	(412.16)	Md.	(42)	Mont.	(.37
Idaho	(701)	Ariz.	(14.9)	W.Va.	(521)	Ky.	(-1.042)	N.H.	(411)	Tenn.	(41)	Mo.	(.37
Mont.	(699)	Utah	(12.7)	Nebr.	(510)	Va.	(-1.062)	Va.	(404)	Conn.	(41)	Del.	(.37
N.H.	(691)	N.Dak.	(8.9)	N.C.	(506)	N.C.	(-1.079)	Tex.	(401)	Penn.	(40)	N.Mex.	(.37
S.Dak.	(668)	Idaho	(8.7)	Okla.	(496)	Ark.	(-1.263)	Maine	(400)	Ohio	(40)	Okla.	(.36
N.Dak.	(632)	S.Dak.	(8.7)	Ark.	(486)	W.Va.	(-1.350)	Ala.	(374)	Ind.	(39)	S.Dak.	(.36
Del.	(524)	N.Mex.	(8.2)	Tenn.	(485)	Ga.	(-1.452)	Tenn.	(372)	Mo.	(39)	Tex.	(.36
Nev.	(438)	Mont.	(4.8)	Tex.	(480)	S.C.	(-1.580)	Miss.	(363)	Ky.	(37)	S.C.	(.34
Vt.	(420)	Nev.	(4.2)	S.C.	(478)	Tenn.	(-1.738)	N.C.	(362)	Va.	(37)	Wyo.	(.32
Wyo.	(319)	Wyo.	(3.3)	Miss.	(465)	Ala.	(-1.753)	Ark.	(351)	R.I.	(37)	Nev.	(.32
Alaska	(271)	Alaska	(0.5)	Ala.	(380)	Miss.	(-2.432)	S.C.	(326)	N.J.	(36)	Miss.	(.29

*Data not included for Alaska and Hawaii in the original study. In these instances, Alaska and Hawaii were given the mean value for correlation purposes.

To obtain a fuller treatment of the assumptions, rationale, and related research that underlie the construction of the scales used, and which help to justify their selection for use in this study, the reader may wish to consult the source cited for each variable. Table 10 recapitulates the list and provides state scores and rank-order positions for each index. The number of the scales in the text and in the table are identical to facilitate cross reference.

Historical Cultural Factors

The Sharkansky-Elazar political culture scale (no. 1 on the table) is taken from Ira Sharkansky, "The Utility of Elazar's Political Culture." The scale ranges from 1.0 (most moralist) to 9.0 (most traditionalist).

Political Factors

The centralization index for state legislatures (no. 2 on the table) is taken from Wayne Francis, Legislative Issues in the Fifty States (Chicago: Rand-McNally, 1967). This index is based on responses to a questionnaire from a 1963 sample of 838 state legislators representing each house in all fifty states. Legislators were asked where they thought the most significant decisions were made in their legislature. Responses were graded as follows:

In the governor's office.

In policy committees of the
legislature, with only legislative leaders represented.
$\left\{\begin{array}{l} 1.00 \\ \text{(most} \\ \text{centralized)} \end{array}\right.$

Party caucus.   .50

Regular committee meetings. $\left\{\begin{array}{l} 0.00 \\ \\ \text{(least} \\ \text{centralized)} \end{array}\right.$

On the floor.

Centralization index scores for each state were found by summing individual scores for each state and dividing the total by the number of responses from each state.

The combined index of governor's formal powers (no. 3 on the table) is taken from Joseph Schlesinger, "The Politics of the Executive," in Politics in the American States, H. Jacob and K. Vines, eds. (Boston: Little, Brown and Co., 1965). This index combines four measures of each governor's formal powers: tenure potential and appointive, budgetary, and veto powers.

The legislative professionalism index (no. 4 on the table) is taken from John Grumm, "Structural Determinants of Legislative Output," in Legislatures in Developmental Perspective, Allan Kornberg and Lloyd Musolf, eds. (Durhum, N.C.: Duke University Press, 1970). Grumm's first step in constructing his legislative professionalism index was to identify five variables that were most obviously connected with legislative professionalism: (1) compensation of legislators (1964-65); (2) total length of sessions during the 1963-64 biennium; (3) expenditures for legislative services and operations during the same biennium; (4) number of bills introduced in the 1963-64 session; (5) a legal services score (based on Calvin Clark's 1967 CCSL study, which developed a point system by which state legislators were graded on the extent of services actually provided, size of staff involved, and extent of utilization by legislators). The next step was to factor-analyze the five variables, using the unrotated first factor loadings to compute factor scores for each state. These scores constitute the professionalism index. (Note: Factor analysis takes a large number of operational indexes and reduces them to a smaller number of conceptual variables. These underlying conceptual variable known as factors, represent the common element associated with a cluster of discrete indicators, each measuring a different facet of the same thing--e.g. professionalism. Thus we can triangulate on a complex phenomenon and construct a single scale for measuring it.)

The professionalism-local reliance factor (no. 5 on the table) is taken from Ira Sharkansky and Richard Hofferbert, "Dimensions of State Politics, Economics, and Public Policy," American Political Science Review, LXIII, 3 (September, 1969). The original data base from which this factor and the competition-turnout factor were extracted comprises fifty-three political-governmental variables. The professionalism-local reliance factor draws its name from "the positively-loaded measures of judicial and legislative compensation, expenditures on legislative services, and legislative activity; and from negatively loaded measures of reliance upon state government expenditures and federal aids."[11] In other words, states scoring high on this factor show high salaries for judges and legislators, well-financed legislative staffs, and primary reliance on locally raised and spent revenues.

The competition-turnout factor (no. 6 on the table) has the same source as no. 5. This factor "has as its highest-loaded variables the measures of turnout in a gubernatorial election, an index of suffrage liberality, and (negatively) one-party dominance in the state legislature and in recent elections for governor."[12]

The party integration index (no. 7 on the table) is taken from Duane Lockard, "State Party Systems and Policy Outputs," in Political Research and Political Theory, Oliver Garceau, ed., (Cambridge, Massachusetts: Harvard University Press, 1968). States scoring high on this index have competitive and cohesive political parties in state legislatures; states scoring low are characterized by one-party domination and party factionalism. On the index used here, states falling in Lockard's groups I-X are assigned the values 1-10, respectively.

The index of resource fluidity (no. 8 on the table) is taken from Tax Foundation, Inc., Earmarked State Taxes (New York: Tax Foundation, Inc., 1965). Scores for each state are given as 1 minus the percent of state government taxes earmarked in 1963. Low-scoring states on this index have lows which earmark or "dedicate" large portions of the budget to specific policy programs, thus reducing the size of the budget that is controllable by state legislative and executive officials.

The partisanship index (no. 9 on the table) is taken from Austin Ranney, "Parties in State Politics," in H. Jacob and K. Vines, op. cit. High-scoring states are mostly Democratic, low-scoring states mostly Republican. This is a composite index based on average percentage figures for popular vote won by Democratic gubernatorial candidates, for percent of seats held by Democrats in state house and senate, and for percent of all terms for governor, house, and senate in which Democrats had control. The base time period is 1946-63.

Demographic/Socieoeconomic Factors

The metro-urbanism factor scores (no. 10 on the table) are taken from John Crittenden, "Dimensions of Modernization in the American States," American Political Science Review, LXI, 4. Highest loadings on this factor include executive salaries, population, ethnic diversity, and urbanization. States scoring high on this index have large metropolitan communities and the characteristics associated with such communities: density, ethnicity, wealth, size. States which have a predominance of what the Census Bureau calls "urban areas" can still score low on the metro-urban index.

The integrative exchange factor scores (no. 11 on the table) is taken from Crittenden. Highest loadings on this factor are number of telephones, voting turnout, income, good housing, education. High-scoring states have complex communication networks serving populations which possess a high level of literacy and enjoy a high standard of living.

The industrialization factor scores (no. 12 on the table) is taken from Richard Hofferbert, "Socioeconomic Dimensions of the American States: 1890-1960," Midwest Journal of Political Science, XII, 3 (August, 1968). Hofferbert extracted this and the cultural enrichment factor from an original data base of twenty-one indicators of socio-economic development. Major components of the industrialization factor include proportion of the state's population in manufacturing employment and value-added per capita by manufacturers.

The cultural enrichment (affluence) factor scores (no. 13 on the table) have the same source as the industrialization factor scores. Highest positive loadings on this factor include education, property value, personal income; highest negative loadings include percent Negro, percent illiterate. This factor is similar to Crittenden's integrative exchange factor, but has greater weight given to measures of income and wealth.

The Gini index of state income inequality (no. 14 on the table) is taken from Thomas Dye, "Income Inequality and American State Politics," in Policy Analysis in Political Science, Ira Sharkansky, ed. op. cit. States scoring high on this index display a high degree of inequality in the distribution of income and wealth.

State population, 1970 (no. 15 on the table) is taken from Bureau of the Census, 1970 Preliminary Reports.

Population density (no. 16 on the table) is taken from Book of the States, 1970-71.

Public Policy Indicators

Expenditures per pupil in ADA, 1968-69 (no. 17 on the table) are taken from Book of the States, 1970-71.

The welfare-education factor (no. 18 on the table) is taken from Sharkansky-Hofferbert, the same source as nos. 5 and 6 on the table. This factor emphasizes generous state and local government welfare payments, the "tendency of high school pupils to remain until graduation, and the success of state residents on national examination."[13] These last two measures reflect the extent and success of public investment in high-quality educational programs.

Per capita direct general expenditures of state and local governments (no. 19 on the table) is taken from Book of the States, 1970-71.

The scope of government factor scores (no. 20 on the table) is taken from Crittenden, op. cit. Highest loadings on this factor include state and local taxes per capita, spending level per capita, and government employment levels per capita.

The innovation index (no. 21 on the table) is taken from Jack Walker, "The Diffusion of Innovations Among the American States," American Political Science Review, LXIII, 3 (September, 1969). Walker's innovation index is designed to represent the relative speed with which state governments adopt innovations. The innovation score is based on the analysis of eighty-eight different programs (ranging from "Accountants' Licensing" to "Zoning in Cities") which were enacted by at least twenty state legislatures prior to 1965. Six to eight pieces of legislation were studied in each of the following areas: welfare, health, education, conservation, planning, administrative organization, highways, civil rights, corrections and police, labor, taxes, and professional regulation. Construction of the innovation index for each state involved three basic steps: (a) counting the total number of years which elapsed between the first and last recorded legislative enactment of a program; (b) assignment to each program in each state a number representing the percentage of time which elapsed between the first adoption and its own acceptance of the program (first states to adopt received a score of 0.000; last states to adopt, and states which did not adopt, a program, received a score of 1.000); (c) the innovation score is then calculated for each state as 1.000 minus the average of the sum of the state's scores on all issues. The larger the score, the faster a state responds to new ideas or programs.

It should be noted that on many of the indexes discussed above, scores are not provided for Alaska and Hawaii. Since our program for calculating correlation coefficients requires values for these two states, they were arbitrarily assigned the mean value on most indexes; and where factor scores were employed, they were assigned a factor score of 0.00. This procedure in no significant way distorts the findings reported below.

METHOD

Mainly for its ease of computation, Spearman's rank-order correlation coefficient (r_s) was selected as the measure of association to be used in this comparison of the LES results with those of other analysts. The principle behind Spearman's r_s is simple. "We compare the rankings on the two sets of scores by taking the differences of ranks, squaring these differences and then adding, and finally manipulating the measure so that its value will be +1.0 whenever the rankings are in perfect agreement, -1.0 if they are in perfect disagreement, and zero if there is no relationship whatsoever."[14]

If we symbolize the difference between any pair of ranks as D_i, then we find the value of

$$\sum_{i=1}^{N} D_i^2$$

and compute r_s using the formula

$$r_s = 1 - \frac{6 \sum_{i=1}^{N} D_i^2}{N(N^2-1)}$$

where N, in this study, equals 50.

How shall we evaluate the correlation coefficients we obtain for any two rank orders (say, for industrialization and accountability)? What significance shall we attach to them? Following standard procedure, our first step in evaluating a coefficient of correlation between two variables is to test the null hypothesis. In plain words, the null hypothesis states that the coefficient could have been obtained by chance alone-- i.e., that no relationship exists between the two variables. Based on a population of fifty states, for example, there is one chance out of 100 that a .333 coefficient could be obtained when in fact no relationship at all exists between the two variables. If we are conservative, perhaps we will insist on one chance out of 1,000 as our criterion in order to guard against the possibility that our statistics might be misleading. Or if we follow common practice, perhaps we will tolerate five chances out of 100 that our judgment is wrong when we assert that a relationship exists between two variables. But we do know that, for any given study, the larger r_s becomes, the smaller the chances are that we could have obtained such a result by chance alone, and thus the more confident we may be that a relationship exists, the strength of that relationship varying with the magnitude of r_s.

Spearman's r_s permits a test of statistical significance that offers a basis for accepting or rejecting the null hypothesis. The test involves calculating z scores for the normal curve distribution for values of N (=50) and r_s.[15] Associated with each z score is the probability (e.g., p = .05) that a relationship of strength r_s could have been obtained by chance alone. In order to conclude that a given coefficient is statistically significant, we must first agree on a criteri (i.e., the odds we are willing to accept that we are wrong in rejecting the null hypothesis). In the present study, any r_s for which $p \leq .05$ is considered statistically significant. Where $p \leq .05$, we reject the null hypothesis and assert that a relationship exists between two variables. Where one of those variables is legislative capability, we call the other variable a correlate of capability. If p is greater than .05, however, we accept the null hypothesis and assert that no relationship exists. For N = 50, (a) $p \leq .05$ if $r_s \geq .236$ and (b) $p \leq .01$ if $r_s \geq .333$. In Table 11 below, all coefficients which are greater than or equal to .236 are found to be statistically significant by our criterion and are thus to be considered correlates of legislative capability.

Identifying a set of statistical correlates is, of course, only the first step in the more difficult task of assessing the theoretical and practical significance of our results.

FINDINGS

Table 11 reports correlations between socioeconomic, cultural, and political variables and state positions on each of the FAIIR and overall schedules. Let us examine the coefficient of correlation between the "Political Culture Scale" and the overall final ranking to illustrate how entries in Table 11 should be interpreted. The entry in this case, $r_s = .415^*$, means two things. (1) It means that traditionalist political cultures are inversely related to legislative capability (or moralist political cultures are positively related to capability). (2) It means that the relationship between culture and capability is strong ($p \leq .01$). (More than this we cannot say on the basis of Table 11 alone. An r_s of .415 does not permit us to conclude, for example, that moralist political cultures cause or in some way bring about legislative capability. But we can say that moralist culture is a strong correlate of capability.) In contrast, the coefficient of correlation between the "Fluid Resources Scale" and the final ranking ($r_s = -.038$) is not, by the criterion which we have established, a correlate of capability.

To facilitate the discussion that follows, Table 12 ranks the significant explanatory variables (all $r_s \geq .236$) according to the strength of their relationship with state positions on the final ranking and on the individual FAIIR schedules. Table 12 therefore offers a concise summary of the correlates of legislative capability.

Correlates of Capability: Final Ranking

The summary of our results shown in Table 12 suggests the

TABLE 11

Coefficients of Correlation Between Selected Socioeconomic, Cultural, and Political Variables
and State Positions on the Five FAIIR Schedules, and the Final Ranking
(Overall) of Legislative Capability

Explanatory Variables	Overall	Functional	Accountability	Information	Independence	Representativeness
(1) Sharkansky-Elazar's Political Culture Scale	+.415**	.315*	.495**	.426**	.085	.129
(2) Francis' Centralization Index	-.119	-.099	-.352**	-.002	.116	.163
(3) Schlesinger's Formal Governor's Powers Index	.292*	.170	.298*	.345**	.140	.125
(4) Grumm's Legislative Professionalism Index	.245*	.114	-.041	.262*	.385**	.381**
(5) Sharkansky-Hofferbert's Professionalism/Local-Reliance Factor	.319*	.170	.010	.401**	.435**	.327*
(6) Sharkansky-Hofferbert's Competition - Turnout Factor Scores	.331*	.159	.418**	.318*	-.057	.221
(7) Lockard's Party Integration Index	.332*	.308*	.130	.355**	.165	.358**
(8) DeLeon's Fluid Resources Scale	-.038	.205	.019	-.101	-.105	.118
(9) Ranney's Partisanship Index	-.360**	-.284*	-.431**	-.389**	-.012	-.124
(10) Crittenden's Metro-Urbanism Factor	.375**	.211	.095	.478**	.371**	.349**
(11) Crittenden's Integrative Exchange Factor	.314*	.135	.348**	.377**	-.045	.148
(12) Hofferbert's Industrialization Factor	.118	.035	.147	.246*	.234	.270*
(13) Hofferbert's Affluence Factor	.424**	.365**	.497**	.399**	.098	.112
(14) Gini's Index of Income Inequality	-.256*	-.196	-.252*	-.292*	.004	-.112
(15) State Population	.199	.037	.024	.289*	.238*	.337**
(16) Population Density	.022	-.042	-.199	.142	.196	.248*

*p ≤ .05
**p ≤ .01

70

TABLE 12

Explanatory Variables Ranked in Order of Importance for
FAIIR Schedules and Final Ranking on Legislative Capability

Final Ranking	Functional	Accountability	Information	Independence	Representativeness
(13) Affluence	(13) Affluence	(13) Affluence	(10) Metro-Urbanism	(5) Professionalism-Local Reliance	(4) Legislative Professionalism
(1) Political Culture	(1) Political Culture	(1) Political Culture	(1) Political Culture	(4) Legislative Professionalism	(7) Party Integration
(10) Metro-Urbanism	(7) Party Integration	(9) Partisanship (-)	(5) Professionalism-Local Reliance	(10) Metro-Urbanism	(10) Metro-Urbanism
(9) Partisanship (-)	(9) Partisanship (-)	(6) Competition-Turnout	(13) Affluence	(15) Population	(15) Population
(7) Party Integration		(2) Legislative Centralization	(9) Partisanship (-)		(5) Professionalism-Local Reliance
(6) Competition-Turnout		(11) Integrative Exchange	(11) Integrative Exchange		(12) Industrialization
(5) Professionalism-Local Reliance		(3) Governor's Powers	(7) Party Integration		(16) Population Density
(11) Integrative Exchange		(14) Inequality (-)	(3) Governor's Powers		
(3) Governor's Powers			(6) Competition-Turnout		
(14) Inequality (-)			(14) Inequality (-)		
(4) Legislative Professionalism			(15) Population		
			(4) Legislative Professionalism		
			(12) Industrialization		

Notes: Relationships with all variables are statistically significant at .05 level.

Relationships with underlined variables are statistically significant at .01 level.

(-) indicates negative correlation.

following general statement regarding the correlates of legislative capability.

· Those state legislatures ranking high in technical capability tend to be in wealthy states whose citizens live predominantly in urban areas. The political culture in such states tends to encourage innovation, popular political participation, bureaucratic efficiency, and government activism. Citizens in these states are generally well-educated, politically active, and involved in public affairs. The political systems in such states tend to have strong governors, professional legislatures, competitive and cohesive political parties, and strong local governments. Finally, these states tend to lack rigid stratification by income class.

· Factors which are not associated with legislative capability include population size, population density, level of industrialization, legislative centralization, and resource fluidity.

· We also find that legislative capability is inversely related to one-party dominance. This is, of course, an expected result, since our two measures of interparty competition correlate significantly with capability.

Is regional affiliation related to a state's position on the final ranking of legislative capability? Figure 3 shows the regional distribution of legislative capability throughout the American states. Positions on the final ranking are arranged by quintiles, the first quintile comprising those ten states possessing the greatest legislative capability, the last quintile comprising those ten states having the least. Careful study of the map reveals several clusters of regionally affiliated states all having approximately the same level of capability. Regional clustering seems especially pronounced in the north central and Southeastern sections of the United States, with "most capable" legislatures dominating the former region and "least capable" the latter. In other sections of the country, however, nothing approximating a regional pattern emerges. Florida, for example, is an island of legislative capability unto itself. And the borders of California touch upon states whose legislatures run the gamut of technical achievement. The relationship between region and capability, therefore, does not appear to be very significant for the United States as a whole. Jack Walker, who also failed to find clear-cut regional clustering in his study of innovation diffusion in the American states, offers a possible explanation:

> During the last thirty years many new professional associations (CCSL is cited by Walker as an example) have been formed and more inter-state and federal agencies

FIGURE 3

The Regional Distribution of Legislative Capability:
Final Ranking

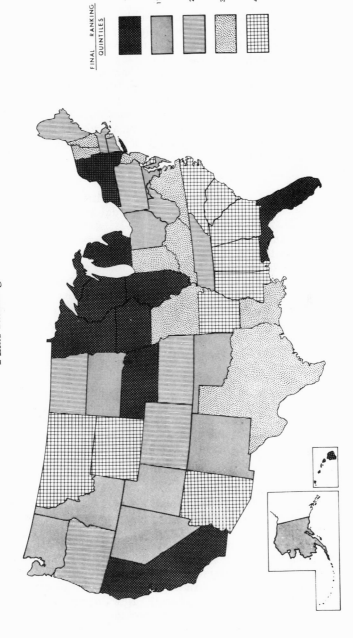

FINAL RANKING
QUINTILES

1 - 10
11 - 20
21 - 30
31 - 40
41 - 50

have begun facilitating communications and encouraging
national uniformity. The diffusion process is operating
much faster today than ever before, especially among those
states which have traditionally lagged behind in adopting
new ideas. The older, established modes of communication and evaluation, based on traditional ties of region and
common culture, are persisting, but there are indications
. . . that the system is slowly changing. Decision makers
in the states seem to be adopting a broader, national focus
based on new lines of communications which extend beyond
regional boundaries.[16]

Correlates of Capability:
The FAIIR Schedules

If we analyze the component factors associated with each of the
FAIIR schedules, we find (1) that correlates of the final ranking are
by no means identical with correlates found for individual schedules,
and (2) that state positions on individual schedules appear to be influenced by overlapping but nonetheless distinct sets of factors. For
example, we see in Table 12 that affluence correlates strongly with
the final ranking and the functionality, accountability, and information-
handling schedules, but appears to have little or no relationship to
the independence and representativeness schedules. The same is
true of political culture, the effects of which apparently do not extend
to independence and representativeness. On the other hand, our two
measures of governmental professionalism correlate significantly
with information-handling, independence, and representativeness,
but not with functionality and accountability. From these observations
we conclude that, in general, no single set of factors can be said to
have uniform impact upon capability across all five of the FAIIR
criteria.

One further observation should be made regarding the coefficients of correlation reported in Table 11. While many of these
coefficients reflect moderately strong relationships, considerable
interstate variation in rank-order positions remains; it can be neither
explained nor predicted by the correlates we have identified. "Deviant"
cases appear on every schedule. Florida, for example, possesses
essentially a traditionalist political culture, yet ranks very high on
the final ranking of legislative capability and on four of the five
individual FAIIR schedules as well. New Jersey, which ranks near
the top in affluence, falls near the bottom in legislative capability.
The first case suggests that a moralist type of political culture is
not a necessary condition for achieving legislative capability. And
the second case suggests that affluence is not a sufficient condition
for developing such capability.

Our ability to explain state positions on the FAIIR rankings, therefore, varies with (1) the particular schedule examined, and (2) the strength of the correlates found.

Let us consider first the functionality schedule. As can be seen in Table 12, our collection of sixteen political and socioeconomic indicators fails to shed much light on the forces shaping functionality in state legislatures. We find only one correlate of functionality at the .01 level of statistical significance: affluence. Three more correlates appear at the .05 level. All three are political indicators, two of them measuring different facets of interparty competition. Although these results are less than overwhelming, they do offer tentative support for the following generalization:

• Functional legislatures tend to be found in wealthy states whose citizens are educated, politically active, receptive to innovation, and appreciative of government efficiency. The political systems in such states tend to be characterized by competitive and cohesive political parties.

• Factors that do not appear to influence legislative functionality include urbanization, population size and density, and industrialization. In addition, legislative professionalism is not discernibly related to functionality.

Turning to the accountability schedule, the results summarized in Table 12 are more impressive. Eight of our sixteen indicators correlate significantly with accountability, six of them at the .01 level.

• Accountable legislatures tend to be found in wealthy states whose citizens are educated, politically active, receptive to innovation, and appreciative of government efficiency. The political systems in such states are characterized by decentralized legislative decision-making, strong governors, and competitive if not cohesive political parties.

• Factors not associated with legislative accountability include urbanization, population size and density, and industrialization. Further, no relationship exists between professionalism and accountability in state legislatures.

• As can be seen in Table 12, the schedule which deals with information-handling capability yields our most satisfying results. Thirteen of the sixteen indicators correlate significantly with information-handling capability, eight of them at the .01 level. (The centrality of information-handling policies within a strategy of legislative reform is discussed below.)

• Legislatures with high information-handling capabilities tend
to be found in wealthy, highly populated, urbanized, and industrialized
states whose citizens are educated, politically active, receptive to
innovation, and appreciative of government efficiency. Political
systems in such states tend to be characterized by strong governors,
competitive and cohesive political parties, and governmental professionalism.

• Factors not associated with information-handling capability
include population density, resource fluidity, and legislative centralization.

Turning now to the independence schedule, we find in Table 12
that four factors correlate significantly with our measure of legislative independence, three of them at the .01 level.

• Independent state legislatures tend to evidence a high degree
of professionalism and are found predominantly in heavily urbanized
states having large populations.

Factors not associated with legislative independence include
political culture, industrialization, economic wealth, legislative
centralization, and characteristics of political party systems. In
addition, no relationship is found between the independence of legislatures and the formal powers of governors--a finding of considerable
interest to those who might view legislative independence and gubernatorial authority as mutually incompatible.

Finally, on the representativeness schedule of legislative
capability, we find in Table 12 that seven factors correlate significantly with our measure of representativeness, four of them at the
.01 level.

• Representative legislatures tend to show a high degree of
professionalism and are found predominantly in industrialized,
urbanized, heavily populated states. The political systems in such
states tend to be characterized by competitive and cohesive political
parties.

• Factors not associated with legislative representativeness
include political culture, economic wealth, legislative centralization,
and gubernatorial strength.

It is worth noting at this point that two of the more widely used
measures of legislative capability (the Grumm index and Hofferbert-
Sharkansky's professionalism-local reliance factor) correlate
significantly only with information-handling capability, independence,

and representativeness. And even on these three schedules the magnitude of the correlation is hardly earth-shaking. The FAIIR schedules, therefore, seem to capture dimensions of legislative capability which have not heretofore been systematically measured and assessed on a comparative basis for the fifty American states.

Correlates of Capability:
Policy Consequences

Is there any relationship between legislative capability and the policy outputs of legislative institutions? Although it is true that the types of policies examined here are not exclusively the product of American state legislatures, the centrality of legislatures in the policy-making process is not disputed. Looking at Table 13, we find results that strongly support the propositions advanced earlier in the chapter. Highly capable legislatures tend to be generally innovative in many different areas of public policy, generous in welfare and education spending and services, and "interventionist" in the sense of having powers and responsibilities of broad scope. Further analysis of Table 13 reveals that the relative independence and representativeness of legislatures explains little of the interstate variation in substantive policy outcomes. These two dimensions of legislative capability are evidently more important in determining how laws are made than which laws are made.

Cross-Correlating the
FAIIR Criteria

How independent are the FAIIR schedules of each other? Where two or more schedules respond similarly to specific socioeconomic and political forces, is it possible that these schedules are tapping essentially the same dimension of legislative capability? Although this possibility is masked, to some degree, by the deliberate use of the same subcriteria in more than one evaluative schedule, cross-correlating state positions on the five FAIIR schedules does shed light on these questions, as shown in Table 14.

If we take individual schedules two at a time and rank them by the strength of their relationship to each other, as measured by coefficients of correlation, we get the array shown in Table 15.

As can be seen in Table 15, information-handling capability, independence, functionality, and accountability cluster together, whereas representativeness seems to stand apart, something different from that which is tapped by the other schedules. Most removed from

TABLE 13

Coefficients of Correlation Between Selected Policy Indicators and State Positions on the Five FAIIR Schedules, and Final Ranking (Overall) on Legislative Capability

	Overall	Functional	Accountable	Information	Independence	Representativeness
(17) Expenditure per Pupil in ADA, 1968-69	.331*	.414**	.173	.399	.294	.079
(18) Sharkansky-Hofferbert's Welfare-Education Factor	.549**	.405**	.434**	.555**	.192	.383**
(19) Per Capita General Revenue, State and Local Governments	.462**	.535**	.410**	.401**	.199	.111
(20) Crittenden's Scope of Government Factor	.214	.254*	.294*	.144	.138	-.018
(21) Walker's Innovation Index	.370**	.225	.239*	.473**	.253*	.308*

*p ≤ .05
**p ≤ .01

TABLE 14

Coefficients of Correlation Between
State Positions on Individual FAIIR Schedules

	F	A	IHC	I	R
F	-	.457**	.654**	.490**	.166
A	-	-	.595**	.336**	.361**
IHC	-	-	-	.658**	.320*
I	-	-	-	-	.130
R	-	-	-	-	-

*p ≤ .05
**p ≤ .01

TABLE 15

Degrees of Connection Among Individual FAIIR Schedules

Most Connected	IHC-I	.658
	IHC-F	.654
	IHC-A	.595
	I-F	.490
	F-A	.457
	A-R	.361
	A-I	.336
	IHC-R	.320
	F-R	.166
Least Connected	I-R	.130

the representativeness schedule are the functionality and independence schedules. What is most striking about Table 15, however, is the apparent centrality of information-handling capability in the matrix of relationships connecting the five FAIIR schedules. Illustrating this point graphically is Figure 4, in which linkages are shaded to reflect the strengths of the relationships.

It is tempting to draw certain causal inferences from the relationships depicted in Figure 4. Specifically, it is very tempting indeed to see in this centrality of information-handling capability a clue to efficient tactics of reform. For example, successful efforts to improve the information-handling aspects of legislative capability may improve three other aspects as well. Further, efforts to improve representativeness might require the use of devices other than those broadly applicable to other aspects of structural improvement. Although our speculations here cannot be put to a definitive test, the implications for a strategy of reform are certainly worth pondering.

FURTHER ANALYSES

Two sorts of questions are explored in this section. First, it seems reasonable that the various correlates of legislative capability,

FIGURE 4

Linkages Connecting Individual
FAIIR Schedules Which Illustrate the
Centrality of Information-handling Capability

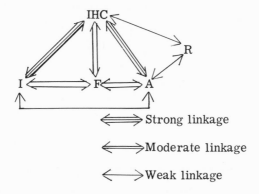

$\Longleftrightarrow$ Strong linkage

$\longleftrightarrow$ Moderate linkage

$\longleftrightarrow$ Weak linkage

taken together, should provide a fuller explanation of capability than
any single correlate taken by itself. Several experiments were conducted to test this idea, and the results are reported here. Second,
it is possible that some of the relationships which we have discovered
might hold only under certain conditions. Experiments were conducted
to assess this possibility also. What follows, therefore, are some
tentative explorations which, hopefully, will stimulate reflection and
further research. We do not regard them as more than tentative,
nor should the reader.

Let us begin with the assumption that two pieces of information
about a state legislature should permit greater accuracy in predicting
technical capability than only one piece of information. A simple test
of this notion, using information on a state's relative affluence and
political culture, is the following: Divide states into "high affluence"
and "low affluence" groups (each group n = 24). Next, divide each of
these groups into "moralistically inclined political cultures" (high)
and "traditionalistically inclined political cultures" (low). Now, if
knowing both pieces of information improves our predictive ability,
states which are high on both indicators should, as a group, have a
higher average rank in legislative capability than those states which
are "high, low," "low, high," and "low, low." "Low, low" states, by a
similar reasoning, should score the lowest average rank in capability.
The actual results of this sorting experiment are shown in Table 16.

As can be seen in Table 16, our predictions are borne out for

TABLE 16

Average State Rank Positions on
Final Ranking of Legislative Capability

		Political Culture	
		High	Low
A f f l u e n c e	High	20.1 (n=17)	19.7 (n=7)
	Low	26.6 (n=7)	34.8 (n=17)

states in the "low, low" cell. Knowing that a state is relatively less
affluent and relatively more traditionalistic in its political culture
increases the accuracy of our prediction beyond that which we could
have achieved knowing only one piece of information alone. But we
find in the "high, high" cell that our prediction of highest capability
is off the mark. How can this be explained? Although the experiment
we have conducted is crude, the results suggest thoughts which are
worth reflection. (1) States that surpass some minimal threshold of
economic and political development are less constrained by economic
and cultural limitations that states that are located at or below such
a threshold. (2) Political factors appear to constitute less of an
important influence on capability than economic factors. Both of
these ideas are explored further below.

In an effort to capture some of the additive effects of our socioeconomic and political indicators, two composite indexes were constructed: (1) a composite index of socioeconomic development on
which each state's score is calculated as the average rank position
on three political indicators: political culture, competition-turnout,
and professionalism-local reliance; and (2) a composite index of
socioeconomic development on which each state's score is calculated
as the average rank on three socioeconomic indicators: metro-
urbanism, affluence, and industrialization. Rank-order positions for
the forty-eight states (Alaska and Hawaii are excluded for lack of
sufficient data) on each of the composite indexes are shown in Table 17

TABLE 17

State Rank-Order Positions on Composite Measures
of Political and Economic Development

State	Composite Index of Political Development	Composite Index of Economic Development
Calif.	4.5	1
N.J.	7	3
Ill.	6	5
Mich.	3	9.5
Conn.	9	4
Minn.	1	14
Wash.	4.5	8
Mass.	12	6
N.Y.	19.5	2
Wis.	2	19
Ohio	17	7
Colo.	10	12
Penn.	14	9.5
Oreg.	8	18
Ind.	15.5	20
Iowa	11	23
Nebr.	15.5	25
Fld.	28	11
Kan.	19.5	22
Utah	13	27
Del.	23	15.5
Mo.	24	15.5
Fla.	34	13
R.I.	25	24
Tex.	30	17
Nev.	31	21
Mont.	22	33
Ariz.	29	29
N.H.	27	34
Idaho	21	38
Wyo.	32	35
Maine	26	40
N.Dak.	18	47
Va.	38	31
La.	41.5	26
Ga.	41.5	28
Tenn.	43	30
N.C.	37	36
Ohio	44.5	32
W.Va.	35	42
S.Dak.	33	45
Vt.	36	44
Ky.	39	41
N.Mex.	40	39
S.C.	44.5	43
Ala.	47	37
Miss.	46	46
Ark.	48	48

Table 18 reports coefficients of correlation between the two composite measures of political and socioeconomic development and state positions on the legislative capability schedules.

Keeping in mind the results reported in Table 11 we look at the coefficients in Table 18 and find that combining indicators as we have done improves our predictive ability considerably for political variables and marginally so for socioeconomic variables. Furthermore, we see that political factors appear to have greater impact on the final ranking, functionality, and accountability schedules than socioeconomic factors, whereas socioeconomic factors seem clearly to overshadow political factors only on the independence schedule.

It is useful at this point to consider the possibility of spurious correlations. It might be the case, for example, that socioeconomic development determines both the level of political development in a state and the degree of legislative capability, yielding a high co-efficient of correlation between political development and capability that is little more than a statistical artifact. Indeed, one of the central generalizations adduced from comparative state policy research is precisely this: socioeconomic development appears to shape both political institutions and public policy outcomes, the relationship between politics and policy disappearing when controlling for socioeconomic development.[17]

To test the validity of this generalization for the present study, states were divided into high, medium, and low categories (n = 16 for all groups) for both the political and the socioeconomic development indicators. Table 19 shows coefficients of correlation between socioeconomic development and legislative capability, controlling for the level of political development. Table 20 shows coefficients of correlation between political development and legislative capability, controlling for the level of socioeconomic development.

Although only one of the coefficients in Tables 19 and 20 is statistically significant, it is clear that political factors survive socioeconomic controls more handily than socioeconomic factors survive political controls. This finding should be of particular interest to researchers in the field of comparative state policy. Political factors, more than socioeconomic factors, account for interstate differences in legislative capability. And as Table 20 suggests, political factors appear to be most crucial as determinants of legislative capability in the socioeconomically less-developed states. Although the pattern is less clear, a similar relationship seems to hold in Table 19: socioeconomic factors exert their strongest influence on legislative capability in the politically less-developed states.

TABLE 18

Coefficients of Correlation Between Composite Indexes
of Political and Socioeconomic Development and
State Positions on Legislative Capability Schedules

	O	F	A	IHC	I	R
Composite Index of Political Development	.535**	.359**	.433**	.482**	.202	.369**
Composite Index of Socioeconomic Development	.439**	.311*	.167	.490**	.276*	.374**

**p ≤ .01
* p ≤ .05

TABLE 19

Coefficients of Correlation Between Socioeconomic Development
and Legislative Capability (Final Ranking), Controlling
for Level of Political Development

	Level of Political Development	
High	Medium	Low
-.030	.324	.232

Note: For forty-eight states, r_s = .439.

TABLE 20

Coefficients of Correlation Between Political Development
and Legislative Capability (Final Ranking), Controlling
for Level of Socioeconomic Development

	Level of Socioeconomic Development		
	High	Medium	Low
	.300	.367	.459*

Note: For forty-eight states, $r_s = .535$.

*p < .05

On the basis of these findings, it is interesting to speculate whether states must first achieve some minimal threshold of political and socioeconomic development in order for policies affecting legislative capability to become a matter primarily of choice rather than circumstances. The lowest coefficients reported in Tables 19 and 20 are for states which have achieved the highest levels of political and socioeconomic development. It must be stressed once again, of course, that considerable latitude for public choice exists at all levels of political and socioeconomic development. But if political and socioeconomic circumstances impose even modest constraints on choice in upgrading state legislatures, then tactics, expectations, and evaluations should take these constraints into account.

THE HYPOTHESES REVISITED

At the beginning of this chapter a number of general hypotheses were advanced to guide our research. Since many of these propositions have received substantial empirical support in the comparative state policy research literature, a summary of our own results will be useful. In addition, many concerned legislators, professionals, and laymen will want to know what practical import the findings of this chapter have for a strategy of legislative reform. Both kinds of information are contained in Table 21, which provides a general summary of the propositions examined in this study, our findings relating to those propositions, and some interpretive notes on the implications for reform strategies.

NOTES

1. Two useful surveys of this literature are John Fenton and Donald Chamberlayne, "The Literature Dealing with the Relationships Between Political Processes, Socioeconomic Conditions and Public Policies in the American States: A Bibliographical Essay," Polity, I, 3 (Spring, 1969), 388-404; and Herbert Jacob and Michael Lipsky, "Outputs, Structure and Power: An Assessment of Changes in the Study of State and Local Politics," Journal of Politics, XXX, 2 (1968), 510-38.

2. See Herbert Blalock, Jr., Causal Inferences in Nonexperimental Research (Chapel Hill: University of North Carolina Press, 1964).

3. See, for example, Richard Hofferbert, "Elite Influence in State Policy Formation: A Model for Comparative Inqiry," Polity, II, 3 (1970), 316-44.

TABLE 21

Summary of Findings and Their Implications

Major Hypotheses	=	Basic Findings (Positive, Negative, Mixed)	Implications for Legislative Reform
1. Regional affiliations are related to equivalent levels of legislative capability.		MIXED-NEGATIVE. Some regional clustering occurs on schedules of legislative capability, particularly in the South and the Great Lakes area, but a nationwide pattern of regionalism is hard to discern.	Continued development of programs and organizations designed to establish nationwide standards of legislative capabilities and to facilitate information diffusion and reform will further reduce the salience of regional norms and regional patterns of emulation.
2. Certain demographic and socioeconomic factors are positively associated with FAIIR measures of legislative capability.		POSITIVE-MIXED. Factors such as a state's economic wealth, urbanization, and industrialization are related to legislative capability. Representativeness and independence are less affected by these factors than are the other FAIIR criteria. These factors impose modest constraints on legislative reform at the lowest levels of socioeconomic and political development; at higher levels of development, however, socioeconomic factors appear to impose no constraints at all on the range of public choice.	States that are politically and economically developed but that rank low in legislative capability offer promising targets for legislative reform, for it is in these states that socioeconomic and political cultural constraints appear to be minimal. The range of choice open to states which are less developed socioeconomically and politically is moderately constrained by scarce economic resources and a non-supportive political environment. The economic and political "costs" of reform, in other words, are very likely higher in these states than in states which are more developed economically and politically. These constraining factors might therefore be taken into account when evaluating a state's progress toward legislative capability.
3. Indexes of political culture are associated with levels of legislative capability.		POSITIVE-MIXED. Features of a state's political party system, of its political cultural environment, and of the political activity of its citizenry all have a considerable impact on legislative capability. Functionality, accountability, and information-handling capability appear especially sensitive to these and other political variables.	
4. High voter participation, competitive party organizations, strong executive leadership, and other political variables are positively associated with legislative capability.			
5. The more capable legislatures are innovative, spend more, and are governmentally interventionist.			
6. Population size is directly related to legislative capability.		NEGATIVE. Small as well as large states rank toward the top of the overall ranking. Low population alone seems no deterrent to high technical capability.	Small states offer as promising targets for structural and procedural reform as do larger states, even though the fruits of reform may be spread over fewer beneficiaries.
7. Information-handling capability is a central feature of overall legislative strength.		POSITIVE. Only representativeness seems unconnected to the level of information-handling capability in state legislatures.	Improvements in information-handling capability might offer the single most important lever for upgrading state legislatures. Programs designed to enhance information-handling capabilities are likely to generate a multiplier effect across other areas of legislative capability as well.

4. Ira Sharkansky, Spending in the American States (Chicago: Rand McNally, 1968), p. 108.

5. See Ira Sharkansky, "Regionalism, Economic Status, and Public Policies," in Policy Analysis in Political Science, (Chicago: Markham Publishing Co., 1970).

6. Thomas Dye, Politics, Economics, and the Public: Policy Outcomes in the American States (Chicago: Rand-McNally, 1966), p. 293.

7. Ira Sharkansky, "The Utility of Elazar's Political Culture: A Research Note," Polity, II, 1 (1969); Daniel J. Elazar, American Federalism: A View from the States (New York: Thomas Cromwell, 1966).

8. Elazar, op. cit., pp. 84-85.

9. Sharkansky, "The Utility of Elazar's Political Culture: A Research Note," op. cit., p. 67.

10. See works by Lockard, Dawson and Robinson, Dye, and Francis cited in the bibliography.

11. Ira Sharkansky and Richard Hofferbert, "Dimensions of State Politics, Economics, and Public Policy," American Political Science Review, LXIII, 3 (September, 1969), 870.

12. Ibid.

13. Ibid., p. 874.

14. Herbert Blalock, Jr., Social Statistics (New York: McGraw-Hill, 1960), p. 316.

15. Ibid., p. 319.

16. Jack L. Walker, "The Diffusion of Innovations Among the American States," American Political Science Review, LXIII, 3 (September, 1969), 896.

17. See Dye, op. cit.

6

**RECOMMENDATIONS
FOR
EACH
STATE**

The evaluation of state legislatures was undertaken by the CCSL to serve a number of interrelated purposes. First, it was intended to compile a comprehensive body of information about the structure, organization, procedures, and practices of all fifty legislatures.

Whatever the deficiencies of this study as a source of specific, comparative information may be--and they are many--it nevertheless represents the largest, most detailed, and most complete body of data about all fifty state legislatures in existence. Prior to this, any effort to understand the condition of legislatures or to consider what, if anything, should or could be done to affect that condition, was disrupted by the lack of consistent, reliable, and usable information.

The second purpose of the study was to organize this information into useful categories which would render it accessible and manageable. The study involves the handling of 35,000 separate items of information-- approximately 700 per state. The legislative process is so complex and involves so many interactions that understanding it in a single state becomes a problem in handling a massive amount of information. Practices vary so greatly from one state to another that unless the information is categorized, it is impossible to be aware of it, let alone understand it.

For these reasons, the main elements of structure, organization, and procedure studied--time, staffing, compensation, committee structure, facilities, leadership, rules and procedures, overall legislative structure, and ethics--were categorized under five major criteria defined as essential characteristics of legislatures. These major categories are functional, accountable, informed, independent, and representative (FAIIR).

The third purpose for which the study was undertaken was to support efforts to improve legislatures. The study was not intended as, nor designed to be, an abstract or academic exercise conducted purely for the sake of increasing knowledge about legislatures but, rather, as an instrument for improving their operations so that they can fulfill the expectations of the citizens of a democratic society.

The fourth purpose of the study has a much wider focus than the others. It grows out of the following convictions:

America's most profound problems stem from the breakdown and the deficiencies of its formal decision-making processes.

These deficiencies are most crippling at the state level of government.

The legislature is at once the most important area of decision-making at the state level and the most dysfunctional.

The relationship between dysfunctional and unresponsive legislatures is not well understood by most Americans, their opinion leaders, and their information media.

The steps which must and can be taken to correct these deficiencies are not taken because of this lack of understanding of the importance of legislatures and of the conditions which make them dysfunctional and unresponsive.

In order to render the vast and complex body of information about legislatures comprehensible and in order to have impact on the information media and, through them, on public attention and understanding, the third method of organizing the information--ranking--was used.

The fifth purpose was to create a specific agenda for action and a set of priorities for those who are dissatisfied with the conditions under which legislatures operate and would change them: CCSL, legislative leaders, rank-and-file legislators, civic organizations, information media, and the citizens of individual states. This purpose is the central focus of this chapter and is discussed in greater detail below.

The sixth and final purpose for which this study was undertaken was to create the beginnings of a matrix in which to locate the fifty state legislatures in terms of their present condition. Having such a matrix will make possible the evaluation of progress in the future. This will provide a yardstick by which to measure legislative reform

efforts--an opportunity for cost/benefit analyses, if you will, something
rare for good government or reform enterprises.

Too often, appeals for reform of governmental institutions are
compelled to stop short of telling us what, specifically, can and should
be done and where it should be done. They dramatize the evils which
stem from the present condition and glorify the benefits which will
flow from the improvement of these conditions, but usually they tell
us nothing about what to do if we want to change things or how to go
about changing them. They usually dissolve into exhortations that we
must interest ourselves in this or that problem and do something about
it; and finally, we are told that what is needed is more public education.

The way in which this study was constructed and the uses to
which its results are being put, avoid generalized exhortations and
appeals to undefined education. We present here a set of detailed
recommendations for each state, describing what specific steps
should be taken to improve the organization, procedures, and practices
of its legislature.

Much of what is wrong with state legislatures is wrong with all,
or most, or many of them. The purposes or functions of the legislature
tend to be similar in all states and, as a consequence, many prescrip-
tions for change will be similar from state to state.

On the other hand, there are many differences in practice or in
the conditions under which legislatures operate and, therefore, in
some of the recommendations concerning what should be done to
improve their operations. Thus, the recommendations which follow
address themselves to priority needs of state legislatures whether
these needs are particular to a given state or held in common with
other states.

The recommendations are derived from a number of sources.
The primary source is, of course, the LES. The answers to specific
questions are drawn from interviews conducted in each state and an
examination of the rules, statutes, and constitution for each state.
These answers, when compared with the preferred answer, reveal
the gap which the recommendation is designed to fill. For example,
the questionnaire asks "How many standing committees are there in
the Senate?" In the case of Missouri, the answer is thirty-one. The
preferred answer is ten to fifteen and Missouri's answer is considerably larger. Therefore, in the section on state recommendations for
Missouri, there is a recommendation to reduce the number of Senate
committees to ten or fifteen.

In addition to the study itself, the recommendations have been shaped by discussion with many individuals, especially legislative leaders and members, who are knowledgeable about particular legislatures. In a number of states, citizens' commissions, legislative committees, and other organizations have made recommendations for the improvement of the legislature. These have been taken into account, though not necessarily followed in each case, in drawing up this list of recommendations.

The recommendations made here cover a signigicant volume of legislative activity in each state, but they are not exhaustive. A given recommendation may be listed for one state but not another even though the second state may well benefit from the same reform. This may come about for several reasons. It may be, for example, that more urgent matters had to be covered; or that details about a particular question may have been unclear in a given state; or that unusual circumstances surround a question in that state; or that other procedures exist which may overcome parts of a given problem.

In some cases we omitted certain recommendations even though a given state does not have the benefits they would bring. We did this because there are prerequisites to making adequate use of those benefits. For example, there is no justification in recommending electronic data-processing equipment in the Wyoming Legislature if there is no professional staff and if the legislature is restricted to meeting only forty days every two years. There is likewise no point in recommending salaries in the range of $20,000 to $30,000 a year for the New Hampshire Legislature when the salaries currently average only $100 a year. In principle, however, there is no justification for paying New Hampshire legislators less than lawmakers in California or New York or Michigan are paid, at least in terms of rate applied to the amount of their time which is demanded.

If all the recommendations we make were implemented, there would still be more to be done to improve legislatures. Some features of legislative activity were not a part of the study because they were not well enough understood or because obtaining information about them for all fifty states was beyond the scope of the study or because the effect of changing such features would be too ambiguous to warrant suggesting that they be changed.

Those who would strengthen and modernize the legislature of their state would do well to look beyond the recommendations listed expressly for their state and consider those listed for other states in order to weigh their relevance for their own.

ALABAMA (50)

Functional, 48; Accountable, 50; Informed, 49; Independent, 50; Representative, 41

GENERAL: The Legislative Reform Study Committee, created by the 1969 session of the legislature, has submitted a thorough analysis of the deficiencies of the Alabama Legislature's operations and procedures with its recommendations (sixty-eight in all) as to how they can be corrected.

The Study Committee's report, "Improving the Alabama Legislature," groups its recommendations into six catogories: the legislature and the constitution, rules and procedures, legislative staffing, the committee system, facilities and space, and records and documents.

The fact of this committee's existence and the quality of its effort are firm indicators of a recognition within the Alabama Legislature of that institution's increasingly moribund state and the will, desire, and intent to breathe new life into the body.

The recommendations, some similar to those made by the Study Committee, are aimed at the overall improvement of the Alabama Legislature.

1. REMOVE CONSTITUTIONAL RESTRICTIONS ON SESSION AND INTERIM TIME. The legislature should have authority to function throughout a two-year term; ideally, this authority should provide a flexible biennial session pattern that permits the legislature to convene, recess, and reconvene as it deems desirable. The legislature should be able to meet in general session or conduct interim work as it deems necessary at any time throughout the period.

    Permit annual general sessions, limited to no fewer than ninety legislative days.

2. LEGISLATIVE POWER TO CALL SPECIAL SESSIONS. Amend the constitution to permit the legislature to convene special sessions either by petition of a majority of the members of both houses or by the call of the presiding officer of each house.

3. PRE-SESSION ORGANIZATIONAL MEETING. Amend the constitution to provide a pre-session organizing session following a general election. Some states make advantageous use of such a session during November or December of a general election

year for the purpose of electing leaders, appointing committee chairmen, assigning members to committees, referring pre-filed bills to committee, holding committee organizational meetings, and conducting orientation conferences for new, as well as returning members of the legislature. Through such pre-session meetings the committees can begin their work before the regular session convenes. This makes it possible to delay the start of the regular session until legislation is ready for floor action.

4.   PRE-SESSION ORIENTATION CONFERENCE. The legislature should hold an orientation conference for new legislators, preferably after each general election. Orientation conferences enable members to speed the process of becoming more effective representatives and provide an opportunity for legislators to examine large policy areas apart from the pressure of the regular session.

5.   REDUCE THE NUMBER OF COMMITTEES. Ideally, there should be from ten to fifteen committees in each house parallel in jurisdiction. This would reduce the general complexity of the legislature and would permit reducing the number of committee assignments per member.

With twenty-one committees in the House and thirty-one in the Senate, there are more committees than should be necessary for the effective organization of the work. This problem is more severe in relation to the Senate than it is to the House.

6.   REDUCE THE NUMBER OF COMMITTEE ASSIGNMENTS. In order to make it possible for members to concentrate their attention and contribute effectively, there should be no more than three committee assignments for each member of the lower house or four committee assignments for each member of the Senate. The multiplicity of assignments introduces problems of scheduling, strains the focus of attention on the part of members, and creates an inordinately heavy workload for members if committees are as active as they should be.

At present, nine percent of the members of the House have more than three committee assignments each, and 100 percent of the members of the Senate have more than four committee assignment each.

7.   UNIFORM COMMITTEE RULES. There should be uniform published rules of committee procedure in both chambers.

8.   COMMITTEE JURISDICTION. A description of the jurisdiction of committees should be contained in the rules of both houses

and assignment of bills should be made in accord with the jurisdiction of committees as described in the rules.

9. OPEN COMMITTEES. The rules of each house should prohibit
    secret meetings except in matters affecting the security of the
    state, or which could unnecessarily damage the reputation of
    individuals in personnel matters. Such exceptions should be
    sparingly and responsibly employed.

10. NOTICE OF MEETINGS. The rules should require a minimum
    notice of five legislative days for committee meetings and hearings,
    with widely disseminated announcement of schedule, location,
    agenda, and availability of public participation.

    The Senate should require, as the House already does, a minimum
    notice of five legislative days for committee meetings and hearings,
    with widely disseminated announcement of schedule, location,
    agenda, and availability of public participation.

11. ACT ON ALL BILLS. Committees should be required to report
    on all bills assigned to them, recommending for passage by the
    parent body those bills which enjoy the support of a majority of
    the members of the committee and killing all others.

12. COMMITTEE HEARINGS. There is no justification for permitting
    any major piece of legislation to become law without having been
    subjected to extensive, thorough, well-planned, and well-prepared
    public hearings, in which representatives of the public, civic
    organizations and interest groups are not only invited but encour-
    aged to participate.

13. RECORD AND PUBLISH PROCEEDINGS OF COMMITTEES.
    Record and publish the record of committee hearings, proceedings,
    and votes.

14. PUBLISH COMMITTEE ROLL CALLS. The committee report of
    action on bills to the respective houses should include those roll
    calls which are taken, showing how each member voted. These
    committee reports should be available to the press and public.
    Published roll calls should apply to those bills recommended
    for approval as well as those killed.

15. DUAL COMMITTEE CONSIDERATION OF APPROPRIATION
    BILLS. There should be a rule requiring dual committee con-
    sideration of legislation affecting significant sums of money.
    Such legislation, when considered and acted upon favorably by a
    substantive policy committee, should then automatically be

referred to the Finance Committee for consideration of its fiscal impact.

16. INTERIM COMMITTEES. When the legislature is not in session, the standing committees should become the interim committees for the purpose of conducting long-range studies of state policy issues. The Legislative Council or some similarly constituted bi-partisan committee should serve as the supervising agency for interim committees and their studies, budgets, and personnel. The major committees should be staffed on a year-round basis.

17. PROVIDE SINGLE-MEMBER DISTRICTS. Legislative districts in both houses should be single-member.

Legislative districts in the House (forty-one percent) and the Senate (seventy-four percent) are multi-member. They should be single-member. Accomplishing this requires an amendment to the state constitution.

18. LEGISLATIVE SALARIES. Legislative salaries should be set by statute and paid in equal monthly installments throughout the biennium, and all unvouchered expense allowances should be incorporated into an annual salary. Actual and necessary expenses incurred in the process of carrying out legislative duties should be reimbursed upon submission and approval of properly vouchered evidence of expenditures.

The constitution should be amended to permit the legislature to establish legislative compensation by statute.

19. INCREASE LEGISLATIVE COMPENSATION. No legislative salaries in the United States should be below the $10,000 a year level. Compensation of legislators in the larger states should be in the $20,000 to $30,000 range.

20. CONSENT CALENDAR. A consent calendar should be used in both houses.

21. BILL DEADLINES. The orderly flow of work through the legislature depends upon the existence of a series of deadlines at various critical stages throughout the legislative process. These deadlines should be adopted as part of the rules and should be consistently enforced.

22. ESTABLISH AN AUTOMATIC CALENDAR OF BILLS. When a bill is favorably reported out of committee to the floor, it should go automatically onto the calendar in the order in which it was reported out. It should require a vote of an extraordinary majority

to move a bill from its position on calendar or to bypass it. The Rules Committee should have no part in the scheduling of bills. No session should adjourn until all bills on calendar have been voted up or down or, by the vote of an extraordinary majority, have been moved from the calendar.

23. REMOVE LEGISLATIVE POWERS FROM LIEUTENANT GOVERNOR. The exercise of legislative powers, including such pro forma powers as presiding, casting tie-breaking votes, and signing enacted legislation, by the Lieutenant Governor, whether the powers derive from the constitution or rule book, would seem to be a particularly serious breach of the separation of powers and the independence of the legislature. The constitution and/or rule book should be amended to permit these legislative powers presently exercised by the lieutenant governor to be set as the responsibility of the office of the president pro tem of the Senate.

24. PRINTED BILL DOCUMENT FORMAT. The bill document printing procedure should permit the clear identification of the text of the existing statute which is being amended as well as the material which the bill proposes to delete or add. This is usually accomplished through the use of varying type faces, such as "strike-through", italics, underlining, or bracketing. It should not be necessary to compare the text of a bill with the text of the existing code in order to determine what the bill does.

25. REPRINT AMENDED BILLS. When a bill is amended substantially, it should be reprinted and returned to the legislature with no more than an overnight delay. The reprint should show clearly the original text of the bill as well as the change created by the amendment.

26. STATEMENT OF INTENT BY AUTHOR OF A BILL. The form in which a bill is introduced should include a statement by the author describing, in laymen's language, what the bill is intended to accomplish.

27. BILL SUMMARY BY BILL-DRAFTING SERVICE. The form in which bills are introduced should include a more extensive summary of the provisions of the bill prepared by the bill-drafting service.

28. STRENGTHEN STAFF SUPPORT. Legislative research, fiscal, legal, and planning agencies should be adequately staffed to full utility and at suitable salary levels for professional qualification. Professional staffing should be at a level to enable the legislature to conduct continuous, year-round examination of state resources

and expenditures as well as program review and evaluation of state agencies. This staff should also prepare fiscal notes accompanying all appropriation bills, evaluating their fiscal impact over the short and long term. Staff agencies should be upgraded to the level at which competent and timely service can be provided to every member of the legislature.

COMMITTEE STAFFING. Standing committees should be staffed on a permanent, year-round basis.

STRENGTHEN STAFF SUPPORT (LEADERS). Staff assistance should be provided to all leaders of both the majority and minority parties. Such assistance should include a secretary and an administrative assistant at the professional level, with space to work reasonably adjacent to the offices of members and leaders.

STRENGTHEN STAFF (RANK-AND-FILE MEMBERS). Rank-and-file members (majority and minority party on an equal basis) should be provided with individual staff assistance consisting of a minimum of an administrative assistant at the professional level and a secretary. Eventually, this should increase to the stated level of support both in the capital and in a district office.

The entire professional staff of the legislature is made up of four professionals in the Legislative Reference Service. The legislature needs to create research fiscal and legal positions within a greatly expanded Reference Service Bureau if it can ever hope to be in a position to conduct effective oversight of executive operations through the ability to maintain continuous program review and evaluation. In addition, qualifications and salary levels for all existing or additional positions should be increased. Other forms of legislative staffing beyond the Legislative Reference Service are needed. Leaders (at least presiding officers, majority and minority leaders) should be provided with assistants at a professional level. A beginning should be made toward permanent, year-round committee staffing for some of the major committees. In addition, some movement toward the staffing of individual members is also in order, perhaps beginning on a shared basis, but ultimately for each member, majority and minority alike.

29. INDIVIDUAL OFFICES. Provide private, individual offices for every member of the legislature, with nearby space for their assistants. The quality and amount of office space should not differ substantially between majority and minority party members.

At a minimum, leaders should have private offices for themselves, with separate, nearby offices for their assistants. A beginning can be made toward providing offices for members by making space available for shared offices among small numbers of members at first, then gradually reducing the number who share space until a private office is provided for each member.

30. FACILITIES FOR COMMITTEES. Legislative effectiveness requires that committees have adequate physical facilities in which to do their work. This includes an adequate number of committee rooms and an adequate number of hearing rooms that will permit the seating of larger audiences.

31. SERVICE AGENCY FACILITIES. Space for service agencies should provide adequate working space for professional and clerical staff as well as library, files, and other storage requirements.

32. IMPROVE PRESS FACILITIES. Improved press facilities aid in the coverage of the work of the legislature. Committee rooms, and both chambers or galleries, should provide adequate space for the news media as well as lighting and electrical power connections for their equipment. Conference or interview rooms and office space should also be provided for the news media.

33. PRACTICE BEFORE REGULATORY AGENCIES. Legislators or their firms should be prohibited from practicing before state regulatory agencies or in matters concerning state agencies for a fee.

PROHIBIT DOING BUSINESS WITH THE STATE. There should be a prohibition against legislators or the firms in which they own a major interest doing business with state agencies.

ALASKA (12)

Functional, 8; Accountable, 29; Informed, 12; Independent, 6; Representative, 40

GENERAL: Ranked twelfth, Alaska's legislature exhibits the benefits of a modern constitution. The structure, organization, and procedures of the Alaska Legislature approach those of a model legislature. Such deficiencies as exist tend to relate to resources in staffing and facilities. Most of the improvements needed could be accomplished by the legislature itself. Only one change, the provision of single-member districts (recommendation no. 9 below), would require an amendment to the constitution.

Alaska voters approved the call of a constitutional convention November 3, 1970. Alaska has one of the smaller legislatures (House, forty; Senate, twenty); a limited number of committees (house, nine; Senate, nine); unlimited annual sessions; and salaries set by statute (currently $9,000 per year). The legislature can call a special session by a vote of two-thirds of its members.

The House and Senate use a common set of rules, the Uniform Rules, backed up by Mason's Manual. There are uniform committee rules, including a description of the jurisdiction of each committee, and bills are always assigned in keeping with these rules.

No Senator has more than four committee assignments and no House member has more than three. The consideration of two committees (finance and policy) is required for all legislation appropriating significant sums of money.

Bills are printed in clear, standard format; amended bills are printed and available to the legislature without delay. Bills are restricted to a single subject, skeleton bills are prohibited, and bills are printed in sufficient quantity as to be available to legislators, press, and public without delay or restriction.

The areas in which improvements could be made are the subject of the following recommendations.

1. STRENGTHEN MINORITY PARTY ROLE. Internal accountability, as well as the capacity of all legislators to represent their constituents effectively, depends upon the opportunity of minority party members to have an effective part in internal legislative affairs.

   MINORITY REPRESENTATION ON COMMITTEE ON RULES. Minority representation on the Committee on Rules should approximate the minority party proportion of the membership of the appropriate house.

   MINORITY PARTY MEMBERS ON COMMITTEE. Minority party members should be assigned to committees by the minority leader in consultation with the minority caucus.

2. INTERIM COMMITTEES. When the legislature is not in session, the standing committees should become the interim committees for the purpose of conducting long-range studies of state policy issues. The Legislative Council or some similarly constituted, bi-partisan committee should serve as the supervising agency for interim committees and their studies, budgets, and personnel.

The major committees should be staffed on a year-round basis.

3. **STRENGTHEN STAFF SUPPORT.** Legislative research, fiscal, legal, and planning agencies should be adequately staffed to full utility and at suitable salary levels for professional qualification. Professional staffing should be at a level to enable the legislature to conduct continuous, year-round examination of state resources and expenditures as well as program review and evaluation of state agencies. This staff should also prepare fiscal notes accompanying all appropriation bills, evaluating their fiscal impact over the short and long term. Staff agencies should be upgraded to the level at which competent and timely service can be provided to every member of the legislature.

Staff agencies should be augmented to the level at which competent and timely service can be provided to every member of the legislature.

4. **ESTABLISH AN AUTOMATIC CALENDAR OF BILLS.** When a bill is favorably reported out of committee to the floor, it should go automatically onto the calendar in the order in which it was reported out. It should require a vote of an extraordinary majority to move a bill from its position on calendar or to bypass it. The Rules Committee should have no part in the scheduling of bills. No session should adjourn until all bills on calendar have been voted up or down or, by the vote of an extraordinary majority, have been moved from the calendar.

5. **PUBLISH COMMITTEE ROLL CALLS.** The committee report of action on bills to the respective houses should include those roll calls which are taken, showing how each member voted. These committee reports should be available to the press and public. Published roll calls should apply to those bills recommended for approval as well as those killed.

6. **CONSENT CALENDAR.** A consent calendar for bills as well as resolutions should be used in the House and Senate.

7. **INDIVIDUAL OFFICES.** Provide private, individual offices for every member of the legislature, with nearby space for their assistants. The quality and amount of office space should not differ substantially between majority and minority party members.

8. **COMMITTEE BILL REPORTS.** Require committees to issue reports describing and explaining the committees action on bills recommended for passage at the time the bill moves from the committee to the floor.

9. PROVIDE SINGLE-MEMBER DISTRICTS. Some legislative districts in the House and the Senate are multi-member. They should be single-member. Accomplishing this requires an amendment to the state constitution.

10. DISCONTINUE ROTATING LEADERSHIP. The practice of limiting presiding officers to a single, two-year term in that position weakens the legislature in its capacity to confront other branches and levels of government as a partner of equal stature and diffuses and disrupts the continuity of leadership within the legislative bodies. Although it is extremely difficult to change a practice such as this, because of its profoundly adverse effects on many aspects of legislative performance, it should be discontinued.

Alaska is one of the remaining states which, by custom, still limits the presiding officer of the Senate to a single, two-year term in that position. The practice should be discontinued.

11. IMPROVE PRESS FACILITIES. Improved press facilities aid in the coverage of the work of the legislature. Committee rooms, and both chambers or galleries, should provide adequate space for the news media as well as lighting and electrical power connections for their equipment. Conference or interview rooms and office space should also be provided for the news media.

Specifically for Alaska, committee rooms should provide adequate space for the news media as well as lighting and electrical power connections for their equipment. Conference or interview rooms should also be provided for the news media.

12. SPECIAL PROVISIONS. In addition to standard laws governing criminal behavior, there should be special provisions regulating legislative conflicts of interest.

PROHIBIT DOING BUSINESS WITH THE STATE. There should be a prohibition against legislators or the firms in which they own a major interest doing business with state agencies.

PROHIBIT APPOINTMENT TO STATE OFFICE. There should be a prohibition against a legislator's accepting appointment to other state office during the term for which he is elected or within two years of the termination of his service as a member of the legislature.

FAMILY EMPLOYMENT. Members of a legislator's immediate family should be barred from employment by the legislature.

13. BILL DEADLINES. The orderly flow of work through the legis-
    lature depends upon the existence of a series of deadlines at
    various critical stages throughout the legislative process. These
    deadlines should be adopted as part of the rules and should be
    consistently enforced.

    Alaska appears not to have as severe a problem as many other
    states have with end of session logjams; in the 1969-70 biennium
    only seventeen percent of all the bills were passed and thirteen
    percent of the conference committees convened in the final week
    of the session. However, the orderly flow of work through the
    legislature depends upon the existence of a series of bill deadlines.
    Such deadlines should be installed and consistently enforced.

ARIZONA (43)

Functional, 11; Accountable, 47; Informed, 38; Independent, 17; Representative, 50

GENERAL: The forty-third-ranked Arizona Legislature meets in
annual session and is small in size, giving it a base for general improvement. Plenary sessions are conducted in chambers rated as
superior overall and specifically in regard to the adequacy of working and circulation space for members, visitors' galleries, and the
working area for the chief administrative officer of each house. It
has a small but well-regarded central staff bureau and provides
five professional staff members for the joint Legislative Budget Committee.

In November, 1970, the electorate approved the creation of a compensation commission to recommend salary levels for the legislative,
executive, and judicial branches, which presumably will improve the
compensation factors.

Recommendations suggested for Arizona are the following.

1. REDUCE THE NUMBER OF COMMITTEE ASSIGNMENTS. In
   order to make it possible for members to concentrate their attention and contribute effectively, there should be no more than
   three committee assignments for each member of the lower
   house and four committee assignments for each member of the
   Senate. The multiplicity of assignments introduces problems of
   scheduling, strains the focus of attention on the part of members,
   and creates an inordinately heavy workload for members if committees are as active as they should be.

At present, twenty-five percent of the members of the House have more than three assignments each and fifty percent of the Senators have more than four.

2. UNIFORM COMMITTEE RULES. There should be uniform published rules of committee procedure in both chambers.

3. OPEN COMMITTEES. The rules of each house should prohibit secret meetings except in matters affecting the security of the state, or which could unnecessarily damage the reputation of individuals in personnel matters. Such exceptions should be sparingly and responsibly employed.

4. ACT ON ALL BILLS. Committees should be required to report on all bills assigned to them, recommending for passage by the parent body those bills which enjoy the support of a majority of the members of the committee and killing all others.

5. COMMITTEE BILL REPORTS. Require committees to issue reports describing and explaining the committee's action on bills recommended for passage at the time the bill moves from the committee to the floor.

6. RECORD AND PUBLISH PROCEEDINGS OF COMMITTEES. Record and publish the record of committee hearings, proceedings, and votes.

7. PUBLISH COMMITTEE ROLL CALLS. The committee report of action on bills to the respective houses should include those roll calls which are taken, showing how each member voted. These committee reports should be available to the press and public. Published roll calls should apply to those bills recommended for approval as well as those killed.

8. DUAL COMMITTEE CONSIDERATION OF APPROPRIATION BILLS There should be a rule requiring dual committee consideration of legislation affecting significant sums of money. Such legislation, when considered and acted upon favorably by a substantive policy committee, should then automatically be referred to the Finance Committee for consideration of its fiscal impact.

9. MANAGEMENT COMMITTEES. There should be an executive or management committee created in each house. Its membership should include the leaders of each party in each house, and the minority party should have representation on the committee in proportion to its numbers in the body as a whole. The Senate/House management committees should combine as a joint

management committee. The purpose of these committees should
be to assume responsibility for the administrative management
(housekeeping) functions relating to personnel, facilities, the
research bureaus, budgets, and expenditures of their respective
houses. The joint management committee should deal with matters
of inter-house coordination.

The Senate and House management committees (House Administration Committee and Senate Administration Committee) should
combine as a joint management committee and at the same time
expand their purview of the operations of their respective houses.

10. LEGISLATIVE SALARIES. Legislative salaries should be set by
    statute and paid in equal monthly installments throughout the
    biennium, and all unvouchered expense allowances should be
    incorporated into an annual salary. Actual and necessary expenses
    incurred in the process of carrying out legislative duties should
    be reimbursed upon submission and approval of properly vouchered
    evidence of expenditures.

    INCREASE LEGISLATIVE COMPENSATION. No legislative
    salaries in the United States should be below the $10,000 a year
    level. Compensation of legislators in the larger states should be
    in the $20,000 to $30,000 range.

    In November, 1970, voters approved a constitutional amendment
    calling for the creation of a commission to recommend legislative,
    judicial, and executive salary levels. Any proposals the commis-
    sion makes regarding legislative salaries will be submitted to
    the people for approval.

11. JOINT RULES. There should be joint rules governing the relation-
    ship and the flow of legislation between the two houses of the
    legislature.

12. ESTABLISH AN AUTOMATIC CALENDAR OF BILLS. When a
    bill is favorably reported out of committee to the floor, it should
    go automatically onto the calendar in the order in which it was
    reported out. It should require a vote of an extraordinary majority
    to move a bill from its position on calendar or to bypass it. The
    Rules Committee should have no part in the scheduling of bills.
    No session should adjourn until all bills on calendar have been
    voted up or down or, by the vote of an extraordinary majority,
    have been moved from the calendar.

13. STRENGTHEN MINORITY PARTY ROLE. Internal accountability,
    as well as the capacity of all legislators to represent their

constituents effectively, depends upon the opportunity of minority
party members to have an effective part in internal legislative
affairs.

14. REPRINT AMENDED BILLS. When a bill is amended substantially,
it should be reprinted and returned to the legislature with no more
than an overnight delay. The reprint should show clearly the
original text of the bill as well as the change created by the
amendment.

15. STATEMENT OF INTENT BY AUTHOR OF A BILL. The form in
which a bill is introduced should include a statement by the author
describing, in laymen's language, what the bill is intended to
accomplish.

16. STRENGTHEN STAFF SUPPORT (LEADERS). Staff assistance
should be provided to all leaders of both the majority and the
minority parties. Such assistance should include a secretary and
an administrative assistant at the professional level, with space
to work reasonably adjacent to the offices of members and leaders.

17. COMMITTEE STAFFING. Standing committees should be staffed
on a permanent year-round basis.

A beginning should be made toward permanent, year-round committee staffing for some of the major committees.

18. STRENGTHEN STAFF (RANK-AND-FILE MEMBERS). Rank-
and-file members (majority and minority party on an equal basis)
should be provided with individual staff assistance consisting of
a minimum of an administrative assistant at the professional
level and a secretary. Eventually, this should increase to the
stated level of support both in the capital and in a district office.

Some movement toward the staffing of individual members is in
order, through the provision of administrative assistants, perhaps
beginning on a shared basis, but ultimately for each member,
majority and minority alike.

19. STRENGTHEN STAFF SUPPORT. Legislative research, fiscal,
legal, and planning agencies should be adequately staffed to full
utility and at suitable salary levels for professional qualification.
Professional staffing should be at a level to enable the legislature
to conduct continuous, year-round examination of state resources
and expenditures, as well as program review and evaluation of
state agencies. This staff should also prepare fiscal notes
accompanying all appropriation bills, evaluating their fiscal

impact over the short and long term. Staff agencies should be upgraded to the level at which competent and timely service can be provided to every member of the legislature.

20. FACILITIES FOR COMMITTEES. Legislative effectiveness requires that committees have adequate physical facilities in which to do their work. This includes an adequate number of committee rooms and an adequate number of hearing rooms that will permit the seating of larger audiences.

The Arizona Legislature's building is a relatively new one (constructed during the early 1960's), but it has several noticeable deficiencies we recommend be corrected.

The generally quality of the committee rooms in both houses should be upgraded; committee rooms should provide lighting and electrical power connections for use by newsmen; each house has only one committee hearng room that will seat as many as fifty spectators, and then not without crowding.

21. INDIVIDUAL OFFICES. Provide private, individual offices for every member of the legislature, with nearby space for their assistants. The quailty and amount of office space should not differ substantially between majority and minority party members.

Only one elected leader does not have a private office by virtue of his leadership office but seventy percent of the House's rank and file have no office space, private or shared, at all; office space for reporters is inadequate, and there are no news conference rooms.

22. PRACTICE BEFORE REGULATORY AGENCIES. Legislators or their firms should be prohibited from practicing before state regulatory agencies or in matters concerning state agencies for a fee.

HOLDING OTHER PUBLIC OFFICE. Legislators should be prohibited from concurrently holding other continuing paid public office.

FAMILY EMPLOYMENT. Members of a legislator's immediate family should be barred from employment by the legislature.

23. REGULATION OF LOBBYISTS. The independence of the legislature and public confidence in its processes require the regulation of special-interest advocates. Lobbyists should be required to register with an agency of the legislature, and should be required

to disclose who employs them, on behalf of what objectives, how much they are paid, and how much they spend and on whom. This information should be available to the press and the public. There should be specific and automatic penalties for failure to comply with these requirements.

The Arizona House currently requires lobbyists to register, after which the facts of such registration are made publicly available.

24. PROVIDE SINGLE-MEMBER DISTRICTS. Legislative districts in both houses should be single-member.

Some legislative districts in the House and the Senate are multi-member. They should be single-member. Accomplishing this requires an amendment to the state constitution.

25. SUPPORT OF DISTRICT OFFICES. District offices are vital to the effective representation by a legislator of his constituency. The legislature should make some contribution to the support of district offices for its members, and the amount of this contributic should be increased over time.

The Arizona Legislature could make a start toward this objective by making a contribution toward the cost of district offices (perhap shared in metropolitan areas, at first) and gradually increasing the amount of that contribution over time.

ARKANSAS (46)

Functional, 41; Accountable, 40; Informed, 46; Independent, 34; Representative, 33

GENERAL: A new state constitution, proposed in 1970 and defeated in November, 1970, contained a number of key provisions which would have substantially enhanced the legislature's capacity to govern. The proposed constitution provided for annual limited general sessions; special sessions to be convened by sixty percent of members of both houses; interim activities of committees and the Legislative Council (the present constitution provides no interim powers for the General Assembly); open meetings of the General Assembly and its committees and for all votes of its members, whether within the chamber or one of its committees, to be recorded and made public. The General Assembly would have been allowed to set compensation rates for its members; a code of ethics would have been established for all elected or appointed state and local government officials; the lieutenant governor would have been removed as the presiding officer of the

Senate; and the vote required of each house to override a gubernatorial veto would have been increased from a simple majority to a three-fifths majority. The notable work of members of the Arkansas Constitutional Revision Commission and the Constitutional Convention which followed the commission's activities, should not be abandoned because of the rejection of the proposed 1970 constitution.

Recent remodeling of the legislative chambers, including the offices of the speaker and lieutenant governor, committee rooms, offices for Senators and for the Legislative Commission, measurably improved the facilities available for legislative activities.

During the 1969-70 biennium the speaker of the House initiated a move to revise and improve the rules of the House (adoption of these recommendations will be considered during the 1971 session of the House). Recommendations for the Arkansas legislature include the following.

1. REMOVE CONSTITUTIONAL RESTRICTIONS ON SESSION AND INTERIM TIME. The legislature should have authority to function throughout a two-year term; ideally, this authority should provide a flexible biennial session pattern that permits the legislature to convene, recess, and reconvene as it deems desirable. The legislature should be able to meet in general session or conduct interim work as it deems necessary at any time throughout the period.

   Amend the constitution to permit annual general sessions, limited to no fewer than ninety legislative days.

2. LEGISLATIVE POWER TO CALL SPECIAL SESSIONS. Amend the constitution to permit the legislature to convene special sessions either by petition of a majority of the members of both houses or by the call of the presiding officer of each house.

3. REDUCE THE NUMBER OF COMMITTEES. Ideally, there should be from ten to fifteen committees in each house, parallel in jurisdiction. This would reduce the general complexity of the legislature and would permit reducing the number of committee assignments per member.

   There are now twenty-five committees in the House and twenty-four in the Senate.

4. REDUCE THE NUMBER OF COMMITTEE ASSIGNMENTS. In order to make it possible for members to concentrate their attention and contribute effectively, there should be no more

than three committee assignments for each member of the lower
house and four committee assignments for each member of the
Senate. The multiplicity of assignments introduces problems of
scheduling, strains the focus of attention on the part of members,
and creates an inordinately heavy workload for members if
committees are as active as they should be.

At present seventy-five percent of the members of the House
have more than three assignments each and 100 percent of the
Senators have more than four.

5. COMMITTEE JURISDICTION. A description of the jurisdiction
   of committees should be contained in the rules of both houses,
   and assignment of bills should be made in accord with the jurisdiction of committees as described in the rules.

6. ACT ON ALL BILLS. Committees should be required to report
   on all bills assigned to them, recommending for passage by the
   parent body those bills which enjoy the support of a majority of
   the members of the committee and killing all others.

7. RECORD AND PUBLISH PROCEEDINGS OF COMMITTEES.
   Record and publish the record of committee hearings, proceedings,
   and votes.

8. PUBLISH COMMITTEE ROLL CALLS. The committee report of
   action on bills to the respective houses should include those roll
   calls which are taken, showing how each member voted. These
   committee reports should be available to the press and public.
   Published roll calls should apply to those bills recommended for
   approval as well as those killed.

9. DUAL COMMITTEE CONSIDERATION OF APPROPRIATION BILLS
   There should be a rule requiring dual committee consideration
   of legislation affecting significant sums of money. Such legislation,
   when considered and acted upon favorably by a substantive policy
   committee, should then automatically be referred to the Finance
   Committee for consideration of its fiscal impact.

10. MANAGEMENT COMMITTEES. There should be an executive
    or management committee created in each house. Its membership
    should include the leaders of each party in each house, and the
    minority party should have representation on the committee in
    proportion to its numbers in the body as a whole. The Senate/
    House management committees should combine as a joint manage-
    ment committee. The purpose of these committees should be to
    assume responsibility for the administrative management

(housekeeping) functions relating to personnel, facilities, the research bureaus, budgets, and expenditures of their respective houses. The joint management committee should deal with matters of inter-house coordination.

While there are a House Management Committee and a Senate Management Committee, there is no joint management committee, as is recommended.

11. INTERIM COMMITTEES. When the legislature is not in session, the standing committees should become the interim committees for the purpose of conducting long-range studies of state policy issues. The Legislative Council or some similarly constituted, bi-partisan committee should serve as the supervising agency for interim committees and their studies, budgets, and personnel. The major committees should be staffed on a year-round basis.

At the present time the Legislative Council is prohibited from meeting more than ninety days per annum.

12. LEGISLATIVE SALARIES. Legislative salaries should be set by statute and paid in equal monthly installments throughout the biennium, and all unvouchered expense allowances should be incorporated into an annual salary. Actual and necessary expenses incurred in the process of carrying out legislative duties should be reimbursed upon submission and approval of properly vouchered evidence of expenditures.

INCREASE LEGISLATIVE COMPENSATION. No legislative salaries in the United States should be below the $10,000 a year level. Compensation of legislators in the larger states should be in the $20,000 to $30,000 range.

13. ESTABLISH AN AUTOMATIC CALENDAR OF BILLS. When a bill is favorably reported out of committee to the floor, it should go automatically onto the calendar in the order in which it was reported out. It should require a vote of an extraordinary majority to move a bill from its position on calendar or to bypass it. The Rules Committee should have no part in the scheduling of bills. No session should adjourn until all bills on calendar have been voted up or down or, by the vote of an extraordinary majority, have been moved from the calendar.

14. SKELETON BILLS. There should be an explicit rule barring introduction of skeleton or "spot" bills. This rule should be enforced by the assigning authority, (the presiding officer or Rules Committee) by refusal to assign bills so identified to committee.

15. STATEMENT OF INTENT BY AUTHOR OF A BILL. The form
    in which a bill is introduced should include a statement by the
    author describing, in laymen's language, what the bill is intended
    to accomplish.

16. BILL SUMMARY BY BILL-DRAFTING SERVICE. The form in
    which bills are introduced should include a more extensive
    summary of the provisions of the bill, prepared by the bill-drafting
    service.

17. STRENGTHEN STAFF SUPPORT. Legislative research, fiscal,
    legal, and planning agencies should be adequately staffed to full
    utility and at suitable salary levels for professional qualification.
    Professional staffing should be at a level to enable the legislature
    to conduct continuous, year-round examination of state resources
    and expenditures as well as program review and evaluation of
    state agencies. This staff should also prepare fiscal notes accom-
    panying all appropriation bills, evaluating their fiscal impact
    over the short and long term. Staff agencies should be upgraded
    to the level at which competent and timely service can be provided
    to every member of the legislature.

    The Legislative Council provides all of the professional staff sup-
    port to the Arkansas General Assembly. It cannot, given its
    present complement of individuals, provide the quantity of services
    required by the legislature. The present Legislative Council
    staff should be enlarged by authorizing additional positions and
    by increasing salary levels and qualifications. Other forms of
    legislative staffing beyond the Legislative Council are needed.

18. COMMITTEE STAFFING. Standing committees should be staffed
    on a permanent year-round basis.

    A beginning should be made toward permanent, year-round
    committee staffing for some of the major committees.

19. STRENGTHEN STAFF SUPPORT (LEADERS). Staff assistance
    should be provided to all leaders of both the majority and the
    minority parties. Such assistance should include a secretary
    and an administrative assistant at the professional level, with
    space to work reasonably adjacent to the offices of members and
    leaders.

20. STRENGTHEN STAFF (RANK-AND-FILE MEMBERS). Rank-and-
    file members (majority and minority party on an equal basis)
    should be provided with individual staff assistance consisting of
    a minimum of an administrative assistant at the professional
    level and a secretary. Eventually, this should increase to the

stated level of support both in the capital and in a district office.

21. INDIVIDUAL OFFICES. Provide private, individual offices for every member of the legislature, with nearby space for their assistants. The quality and amount of office space should not differ substantially between majority and minority party members.

Senators enjoy either individual (for ten senior members) or shared offices, but Representatives have no office space save their desk on the floor of the chamber. Immediate steps should be taken to provide at least shared office space for House members, and then gradually reducing the number of members who share space until a private office is provided for each member.

22. SERVICE AGENCY FACILITIES. Space for service agencies should provide adequate working space for professional and clerical staff as well as library, files, and other storage requirements.

At the present time the Legislative Council staff is squeezed into tight quarters. The expansion of this staff (as we have recommended earlier) will require an expansion of the total office space.

23. FACILITIES FOR COMMITTEES. Legislative effectiveness requires that committees have adequate physical facilities in which to do their work. This includes an adequate number of committee rooms and an adequate number of hearing rooms that will permit the seating of larger audiences.

Committee rooms, although recently remodeled, are far too few in number, have little if any spectator space, no space for the press, no electrical connections and lights for television transmission. The number of committee rooms should be expanded to comfortably allow scheduling of activities for all committees. New rooms should be designed to allow space for spectators, the press, and witnesses. In addition, the number of hearing rooms able to accommodate more than fifty non-committee members should be increased from one to three.

24. IMPROVE PRESS FACILITIES. Improved press facilities aid in the coverage of the work of the legislature. Committee rooms, and both chambers or galleries, should provide adequate space for the news media as well as lighting and electrical power connections for their equipment. Conference or interview rooms and office space should also be provided for the news media.

Offices should be provided for the permanent and sessional members of the capital press corps. New conference or interview rooms should also be made available to the news media.

25. PROVIDE SINGLE-MEMBER DISTRICTS. Legislative districts
in both houses should be single-member.

26. PRACTICE BEFORE REGULATORY AGENCIES. Legislators or
their firms should be prohibited from practicing before state
regulatory agencies or in matters concerning state agencies for
a fee.

PROHIBIT DOING BUSINESS WITH THE STATE. There should
be a prohibition against legislators or the firms in which they
own a major interest doing business with state agencies.

27. DISCONTINUE ROTATING LEADERSHIP. The practice of limiting
presiding officers to a single, two-year term in that position
weakens the legislature in its capacity to confront other branches
and levels of government as a partner of equal stature and diffuses
and disrupts the continuity of leadership within the legislative
bodies. Although it is extremely difficult to change a practice
such as this, because of its profoundly adverse effects on many
aspects of legislative performance, it should be discontinued.

CALIFORNIA (1)

Functional, 1; Accountable, 3; Informed, 2; Independent, 3; Representative, 2

GENERAL: As the state ranked number one in this study, California's
legislature has many of the resources as well as the structural and
organizational requirements for excellence. The areas in which the
California Legislature particularly excels, and therefore provides a
model for many large state's legislatures, are the following.

Professional Staffing. The amount and quality, as well as the extensive
ness of coverage and availability, of professional staff services is
probably the outstanding feature of the California Legislature.

Physical Facilities. The physical facilities provided for leaders,
committees, individual members, legislative staff, and the public
are superior.

Character and Quality of Bill Documents, Other Legislative Documents
and Records. Members of the legislature are provided a wide range
of high-quality records and documents recording the actions of the
legislature and its committees. These records are produced with

speed and accuracy. Although electronic processing equipment is
not extensively used and could facilitate the preparation of these
documents and records, nevertheless these supporting services are
well provided.

Rules and Procedures. Explicit and detailed published rules of procedure exist and are generally followed.

Compensation. Starting in January, 1971, the basic salary of members
of the legislature of $19,200 a year, taken together with other forms
of compensation, more closely approximates appropriate compensation
for legislative service than that which is provided in any other state.

Time. Annual unlimited sessions make it possible for the California
Legislature to use as much time as is required to accomplish its
work.

Automatic Calendar.

The areas in which the California Legislature could improve are the
committee system, inter-house coordination, the role of the minority
party, and information accompanying bills. These and other areas of
potential improvement are spelled out in these specific recommendations.

1.   REDUCE THE NUMBER OF COMMITTEES. Ideally, there should
     be from ten to fifteen committees in each house, parallel in juris-
     diction. This would reduce the general complexity of the legis-
     lature and would permit reducing the number of committee
     assignments per member.

     With twenty-one committees in the Assembly and twenty-one in
     the Senate, California has more committees than should be
     necessary for the effective organization of the work. This surplus
     is more severe in relation to the Senate than it is to the Assembly.

2.   REDUCE THE NUMBER OF COMMITTEE ASSIGNMENTS. In
     order to make it possible for members to concentrate their
     attention and contribute effectively, there should be no more than
     three committee assignments for each member of the lower house
     and four committee assignments for each member of the Senate.
     The multiplicity of assignments introduces problems of scheduling,
     strains the focus of attention on the part of members, and creates
     an inordinately heavy workload for members if committees are
     as active as they should be.

     At present, thirty percent of the members of the Assembly have
     more than three committee assignments each, and ninety-two

percent of the members of the Senate have more than four
committee assignments each.

3. UNIFORM COMMITTEE RULES. There should be uniform published rules of committee procedure in the Senate, as exists in
the Assembly.

4. COMMITTEE JURISDICTION. A description of the jurisdiction
of Assembly committees should be spelled out in the Assembly
rules, as they are in the Senate rules. Assignment of bills should
consistently accord with the jurisdiction of committees as describe
in the rules.

5. PUBLISH COMMITTEE ROLL CALLS. The committee report of
action on bills to the respective houses should include those roll
calls which are taken, showing how each member voted. These
committee reports should be available to the press and public.
Published roll calls should apply to those bills recommended for
approval as well as those killed.

6. STATEMENT OF INTENT BY AUTHOR OF A BILL. The form in
which a bill is introduced should include a statement by the author
describing, in laymen's language, what the bill is intended to
accomplish.

7. BILL SUMMARY BY BILL-DRAFTING SERVICE. The form in
which bills are introduced should include a more extensive
summary of the provisions of the bill, prepared by the bill-drafting
service.

8. SKELETON BILLS. There should be an explicit rule barring
introduction of skeleton or "spot" bills. This rule should be
enforced by the assigning authority (the presiding officer or
Rules Committee) by refusal to assign bills so identified to
committee.

9. MINORITY PARTY MEMBERS ON COMMITTEE. Minority party
members should be assigned to committees by the minority leader
in consultation with the minority caucus.

10. ELECTRIC ROLL CALL RECORDER. There should be an electric
roll call recorder installed in the Senate. This is recommended
not simply because it would speed up the proceedings (worthwhile
as this may be), but because it is an efficient method of producing
an error-free record of roll call votes.

11. INFORMATION OFFICER. Provide an information officer for
the Assembly and the Senate.

12. LEGISLATIVE POWER TO CALL SPECIAL SESSIONS. Amend the constitution to permit the legislature to convene special sessions either by petition of a majority of the members of both houses or the call of the presiding officer of each house.

13. POWER TO EXPAND SPECIAL SESSION AGENDA. Amend the constitution to permit the legislature to broaden the subject matter of a governor's call of a special session by a majority vote in each house, or prohibit the restriction of the agenda by the governor.

14. COMMITTEE BILL REPORTS. Require committees to issue reports describing and explaining the committee's action on bills recommended for passage at the time the bill moves from the committee to the floor.

15. REMOVE CONSTITUTIONAL RESTRICTIONS ON SESSION TIME. Amend the constitution to provide for flexible biennial sessions permitting the legislature to convene, recess, and reconvene as it deems desirable over the two-year period of its term.

16. BILL CARRY-OVER. Amend the constitution to permit the carry-over of bills from one session to the next within the same term.

17. PROHIBIT DOING BUSINESS WITH THE STATE. There should be a prohibition against legislators or the firms in which they own a major interest doing business with state agencies.

PROHIBIT APPOINTMENT TO STATE OFFICE. There should he a prohibition against a legislator accepting appointment to other state office during the term for which he is elected or within two years of the termination of his service as a member of the legislature.

COLORADO (28)

Functional, 21; Accountable, 25; Informed, 21; Independent, 28; Representative, 27

GENERAL: The Colorado Legislature is in a state of transition. Many improvements have been made in the last few years, but much remains to be done to permit the legislature to take its place as an equal partner in state government and an institution capable of providing innovative leadership. At its present stage of development, the Colorado Legislature displays a mixture of strengths and weaknesses.

The legislature gains strength from its small size (House, sixty-five; Senate, thirty-five), consolidated committees (House, fifteen; Senate, sixteen), and single-member districts, which contribute to the reduced complexity of the legislature. Bills and other legislative documents are clear and comprehensible in format. The openness of the legislature is advanced by the accessibility of press and public to its proceedings in the chambers and committee rooms, as well as its facilities for news media coverage. A full set of deadlines governs the flow of work through the legislature and a comprehensive set of centralized staff agencies provides a substantial range of research services for the legislature. A beginning has been made in the use of electronic data-processing equipment to amplify these support services.

Some of the unmet needs of the Colorado legislature are addressed in the following recommendations.

1. IMPROVE AND EXPAND PHYSICAL FACILITIES. During the past few years, some improvements have been made in upgrading the physical facilities of the legislature and in providing offices for legislative leaders, creating committee meeting and hearing rooms, installing electronic media coverage facilities, and expanding the space available to staff agencies. These improvements have been accomplished by occupying and renovating space in the capitol. Nevertheless, space remains one of the pressing problems which interferes with the legislature's ability to make other improvements. Consideration has been given recently to the construction of a new legislative office building or a state office building into which to move administrative agencies now housed in the capitol. The new building would be constructed near the capitol. One or another of these alternatives should be selected and implemented. The feasibility of a number of the following recommendations depends upon that action.

2. INDIVIDUAL OFFICES. Provide private, individual offices for every member of the legislature, with nearby space for their assistants. The quality and amount of office space should not differ substantially between majority and minority party members.

    At a minimum, minority and majority leaders should have private offices for themselves, with separate, nearby offices for their assistants. A beginning can be made toward providing offices for members by making space available for shared offices among small numbers of members at first, then gradually reducing the number who share space until a private office is provided for each member.

3. FACILITIES FOR COMMITTEES. Legislative effectiveness

requires that committees have adequate physical facilities in which to do their work. This includes an adequate number of committee rooms and an adequate number of hearing rooms that will permit the seating of larger audiences.

The number of adequate hearing rooms should be increased.

4. SERVICE AGENCY FACILITIES. Space for service agencies should provide adequate working space for professional and clerical staff as well as library, files, and other storage requirements.

Space for service agencies is inadequate and should be expanded.

5. IMPROVE PRESS FACILITIES. Improved press facilities aid in the coverage of the work of the legislature. Committee rooms, and both chambers or galleries, should provide adequate space for the news media as well as lighting and electrical power connections for their equipment. Conference or interview rooms and office space should also be provided for the news media.

6. REDUCE THE NUMBER OF COMMITTEE ASSIGNMENTS. In order to make it possible for members to concentrate their attention and contribute effectively, there should be no more than three committee assignments for each member of the lower house and four committee assignments for each member of the Senate. The multiplicity of assignments introduces problems of scheduling, strains the focus of attention on the part of members, and creates an inordinately heavy workload for members if committees are as active as they should be.

At present, twenty-six percent of the members of the House have more than three committee assignments each, and ninety-two percent of the members of the Senate have more than four committee assignments each.

7. COMMITTEE JURISDICTION. A description of the jurisdiction of committees should be contained in the rules of both houses, and assignment of bills should be made in accord with the jurisdiction of committees as described in the rules.

8. BALANCED COMMITTEES. Committees, in their composition, should reflect as accurately as possible the makeup of the entire house of which they are a part. There should be no "killer," "graveyard," or "cinch" committees.

9. COMMITTEE BILL REPORTS. Require committees to issue reports describing and explaining the committee's action on bills

recommended for passage at the time the bill moves from the
committee to the floor.

10. ELECTRIC ROLL CALL RECORDER. There should be an electric
roll call recorder in each house. This is recommended not simply because it would speed up the proceedings (worthwhile as
this may be), but because it is an efficient method of producing
an error-free record of roll call votes.

11. INTERIM COMMITTEES. When the legislature is not in session,
the standing committees should become the interim committees
for the purpose of conducting long-range studies of state policy
issues. The Legislative Council or some similarly constituted,
bi-partisan committee should serve as the supervising agency
for interim committees and their studies, budgets, and personnel.
The major committees should be staffed on a year-round basis.

12. LEGISLATIVE SALARIES. Legislative salaries should be set by
statute and paid in equal monthly installments throughout the
biennium, and all unvouchered expense allowances should be incorporated into an annual salary. Actual and necessary expenses
incurred in the process of carrying out legislative duties should
be reimbursed upon submission and approval of properly vouchered
evidence of expenditures.

INCREASE LEGISLATIVE COMPENSATION. No legislative salaries in the United States should be below the $10,000 a year level.
Compensation of legislators in the larger states should be in the
$20,000 to $30,000 range.

Colorado's legislative salaries (currently $7,600 a year) should
be increased to the $10,000 to $15,000 level on an annual basis.
Consideration might be given to the establishment of a public
commission to make appropriate recommendations on all governmental salaries.

13. REPRINT AMENDED BILLS. When a bill is amended substantially
it should be reprinted and returned to the legislature with no
more than an overnight delay. The reprint should show clearly
the original text of the bill as well as the change created by the
amendment.

14. WASHINGTON, D.C., OFFICE FOR THE LEGISLATURE. With
the large and growing volume of activity generated by state-federal
relationships, the legislature, beyond merely reacting to federal
legislation, should be in a position to influence the development
of new programs in accordance with the interests of the state.

To do so, the legislature should have an office in the nation's capital to represent it and to be its most direct liaison with the Congress.

For small states, consideration might be given to joining with a number of sister states (either on a geographical or on a population basis) for the purpose of sharing the services of a Washington office. But in large states, the volume of inter-governmental traffic has reached a stage at which it would benefit the legislature greatly to have a full-time Washington office.

15. ESTABLISH AN AUTOMATIC CALENDAR OF BILLS. When a bill is favorably reported out of committee to the floor, it should go automatically onto the calendar in the order in which it was reported out. It should require a vote of an extraordinary majority to move a bill from its position on calendar or to bypass it. The Rules Committee should have no part in the scheduling of bills. No session should adjourn until all bills on calendar have been voted up or down or, by the vote of an extraordinary majority, have been moved from the calendar.

16. MINORITY PARTY MEMBERS ON COMMITTEE. Minority party members should be assigned to committees by the minority leader in consultation with the minority caucus.

17. STRENGTHEN STAFF SUPPORT (LEADERS). Staff assistance should be provided to all leaders of both the majority and the minority parties. Such assistance should include a secretary and an administrative assistant at the professional level, with space to work reasonably adjacent to the offices of members and leaders.

18. PRE-SESSION ORGANIZATIONAL MEETING. Amend the constitution to provide a pre-session organizing session following a general election. Some states make advantageous use of such a session during November or December of a general election year for the purpose of electing leaders, appointing committee chairmen, assigning members to committees, referring pre-filed bills to committee, holding committee organizational meetings, and conducting orientation conferences for new, as well as returning, members of the legislature. Through such pre-session meetings the committees can begin their work before the regular session convenes. This makes it possible to delay the start of the regular session until legislation is ready for floor action.

Existing plans to widen the scope of pre-session activities should include the items suggested in this general recommendation.

19. **REGULATION OF LOBBYISTS.** The independence of the legislature and public confidence in its processes require the regulation
of special-interest advocates. Lobbyists should be required to
register with an agency of the legislature, and should be required
to disclose who employs them, on behalf of what objectives, how
much they are paid, and how much they spend and on whom. This
information should be available to the press and the public. There
should be specific and automatic penalties for failure to comply
with these requirements.

Lobbyists in Colorado are required only to register with an agency
of the legislature.

20. **LEGISLATIVE POWER TO CALL SPECIAL SESSIONS.** Amend
the constitution to permit the legislature to convene special sessions either by petition of a majority of the members of both
houses or the call of the presiding officer of each house.

21. **POWER TO EXPAND SPECIAL SESSION AGENDA.** Amend the
constitution to permit the legislature to broaden the subject matter
of a governor's call of a special session by a majority vote in
each house, or prohibit the restriction of the agenda by the
governor.

22. **REMOVE LEGISLATIVE POWERS FROM LIEUTENANT GOV-
ERNOR.** The exercise of legislative powers, including such pro
forma powers as presiding, casting tie-breaking votes, and signing
enacted legislation by the lieutenant governor, whether the powers
derive from the constitution or the rule book, would seem to be
a particularly serious breach of the separation of powers and the
independence of the legislature. The constitution and/or rule
book should be amended to permit these legislative powers presently exercised by the lieutenant governor to be set as the responsibility of the office of the president pro tem of the Senate.

Although the present lieutenant governor has considerable legislative experience, having served as both a member and as speaker
of the House, were the people of Colorado to elect a lieutenant
governor with no legislative experience, the exercise of legislative
powers by the lieutenant governor would be particularly awkward.
In any case, this prevents the Senate from developing leadership
of its own choosing from among its own members.

23. **ESTABLISH CITIZENS' COMMISSION ON THE LEGISLATURE.**
As a means of cultivating generalized support for the legislature
as an institution, a citizens' commission should be created by
joint resolution of the legislature, to study its operations,

facilities, and needs and to recommend improvements. The appointive power should be consigned to the speaker and the president pro tem on an equal basis and should include consultation with the minority leader of each house. The citizens' commission should conduct its review over a two-year period, resulting in recommendations to the legislature and the public concerning the role the legislature is expected to perform in development of a truly effective and responsive state government, and the measures required to reach that objective. A key function of the commission is to educate the citizenry to problems, opportunities, and needs of the legislature. This purpose is best served by doing much of its work through public hearings conducted in the population centers of the state. A commission composed of from twenty-five to thirty-five leading citizens, representing various fields of activity, interest groups, and areas of the state can contribute much to the development of public support for a more dynamic legislature.

CONNECTICUT (24)

Functional, 39; Accountable, 26; Informed, 26; Independent, 25; Representative, 6

GENERAL: The momentum for modernization of the Connecticut Legislature has accelerated in the past two years. A number of significant changes have recently been made both by constitutional amendment and by legislative action which are not reflected in these standings. As these improvements and others which continue to be made begin to have impact, it is apparent that the Connecticut Legislature will begin to rapidly progress toward becoming a more effective decision-making institution.

During 1968 and 1969, study of its procedures was commissioned by the Connecticut Legislature and conducted by the Eagleton Institute of Politics at Rutgers University; the Citizens Conference on the General Assembly was organized, conducted its inquiry, and rendered its recommendations; and the legislature undertook an active program of modernization.

The Joint Legislative Management Committee was created, and the beginning of bi-partisan professional staffing has been made under its agencies. An amendment to the constitution providing annual sessions was submitted to the voters and ratified in November, 1970. The current state of transition occasioned by these events implies a considerable mixture of strengths and weaknesses in legislative organization and procedure.

The Connecticut Legislature has clear-cut, well-formulated, published rules of procedure for the respective houses as well as committee operations. There are also joint rules, and the jurisdiction of committees is spelled out. A record of committee deliberations and actions is recorded and available to the public. The format of bills is clear and comprehensible. Connecticut is one of the few states whose legislation contains a statement by the author expressing the intent of the bill. Bills are confined to a single subject matter. They are printed in quantity and easily available. Amended bills are reprinted and returned to the legislature without delay.

The minority leadership and membership in each house have effective roles through involvement in the management committees and control over the appointment of members to other committees.

Implementation of the recommendations to follow will contribute to the development of a more effective legislature.

1. REDUCE THE OVERALL SIZE OF THE LEGISLATURE. Although size reduction in a legislative body is extremely difficult to achieve, it has been done in some states — such as in Vermont and Iowa — and needs to be accomplished in others (New Hampshire, Massachusetts, Georgia, and Pennsylvania). Where reduction in size has occurred, it has most often required a constitutional convention to accomplish it. In a few cases it has been done by legislatively adopted constitutional amendment (Iowa, in 1968, which becomes effective in November, 1971)ratified by the voters. There should be 100 or fewer members in the house. The combined size of both houses should be between 100 and 150.

    With 177 members in the House and thirty-six members in the Senate, a total of 213, Connecticut has the sixth largest legislature in the United States. By reducing the size of the House to under 100, Connecticut could achieve a significant reduction in the complexity of its legislature and facilitate improvements in a number of elements of its operations.

2. INCREASE LEGISLATIVE COMPENSATION. No legislative salaries in the United States should be below the $10,000 a year level. Compensation of legislators in the larger states should be in the $20,000 to $30,000 range.

    Salaries of members of the legislature are far too low. Current compensation -- which includes a salary of $3,250 per biennium, plus an expense allowance of $750 for the same two-year period, making a total compensation of $2,000 per year--should be increased to the $10,000 to $15,000 a year level.

3. REDUCE THE NUMBER OF COMMITTEE ASSIGNMENTS. In order to make it possible for members to concentrate their attention and contribute effectively, there should be no more than three committee assignments for each member of the lower house and four committee assignments for each member of the Senate. The multiplicity of assignments introduces problems of scheduling, strains the focus of attention on the part of members, and creates an inordinately heavy workload for members if committees are as active as they should be.

At present, 33 percent of the members of the House have more than three committee assignments each, and 92 percent of the members of the Senate have more than four committee assignments each.

4. REDUCE THE NUMBER OF COMMITTEES. Ideally, there should be from ten to fifteen committees in each house, parallel in jurisdiction. This would reduce the general complexity of the legislature and would permit reducing the number of committee assignments per member.

All committees of the Connecticut General Assembly operate as joint committees during both the session and the interim. There are thirty of them at present, which is approximately double the number that should be necessary for the effective organization of the work. A reduction in the number of joint committees would facilitate reducing the number of committee assignments.

5. INDIVIDUAL OFFICES. Provide private, individual offices for every member of the legislature, with nearby space for their assistants. The quality and amount of office space should not differ substantially between majority and minority party members.

At a minimum and immediately, leaders should have private offices for themselves, with separate, nearby offices for their assistants.

6. FACILITIES FOR COMMITTEES. Legislative effectiveness requires that committees have adequate physical facilities in which to do their work. This includes an adequate number of committee rooms and an adequate number of hearing rooms that will permit the seating of larger audiences.

The number of committee hearing rooms should be increased to permit the seating of larger audiences.

7. SERVICE AGENCY FACILITIES. Space for service agencies
    should provide adequate working space for professional and cleri-
    cal staff as well as library, files, and other storage requirements.

8. IMPROVE PRESS FACILITIES. Improved press facilities aid in
    the coverage of the work of the legislature. Committee rooms,
    and both chambers or galleries, should provide adequate space
    for the news media as well as lighting and electrical power con-
    nections for their equipment. Conference or interview rooms
    and office space should also be provided for the news media.

9. STAFF (PATRONAGE). Eliminate party patronage from all legis-
    lative staffing and from the staffing of joint legislative committees
    in particular.

10. STRENGTHEN STAFF SUPPORT. Legislative research, fiscal,
    legal, and planning agencies should be adequately staffed to full
    utility and at suitable salary levels for professional qualification.
    Professional staffing should be at a level to enable the legislature
    to conduct continuous, year-round examination of state resources
    and expenditures as well as program review and evaluation of state
    agencies. This staff should also prepare fiscal notes accompany-
    ing all appropriation bills, evaluating their fiscal impact over
    the short and long term. Staff agencies should be upgraded to
    the level at which competent and timely service can be provided
    to every member of the legislature.

11. COMMITTEE STAFFING. Standing committees should be staffed
    on a permanent, year-round basis.

12. STRENGTHEN STAFF SUPPORT (LEADERS). Staff assistance
    should be provided to all leaders of both the majority and the mi-
    nority parties. Such assistance should include a secretary and
    an administrative assistant at the professional level, with space
    to work reasonably adjacent to the offices of members and leaders.

13. STRENGTHEN STAFF (RANK-AND-FILE MEMBERS). Rank-and-
    file members (majority and minority party on an equal basis)
    should be provided with individual staff assistance consisting of
    a minimum of an administrative assistant at the professional
    level and a secretary. Eventually, this should increase to the
    stated level of support both in the capital and in a district office.

14. COMMITTEE BILL REPORTS. Require committees to issue
    reports describing and explaining the committees action on bills
    recommended for passage at the time the bill moves from the
    committee to the floor.

15. PUBLISH COMMITTEE ROLL CALLS. The committee report of action on bills to the respective houses should include those roll calls which are taken, showing how each member voted. These committee reports should be available to the press and public. Published roll calls should apply to those bills recommended for approval as well as those killed.

16. DUAL COMMITTEE CONSIDERATION OF APPROPRIATION BILLS. There should be a rule requiring dual committe consideration of legislation affecting significant sums of money. Such legislation, when considered and acted upon favorably by a substantive policy committee, should then automatically be referred to the Finance Committee for consideration of its fiscal impact.

17. WASHINGTON, D.C., OFFICE FOR THE LEGISLATURE. With the large and growing volume of activity generated by state-federal relationships, the legislature, beyond merely reacting to federal legislation, should be in a position to influence the development of new programs in accordance with the interests of the state. To do so, the legislature should have an office in the nation's capital to represent it and to be its most direct liaison with the Congress.

For small states, consideration might be given to joining with a number of sister states (either on a geographical or on a population basis) for the purpose of sharing the services of a Washington office. But in large states, the volume of inter-governmental traffic has reached a stage at which it would benefit the legislature greatly to have a full-time Washington office.

18. SUPPORT OF DISTRICT OFFICES. District offices are vital to the effective representation by a legislator of his constituency. The legislature should make some contribution to the support of district offices for its members, and the amount of this contribution should be increased over time.

19. BILL DEADLINES. The orderly flow of work through the legislature depends upon the existence of a series of deadlines at various critical stages throughout the legislative process. These deadlines should be adopted as part of the rules and should be consistently enforced.

The adoption and observance of a system of deadlines should alleviate the end of session logjams. In the last (1969) session of the Connecticut Legislature, 40 percent of the bills passed were enacted in the final week of the session.

20. SKELETON BILLS. There should be an explicit rule barring introduction of skeleton or "spot" bills. This rule should be enforced by the assigning authority (the presiding officer or Rules Committee) by refusal to assign bills so identified to committee.

21. REQUIRE ROLL CALL ON PASSAGE OF BILLS. A recorded roll call should be required on final passage of any legislative measure, and it should require a constitutional majority to pass any bill on final action by either house.

22. SPECIAL PROVISIONS. In addition to standard laws governing criminal behavior, there should be special provisions regulating legislative conflicts of interest.

PRACTICE BEFORE REGULATORY AGENCIES. Legislators or their firms should be prohibited from practicing before state regulatory agencies or in matters concerning state agencies for a fee.

PROHIBIT DOING BUSINESS WITH THE STATE. There should be a prohibition against legislators or the firms in which they own a major interest doing business with state agencies.

HOLDING OTHER PUBLIC OFFICE. Legislators should be prohibited from concurrently holding other continuing, paid public office.

FAMILY EMPLOYMENT. Members of a legislator's immediate family should be barred from employment by the legislature.

23. PRE-SESSION ORGANIZATIONAL MEETING. Amend the constitution to provide a pre-session organizing session following a general election. Some states make advantageous use of such a session during November or December of a general election year for the purpose of electing leaders, appointing committee chairmen, assigning members to committees, referring pre-filed bills to committee, holding committee organizational meetings, and conducting orientation conferences for new, as well as returning, members of the legislature. Through such pre-session meetings the committees can begin their work before the regular session convenes. This makes it possible to delay the start of the regular session until legislation is ready for floor action.

24. RETIREMENT BENEFITS FOR LEGISLATORS. A system of retirement benefits should be adopted for members of the legislature which is at least as favorable as that provided for state employees generally.

25. QUANTITY OF BILLS INTRODUCED. An extraordinarily high
    number of bill introductions inevitably clogs the entire legislative
    machinery and should be reduced. One alternative would be to
    use a short bill form (as done in Hawaii); another would be to
    require multiple authorship of bills rather than permit the intro-
    duction of identical bills by separate authors. The short-form
    bill has certain advantages in that it permits a member to intro-
    duce a statement describing the intent of the legislation which
    he proposes, but it is not drafted in legal language. Under this
    system the committees to which such short-form bills are referred
    have the obligation of combining them into omnibus legislation
    sponsored by the committee itself.

    Connecticut's volume of bill introduction is among the five highest
    in the nation.

                          DELAWARE (48)

Functional, 43; Accountable, 48; Informed, 47; Independent, 38;
Representative, 29

GENERAL: Delaware is the only state which permits its legislature
to amend the state constitution without a vote of the people. The
constitution is amended when the legislature proposes and passes any
given amendment at two successive sessions. This presents a unique
opportunity for removing limitations hampering the legislature's
operations and procedures.

Two new wings were added to the legislative building in 1970. They
provide individual offices for all Senators and shared offices for
Representatives. Each wing also contains one new committee room
per house. The space alloted to the Legislative Council and the
comptroller general was also markedly upgraded.

The 1968 session of the House of Representatives reduced the number
of its standing committees from twenty-eight to seventeen. Other
new House rules implemented at that time required lobbyists to
register and changed the vote requirement for suspension of the rules
from a simple majority to a three-fifths majority. The 1969 session
implemented the statute creating the Legislative Council and a new
director for the council was hired. In 1970 a resolution of the legislature created the Commission on Legislative Compensation.

The following recommendations are intended to outline a broad attack
on Delaware's remaining problem.

1. REMOVE CONSTITUTIONAL RESTRICTIONS ON SESSION AND
    INTERIM TIME. The legislature should have authority to function
    throughout a two-year term; ideally, this authority should provide
    a flexible biennial session pattern that permits the legislature
    to convene, recess, and reconvene as it deems desirable.
    The legislature should be able to meet in general session or con-
    duct interim work as it deems necessary at any time throughout
    the period.

    The Delaware constitution restricts regular sessions to the
    period between the second Tuesday in January and June 30.
    Although the legislature convenes a special session by the call
    of the presiding officers, the constitution should provide for
    flexible biennial sessions, permitting the legislature to convene
    and recess as it sees fit over the two-year term.

2. BILL DEADLINES. The orderly flow of work through the legis-
    lature depends upon the existence of a series of deadlines at
    various critical stages throughout the legislative process. These
    deadlines should be adopted as part of the rules and should be
    consistently enforced.

    Delaware has a deadline only for bill introduction.

3. INTERIM COMMITTEES. When the legislature is not in session,
    the standing committees should become the interim committees
    for the purpose of conducting long-range studies of state policy
    issues. The Legislative Council or some similarly constituted,
    bi-partisan committee should serve as the supervising agency
    for interim committees and their studies, budgets, and personnel.
    The major committees should be staffed on a year-round basis.

    At present, the meetings of the Legislative Council constitute the
    only interim activity of the General Assembly.

4. PRE-SESSION ORGANIZATIONAL MEETING. Amend the consti-
    tution to provide a pre-session organizing session following a
    general election. Some states make advantageous use of such a
    session during November or December of a general election
    year for the purpose of electing leaders, appointing committee
    chairmen, assigning members to committees, referring pre-filed
    bills to committee, holding committee organizational meetings,
    and conducting orientation conferences for new, as well as
    returning, members of the legislature. Through such pre-session
    meetings the committees can begin their work before the regular
    session convenes. This makes it possible to delay the start of
    the regular session until legislation is ready for floor action.

5. PRE-SESSION ORIENTATION CONFERENCE. The legislature
    should hold an orientation conference for new legislators, prefer-
    ably after each general election. Orientation conferences enable
    members to speed the process of becoming more effective
    representatives, and they provide an opportunity for legislators
    to examine large policy areas apart from the pressure of the
    regular session.

6. LEGISLATIVE SALARIES. Legislative salaries should be set by
    statute and paid in equal monthly installments throughout the
    biennium, and all unvouchered expense allowances should be in-
    corporated into an annual salary. Actual and necessary expenses
    incurred in the process of carrying out legislative duties should
    be reimbursed upon submission and approval of properly vouchered
    evidence of expenditures.

    INCREASE LEGISLATIVE COMPENSATION. No legislative salaries
    in the United States should be below the $10,000 a year level.
    Compensation of legislators in the larger states should be in the
    $20,000 to $30,000 range.

    Legislative salaries in Delaware should be at the $10,000 to
    $15,000 per year level.

7. EXPENSE ALLOWANCES. Members of the legislature should be
    allowed an expense reimbursement covering their travel and
    living costs while engaged in carrying out their legislative duties.
    The same allowance should obtain during the interim for days in
    attendance at interim committee meetings or other official and
    authorized legislative business. These allowances should be
    provided by statute.

    The constitution limits expenses for legislators to $25 for any
    regular session and $10 for a special session. The constitution
    also allows payment of transportation costs at rates to be estab-
    lished by statute. Legislators should receive an expense allowance
    for interim activities.

8. STRENGTHEN STAFF SUPPORT. Legislative research, fiscal,
    legal, and planning agencies should be adequately staffed to full
    utility and at suitable salary levels for professional qualification.
    Professional staffing should be at a level to enable the legislature
    to conduct continuous, year-round examination of state resources
    and expenditures as well as program review and evaluation of
    state agencies. This staff should also prepare fiscal notes
    accompanying all appropriation bills, evaluating their fiscal
    impact over the short and long term. Staff agencies should be

upgraded to the level at which competent and timely service can be provided to every member of the legislature.

COMMITTEE STAFFING. Standing committees should be staffed on a permanent, year-round basis.

STRENGTHEN STAFF SUPPORT (LEADERS). Staff assistance should be provided to all leaders of both the majority and the minority parties. Such assistance should include a secretary and an administrative assistant at the professional level, with space to work reasonably adjacent to the offices of members and leaders.

STRENGTHEN STAFF (RANK-AND-FILE MEMBERS). Rank-and-file members (majority and minority party on an equal basis) should be provided with individual staff assistance consisting of a minimum of an administrative assistant at the professional level and a secretary. Eventually, this should increase to the stated level of support both in the capital and in a district office.

9. TRANSFER AUDIT FUNCTION TO THE LEGISLATURE. A significant part of the legislature's ability to exercise oversight of executive departments and administrative agencies depends upon the power and capacity to conduct audits (financial and functional) of these units of the state government. These functions and responsibilities should be removed from the duties and resources of the office of auditor and be established under a legislative auditor.

10. STRENGTHEN MINORITY PARTY ROLE. Internal accountability as well as the capacity of all legislators to represent their constituents effectively depends upon the opportunity of minority party members to have an effective part in internal legislative affairs.

11. REDUCE THE NUMBER OF COMMITTEE ASSIGNMENTS. In order to make it possible for members to concentrate there attention and contribute effectively, there should be no more than three committee assignments for each member of the lower house and four committee assignments for each member of the Senate.

The multiplicity of assignments introduces problems of scheduling, strains the focus of attention on the part of members, and creates an inordinately heavy workload for members if committees are as active as they should be.

At present, eight percent of the House members have more than three committee assignments each, and eighty-four percent of the Senate members have more than four assignments each. Since there are only thirty-nine Representatives and nineteen Senators, a reduction in the number of committees (seventeen in the House, eighteen in the Senate) would facilitate reducing the number of committee assignments.

12. ACT ON ALL BILLS. Committees should be required to report on all bills assigned to them, recommending for passage by the parent body those bills which enjoy the support of a majority of the members of the committee and killing all others.

13. OPEN COMMITTEES. The rules of each house should prohibit secret meetings except in matters affecting the security of the state, or which could unnecessarily damage the reputation of individuals in personnel matters. Such exceptions should be sparingly and responsibly employed.

14. COMMITTEE BILL REPORTS. Require committees to issue reports describing and explaining the committee's action on bills recommended for passage at the time the bill moves from the committee to the floor.

15. NOTICE OF MEETINGS. The rules should require a minimum notice of five legislative days for committee meetings and hearings, with widely disseminated announcement of schedule, location, agenda, and availability of public participation.

16. UNIFORM COMMITTEE RULES. There should be uniform published rules of committee procedure in both chambers.

17. FACILITIES FOR COMMITTEES. Legislative effectiveness requires that committees have adequate physical facilities in which to do their work. This includes an adequate number of committee rooms and an adequate number of hearing rooms that will permit the seating of larger audiences.

Even though new office space was created by adding wings to the old capitol building, committees still do not have adequate space.

18. PRACTICE BEFORE REGULATORY AGENCIES. Legislators or their firms should be prohibited from practicing before state regulatory agencies or in matters concerning state agencies for a fee.

PROHIBIT DOING BUSINESS WITH THE STATE. There should be a prohibition against legislators or the firms in which they own a major interest doing business with state agencies.

PROHIBIT APPOINTMENT TO STATE OFFICE. There should

be a prohibition against a legislator accepting appointment to
other state office during the term for which he is elected or
within two years of the termination of his service as a member
of the legislature.

HOLDING OTHER PUBLIC OFFICE. Legislators should be
prohibited from concurrently holding other continuing, paid public
office.

FAMILY EMPLOYMENT. Members of a legislator's immediate
family should be barred from employment by the legislature.

Only immediate families of Representatives are barred from
employment by the legislature.

19. REGULATION OF LOBBYISTS. The independence of the legislature and public confidence in its processes require the regulation
of special interest advocates. Lobbyists should be required to
register with an agency of the legislature, and should be required
to disclose who employs them, on behalf of what objectives, how
much they are paid, and how much they spend and on whom.
This information should be available to the press and the public.
There should be specific and automatic penalties for failure to
comply with these requirements.

At present, lobbyists are only required to register in the House.

20. SUPPORT OF DISTRICT OFFICES. District offices are vital to
the effective representation by a legislator of his constituency.
The legislature should make some contribution to the support of
district offices for its memebers, and the amount of this contribution should be increased over time.

21. REMOVE LEGISLATIVE POWERS FROM LIEUTENANT GOVERNC
The exercise of legislative powers, including such pro forma
powers as presiding, casting tie-breaking votes, and signing
enacted legislation, by the lieutenant governor, whether the
powers derive from the constitution or the rule book, would
seem to be a particularly serious breach of the separation of
powers and the independence of the legislature. The constitution
and/or rule book should be amended to permit these legislative
powers presently exercised by the lieutenant governor to be set
as the responsibility of the office of the president pro tem of the
Senate.

22. MANAGEMENT COMMITTEES. There should be an executive or
management committee created in each house. Its membership

should include the leaders of each party in each house, and the
minority party should have representation on the committee in
proportion to its numbers in the body as a whole. The Senate/
House management committees should combine as a joint management committee. The purpose of these committees should be to
assume responsibility for the administrative management (housekeeping) functions relating to personnel, facilities, the research
bureaus, budgets, and expenditures of their respective houses.
The joint management committee should deal with matters of
inter-house coordination.

23. DUAL COMMITTEE CONSIDERATION OF APPROPRIATION BILLS.
There should be a rule requiring dual committee consideration
of legislation affecting significant sums of money. Such legislation, when considered and acted upon favorably by a substantive
policy committee, should then automatically be referred to the
Finance Committee for consideration of its fiscal impact.

There is a requirement for dual committee consideration of
appropriation bills in the House, but not in the Senate.

24. ESTABLISH AN AUTOMATIC CALENDAR OF BILLS. When a
bill is favorably reported out of committee to the floor, it should
go automatically onto the calendar in the order in which it was
reported out. It should require a vote of an extraordinary majority
to move a bill from its position on calendar or to bypass it. The
Rules Committee should have no part in the scheduling of bills.
No session should adjourn until all bills on calendar have been
voted up or down or, by the vote of an extraordinary majority,
have been moved from the calendar.

25. CONSENT CALENDAR. A consent calendar should be used in
both houses.

26. JOINT RULES. There should be joint rules governing the relationship and the flow of legislation between the two houses of the
legislature.

27. IMPROVE PRESS FACILITIES. Improved press facilities aid in
the coverage of the work of the legislature. Committee rooms,
and both chambers or galleries, should provide adequate space
for the news media as well as lighting and electrical power connections for their equipment. Conference or interview rooms and
office space should also be provided for the news media.

Although legislative proceedings, both in committee and in the
chamber, are accessible to the press, improved press facilities
are needed to aid in coverage of the legislature.

FLORIDA (4)

Functional, 5; Accountable, 8; Informed, 4; Independent, 1; Representative 30

GENERAL: Florida, the fourth-ranked legislature in this study, has made dramatic progress in the last three years toward acquiring the resources and making the structural and organizational improvements necessary for an effective lawmaking environment. The greatest transformations have taken place in those areas which contribute to the independence of the legislature, in which Florida ranks first, and in the availability of information resources.

Some outstanding features of the Florida Legislature are the following.

Legislators, press, and public have access to the work of the legislature aided by the existence of uniform, published rules of committee procedure; the availability of a public record of committee deliberations and actions, including roll call votes; the prohibition against skeleton bills; and the provision of informative summaries contained in the format of bill documents.

Although the constitution limits the annual session to sixty consecutive days, the legislature can extend the session by three-fifths vote, can call itself into session, and can expand the agenda of a special session called by the governor.

The legislature's independence and its capacity to be informed are strengthened by the availability of an extensive array of staff services provided for members and committees. The capacity to conduct legislative oversight of executive agencies is enhanced by its control of a large, well-staffed auditing bureau which conducts functional audits.

The legislature in Florida meets fourteen days following the general election for the purpose of organizing, electing officers, appointing committee chairmen and members, and assigning pre-filed bills to committee, so that the committees can begin to study legislation and hold public hearings in advance of the regular session. During this same period, a full-scale orientation session is conducted for all members, covering legislative procedures as well as state governmental organization and major policy issues. Florida's pre-session activities could serve as a model which most other states would do well to adopt; they have been referred to in the recommendations for other states.

Those characteristics which contribute to the capacity of a legislature to be representative are the ones in which Florida falls farthest behind.

The following recommendations apply to the areas in which the Florida Legislature is most in need of improvement.

1.   PROVIDE SINGLE-MEMBER DISTRICTS. Legislative districts in both houses should be single-member.

     Accomplishing this will require an amendment to the constitution.

2.   REDUCE THE NUMBER OF COMMITTEES. Ideally, there should be from ten to fifteen committees in each house, parallel in jurisdiction. This would reduce the general complexity of the legislature and would permit reducing the number of committee assignments per member.

     REDUCE THE NUMBER OF COMMITTEE ASSIGNMENTS. In order to make it possible for members to concentrate their attention and contribute effectively, there should be no more than three committee assignments for each member of the lower house and four committee assignments for each member of the Senate. The multiplicity of assignments introduces problems of scheduling, strains the focus of attention on the part of members, and creates an inordinately heavy workload for members if committees are as active as they should be.

     At present there are twenty committees in the House (reduced from twenty-nine in December, 1970) and twelve in the Senate. The House should reduce the number of its committees to twelve, as in the Senate, making them parallel in jurisdiction. Adoption of this recommendation would permit a reduction in the number of committee assignments per member of the House. At present, twenty-two percent of the House members serve on more than three committees.

3.   COMMITTEE JURISDICTION. A description of the jurisdiction of committees should be contained in the rules of both houses, and assignment of bills should be made in accord with the jurisdiction of committees as described in the rules.

4.   REPRINT AMENDED BILLS. When a bill is amended substantially, it should be reprinted and returned to the legislature with no more than an overnight delay. The reprint should show clearly the original text of the bill as well as the change created by the amendment.

5. STRENGTHEN MINORITY PARTY ROLE. Internal accountability, as well as the capacity of all legislators to represent their constituents effectively, depends upon the opportunity of minority party members to have an effective party in internal legislative affairs.

MINORITY REPRESENTATION ON COMMITTEE ON RULES. Minority representation on the Committee on Rules should approxi mate the minority party proportion of the membership of the appropriate house.

MINORITY PARTY MEMBERS ON COMMITTEE. Minority party members should be assigned to committees by the minority leader in consultation with the minority caucus.

6. WASHINGTON, D.C., OFFICE FOR THE LEGISLATURE. With the large and growing volume of activity generated by state-federal relationships, the legislature, beyond merely reacting to federal legislation, should be in a position to influence the development of new programs in accordance with the interests of the state. To do so the legislature should have an office in the nation's capital to represent it and to be its most direct liaison with the Congress.

For small states, consideration might be given to joining with a number of sister states (either on a geographical or on a population basis) for the purpose of sharing the services of Washington office But in large states, the volume of inter-governmental traffic has reached a stage at which it would benefit the legislature greatly to have a full-time Washington office.

The Florida Legislature was the first to appoint a coordinator to act as liaison between the legislature and the state's Congressional delegation and federal agencies. Other states have since followed this practice of appointing coordinators for this purpose. The establishment of an office in Washington would be a further develop ment along this same line.

7. DISCONTINUE ROTATING LEADERSHIP. The practice of limiting presiding officers to a single, two-year term in that position weakens the legislature in its capacity to confront other branches and levels of government as a partner of equal stature and diffuses and disrupts the continuity of leadership within the legislative bodies. Although it is extremely difficult to change a practice such as this, because of its profoundly adverse effects on many aspects of legislative performance, it should be discontinued.

Florida is one of the states which still limits its presiding officers to a single, two-year term in that position. This practice should be discontinued.

8. PROHIBIT DOING BUSINESS WITH THE STATE. There should be a prohibition against legislators or the firms in which they own a major interest doing business with state agencies.

PROHIBIT APPOINTMENT TO STATE OFFICE. There should be a prohibition against a legislator accepting appointment to other state office during the term for which he is elected or within two years of the termination of his service as a member of the legislature.

9. SUPPORT OF DISTRICT OFFICES. District offices are vital to the effective representation by a legislator of his constituency. The legislature should make some contribution to the support of district offices for its members, and the amount of this contribution should be increased over time.

Although the Florida Legislature makes some contributions to the support of district offices for its members, the amount of this contribution should be increased.

10. INCREASE LEGISLATIVE COMPENSATION. Gubernatorial and press furor over legislator salaries during 1970 notwithstanding, legislative salaries are low in relationship to the importance of the office of legislator and the increasing public demand, in session and out, made upon members of the legislature. The growing importance and size of the state, together with the increasing complexity of its problems, require that legislative salaries be raised. Legislator salaries for Florida should be in the $20,000 to $30,000 range. Consideration might be given to the establishment of a public commission to make appropriate recommendations on all governmental salaries.

11. BILL CARRY-OVER. Amend the constitution to permit the carry-over of bills from one session to the next within the same term.

GEORGIA (45)

Functional, 40; Accountable, 49; Informed, 36; Independent, 33; Representative, 38

GENERAL: In January, 1970, the Citizens' Committee on the Georgia

General Assembly presented its report, "Strengthening the Georgia General Assembly," to the people and the General Assembly of Georgia. The report contains 113 specific recommendations spread over five subject areas: (1) organization, function, members; (2) legal matters; (3) staffing and space requirements; (4) internal operations; and (5) constituent relations. The commission's members, legislative leaders, and citizens should not let this report gather dust on a bookshelf but should make its recommendations come alive through their active support.

In 1969, the General Assembly created the Office of Budget Analyst, staffed by an experienced director and three professional assistants. It is expected that this staff will be expanded in the future.

There have also been some recent assertions of the independence of the legislature. Notably, in 1969 the House achieved its greatest independence from the executive branch when its speaker was chosen without the victorious candidate having been anointed by the governor.

At the present time, the General Assembly does not have a truly two-party system, but it does appear that it may be on the way to developing one.

Both houses are also to be commended for reducing the number of standing committees, although with twenty-six in the House and twenty-two in the Senate, further reductions should be made.

In the current year, the Georgia General Assembly is conducting an experiment in public information about the legislature. Under a grant from the University of Georgia, a one-hour color television summary of each day's legislative activity is broadcast statewide. Other states, particularly the larger ones, could look attentively to this experiment for its value to citizen awareness of the legislature and the legislative process.

The Georgia General Assembly is in the process of adopting some of the suggestions contained in the Citizens' Committee's report. Some changes occurred after the data collection phase of this study. These recommendations might spur additional improvement.

1. REMOVE CONSTITUTIONAL RESTRICTIONS ON SESSION AND INTERIM TIME. The legislature should have authority to function throughout a two-year term; ideally, this authority should provide a flexible biennial session pattern that permits the legislature to convene, recess, and reconvene as it deems desirable.

    The legislature should be able to meet in general session or conduct interim work as it deems necessary at any time throughout the period.

Permit annual general sessions, limited to no fewer than ninety legislative days.

2. POWER TO EXPAND SPECIAL SESSION AGENDA. Amend the constitution to permit the legislature to broaden the subject matter of a governor's call of a special session by a majority vote in each house, or prohibit the restriction of the agenda by the governor.

3. INTERIM COMMITTEES. When the legislature is not in session, the standing committees should become the interim committees for the purpose of conducting long-range studies of state policy issues. The Legislative Council or some similarly constituted, bi-partisan committee should serve as the supervising agency for interim committees and their studies, budgets, and personnel. The major committees should be staffed on a year-round basis.

    The Legislative Services Committee should serve as the supervising agency for interim committees and their studies, budgets, and personnel. There has been no coordination, supervision, planning, budgeting, and review carried out for all interim committees by one central agency in each house or jointly. Often more than 200 committees are established during the interim. In addition to standing committees that may be given an extended life by a specific assignment, there are many, many ad hoc committees created by the speaker or the lieutenant governor. Whether a standing committee or an ad hoc committee consisting of one or a few legislators, interim committees are usually authorized a specified number of days in which to carry out their assignment.

4. REDUCE THE OVERALL SIZE OF THE LEGISLATURE. Although size reduction in a legislative body is extremely difficult to achieve, it has been done in some states-such as in Vermont and Iowa-and needs to be accomplished in others (New Hampshire, Massachusetts, Georgia, and Pennsylvania). Where reduction in size has occurred, it has most often required a constitutional convention to accomplish it. In a few cases it has been done by legislatively adopted constitutional amendment (Iowa, in 1968, which becomes effective in November, 1971) ratified by the voters. There should be 100 or fewer members in the house. The combined size of both houses should be between 100 and 150.

    With 195 members, the House of the Georgia Legislature is the fourth largest state legislative body in the United States. The size of the House should be reduced to no more than 100 members.

5. LEGISLATIVE SALARIES. Legislative salaries should be set by statute and paid in equal monthly installments throughout the biennium, and all unvouchered expense allowances should be

incorporated into an annual salary. Actual and necessary expenses incurred in the process of carrying out legislative duties should be reimbursed upon submission and approval of properly vouchered evidence of expenditures.

INCREASE LEGISLATIVE COMPENSATION. No legislative salaries in the United States should be below the $10,000 a year level. Compensation of legislators in the larger states should be in the $20,000 to $30,000 range.

Salaries of members of the General Assembly are far too low at $4,200 a year. Legislative salaries should be established by statute at a level of $10,000 to $15,000 annually.

6. REDUCE THE NUMBER OF COMMITTEES. Ideally, there should be from ten to fifteen committees in each house parallel in juris- diction. This would reduce the general complexity of the legis- lature and would permit reducing the number of committee assignments per member.

   With twenty-six committees in the House and twenty-two in the Senate, there are more committees than should be necessary for the effective organization of the work. There should be from ten to fifteen committees in each house parallel in jurisdiction.

7. UNIFORM COMMITTEE RULES. There should be uniform publishe rules of committee procedure in both chambers.

8. OPEN COMMITTEES. The rules of each house should prohibit secret meetings except in matters affecting the security of the state, or which could unnecessarily damage the reputation of individuals in personnel matters. Such exceptions should be sparingly and responsibly employed.

9. NOTICE OF MEETINGS. The rules should require a minimum notice of five legislative days for committee meetings and hearings with widely disseminated announcement of schedule, location, agenda, and availability of public participation.

10. ACT ON ALL BILLS. Committees should be required to report on all bills assigned to them, recommending for passage by the parent body those bills which enjoy the support of a majority of the members of the committee and killing all others.

11. COMMITTEE HEARINGS. There is no justification for permitting any major piece of legislation to become law without having been subjected to extensive, thorough, well-planned, and well-prepared

public hearings, in which representatives of the public, civic
organizations, and interest groups are not only invited but encouraged to participate.

12. PUBLISH COMMITTEE ROLL CALLS. The committee report
    of action on bills to the respective houses should include those
    roll calls which are taken, showing how each member voted.
    These committee reports should be available to the press and
    public. Published roll calls should apply to those bills recom-
    mended for approval as well as those killed.

13. DUAL COMMITTEE CONSIDERATION OF APPROPRIATION BILLS.
    There should be a rule requiring dual committee consideration
    of legislation affecting significant sums of money. Such legislation,
    when considered and acted upon favorably by a substantive policy
    committee, should then automatically be referred to the Finance
    Committee for consideration of its fiscal impact.

14. ADOPT BACK-UP RULES OF PROCEDURES IN BOTH HOUSES.
    There should be officially adopted back-up rules (such as Mason's
    Manual or Jefferson's Manual) which come into operation when
    the standing rules fail to cover the parliamentary problem at
    hand.

15. ESTABLISH AN AUTOMATIC CALENDAR OF BILLS. When a
    bill is favorably reported out of committee to the floor, it should
    go automatically onto the calendar in the order in which it was
    reported out. It should require a vote of an extraordinary
    majority to move a bill from its position on calendar or to bypass
    it. The rules committee should have no part in the scheduling
    of bills. No session should adjourn until all bills on calendar
    have been voted up or down or, by the vote of an extraordinary
    majority, have been moved from the calendar.

16. BILL DEADLINES. The orderly flow of work through the legis-
    lature depends upon the existence of a series of deadlines at
    various critical stages throughout the legislative process. These
    deadlines should be adopted as part of the rules and should be
    consistently enforced.

17. REQUIRE ROLL CALL ON PASSAGE OF BILLS. A recorded roll
    call should be required on final passage of any legislative measure,
    and it should require a constitutional majority to pass any bill on
    final action by either house.

18. STATEMENT OF INTENT BY AUTHOR OF A BILL. The form
    in which a bill is introduced should include a statement by the

author describing, in laymen's language, what the bill is intended
to accomplish.

19. BILL SUMMARY BY BILL-DRAFTING SERVICE. The form in
which bills are introduced should include a more extensive
summary of the provisions of the bill, prepared by the bill-drafting
service.

20. STRENGTHEN STAFF SUPPORT. Legislative research, fiscal,
legal, and planning agencies should be adequately staffed to full
utility and at suitable salary levels for professional qualification.
Professional staffing should be at a level to enable the legislature
to conduct continuous, year-round examination of state resources
and expenditures as well as program review and evaluation of
state agencies. This staff should also prepare fiscal notes
accompanying all appropriation bills, evaluating their fiscal
impact over the short and long term. Staff agencies should be
upgraded to the level at which competent and timely service can
be provided to every member of the legislature.

21. COMMITTEE STAFFING. Standing committees should be staffed
on a permanent, year-round basis.

22. STRENGTHEN STAFF SUPPORT (LEADERS). Staff assistance
should be provided to all leaders of both the majority and the
minority parties. Such assistance should include a secretary
and an administrative assistant at the professional level, with
space to work reasonably adjacent to the offices of members and
leaders.

23. STRENGTHEN STAFF (RANK-AND-FILE MEMBERS). Rank-and-
file members (majority and minority party on an equal basis)
should be provided with individual staff assistance consisting of
a minimum of an administrative assistant at the professional level
and a secretary. Eventually, this should increase to the stated
level of support both in the capital and in a district office.

24. PROVIDE SINGLE-MEMBER DISTRICTS. Legislative districts
in both houses should be single-member.

25. REMOVE LEGISLATIVE POWERS FROM LIEUTENANT GOVERNO
The exercise of legislative powers, including such pro forma
powers as presiding, casting tie-breaking votes, and signing
enacted legislation, by the lieutenant governor, whether the
powers derive from the constitution or the rule book, would seem
to be a particularly serious breach of the separation of powers
and the independence of the legislature. The constitution and/or

rule book should be amended to permit these legislative powers presently exercised by the lieutenant governor to be set as the responsibility of the office of the president pro tem of the Senate.

The lieutenant governor exercises a great many legislative powers. By the constitution, he is designated as president of the Senate and casts the tie-breaking vote. In addition, the rules provide that he act as leader of the Senate, with power to appoint committee chairmen, assign bills to committees and appoint committee membership. The constitution should be amended to permit the reposing of those legislative powers presently exercised by the lieutenant governor in the office of president pro tem of the Senate.

HAWAII (7)

Functional, 2; Accountable, 11; Informed, 20; Independent, 7; Representative, 16

GENERAL: The seventh-ranked legislature in this study is Hawaii. Although one of the smallest states, Hawaii has taken the lead among legislatures in a number of important respects.

Hawaii has the most openly accessible, the most comprehensible, and lest complex legislative system in the nation. Though not the smallest legislature, its fifty-one-member House and twenty-five-member Senate make thoughtful deliberation and rational organization possible and operative. Uniform committee rules of procedure are published and followed. The jurisdiction of committees is defined in the rules, and bills are invariably assigned to committee accordingly. Formal reports are required of all interim committees.

Bills are printed in highly readable form and standard format; they are limited to single subjects, printed in large quantity, and available to legislators, press and public from a central distribution point. Copies of bills are available the day following introduction or amendment, and skeleton bills are prohibited.

The Hawaii Legislature requires a committee report on bills which are recommended for passage. This report could serve as a model for all legislatures, yet no other state follows this practice. The bill report contains a comprehensive history of the legislation to which it relates; it includes the findings of the committee, a report of hearings, a record of decisions to include or exclude provisions, and an explanation of the resulting bill. A majority of the members of the committee are required to sign the report before the bill can reach the floor, and a copy is provided to each member, accompanying the bill, when it reaches the floor calendar.

In addition to the bureau staffing, which serves the entire legislature and its committees, staff assistants are provided for all members; each member has a private office and adjacent space is provided for his staff. An allowance is also provided for each member which may be used to cover a part of his district office expenses.

A pre-session orientation conference is held at the beginning of each term, and most of the organizational activities have taken place prior to the start of the regular session.

The new legislative building (opened in 1969) is far and away the most impressively beautiful and functionally effective legislative structure in the United States.

The legislature has the power to extend the sixty-day annual session by a vote of two-thirds of the members of each house and can convene in special session on the petition of two-thirds of the members.

There are a few significant weaknesses in the form of organization and methods of operation of the Hawaii Legislature. They concern the number of committees and committee assignments, and the limited volume of staffing, which restricts the number of staff services available to members and committees. These and the few other short-comings which this study identifies are covered in the following recommendations.

1. REDUCE THE NUMBER OF COMMITTEES. Ideally, there should be from ten to fifteen committees in each house, parallel in jurisdiction. This would reduce the general complexity of the legislature and would permit reducing the number of committee assignments per member.

    For a legislature as small as Hawaii's (House, fifty-one; Senate, twenty-five) the number of committees (House, nineteen; Senate, sixteen) is too large and should be reduced to ten or twelve committees, parallel in jurisdiction.

2. REDUCE THE NUMBER OF COMMITTEE ASSIGNMENTS. In order to make it possible for members to concentrate their attention and contribute effectively, there should be no more than three committee assignments for each member of the lower house and four committee assignments for each member of the Senate.

The multiplicity of assignments introduces problems of scheduling, strains the focus of attention on the part of members, and creates an inordinately heavy workload for members if committees are as active as they should be.

Reduction in the number of committees would facilitate reducing the number of committee assignments. At present, 77 percent of the members of the House have more than three assignments each and 36 percent of the Senators have more than four.

3. INTERIM COMMITTEES. When the legislature is not in session, the standing committees should become the interim committees for the purpose of conducting long-range studies of state policy issues. The Legislative Council or some similarly constituted, bi-partisan committee should serve as the supervising agency for interim committees and their studies, budgets, and personnel. The major committees should be staffed on a year-round basis.

If the committees of the respective houses are made parallel, consideration could be given to having them work as joint interim committees, affording the opportunity to hold joint hearings and use combined staffing.

4. MANAGEMENT COMMITTEES. There should be an executive or management committee created in each house. Its membership should include the leaders of each party in each house, and the minority party should have representation on the committee in proportion to its numbers in the body as a whole. The Senate/House management committees should combine as a joint management committee. The purpose of these committees should be to assume responsibility for the administrative management (housekeeping) functions relating to personnel, facilities, the research bureaus, budgets, and expenditures of their respective houses. The joint management committee should deal with matters of inter-house coordination.

5. PROVIDE SINGLE-MEMBER DISTRICTS. Legislative districts in both houses should be single-member.

The creation of single-member districts requires an amendment to the Hawaii constitution.

6. DUAL COMMITTEE CONSIDERATION OF APPROPRIATION BILLS. There should be a rule requiring dual committee consideration of legislation affecting significant sums of money.

Such legislation, when considered and acted upon favorably by a substantive policy committee, should then automatically be referred to the Finance Committee for consideration of its fiscal impact.

7. INCREASE LEGISLATIVE COMPENSATION. No legislative salaries in the United States should be below the $10,000 a year level. Compensation of legislators in the larger states should be in the $20,000 to $30,000 range.

Considering the degree to which Hawaii's Legislature stands out as an example which other states would do well to follow, its present legislative salaries ($12,000 per year) are far from exemplary. Legislative salaries should be raised to the $15,000 to $20,000 per year range.

8. SUPPORT OF DISTRICT OFFICES. District offices are vital to the effective representation by a legislator of his constituency. The legislature should make some contribution to the support of district offices for its members, and the amount of this contribution should be increased over time.

Although the legislature makes some contributions to the support of district offices for its members, the amount of this contribution should be increased.

9. STRENGTHEN STAFF SUPPORT. Legislative research, fiscal, legal, and planning agencies should be adequately staffed to full utility and at suitable salary levels for professional qualification. Professional staffing should be at a level to enable the legislature to conduct continuous, year-round examination of state resources and expenditures as well as program review and evaluation of state agencies. This staff should also prepare fiscal notes accompanying all appropriation bills, evaluating their fiscal impact over the short and long term. Staff agencies should be upgraded to the level at which competent and timely service can be provided to every member of the legislature.

The Hawaii Legislature has a small but competent staff which provides a number of necessary services, such as bill drafting, fiscal analysis, and legislative research. To put the legislature in a position to conduct effective oversight of executive operations, the range, volume, and level of those services are in need of expansion. This can be accomplished most directly by authorizing additional staff positions and by increasing salary levels and qualifications.

10. JOINT RULES. There should be joint rules governing the relationship and the flow of legislation between the two houses of the
legislature.

11. BILL SUMMARY BY BILL-DRAFTING SERVICE. The form in
which bills are introduced should include a more extensive summary of the provisions of the bill, prepared by the bill-drafting
service.

12. IMPROVE PRESS FACILITIES. Improved press facilities aid
in the coverage of the work of the legislature. Committee rooms,
and both chambers or galleries, should provide adequate space
for the news media as well as lighting and electrical power connections for their equipment. Conference or interview rooms
and office space should also be provided for the news media.

The overall facilities for the news media are excellent; however,
conference or interview rooms should also be provided.

13. WASHINGTON, D.C., OFFICE FOR THE LEGISLATURE. With
the large and growing volume of activity generated by state-federal
relationships, the legislature, beyond merely reacting to federal
legislation, should be in a position to influence the development
of new programs in accordance with the interests of the state.
To do so, the legislature should have an office in the nation's
capital to represent it and to be its most direct liaison with the
Congress.

For small states, consideration might be given to joining with a
number of sister states (either on a geographical or on a population basis) for the purpose of sharing the services of a Washington
office. But in large states, the volume of inter-governmental
traffic has reached a stage at which it would benefit the legislature
greatly to have a full-time Washington office.

An office of the legislature in Washington, D.C., may be even
more critical for Hawaii than other states because of the physical
distance between the state and national capitals.

14. PRACTICE BEFORE REGULATORY AGENCIES. Legislators
or their firms should be prohibited from practicing before state
regulatory agencies or in matters concerning state agencies for
a fee.

PROHIBIT DOING BUSINESS WITH THE STATE. There should
be a prohibition against legislators or the firms in which they

own a major interest doing business with state agencies.

FAMILY EMPLOYMENT. Members of a legislator's immediate family should be barred from employment by the legislature.

15. RECORD AND PUBLISH PROCEEDINGS OF COMMITTEES. Record and publish the record of committee hearings, proceedings, and votes.

16. ACT ON ALL BILLS. Committees should be required to report on all bills assigned to them, recommending for passage by the parent body those bills which enjoy the support of a majority of the members of the committee and killing all others.

17. BILL DEADLINES. The orderly flow of work through the legislature depends upon the existence of a series of deadlines at various critical stages throughout the legislative process. These deadlines should be adopted as part of the rules and should be consistently enforced.

18. ESTABLISH AN AUTOMATIC CALENDAR OF BILLS. When a bill is favorably reported out of committee to the floor, it should go automatically onto the calendar in the order in which it was reported out. It should require a vote of an extraordinary majority to move a bill from its position on calendar or to bypass it. The Rules Committee should have no part in the scheduling of bills. No session should adjourn until all bills on calendar have been voted up or down or, by the vote of an extraordinary majority, have been moved from the calendar.

IDAHO (18)

Functional, 20; Accountable, 9; Informed, 29; Independent, 27; Representative, 21

GENERAL: The 1969 legislature made a number of improvements following submission of the Idaho Citizens' Committee on the State Legislature's final report (which contained fifty-six specific recommendations): passed a concurrent resolution directing the Legislative Council to utilize the standing committees of the Legislative Council wherever possible; reduced the number of standing committees from fifteen to twelve in the Senate and from fourteen to thirteen in the House; created a joint rule permitting bill carry-over from the odd-to-even-year session; passed a Senate rule requiring that all bills introduced into the Senate must contain a statement of purpose signed by the sponsor; and insured greater public access to committee meetings and hearings.

Other improvements were advanced by the Constitutional Revision
Commission, established by the legislature, which presented a draft
of a new charter to the legislature in 1969. After the legislature
completed its own hearings on the proposal and made some changes,
the amended draft charter was submitted to the voters in November,
1970, but was rejected. The proposed constitution would have made
the legislature a "continuous body" and would have also required
the governor to convene a special session of the legislature when
petitioned by the majority of the members of each house. The proposed document would have lifted the restriction on the number of
days for which a legislator may be compensated during each session
and would have provided that compensation be set by law. The legislature would have been empowered to consider bills vetoed after
adjournment of the legislative session at the convening of its next
session. Furthermore, the new constitution would have authorized
the legislature to appoint a state auditor directly responsible to the
legislature itself.

A serious setback occurred for the Idaho Legislature in the same
1970 general election, when the voters approved an initiative drastically reducing the expense allowance of legislators. Proponents of
the measure claimed that the $35 per diem allowance, set by the Legis-
lative Compensation Commission, which was created in 1967, was a
legislator tactic to increase salaries. Opponents to the pay reduction
said that the compensation commission only set the allowance to
meet average expenses based upon living costs applicable to Idaho,
and that, even more critically, the initiative failed to recognize legislative duties in terms of the full range of activities expected of legislators in Idaho.

The initiative reduces the per diem expense allowance from $35,
which was not limited to days in session, to $25, limited to sixty
calendar days in odd years and thirty days in even years (the constitution limits salary to sixty calendar days each year). The latter
restriction may have the effect of reducing session time in even years
from sixty to thirty days. The initiative also eliminates the $200
per month allowance for maintaining an office, another backward
step.

These following recommendations will serve as a potential list of
improvements.

1. REMOVE CONSTITUTIONAL RESTRICTIONS ON SESSION AND
    INTERIM TIME. The legislature should have authority to func-
    tion throughout a two-year term; ideally, this authority should
    provide a flexible biennial session pattern that permits the
    legislature to convene, recess, and reconvene as it deems
    desirable. The legislature should be able to meet in general

session or conduct interim work as it deems necessary at any
time throughout the period.

2. LEGISLATIVE POWER TO CALL SPECIAL SESSIONS. Amend
    the constitution to permit the legislature to convene special ses-
    sions either by petition of a majority of the members of both
    houses or the call of the presiding officer of each house.

    The constitution might also be amended, as in the 1970 proposed
    constitution, to provide for bills vetoed after adjournment of the
    session to be considered at the convening of the next session, or
    the legislature might be allowed to reconvene following the signing
    of bills to consider overriding vetoes.

3. POWER TO EXPAND SPECIAL SESSION AGENDA. Amend the
    constitution to permit the legislature to broaden the subject
    matter of a governor's call of a special session by a majority
    vote in each house, or prohibit the restriction of the agenda by
    the governor.

4. BILL CARRY-OVER. Amend the constitution to permit the
    carry-over of bills from one session to the next within the same
    term.

5. INTERIM COMMITTEES. When the legislature is not in ses-
    sion, the standing committees should become the interim com-
    mittees for the purpose of conducting long-range studies of state
    policy issues. The Legislative Council or some similarly con-
    stituted, bi-partisan committee should serve as the supervising
    agency for interim committees and their studies, budgets, and
    personnel. The major committees should be staffed on a year-
    round basis.

6. INCREASE LEGISLATIVE COMPENSATION. No legislative
    salaries in the United States should be below the $10,000 a year
    level. Compensation of legislators in the larger states should
    be in the $20,000 to $30,000 range.

    Legislative salaries should be provided by statute at the $10,000
    to $15,000 level on an annual basis. Consideration might be given
    to the establishment of a public commission to make appropriate
    recommendations on all governmental salaries. The Idaho con-
    stitution sets the salary for legislators at $10.00 a day and limits
    the total received for any one session to $600.00. This limitation
    has the effect of limiting the length of the regular session to sixty
    calendar days where no limitation would otherwise exist.

7. EXPENSE ALLOWANCES. Members of the legislature should be allowed an expense reimbursement covering their travel and living costs while engaged in carrying out their legislative duties. The same allowance should obtain during the interim for days in attendance at interim committee meetings or other official and authorized legislative business. These allowances should be provided by statute.

8. STRENGTHEN STAFF SUPPORT. Legislative research, fiscal, legal, and planning agencies should be adequately staffed to full utility and at suitable salary levels for professional qualification. Professional staffing should be at a level to enable the legislature to conduct continuous, year-round examination of state resources and expenditures as well as program review and evaluation of state agencies. This staff should also prepare fiscal notes accompanying all appropriation bills, evaluating their fiscal impact over the short and long term. Staff agencies should be upgraded to the level at which competent and timely service can be provided to every member of the legislature.

9. STRENGTHEN STAFF SUPPORT (LEADERS). Staff assistance should be provided to all leaders of both the majority and the minority parties. Such assistance should include a secretary and an administrative assistant at the professional level, with space to work reasonably adjacent to the offices of members and leaders.

10. STRENGTHEN STAFF (RANK-AND-FILE MEMBERS). Rank-and-file members (majority and minority party on an equal basis) should be provided with individual staff assistance consisting of a minimum of an administrative assistant at the professional level and a secretary. Eventually, this should increase to the stated level of support both in the capital and in a district office.

11. COMMITTEE STAFFING. Standing committees should be staffed on a permanent, year-round basis.

12. INDIVIDUAL OFFICES. Provide private, individual offices for every member of the legislature, with nearby space for their assistants. The quality and amount of office space should not differ substantially between majority and minority party members.

A beginning can be made toward providing offices for members by making space available for shared offices, then gradually reducing the number of members who share space until each member has a private office.

13. FACILITIES FOR COMMITTEES. Legislative effectiveness requires that committees have adequate physical facilities in which to do their work. This includes an adequate number of committee rooms and an adequate number of hearing rooms that will permit the seating of larger audiences.

14. PROVIDE SINGLE-MEMBER DISTRICTS. Legislative districts in both houses should be single-member.

The House should be elected from single-member districts, as is the Senate.

15. ACT ON ALL BILLS. Committees should be required to report on all bills assigned to them, recommending for passage by the parent body those bills which enjoy the support of a majority of the members of the committee and killing all others.

16. WASHINGTON, D.C., OFFICE FOR THE LEGISLATURE. With the large and growing volume of activity generated by state-federal relationships, the legislature, beyond merely reacting to federal legislation, should be in a position to influence the development of new programs in accordance with the interests of the state. To do so, the legislature should have an office in the nation's capital to represent it and to be its most direct liaison with the Congress.

For small states, consideration might be given to joining with a number of sister states (either on a geographical or on a population basis) for the purpose of sharing the services of a Washington office. But in large states, the volume of inter-governmental traffic has reached a stage at which it would benefit the legislature greatly to have a full-time Washington office.

17. DUAL COMMITTEE CONSIDERATION OF APPROPRIATION BILLS. There should be a rule requiring dual committee consideration of legislation affecting significant sums of money. Such legislation, when considered and acted upon favorably by a substantive policy committee, should then automatically be referred to the Finance Committee for consideration of its fiscal impact.

18. REMOVE LEGISLATIVE POWERS FROM LIEUTENANT GOVERNOR. The exercise of legislative powers, including such pro form powers as presiding, casting tie-breaking votes, and signing

enacted legislation, by the lieutenant governor, whether the powers derive from the constitution or the rule book, would seem to be a particularly serious breach of the separation of powers and the independence of the legislature. The constitution and/or rule book should be amended to permit these legislative powers presently exercised by the lieutenant governor to be set as the responsibility of the office of the president pro tem of the Senate.

19. MANAGEMENT COMMITTEES. There should be an executive or management committee created in each house. Its membership should include the leaders of each party in each house, and the minority party should have representation on the committee in proportion to its numbers in the body as a whole. The Senate/House management committees should combine as a joint management committee. The purpose of these committees should be to assume responsibility for the administrative management (housekeeping) functions relating to personnel, facilities, the research bureaus, budgets, and expenditures of their respective houses. The joint management committee should deal with matters of interhouse coordination.

20. COMMITTEE BILL REPORTS. Require committees to issue reports describing and explaining the committee's action on bills recommended for passage at the time the bill moves from the committee to the floor.

PUBLISH COMMITTEE ROLL CALLS. The committee report of action on bills to the respective houses should include those roll calls which are taken, showing how each member voted. These committee reports should be available to the press and public. Published roll calls should apply to those bills recommended for approval as well as those killed.

21. UNIFORM COMMITTEE RULES. There should be uniform published rules of committee procedure in both chambers.

22. ELECTRIC ROLL CALL RECORDER. There should be an electric roll call recorder in the Senate, as in the House. This is recommended not simply because it would speed up the proceedings (worthwhile as this may be), but because it is an efficient method of producing an error-free record of roll call votes.

23. REPRINT AMENDED BILLS. When a bill is amended substantially, it should be reprinted and returned to the legislature with no more than an overnight delay. The reprint should show clearly the original text of the bill as well as the change created by the amendment.

24. BILL DEADLINES. The orderly flow of work through the legis-
     lature depends upon the existence of a series of deadlines at
     various critical stages throughout the legislative process. These
     deadlines should be adopted as part of the rules and should be
     consistently enforced.

25. IMPROVE PRESS FACILITIES. Improved press facilities aid in
     the coverage of the work of the legislature. Committee rooms,
     and both chambers of galleries, should provide adequate space
     for the news media as well as lighting and electrical power con-
     nections for their equipment. Conference or interview rooms and
     office space should also be provided for the news media.

26. CONSENT CALENDAR. A consent calendar should be used in
     both houses.

27. BILL SUMMARY BY BILL-DRAFTING SERVICE. The form in
     which bills are introduced should include a more extensive summary
     of the provisions of the bills, prepared by the bill-drafting service.

ILLINOIS (3)

Functional, 17; Accountable, 4; Informed, 6; Independent, 2; Representative, 13

GENERAL: If this study had been done five years ago, it is doubtful
that the Illinois Legislature would have ranked third, or anything
approaching that level of attainment. The fact that it now ranks that
high testifies to the rapid rate of improvement which has been maintained since reapportionment, the statewide election of legislators,
and the founding of the Commission on Organization of the General
Assembly (1965).

Ratification of the revised Illinois constitution on December 15, 1970,
adds further to progress of legislative improvement because of changes
in the legislative article which were included. The new constitution
provides for a redistricting plan to be effected after every federal
census; authorizes the legislature to call itself into special session;
specifically grants subpoena power to the legislature and legislative
committees; requires committees to give adequate public notice of
meetings; requires that bills be read on three different days by title,
rather than in full, as formerly provided (the legislature traditionally
has waived reading in full); and removes the lieutenant governor as
presiding officer of the Senate.

Some of the better features of the Illinois Legislature are the following:

The Illinois Legislature has one of the stronger staffing patterns among
the legislatures in the United States. The variety of professional
staff services permits the continuous, year-round examination of
state resources and expenditures and provides program review and
evaluation of executive agencies. A start on the staffing of major
committees has been made through the provision of majority and
minority party staff representatives for five committees in each house.

Legislators, the news media, and the public have access to the work
of the legislature, aided by the existence of published, uniform rules
of committee procedure and the availability of a published record of
committee roll call votes. Coverage of floor proceedings is permitted
by the electronic media as well as the press, and facilities for such
coverage are available in each chamber. There is a press officer
assigned by each house to facilitate media access to information about
the work of the legislature.

Annual unlimited sessions enable the Illinois Legislature to use as
much time as is required to accomplish its work. Through the practice
of recessing and reconvening a degree of flexibility has also been
achieved in scheduling its work. Control by the legislature of its
appropriated funds, its staff, and its facilities supports the legislature's
independence.

The areas in which improvements are recommended are the following.

1. REDUCE THE OVERALL SIZE OT THE LEGISLATURE. Although
    size reduction in a legislative body is extremely difficult to
    achieve, it has been done in some states-such as in Vermont and
    Iowa-and needs to be accomplished in others (New Hampshire,
    Massachusetts, Georgia, and Pennsylvania). Where reduction in
    size has occurred, it has most often required a constitutional
    convention to accomplish it. In a few cases it has been done by
    legislatively adopted constitutional amendment (Iowa, in 1968,
    which becomes effective in November, 1971) ratified by the voters.
    There should be 100 or fewer members in the house. The com-
    bined size of both houses should be between 100 and 150.

    With 177 members, the House of the Illinois Legislature is the
    fifth largest state legislative body in the United States. Despite
    the difficulty of bringing about reduction in size, and recognizing
    that a recent constitutional convention bypassed this question, it
    is nevertheless recommended that the House be reduced in numbers
    from its present 177 to 100 or fewer.

2. COMMITTEE JURISDICTION. A description of the jurisdiction
    of committees should be contained in the rules of both houses,

and assignment of bills should be made in accord with the jurisdiction of committees as described in the rules.

3. PRACTICE BEFORE REGULATORY AGENCIES. Legislators or
    their firms should be prohibited from practicing before state
    regulatory agencies or in matters concerning state agencies for
    a fee.

4. AMENDING THE RULES. A due regard for the rights of the
    minority, one of the means of insuring internal accountability,
    requires stable rules of procedure. Although it is consistent
    with majority rule to permit the adoption of rules of procedure
    at the beginning of a term by a majority vote, once adopted, the
    requirement to change the rules should be by a two-thirds vote,
    as is the case in most legislatures.

5. REDUCE THE NUMBER OF COMMITTEES. Ideally, there should
    be from ten to fifteen committees in each house, parallel in
    jurisdiction. This would reduce the general complexity of the
    legislature and would permit reducing the number of committee
    assignments per member.

    In Illinois there are twenty-three committees in the House and
    eighteen in the Senate. A small improvement could be achieved
    by reducing the number of House committees to eighteen; as in
    the Senate, making them parallel in jurisdiction. Greater improve-
    ment would result from reducing the number in both houses to the
    twelve to fifteen range.

6. PROVIDE SINGLE-MEMBER DISTRICTS. Legislative districts
    in both houses should be single-member.

    Although single-member districts contribute to a more direct
    and focused relationship between a legislator and his constituents
    than do multi-member districts, the voters of Illinois turned down
    such a proposal as recently as December 15, 1970. The Illinois
    legislative district system involves cumulative voting and a limit
    of three House seats per district. In these respects, this arrange-
    ment is preferable to the multi-member districts in other states
    (some of which contain as many as thirty seats in one district, as
    in Arizona).

7. INDIVIDUAL OFFICES. Provide private, individual offices for
    every member of the legislature, with nearby space for their
    assistants. The quality and amount of office space should not
    differ substantially between majority and minority party members.

A plan currently exists for building underground office space for the legislature connecting the capitol with the Executive Office Building across the plaza. This plan or some other means of acquiring added space should be implemented promptly.

8. IMPROVE PRESS FACILITIES. A room equipped with lighting and sound outlets, suitable for the holding of press conferences, briefings, or interviews should be available to each house. Committee hearing rooms should also be equipped for news media coverage of the proceedings which take place in them.

9. ELECTRIC ROLL CALL RECORDER. In a Senate as large as Illinois' (second largest in the United States) it would improve voting procedure to install and use an electric roll call recorder. This is recommended not simply because it would speed up the proceedings (worthwhile as this may be), but because it is an efficient method of producing an error-free record of roll call votes.

10. COMMITTEE BILL REPORTS. Require committees to issue reports describing and explaining the committee's action on bills recommended for passage at the time the bill moves from the committee to the floor.

11. REPRINT AMENDED BILLS. When a bill is amended substantially, it should be reprinted and returned to the legislature with no more than an overnight delay. The reprint should show clearly the original text of the bill as well as the change created by the amendment.

12. STATEMENT OF INTENT BY AUTHOR OF A BILL. The form in which a bill is introduced should include a statement by the author describing, in laymen's language, what the bill is intended to accomplish.

13. SKELETON BILLS. There should be an explicit rule barring introduction of skeleton on "spot" bills. This rule should be enforced by the assigning authority (the presiding officer or Rules Committee) by refusal to assign bils so identified to committee.

14. WASHINGTON, D.C., OFFICE FOR THE LEGISLATURE. With the large and growing volume of activity generated by state-federal relationships, the legislature, beyond merely reacting to federal legislation, should be in a position to influence the development of new programs in accordance with the interests of the state. To do so, the legislature should have an office in the nation's

capital to represent it and to be its most direct liaison with the
Congress.

For small states, consideration might be given to joining with a
number of sister states (either on a geographical or on a population
basis) for the purpose of sharing the services of a Washington
office. But in large states, the volume of inter-governmental
traffic has reached a stage of which it would benefit the legislature
greatly to have a full-time Washington office.

15. INCREASE LEGISLATIVE COMPENSATION. No legislative salaries in the United States should be below the $10,000 a year level.
Compensation of legislators in the larger states should be in the
$20,000 to $30,000 range.

The salaries of Illinois legislators should be increased to the
$20,000 to $30,000 level.

16. SUPPORT OF DISTRICT OFFICES. District offices are vital to
the effective representation by a legislator of his constituency.
Although the legislature makes some contributions to the support
of district offices for its members, the amount of this contribution
should be increased.

17. PROHIBIT PROXY VOTING IN COMMITTEE.

18. ADOPTION OF RULES. Rules should be adopted on the first
day of the session or, at the very latest, within the first week of
the session.

19. CONSENT CALENDAR. A formal consent calendar should be
used in both houses. The House presently uses an informal consent
calendar: the speaker accumulates a list of non-controversial
items.

20. MANAGEMENT COMMITTEES. There should be an executive
or management committee created in each house. Its membership
should include the leaders of each party in each house, and the
minority party should have representation on the committee in
proportion to its numbers in the body as a whole. The Senate/House
management committees should combine as a joint management
committee. The purpose of these committees should be to assume
responsibility for the administrative management (housekeeping)
functions relating to personnel, facilities, the research bureaus,
budgets, and expenditures of their respective houses. The joint
management committee should deal with matters of interhouse
coordination.

A management committee should be created in the House; such
a committee already exists in the Senate.

21. EXPENSE ALLOWANCE. Illinois legislators now receive a $25
per diem expense allowance plus expense reimbursement for
travel during the interim. The same allowance should obtain
during the regular session.

INDIANA (40)

Functional, 44; Accountable, 38; Informed, 41; Independent 43;
Representative 20

GENERAL: In November, 1970, Indiana voters approved a constitutional
amendment which will permit the General Assembly to establish the
length and frequency of legislative sessions. The amendment also
removes the restriction (forty calendar days) on special session length.
The amendment did not alter the arrangement whereby only the governor
can convene the legislature in extraordinary session; however, the
governor will no longer be able to limit the agenda of a special session.

Indiana's greatest potential strength in modernizing its legislature,
which ranked fortieth of the fifty states, lies in the clearly discernible
mood and intent of legislators and civic leaders, as demonstrated by
their persistant and successful efforts to alter the General Assembly's
session pattern.

Indiana is an example of a state poised for improvement of its legislature. Therefore, these recommendations may serve as an agenda
for the citizens of that state.

1. PRE-SESSION ORGANIZATIONAL MEETING. Amend the constitution to provide a pre-session organizing session following a
general election. Some states make advantageous use of such a
session during November or December of a general election year
for the purpose of electing leaders, appointing committee chairmen,
assigning members to committees, referring pre-filed bills to
committee, holding committee organizational meetings, and conducting orientation conferences for new, as well as returning,
members of the legislature. Through such pre-session meetings
the committees can begin their work before the regular session
convenes. This makes it possible to delay the start of the regular
session until legislation is ready for floor action.

2. INTERIM COMMITTEES. When the legislature is not in session,
the standing committees should become the interim committees
for the purpose conducting long-range studies of state policy

issues. The Legislative Council or some similarly constituted, bi-partisan committee should serve as the supervising agency for interim committees and their studies, budgets, and personnel. The major committees should be staffed on a year-round basis.

3. INTERIM COMMITTEE REPORTING. Interim committees should be required to render formal reports concerning the topics they were charged with responsibility for investigating. These reports should cover the committee's recommendations, including drafts of proposed legislation where appropriate.

4. LEGISLATIVE SALARIES. Legislative salaries should be set by statute and paid in equal monthly installments throughout the biennium, and all unvouchered expense allowances should be incorporated into an annual salary. Actual and necessary expenses incurred in the process of carrying out legislative duties should be reimbursed upon submission and approval of properly vouchered evidence of expenditures.

    INCREASE LEGISLATIVE COMPENSATION. No legislative salarie in the United States should be below the $10,000 a year level. Compensation of legislators in the larger states should be in the $20,000 to $30,000 range.

    Salaries of members of the legislature are far too low in comparison with states of similar size and development. Current salaries of $4,000 should be doubled immediately and increased again within the next few years as other improvements in the legislature are made. Actual and necessary travel expenses incurred in the process of carrying out legislative duties should be reimbursed upon submission and approval of properly vouchered evidence of expenditures.

5. STRENGTHEN STAFF SUPPORT. Legislative research, fiscal, legal, and planning agencies should be adequately staffed to full utility and at suitable salary levels for professional qualification. Professional staffing should be at a level to enable the legislature to conduct continuous, year-round examination of state resources and expenditures as well as program review and evaluation of state agencies. This staff should also prepare fiscal notes accompanying all appropriation bills, evaluating their fiscal impact over the short and long term. Staff agencies should be upgraded to the level at which competent and timely service can be provided to every member of the legislature.

    COMMITTEE STAFFING. Standing committees should be staffed on a permanent, year-round basis.

6. INDIVIDUAL OFFICES. Provide private, individual offices for
   every member of the legislature, with nearby space for their
   assistants. The quality and amount of office space should not
   differ substantially between majority and minority party members.

   A beginning can be made toward providing offices for members
   by making space available for shared offices among small numbers
   of members at first, then gradually reducing the members who
   share space until a private office is provided for each member.

7. FACILITIES FOR COMMITTEES. Legislative effectiveness
   requires that committees have adequate physical facilities in
   which to do their work. This includes an adequate number of
   committee rooms and an adequate number of hearing rooms that
   will permit the seating of larger audiences.

8. PROVIDE SINGLE-MEMBER DISTRICTS. Legislative districts
   in both houses should be single-member.

9. WASHINGTON, D.C., OFFICE FOR THE LEGISLATURE. With
   the large and growing volume of activity generated by state-federal
   relationships, the legislature, beyond merely reacting to federal
   legislation, should be in a position to influence the development
   of new programs in accordance with the interests of the state.
   To do so, the legislature should have an office in the nation's
   capital to represent it and to be its most direct liaison with the
   Congress.

   For small states, consideration might be given to joining with a
   number of sister states (either on a geographical of on a population
   basis) for the purpose of sharing the services of a Washington
   office. But in large states, the volume of inter-governmental
   traffic has reached a stage at which it would benefit the legislature
   greatly to have a full-time Washington office.

10. ESTABLISH AN AUTOMATIC CALENDAR OF BILLS. When a
    bill is favorably reported out of committee to the floor, it should
    go automatically onto the calendar in the order in which it was
    reported out. It should require a vote of an extraordinary majority
    to move a bill from its positon on calendar or to bypass it. The
    Rules Committee should have no part in the scheduling of bills.
    No session should adjourn until all bills on calendar have been
    voted up or down or, by the vote of an extraordinary majority,
    have been moved from the calendar.

11. OPEN COMMITTEES. The rules of each house should prohibit
    secret meetings except in matters affecting the security of the

state, or which could unnecessarily damage the reputation of individuals in personnel matters. Such exceptions should be sparingl
and responsibly employed.

12. NOTICE OF MEETINGS. The rules should require a minimum
    notice of five legislative days for committee meetings and hearings
    with widely disseminated announcement of schedule, location,
    agenda, and availability of public participation.

13. UNIFORM COMMITTEE RULES. There should be uniform publishe
    rules of committee procedure in both chambers.

14. ACT ON ALL BILLS. Committees should be required to report on
    all bills assigned to them, recommending for passage by the
    parent body those bills which enjoy the support of a majority of
    the members of the committee and killing all others.

15. REDUCE THE NUMBER OF COMMITTEES. Ideally, there should
    be from ten to fifteen committees in each house parallel in juris-
    diction. This would reduce the general complexity of the legislatur
    and would permit reducing the number of committee assignments
    per member.

    With twenty-eight committees in the House and twenty-six in the
    Senate, there are more committees than should be necessary for
    the effective organization of the work.

16. REDUCE THE NUMBER OF COMMITTEE ASSIGNMENTS. In
    order to make it possible for members to concentrate their
    attention and contribute effectively, there should be no more than
    three committee assignments for each member of the lower house
    and four committee assignments for each member of the Senate.
    The multiplicity of assignments introduces problems of scheduling,
    strains the focus of attention on the part of members, and creates
    an inordinately heavy workload for members if committees are
    as active as they should be.

    Reduction in the number of committees would permit reducing
    the number of committee assignments per member. At present,
    seventy-five percent of the members of the House have more
    than three assignments each and thirty-four percent of the Senators
    have more than four.

17. MINORITY PARTY MEMBERS ON COMMITTEE. Minority party
    members should be assigned to committees by the minority
    leader in consultation with the minority caucus.

18. COMMITTEE BILL REPORTS. Require committees to issue reports describing and explaining the committees action on bills recommended for passage at the time the bill moves from the committee to the floor.

19. RECORD AND PUBLISH PROCEEDINGS OF COMMITTEES. Record and publish the record of committee hearings, proceedings, and votes.

20. PUBLISH COMMITTEE ROLL CALLS. The committee report of action on bills to the respective houses should include those roll calls which are taken, showing how each member voted. These committee reports should be available to the press and public. Published roll calls should apply to those bills recommended for approval as well as those killed.

21. REMOVE LEGISLATIVE POWERS FROM LIEUTENANT GOVERNOR. The exercise of legislative powers including, such pro forma powers as presiding, casting tie-breaking votes, and signing enacted legislation, by the lieutenant governor, whether the powers derive from the constitution or the rule book, would seem to be a particularly serious breach of the separation of powers and the independence of the legislature. The constitution and/or rule book should be amended to permit these legislative powers presently exercised by the lieutenant governor to be set as the responsibility of the office of the president pro tem of the Senate.

In Indiana, the lieutenant governor is also empowered by the constitution to join in debate and vote on all subjects when the Senate is meeting in the committee of the whole. He also assigns bills to committee and appoints members to committees when he is of the majority party, and is an ex-officio member of the Legislative Council. These powers should be removed to the office of president pro tem.

22. SPECIAL PROVISIONS. In addition to standard laws governing criminal behavior, there should be special provisions regulating legislative conflicts of interest.

PRACTICE BEFORE REGULATORY AGENCIES. Legislators or their firms should be prohibited from practicing before state regulatory agencies or in matters concerning state agencies for a fee.

PROHIBIT DOING BUSINESS WITH THE STATE. There should be a prohibition against legislators or the firms in which they own a major interest doing business with state agencies.

PROHIBIT APPOINTMENT TO STATE OFFICE. There should be a prohibition against a legislator accepting appointment to other state office during the term for which he is elected or within two years of the termination of his service as a member of the legislature.

23. DUAL COMMITTEE CONSIDERATION OF APPROPRIATION BILLS. There should be a rule requiring dual committee consideration of legislation affecting significant sums of money. Such legislation, when considered and acted upon favorably by a substantive policy committee, should then automatically be referred to the Finance Committee for consideration of its fiscal impact.

24. BILL DEADLINES. The orderly flow of work through the legislature depends upon the existence of a series of deadlines at various critical stages throughout the legislative process. These deadlines should be adopted as part of the rules and should be consistently enforced.

Although the General Assembly has deadlines for second and third readings, approximately seventy-five percent of the bills passed in the last session were enacted in the final week of the session. Additional deadlines, or time limits, should be established to create an even flow of work through the legislature.

25. SKELETON BILLS. There should be an explicit rule barring introduction of skeleton or "spot" bills. This rule should be enforced by the assigning authority (the presiding officer or Rules Committee) by refusal to assign bills so identified to committee.

26. MANAGEMENT COMMITTEES. There should be an executive or management committee created in each house. Its membership should include the leaders of each party in each house, and the minority party should have representation on the committee in proportion to its numbers in the body as a whole. The Senate/ House management committees should combine as a joint management committee. The purpose of these committees should be to assume responsibility for the administrative management (housekeeping) functions relating to personnel, facilities, the research bureaus, budgets, and expenditures of their respective houses. The joint management committee should deal with matters of inter-house coordination.

27. IMPROVE PRESS FACILITIES. Improved press facilities aid in the coverage of the work of the legislature. Committee rooms, and both chambers of galleries, should provide adequate space for the news media as well as lighting and electrical power

connections for their equipment. Conference or interview rooms
and office space should also be provided for the news media.

28. CONSENT CALENDAR. A consent calendar should be used in
both houses.

IOWA (6)

Functional, 6; Accountable, 6; Informed, 5; Independent, 11; Representative, 25

GENERAL: The Iowa Legislature occupies position number six in the
overall ranking. It is the highest-ranking of the smaller states and
indicates that size alone, or volume of resources is not itself a deter-
minant of improved legislative organization and decision-making
capability. In 1968, five amendments to the Iowa constitution were
adopted by the legislature and ratified by the voters. Two of these
amendments removed restrictions on the legislature (sessions and
compensation), and the others affected the operations of the legislature
indirectly, including a small reduction in the membership of both
houses. Another amendment, creating single-member districts, was
approved by the voters November 3, 1970. The passage of these
amendments, together with internal changes has created a momentum
for improvement in the Iowa Legislature which shows in these rankings.

Some of the features which contribute to the relatively high position
occupied by the Iowa Legislature are the following.

There are eighteen standing committees in the House and eighteen in
the Senate. (Although eighteen may be somewhat higher than the ideal
number, it is nevertheless a considerably smaller number than appears
in many legislatures.) These committees are parallel in jurisdiction
between the houses and operate as joint committees during the interim.
They act under uniform, published rules of procedure, and the interim
committees are required to publish formal reports of their investigations. No member of the Senate has more than four committee
assignments, and only eighteen percent of the members of the House
have more than three.

Legislators, press, and public have access to the work of the legislature, aided by the availability of a public record of committee
deliberations and actions, including roll. calls; the prohibition against
skeleton bills; and the provision of informative summaries in the
format of bill documents.

Annual, unlimited sessions enable the Iowa Legislature to use as much time as is required to accomplish its work. The legislature can expand the agenda of a special session because the governor is not permitted to limit the agenda.

Single-member districts contribute to a focused relationship between legislators and their constituents. The rules prohibit legislators or their firms from practicing before state regulatory agencies for a fee and doing business with the state.

There are a number of areas in which improvements can be made in the Iowa Legislature. The following are specific recommendations toward that end.

1. COMMITTEE JURISDICTION. A description of the jurisdiction of committees should be contained in the rules of both houses, and assignment of bills should be made in accord with the jurisdiction of committees as described in the rules.

2. REPRINT AMENDED BILLS. When a bill is amended substantially, it should be reprinted and returned to the legislature with no more than an overnight delay. The reprint should show clearly the original text of the bill as well as the change created by the amendment.

3. PRE-SESSION ORIENTATION CONFERENCE. The legislature should hold an orientation conference for new legislators, preferably after each general election. Orientation conferences enable members to speed the process of becoming more effective representatives, and they provide an opportunity for legislators to examine large policy areas apart from the pressure of the regular session.

4. STRENGTHEN STAFF SUPPORT. The Iowa Legislature has a small but competent staff (organized under the Legislative Council) which provides a number of necessary services, such as bill drafting, fiscal analysis and fiscal note preparation, and legislative research. To put the legislature in a position to conduct effective oversight of executive operations through continuous program review and evaluation, the range, volume, and level of these services are in need of expansion. This can be accomplished most directly by authorizing additional staff positions and by increasing salary levels and qualifications.

5. STRENGTHEN STAFF SUPPORT (LEADERS). Staff assistance should be provided to all leaders of both the majority and minority parties. Such assistance should include a secretary and an administrative assistant at the professional level, with space to

work reasonably adjacent to the offices of members and leaders.

6. STRENGTHEN STAFF (RANK-AND-FILE MEMBERS). Rank-and-file members (majority and minority party on an equal basis) should be provided with individual staff assistance consisting of a minimum of an administrative assistant at the professional level and a secretary. Eventually, this should increase to the stated level of support both in the capital and in a district office.

   Some movement toward the staffing of individual members can be made through the provision of administrative assistants, perhaps beginning on a shared basis, but ultimately for each member, majority and minority alike.

7. COMMITTEE STAFFING. A beginning should be made toward permanent, year-round committee staffing for some of the major committees.

8. INCREASE LEGISLATIVE COMPENSATION. No legislative salaries in the United States should be below the $10,000 a year level. Compensation of legislators in the larger states should be in the $20,000 to $30,000 range.

   Current salaries for Iowa legislators of $5,500 a year are considerably lower than those in any state ranked higher than Iowa in this study (California, $19,200; New York, $15,000; Illinois, $12,000; Wisconsin, $8,900). It would require a doubling of legislative salaries merely to equal the average in the states among which Iowa ranks favorably (i.e., the top ten). Legislative salaries in Iowa should be increased to the $12,000 to $15,000 annual range.

9. INDIVIDUAL OFFICES. Provide private, individual offices for every member of the legislature, with nearby space for their assistants. The quality and amount of office space should not differ substantially between majority and minority party members.

10. FACILITIES FOR COMMITTEES. Legislative effectiveness requires that committees have adequate physical facilities in which to do their work. This includes an adequate number of committee rooms and an adequate number of hearing rooms that will permit the seating of larger audiences.

11. SUPPORT OF DISTRICT OFFICES. District offices are vital to the effective representation by a legislator of his constituency. The legislature should make some contribution to the support of district offices for its members, and the amount of this contribution should be increased over time.

The Iowa Legislature could make a start toward this objective
by making a contribution toward the cost of district offices (perhaps
shared in metropolitan areas, at first) and gradually increasing
the amount of that contribution over time.

12. WASHINGTON, D.C., OFFICE FOR THE LEGISLATURE. With
the large and growing volume of activity generated by state-federal
relationships, the legislature, beyond merely reacting to federal
legislation, should be in a position to influence the development
of new programs in accordance with the interests of the state.
To do so, the legislature should have an office in the nation's
capital to represent it and to be its most direct liaison with the
Congress.

For small states, consideration might be given to joining with a
number of sister states (either on a geographical or on a population
basis) for the purpose of sharing the services of a Washington
office. But in large states, the volume of inter-governmental
traffic has reached a stage at which it would benefit the legislature greatly to have a full-time Washington office.

13. ELECTRIC ROLL CALL RECORDER. An electric roll call
recorder should be installed in the Senate, as in the House. This
is recommended not simply because it would speed up the proceedings (worthwhile as this may be), but because it is an efficient
method of producing an error-free record of roll call votes.

14. STATEMENT OF INTENT BY AUTHOR OF A BILL. The form in
which a bill is introduced should include a statement by the author
describing, in laymen's language, what the bill is intended to
accomplish.

15. IMPROVE PRESS FACILITIES. Committee rooms should provide
adequate space for the news media and lighting and electrical
power connections for their equipment, as is provided in the
chambers. Conference or interview rooms and office space should
also be available to the news media.

16. DUAL COMMITTEE CONSIDERATION OF APPROPRIATION BILLS.
There should be a rule requiring dual committee consideration
of legislation affecting significant sums of money. Such legislation,
when considered and acted upon favorably by a substantive policy
committee, should then automatically be referred to the Finance
Committee for consideration of its fiscal impact.

17. LEGISLATIVE POWER TO CALL SPECIAL SESSIONS. Amend
the constitution to permit the legislature to convene special

sessions either by petition of a majority of the members of both houses or the call of the presiding officer of each house.

18. PROHIBIT APPOINTMENT TO STATE OFFICE. There should be a prohibition against a legislator accepting appointment to other state office during the term for which he is elected or within two years of the termination of his service as a member of the legislature.

KANSAS (23)

Functional, 31; Accountable, 15; Informed, 14; Independent, 32; Representative, 34

GENERAL: Newly elected legislators in Kansas have the advantage of an extensive, well-planned pre-session orientation. These week-long meetings cover many topics, from parliamentary procedures to a summary of the last interim's activities. Kansas is one of the few states (also Florida and North Dakota) that provide for such activities by law, not custom.

One recent improvement in the legislature was the establishment of a permanent Joint Committee on Legislative Services and Facilities. The committee will make studies and, from time to time, provide reports with recommendations to the legislature concerning facilities, services, and the organization and operation of the legislature. In November, 1970, the voters approved a constitutional amendment that requires the governor to call a special session upon petition of two-thirds of the members of each house and another amendment that increases from three to five the number of amendments that may be submitted to the voters at one time. The latter provision lends greater impetus to the amount of legislative reform that can be accomplished through the amending process.

The Legislative Council provides year-round staffing for the legislature and interim committees, the latter of which are always joint. An increasing number of House and Senate standing committees are beginning to gain interim status. A bill has been introduced in the 1971 session to eliminate the Legislative Council, replacing it with a similar body with broad management powers and creating fully staffed, year-round standing committees. A similar bill was defeated in 1970.

State Senators in Kansas have the advantage of individual secretarial help during the session, and each Senate committee has a clerk. Staffing for the House has not nearly reached this level. To streamline

the flow of bills through the legislative process, Kansas has adopted
deadline and pre-session systems. Bills may be filed, drafted, and
printed before the session begins, and, if the relevant committee has
interim status, actual committee work may begin.

Recommendations which will improve the Kansas Legislature are the
following.

1.   REMOVE CONSTITUTIONAL RESTRICTIONS ON SESSION AND
     INTERIM TIME. The legislature should have authority to function
     throughout a two-year term; ideally, this authority should provide
     a flexible biennial session pattern that permits the legislature to
     convene, recess, and reconvene as it deems desirable. The
     legislature should be able to meet in general session or conduct
     interim work as it deems necessary at any time throughout the
     period.

     Currently, the Kansas Legislature is limited to ninety calendar
     days in odd years and sixty in even years, with a sixty calendar
     day extension possible only for even-year sessions. The consti-
     tution should be amended to permit unlimited annual sessions.

2.   LEGISLATIVE POWER TO CALL SPECIAL SESSIONS. Amend
     the constitution to permit the legislature to convene special
     sessions either by petition of a majority of the members of both
     houses or the call of the presiding officer of each house.

3.   REDUCE THE NUMBER OF COMMITTEES. Ideally, there should
     be from ten to fifteen committees in each house, parallel in juris-
     diction. This would reduce the general complexity of the legis-
     lature and would permit reducing the number of committee
     assignments per member.

     There are twenty-five committees in the House and nineteen in
     the Senate. If the committees in both houses were reduced to
     the same number and given parallel subject matter jurisdictions,
     the pending move to full-time standing committees could be made
     smoothly and successfully in that they could act jointly.

4.   REDUCE THE NUMBER OF COMMITTEE ASSIGNMENTS. In
     order to make it possible for members to concentrate their
     attention and contribute effectively, there should be no more than
     three committee assignments for each member of the lower house
     and four committee assignments for each member of the Senate.
     The multiplicity of assignments introduces problems of scheduling
     strains the focus of attention on the part of members, and creates
     an inordinately heavy workload for members if committees are
     as active as they should be.

At present, twenty-two percent of the House members have more than three committee assignments each, and twenty-eight percent of the Senate members have more than four.

5. STRENGTHEN STAFF SUPPORT. Legislative research, fiscal, legal, and planning agencies should be adequately staffed to full utility and at suitable salary levels for professional qualification. Professional staffing should be at a level to enable the legislature to conduct continuous, year-round examination of state resources and expenditures as well as program review and evaluation of state agencies. This staff should also prepare fiscal notes accompanying all appropriation bills, evaluating their fiscal impact over the short and long term. Staff agencies should be upgraded to the level at which competent and timely service can be provided to every member of the legislature.

6. STRENGTHEN STAFF SUPPORT (LEADERS). Staff assistance should be provided to all leaders of both the majority and minority parties. Such assistance should include a secretary and an administrative assistant at the professional level, with space to work reasonably adjacent to the offices of members and leaders.

7. STRENGTHEN STAFF (RANK-AND-FILE MEMBERS). Rank-and-file members (majority and minority party on an equal basis) should be provided with individual staff assistance consisting of a minimum of an administrative assistant at the professional level and a secretary. Eventually, this should increase to the stated level of support both in the capital and in a district office.

8. COMMITTEE STAFFING. Standing committees should be staffed on a permanent, year-round basis.

9. WASHINGTON, D.C., OFFICE FOR THE LEGISLATURE. With the large and growing volume of activity generated by state-federal relationships, the legislature, beyond merely reacting to federal legislation, should be in a position to influence the development of new programs in accordance with the interests of the state. To do so, the legislature should have an office in the nation's capital to represent it and to be its most direct liaison with the Congress.

For small states, consideration might be given to joining with a number of sister states (either on a geographical or on a population basis) for the purpose of sharing the services of a Washington office. But in large states, the volume of inter-governmental traffic has reached a stage at which it would benefit the legislature greatly to have a full-time Washington office.

10. INDIVIDUAL OFFICES. Provide private, individual offices for
     every member of the legislature, with nearby space for their
     assistants. The quality and amount of office space should not
     differ substantially between majority and minority party members.

11. FACILITIES FOR COMMITTEES. Legislative effectiveness
     requires that committees have adequate physical facilities in
     which to do their work. This includes an adequate number of
     committee rooms and an adequate number of hearing rooms that
     will permit the seating of larger audiences.

12. SERVICE AGENCY FACILITIES. Space for service agencies
     should provide adequate working space for professional and clerical
     staff as well as library, files, and other storage requirements.

13. IMPROVE PRESS FACILITIES. Improved press facilities aid in
     the coverage of the work of the legislature. Committee rooms,
     and both chambers or galleries, should provide adequate space
     for the news media as well as lighting and electrical power con-
     nections for their equipment. Conference or interview rooms
     and office space should also be provided for the news media.

     Specifically, the legislature should provide adequate space in
     committee rooms with lighting and electrical power connections
     for media equipment, conference or interview rooms, and office
     space for the news media.

14. INCREASE LEGISLATIVE COMPENSATION. No legislative
     salaries in the United States should be below the $10,000 a year
     level. Compensation of legislators in the larger states should be
     in the $20,000 to $30,000 range.

     Current salaries total $1,500 per biennium plus expenses. Since
     compensation, set by statute in Kansas, is difficult to raise, con-
     sideration should be given to the establishment of a compensation
     commission to make appropriate recommendations on all govern-
     ment services.

15. SPECIAL PROVISIONS. In addition to standard laws governing
     criminal behavior, there should be special provisions regulating
     legislative conflicts of interest.

     PRACTICE BEFORE REGULATORY AGENCIES. Legislators or
     their firms should be prohibited from practicing before state
     regulatory agencies or in matters concerning state agencies for
     a fee.

PROHIBIT APPOINTMENT TO STATE OFFICE. There should be a prohibition against a legislator accepting appointment to other state office during the term for which he is elected or within two years of the termination of his service as a member of the legislature.

FAMILITY EMPLOYMENT. Members of a legislator's immediate family should be barred from employment by the legislature.

16. REGULATION OF LOBBYISTS. The independence of the legislature and public confidence in its processes require the regulation of special interest advocates. Lobbyists should be required to register with an agency of the legislature, and should be required to disclose who employs them, on behalf of what objectives, how much they are paid, and how much they spend and on whom. This information should be available to the press and the public. There should be specific and automatic penalties for failure to comply with these requirements.

17. JOINT RULES. There should be joint rules governing the relationship and the flow of legislation between the two houses of the legislature.

18. OPEN COMMITTEES. The rules of each house should prohibit secret meetings except in matters affecting the security of the state, or which could unnecessarily damage the reputation of individuals in personnel matters. Such exceptions should be sparingly and responsibly employed.

19. NOTICE OF MEETINGS. The rules should require a minimum notice of five legislative days for committee meetings and hearings, with widely disseminated announcement of schedule, location, agenda, and availability of public participation.

20. CONSENT CALENDAR. A consent calendar should be used in both houses.

21. PUBLISH COMMITTEE ROLL CALLS. The committee report of action on bills to the respective houses should include those roll calls which are taken, showing how each member voted. These committee reports should be available to the press and public. Published roll calls should apply to those bills recommended for approval as well as those killed.

22. DUAL COMMITTEE CONSIDERATION OF APPROPRIATION BILLS. There should be a rule requiring dual committee consideration

of legislation affecting significant sums of money. Such legislation, when considered and acted upon favorably by a substantive policy committee, should then automatically be referred to the Finance Committee for consideration of its fiscal impact.

23. MANAGEMENT COMMITTEES. There should be an executive or management committee created in each house. Its membership should include the leaders of each party in each house, and the minority party should have representation on the committee in proportion to its numbers in the body as a whole. The Senate/House management committees should combine as a joint management committee. The purpose of these committees should be to assume responsibility for the administrative management (housekeeping) functions relating to personnel, facilities, the research bureaus, budgets, and expenditures of their respective houses. The joint management committee should deal with matters of inter-house coordination.

24. BILL SUMMARY BY BILL-DRAFTING SERVICE. The form in which bills are introduced should include a more extensive summary of the provisions of the bill, prepared by the bill-drafting service.

25. STATEMENT OF INTENT BY AUTHOR OF A BILL. The form in which a bill is introduced should include a statement by the author describing, in laymen's language, what the bill is intended to accomplish.

26. TRANSFER AUDIT FUNCTION TO THE LEGISLATURE. A significant part of the legislature's ability to exercise oversight of executive departments and administrative agencies depends upon the power and capacity to conduct audits (financial and functional) of these units of the state government. These functions and responsibilities should be removed from the duties and resources of the Office of Auditor and be established under a legislative auditor.

KENTUCKY (31)

Functional, 49; Accountable, 2; Informed, 48; Independent, 44; Representative, 7

GENERAL: Kentucky, although ranked thirty-first overall, showed remarkable strength in two areas: accountability (second) and representativeness (seventh). Among the reasons the General Assembly is regarded as so able to be held accountable are the size of the House is 100 members; the number of standing committees is within the desirable range (fourteen and they are parallel in jurisdiction; there are rules describing the jurisdictions of committees, and they are always followed in assigning legislation to committees; roll calls are required on final passage of any bill; and the results of interim committee actions are recorded and made public.

Some of the index of the high degree of representativeness of the General Assembly are the number of staff services it provides members; the practice of holding a pre-session orientation conference that has a comprehensive agenda covering five critical areas; uniform committee rules; and only single-member districts in both the House and Senate.

A 1968 revision of the House and Senate rules provided that not only should House and Senate committees be identical in name, number, and jurisdiction, but that during the interim, the standing committees of both be combined to operate as subcommittees of the Legislative Research Commission.

The low rank of the Kentucky Legislature in functionality (49), informed (48), and independence (44) creates an especially erratic profile when viewed across the FAIIR scheme and accounts for the state's low overall ranking.

The recommendations proposed attempt to correct some of these shortcomings.

1. REMOVE CONSTITUTIONAL RESTRICTIONS ON SESSION AND INTERIM TIME. The legislature should have authority to function throughout a two-year term; ideally, this authority should provide a flexible biennial session pattern that permits the legislature to convene, recess, and reconvene as it deems desirable. The legislature should be able to meet in general session or conduct interim work as it deems necessary at any time throughout the period.

    In 1968 the General Assembly proposed a constitutional amendment to provide annual legislative sessions, limited to sixty legislative days, that must adjourn by June 30. The amendment was defeated at the general election in November, 1969. We recommend that the General Assembly meet in annual session of not less than ninety legislative days and that no mandatory adjournment deadline short of the end of the year be imposed. In addition, we recommend that for each term of the General Assembly, bill carry-over from the first annual session to the second be authorized.

2.   LEGISLATIVE POWER TO CALL SPECIAL SESSIONS. Amend
     the constitution to permit the legislature to convene special
     sessions either by petition of a majority of the members of both
     houses or the call of the presiding officer of each house.

3.   POWER TO EXPAND SPECIAL SESSION AGENDA. Amend the
     constitution to permit the legislature to broaden the subject
     matter of a governor's call of a special session by a majority
     vote in each house, or prohibit the restriction of the agenda by
     the governor.

4.   STRENGTHEN STAFF SUPPORT. Legislative research, fiscal,
     legal, and planning agencies should be adequately staffed to full
     utility and at suitable salary levels for professional qualification.
     Professional staffing should be at a level to enable the legislature
     to conduct continuous, year-round examination of state resources
     and expenditures as well as program review and evaluation of
     state agencies. This staff should also prepare fiscal notes
     accompanying all appropriation bills, evaluating their fiscal
     impact over the short and long term. Staff agencies should be
     upgraded to the level at which competent and timely service can
     be provided to every member of the legislature.

     Although the Legislative Research Commission has a relatively
     large and capable professional staff, it is the only bureau providing
     legislative services; thus the number of professional services
     available to legislative leaders and members is below par. We
     recommend a strengthening of professional services by providing
     a slightly enlarged commission staff. The commission's chronic
     space problems have been generally eased in the past few years,
     but at a price of scattering offices- including the use of the
     capitol's attic-over several floors. There is a continuing effort
     to provide adequate space for those few still ill-housed and, as
     well, to make room for additional staff.

5.   COMMITTEE STAFFING. Standing committees should be staffed
     on a permanent, year-round basis.

6.   INDIVIDUAL OFFICES. Provide private, individual offices for
     every member of the legislature, with nearby space for their
     assistants. The quality and amount of office space should not
     differ substantially between majority and minority party members.

     The state capitol's severe space shortages deny the General
     Assembly basic and pressing space needs. Individual, private
     offices ought to be furnished every member of the legislature.
     Presently, only the top two elected leaders of the majority party

in either house have private offices, and no member of the rank and file has any space at all.

7. FACILITIES FOR COMMITTEES. Legislative effectiveness requires that committees have adequate physical facilities in which to do their work. This includes an adequate number of committee rooms and an adequate number of hearing rooms that will permit the seating of larger audiences.

Committees meet in one of three recently remodeled rooms which, while well-lighted and moderately comfortable for committee members, provide very little space-and then around the perimeter of the room-for spectators and members of the press. Moreover, there are no hearing rooms capable of seating as many as fifty non-committee members.

8. IMPROVE PRESS FACILITIES. Improved press facilities aid in the coverage of the work of the legislature. Committee rooms, and both chambers or galleries, should provide adequate space for the news media as well as lighting and electrical power connections for their equipment. Conference or interview rooms and office space should also be provide for the news media.

The press accommodations in the chambers of both houses are inadequate.

9. LEGISLATIVE SALARIES. Legislative salaries should be set by statute and paid in equal monthly installments throughout the biennium, and all unvouchered expense allowances should be incorporated into an annual salary. Actual and necessary expenses incurred in the process of carrying out legislative duties should be reimbursed upon submission and approval of properly vouchered evidence of expenditures.

INCREASE LEGISLATIVE COMPENSATION. No legislative salaries in the United States should be below the $10,000 a year level. Compensation of legislators in the larger states should be in the $20,000 to $30,000 range.

10. JOINT RULES. There should be joint rules governing the relationship and the flow of legislation between the two houses of the legislature.

11. BILL DEADLINES. The orderly flow of work through the legislature depends upon the existence of a series of deadlines at various critical stages throughout the legislative process. These deadlines should be adopted as part of the rules and should be consistently enforced.

12. ESTABLISH AN AUTOMATIC CALENDAR OF BILLS. When a
    bill is favorably reported out of committee to the floor, it should
    go automatically onto the calendar in the order in which it was
    reported out. It should require a vote of an extraordinary majority
    to move a bill from its position on calendar or to bypass it. The
    Rules Committee should have no part in the scheduling of bills.
    No session should adjourn until all bills on calendar have been
    voted up or down or, by the vote of an extraordinary majority,
    have been moved from the calendar.

13. DUAL COMMITTEE CONSIDERATION OF APPROPRIATION BILLS.
    There should be a rule requiring dual committee consideration
    of legislation affecting significant sums of money. Such legislation,
    when considered and acted upon favorably by a substantive policy
    committee, should then automatically be referred to the Finance
    Committee for consideration of its fiscal impact.

14. STATEMENT OF INTENT BY AUTHOR OF A BILL. The form
    in which a bill is introduced should include a statement by the
    author describing, in laymen's language, what the bill is intended
    to accomplish.

15. BILL SUMMARY BY BILL-DRAFTING SERVICE. The form in
    which bills are introduced should include a more extensive summary
    of the provisions of the bill prepared by the bill-drafting service.

16. CONSENT CALENDAR. A consent calendar should be used in both
    houses.

17. PUBLISH COMMITTEE ROLL CALLS. The committee report of
    action on bills to the respective houses should include those roll
    calls which are taken, showing how each member voted. These
    committee reports should be available to the press and public.
    Published roll calls should apply to those bills recommended for
    approval as well as those killed.

    The committee report of action on bills to the Senate should
    include those roll calls which are taken, showing how each member
    voted. Such roll calls are often available from House committees;
    they should be available for all committee reports.

18. STRENGTHEN MINORITY PARTY ROLE. Internal accountability
    as well as the capacity of all legislators to represent their con-
    stituents effectively depends upon the opportunity of minority
    party members to have an effective part in internal legislative
    affairs.

MINORITY REPRESENTATION ON COMMITTEE ON RULES.
Minority representation on the Committee on Rules should approximate the minority party proportion of the membership of the
appropriate house.

19. WASHINGTON, D.C., OFFICE FOR THE LEGISLATURE. With
the large and growing volume of activity generated by state-federal
relationships, the legislature, beyond merely reacting to federal
legislation, should be in a position to influence the development
of new programs in accordance with the interests of the state.
To do so, the legislature should have an office in the nation's
capital to represent it and to be its most direct liaison with the
Congress.

For small states, consideration might be given to joining with a
number of sister states (either on a geographical or on a population
basis) for the purpose of sharing the services of a Washington
office. But in large states, the volume of inter-governmental
traffic has reached a stage at which it would benefit the legislature
greatly to have a full-time Washington office.

20. PRACTICE BEFORE REGULATORY AGENCIES. Legislators or
their firms should be prohibited from practicing before state
regulatory agencies or in matters concerning state agencies for
a fee.

21. ESTABLISH CITIZENS COMMISSION ON THE LEGISLATURE.
As a means of cultivating generalized support for the legislature
as an institution, a citizens' commission should be created by
joint resolution of the legislature, to study its operations, facilities,
and needs and to recommend improvements. The appointive power
should be consigned to the speaker and the president pro tem on
an equal basis and should include consultation with the minority
leader of each house. The citizens' commission should conduct
its review over a two-year period, resulting in recommendations
to the legislature and the public concerning the role the legislature
is expected to perform in development of a truly effective and
responsive state government, and the measures required to
reach that objective. A key function of the commission is to
educate the citizenry to problems, opportunities, and needs of
the legislature. This purpose is best served by doing much of
its work through public hearings conducted in the population
centers of the state. A commission composed of from twenty-
five to thirty-five leading citizens, representing various fields
of activity, interest groups, and areas of the state can contribute
much to the development of public support for a more dynamic
legislature.

The Kentucky Committee on the State Legislature, in existence
since September, 1967, should be rejuvenated to undertake a
more vigorous attempt at launching a full-scale modernization
effort to aid in the development of the Kentucky General Assembly
as a more effective and responsive body.

LOUISIANA (33)

Functional, 47; Accountable, 39; Informed, 33; Independent, 13;
Representative, 14

GENERAL: The Louisiana Legislature has relatively small houses
and a well-qualified but undermanned central staff bureau. Bill summaries accompany each piece of legislation introduced, and every bill
favorably reported from committee is taken up on the floor according
to an automatic calendaring system.

In 1970, both houses began to use an electronic data-processing system
to monitor the status of all bills. During 1970, the House planned to
give a considerable amount of attention to a complete revision of its
rules.

Steps to improve the Louisiana Legislature are included in the following recommendations.

1. REMOVE CONSTITUTIONAL RESTRICTIONS ON SESSION AND
    INTERIM TIME. The legislature should have authority to function
    throughout a two-year term; ideally, this authority should provide
    a flexible biennial session pattern that permits the legislature
    to convene, recess, and reconvene as it deems desirable. The
    legislature should be able to meet in general session or conduct
    interim work as it deems necessary at any time throughout the
    period.

    The constitution should be amended to provide for annual unlimited
    sessions.

2. REDUCE THE NUMBER OF COMMITTEES. Ideally, there should
    be from ten to fifteen committees in each house parallel in juris-
    diction. This would reduce the general complexity of the legis-
    lature and would permit reducing the number of committee as-
    signments per member.

    With twenty-three committees in the House and twenty in the
    Senate, there are more committees than should be necessary
    for the effective organization of the work. This condition is more
    severe in relation to the Senate than it is in relation to the House.

3. REDUCE THE NUMBER OF COMMITTEE ASSIGNMENTS. In
    order to make it possible for members to concentrate their
    attention and contribute effectively, there should be no more than
    three committee assignments for each member of the lower house
    and four committee assignments for each member of the Senate.
    The multiplicity of assignments introduces problems of scheduling,
    strains the focus of attention on the part of members, and creates
    an inordinately heavy workload for members if committees are
    as active as they should be.

    At present, fifty-seven percent of the House members serve on
    more than three committees, and ninety-seven of the Senate
    members serve on more than four committees.

4. PUBLISH COMMITTEE ROLL CALLS. The committee report
    of action on bills to the respective houses should include those
    roll calls which are taken, showing how each member voted.
    These committee reports should be available to the press and
    public. Published roll calls should apply to those bills recom-
    mended for approval as well as those killed.

5. RECORD AND PUBLISH PROCEEDINGS OF COMMITTEES.
    Record and publish the record of committee hearings, proceedings,
    and votes.

6. INTERIM COMMITTEES. When the legislature is not in session,
    the standing committees should become the interim committees
    for the purpose of conducting long-range studies of state policy
    issues. The Legislative Council or some similarly constituted,
    bi-partisan committee should serve as the supervising agency
    for interim committees and their studies, budgets, and personnel.
    The major committees should be staffed on a year-round basis.

    INTERIM COMMITTEE REPORTING. Interim committees should
    be required to render formal reports concerning the topics
    they were charged with responsibility for investigating. These
    reports should cover the committee's recommendations, including
    drafts of proposed legislation where appropriate.

7. MANAGEMENT COMMITTEES. There should be an executive
    or management committee created in each house. Its membership
    should include the leaders of each party in each house, and the
    minority party should have representation on the committee in
    proportion to its numbers in the body as a whole. The Senate/
    House management committees should combine as a joint manage-
    ment committee. The purpose of these committees should be to
    assume responsibility for the administrative management

(housekeeping) functions relating to personnel, facilities, the research bureaus, budgets, and expenditures of their respective houses. The joint management committee should deal with matters of inter-house coordination.

8. STRENGTHEN STAFF SUPPORT. Legislative research, fiscal, legal, and planning agencies should be adequately staffed to full utility and at suitable salary levels for professional qualification. Professional staffing should be at a level to enable the legislature to conduct continuous, year-round examination of state resources and expenditures as well as program review and evaluation of state agencies. This staff should also prepare fiscal notes accompanying all appropriation bills, evaluating their fiscal impact over the short and long term. Staff agencies should be upgraded to the level at which competent and timely service can be provided to every member of the legislature.

9. COMMITTEE STAFFING. Standing committees should be staffed on a permanent year-round basis.

10. INDIVIDUAL OFFICES. Provide private, individual offices for every member of the legislature, with nearby space for their assistants. The quality and amount of office space should not differ substantially between majority and minority party members.

11. FACILITIES FOR COMMITTEES. Legislative effectiveness requires that committees have adequate physical facilities in which to do their work. This includes an adequate number of committee rooms and an adequate number of hearing rooms that will permit the seating of larger audiences.

12. IMPROVE PRESS FACILITIES. Improved press facilities aid in the coverage of the work of the legislature. Committee rooms, and both chambers or galleries, should provide adequate space for the news media as well as lighting and electrical power connections for their equipment. Conference or interview rooms and office space should also be provided for the news media.

Although legislative proceedings, both in committee and in the chamber, are accessible to the press, there is need for improved press facilities to aid in the coverage of the work of the legislature.

13. LEGISLATIVE SALARIES. Legislative salaries should be set by statute and paid in equal monthly installments throughout the biennium, and all unvouchered expense allowances should be incorporated into an annual salary. Actual and necessary expenses

incurred in the process of carrying out legislative duties should be reimbursed upon submission and approval of properly vouchered evidence of expenditures.

INCREASE LEGISLATIVE COMPENSATION. No legislative salaries in the United States should be below the $10,000 a year level. Compensation of legislators in the larger states should be in the $20,000 to $30,000 range.

14. SUPPORT OF DISTRICT OFFICES. District offices are vital to the effective representation by a legislator of his constituency. The legislature should make some contribution to the support of district offices for its members, and the amount of this contribution should be increased over time.

The Louisiana Legislature could make a start toward this objective by making a contribution toward the cost of district offices, perhaps shared in metropolitan areas at first, and gradually increasing the amount of that contribution over time.

15. REGULATION OF LOBBYISTS. The independence of the legislature and public confidence in its processes require the regulation of special-interest advocates. Lobbyists should be required to register with an agency of the legislature, and should be required to disclose who employs them, on behalf of what objectives, how much they are paid, and how much they spend and on whom. This information should be available to the press and the public. There should be specific and automatic penalties for failure to comply with these requirements.

16. BILL DEADLINES. The orderly flow of work through the legislature depends upon the existence of a series of deadlines at various critical stages throughout the legislative process. These deadlines should be adopted as part of the rules and should be consistently enforced.

Orderly flow of work through the legislature depends upon a series of deadlines at various critical stages throughout the legislative process. So far, both the House and the Senate have instituted only the most basic deadlines, as evidenced by the high percentage of bills — 68 percent in both houses — passed during the final week of the regular session.

17. CONSENT CALENDAR. A consent calendar should be used in both houses.

18. SKELETON BILLS. There should be an explicit rule barring

introduction of skeleton or "spot" bills. This rule should be
enforced by the assigning authority (the presiding officer or
Rules Committee) by refusal to assign bills so identified to
committee.

19. UNIFORM COMMITTEE RULES. There should be uniform published rules of committee procedure in both chambers.

The House should institute uniform committee rules; the Senate
already provides for them.

20. COMMITTEE JURISDICTION. A description of the jurisdiction
of committees should be contained in the rules of both houses,
and assignment of bills should be made in accord with the jurisdiction of committees as described in the rules.

21. STATEMENT OF INTENT BY AUTHOR OF A BILL. The form
in which a bill is introduced should include a statement by the
author describing,in laymen's language, what the bill is intended
to accomplish.

22. QUANTITY OF BILLS INTRODUCED. An extraordinarily high
number of bill introductions inevitably clogs the entire legislative
machinery and should be reduced. One alternative would be to
use short bill form (as done in Hawaii); another would be to require multiple authorship of bills rather than permit the introduction of identical bills by separate authors. The short-form
bill has certain advantages, in that it permits a member to in-
troduce a statement describing the intent of the legislation which
he proposes, but it is not drafted in legal language. Under this
system the committees to which such short-form bills are referred have the obligation of combining them into omnibus legislation sponsored by the committee itself.

23. DUAL COMMITTEE CONSIDERATION OF APPROPRIATION
BILLS. There should be a rule requiring dual committee consideration of legislation affecting significant sums of money.
Such legislation, when considered and acted upon favorably by a
substantive policy committee, should then automatically be referred to the Finance Committee for consideration of its fiscal
impact.

24. POWER TO EXPAND SPECIAL SESSION AGENDA. Amend the
constitution to permit the legislature to broaden the subject
matter of a governor's call of a special session by a majority
vote in each house, or prohibit the restriction of the agenda by
the governor.

25. PROHIBIT APPOINTMENT TO STATE OFFICE. There should
     be a prohibition against a legislator accepting appointment to
     other state office during the term for which he is elected or
     within two years of the termination of his service as a member
     of the legislature.

     HOLDING OTHER PUBLIC OFFICE. Legislators should be pro-
     hibited from concurrently holding other continuing, paid public
     office.

     FAMILY EMPLOYMENT. Members of a legislator's immediate
     family should be barred from employment by the legislature.

26. PROVIDE SINGLE-MEMBER DISTRICTS. Legislative districts
     in both houses should be single-member.

     At present only 47 percent of the House's districts and 69 percent
     of the Senate's are single-member.

                          MAINE (30)

Functional, 29; Accountable, 34; Informed, 32; Independent, 18; Representative, 22

GENERAL: Maine exhibits a number of glaring weaknesses one would
expect from a state ranked at the sixtieth percentile. However, some
of the Maine Legislature's operations and procedures, probably by
happenstance more than design, work to mitigate the effect of some
of its handicaps. The legislature is severely understaffed — it employs
only four professional staff members. But since the substantive committees of both houses always meet and act jointly, the net result is
not quite as debilitating as it would be if they met as separate committees. Too, the legislature does not face a time limitation during its
biennial session, so staff workloads can be eased slightly.

Committee procedures are generally open, and although final committee votes taken in executive session, roll calls of those votes are
made public. Each committee room, although spare by some standards,
contains enough room to accomodate well over fifty spectators. As
one might expect in a New England state, committee hearings are
ordinarily well attended.

Maine voters approved a constitutional amendment in November, 1970,
that will allow the legislature to call itself into special session by
concurrent action of the presiding officer of each house, with the
consent of a majority of each party in each house. Approval of this

amendment attests to a growing awareness on the part of the people
of Maine of the need for the legislature to be able to respond independently to pressing state needs.

The recommendations which follow are addressed to some of the major areas in need of improvement in the operations, procedures, and
facilities of the Maine Legislature:

1. ESTABLISH CITIZENS' COMMISSION ON THE LEGISLATURE.
    As a means of cultivating generalized support for the legislature
    as an institution, a citizens' commission should be created by
    joint resolution of the legislature, to study its operations, facili-
    ties, and needs and to recommend improvements. The appointive
    power should be consigned to the speaker and the president pro
    tem on an equal basis, and should include consultation with the
    minority leader of each house. The citizens' commission should
    conduct its review over a two-year period, resulting in recom-
    mendations to the legislature and the public concerning the role
    the legislature is expected to perform in development of a truly
    effective and responsive state government, and the measures
    required to reach that objective. A key function of the commissio
    is to educate the citizenry on problems, opportunities, and needs
    of the legislature. This purpose is best served by doing much
    of its work through public hearings conducted in the population
    centers of the state. A commission composed of from twenty-
    five to thirty-five leading citizens, representing various fields
    of activity, interest groups, and areas of the state, can contribute
    much to the development of public support for a more dynamic
    legislature.

    During the last regular session of the legislature, a bill to create
    a citizens' commission on the legislature was defeated by a very
    narrow margin. That proposal (which carried a $30,000 appro-
    priation to support the staff, facility, and supply needs of the
    commission) should be reintroduced and passed, because the
    legislature needs to educate and inform the electorate if it is to
    solve the operational, procedural, and facility problems that
    retard its development as an effective and responsive part of
    state government.

2. REMOVE CONSTITUTIONAL RESTRICTIONS ON SESSION AND
    INTERIM TIME. The legislature should have authority to functio
    throughout a two-year term; ideally, this authority should provide
    a flexible biennial session pattern that permits the legislature
    to convene, recess, and reconvene as it deems desirable. The
    legislature should be able to meet in general session or conduct
    interim work as it deems necessary at any time throughout the
    period.

While the legislature can meet for an unlimited amount of time during the first year of a biennium, the recent experience of having to convene one or more special sessions during the second year of the biennium underscores the legislature's need for the freedom to meet in a series of sessions that are part of an ordered plan. The constitution should be amended to provide for flexible biennial sessions, permitting the legislature to convene, recess, and reconvene as it deems desirable over not one but both years of its terms.

3. INTERIM COMMITTEES. When the legislature is not in session, the standing committees should become the interim committees for the purpose of conducting long-range studies of state policy issues. The Legislative Council or some similarly constituted, bi-partisan committee should serve as the supervising agency for interim committees and their studies, budgets, and personnel. The major committees should be staffed on a year-round basis.

4. REDUCE THE OVERALL SIZE OF THE LEGISLATURE. Although size reduction in a legislative body is extremely difficult to achieve, it has been done in some states - such as Vermont and Iowa - and needs to be accomplished in others (New Hampshire, Massachusetts, Georgia and Pennsylvania). Where reduction in size has occurred, it has most often required a constitutional convention to accomplish it. In a few cases it has been done by legislatively adopted constitutional amendment (Iowa, in 1968, which becomes effective in November, 1971) ratified by the voters. There should be 100 or fewer members in the house. The combined size of both houses should be between 100 and 150.

With 151 members, the House of the Maine Legislature is the eighth largest state legislative body in the United States. (The adverse effects of inordinate size upon many phases of legislative work are discussed in Chapter 3.)

5. MANAGEMENT COMMITTEES. There should be an executive or management committee created in each house. Its membership should include the leaders of each party in each house, and the minority party should have representation on the committee in proportion to its numbers in the body as a whole. The Senate/House management committees should combine as a joint management committee. The purpose of these committees should be to assume responsibility for the administrative management (housekeeping) functions relating to personnel, facilities, the research bureaus, budgets, and expenditures of their respective houses. The joint management committee should deal with matters of interhouse coordination.

6. **STRENGTHEN STAFF SUPPORT.** Legislative research, fiscal, legal, and planning agencies should be adequately staffed to full utility and at suitable salary levels for professional qualification. Professional staffing should be at a level to enable the legislature to conduct continuous, year-round examination of state resources and expenditures as well as program review and evaluation of state agencies. This staff should also prepare fiscal notes accompanying all appropriation bills, evaluating their fiscal impact over the short and long term. Staff agencies should be upgraded to the level at which competent and timely service can be provided to every member of the legislature.

There are two staff bureaus to assist the Maine Legislature: the Legislative Research Committee, with a two-man staff (both attorneys), and the Legislative Fiscal Office, also with a two-man staff, neither of whom is a professional accountant. The legislative reference librarian also assists legislators. To put the legislature in a position to conduct effective oversight of executive operations and to establish timely, responsive, and innovative programs to state-wide problems, the range, volume, and level of these services are in dire need of expansion. This can be accomplished most directly by augmenting and enlarging the present staff by authorizing additional positions and by increasing salary levels and qualifications.

7. **COMMITTEE STAFFING.** Standing committees should be staffed on a permanent, year-round basis.

The legislature should consider, immediately, the staffing of the major committees. Because of the joint committee system, the cost of initially staffing committees will not be as great if there were separate House and Senate committees. All remaining standing committees should be staffed as soon thereafter as possible.

8. **STRENGTHEN STAFF SUPPORT (LEADERS).** Staff assistance should be provided to all leaders of both the majority and minority parties. Such assistance should include a secretary and an administrative assistant at the professional level, with space to work reasonably adjacent to the offices of members and leaders.

9. **STRENGTHEN STAFF (RANK-AND-FILE MEMBERS).** Rank-and-file members (majority and minority party on an equal basis) should be provided with individual staff assistance consisting of a minimum of an administrative assistant at the professional level and a secretary. Eventually, this should increase to the stated level of support both in the capital and in a district office.

As soon as possible, a start should be made toward providing each member (majority and minority on an equal basis) with secretarial and professional staff assistance.

10. IMPROVE PRESS FACILITIES. Improved press facilities aid in the coverage of the work of the legislature. Committee rooms, and both chambers or galleries, should provide adequate space for the news media as well as lighting and electrical power connections for their equipment. Conference or interview rooms and office space should also be provided for the news media.

    Although legislative proceedings, both in committee and in the chamber, are accessible to the press, there is need for improved press facilities to aid in the coverage of the work of the Maine Legislature.

11. COMMITTEE JURISDICTION. A description of the jurisdiction of committees should be contained in the rules of both houses, and assignment of bills should be made in accord with the jurisdiction of committees as described in the rules.

12. OPEN COMMITTEES. The rules of each house should prohibit secret meetings except in matters affecting the security of the state, or which could unnecessarily damage the reputation of individuals in personnel matters. Such exceptions should be sparingly and responsibly employed.

    Although roll calls are taken and made public on final committee actions, open committees could be improved by implementation of general recommendations.

13. NOTICE OF MEETINGS. The rules should require a minimum notice of five legislative days for committee meetings and hearings, with widely disseminated announcement of schedule, location, agenda, and availability of public participation.

14. DUAL COMMITTEE CONSIDERATION OF APPROPRIATION BILLS. There should be a rule requiring dual committee consideration of legislation affecting significant sums of money. Such legislation, when considered and acted upon favorably by a substantive policy committee, should then automatically be referred to the Finance Committee for consideration of its fiscal impact.

15. LEGISLATIVE SALARIES. Legislative salaries should be set by statute and paid in equal monthly installments throughout the biennium, and all unvouchered expense allowances should be incorporated into an annual salary. Actual and necessary expenses

incurred in the process of carrying out legislative duties should
be reimbursed upon submission and approval of properly vouchered
evidence of expenditures.

INCREASE LEGISLATIVE COMPENSATION. No legislative salaries in the United States should be below the $10,000 a year level.
Compensation of legislators in the larger states should be in the
$20,000 to $30,000 range.

Maine's current salaries of $2,500 (as of 1971, up from $2,000)
should be doubled immediately and increased again within the
next few years as other improvements are made.

16. CONSENT CALENDAR. A consent calendar should be used in
    both houses.

17. MINORITY PARTY MEMBERS ON COMMITTEE. Minority party
    members should be assigned to committees by the minority leader
    in consultation with the minority caucus.

18. STATEMENT OF INTENT BY AUTHOR OF A BILL. The form in
    which a bill is introduced should include a statement by the author
    describing, in laymen's language, what the bill is intended to
    accomplish.

19. SPECIAL PROVISIONS. In addition to standard laws governing
    criminal behavior, there should be special provisions regulating
    legislative conflicts of interest.

    PRACTICE BEFORE REGULATORY AGENCIES. Legislators or
    their firms should be prohibited from practicing before state
    regulatory agencies or in matters concerning state agencies for
    a fee.

    PROHIBIT DOING BUSINESS WITH THE STATE. There should
    be a prohibition against legislators or the firms in which they
    own a major interest doing business with state agencies.

    PROHIBIT APPOINTMENT TO STATE OFFICE. There should
    be a prohibition against a legislator accepting appointment to
    other state office during the term for which he is elected or
    within two years of the termination of his service as a member
    of the legislature.

    HOLDING OTHER PUBLIC OFFICE. Legislators should be
    prohibited from concurrently holding other continuing, paid
    public office.

FAMILY EMPLOYMENT. Members of a legislator's immediate family should be barred from employment by the legislature.

20. TRANSFER AUDIT FUNCTION TO THE LEGISLATURE. A significant part of the legislature's ability to exercise oversight of executive departments and administrative agencies depends upon the power and capacity to conduct audits (financial and functional) of these units of the state government. These functions and responsibilities should be removed from the duties and resources of the Office of Auditor and be established under a legislative auditor.

21. REQUIRE ROLL CALL ON PASSAGE OF BILLS. A recorded roll call should be required on final passage of any legislative measure, and it should require a constitutional majority to pass any bill on final action by either house.

MARYLAND (20)

Functional, 16; Accountable, 31; Informed, 10; Independent, 15; Representative, 45

GENERAL: At the 1970 general election Maryland voters approved several important constitutional amendments. One amendment extended the length of Maryland's annual session from seventy to ninety consecutive days; gave the General Assembly the power to extend sessions to 120 days by a three-fifths vote of both houses; and granted the legislature the power to call itself into extraordinary session by a three-fifths vote of both houses. The amendment also created a commission to set legislative compensation: the General Assembly will be able to reduce or reject, but not increase, the amounts proposed by the commission. A second amendment provides for forty-seven legislative districts with one Senator and three Delegates from each.

Although the General Assembly has yet to provide all of its members with professional-level assistance, it has been able to develop through its service agencies the ability to perform continuous studies of resources and expenditures as well as ongoing program review and evaluation.

Many of the recent improvements made in the General Assembly are the result of the efforts of the Maryland Citizens' Commission on the General Assembly and the work of the 1967 Constitutional Convention. In fact, some of the legislative amendments approved in 1970 were contained in the constitution rejected in May, 1968.

Recommendations for further improvement of the Maryland Legislatur
include the following.

1. REMOVE CONSTITUTIONAL RESTRICTIONS ON SESSION AND
   INTERIM TIME. The legislature should have authority to function
   throughout a two-year term; ideally, this authority should provide
   a flexible biennial session pattern that permits the legislature to
   convene, recess, and reconvene as it deems desirable. The
   legislature should be able to meet in general session or conduct
   interim work as it deems necessary at any time throughout the
   period.

2. INTERIM COMMITTEES. When the legislature is not in session,
   the standing committees should become the interim committees
   for the purpose of conducting long-range studies of state policy
   issues. The Legislative Council or some similarly constituted,
   bi-partisan committee should serve as the supervising agency
   for interim committees and their studies, budgets, and personnel.
   The major committees should be staffed on a year-round basis.

3. PRE-SESSION ORGANIZATIONAL MEETING. Amend the constitution to provide a pre-session organizing session following a
   general election. Some states make advantageous use of such
   a session during November or December of a general election
   year for the purpose of electing leaders, appointing committee
   chairmen, assigning members to committees, referring pre-filed
   bills to committee, holding committee organizational meetings,
   and conducting orientation conferences for new, as well as
   returning, members of the legislature. Through such pre-session
   meetings the committees can begin their work before the regular
   session convenes. This makes it possible to delay the start of
   the regular session until legislation is ready for floor action.

4. STRENGTHEN STAFF SUPPORT (LEADERS). Staff assistance
   should be provided to all leaders of both the majority and minority
   parties. Such assistance should include a secretary and an
   administrative assistant at the professional level, with space to
   work reasonably adjacent to the offices of members and leaders.

5. STRENGTHEN STAFF (RANK-AND-FILE MEMBERS). Rank-and-
   file members (majority and minority party on an equal basis)
   should be provided with individual staff assistance consisting of
   a minimum of an administrative assistant at the professional
   level and a secretary. Eventually, this should increase to the
   stated level of support both in the capital and in a district office.

6. COMMITTEE STAFFING. Standing committees should be staffed
   on a permanent, year-round basis.

7. INCREASE LEGISLATIVE COMPENSATION. No legislative
   salaries in the United States should be below the $10,000 a year
   level. Compensation of legislators in the larger states should
   be in the $20,000 to $30,000 range.

   Current salaries, which average $2,400 a year, should be doubled
   immediately and increased again within the next few years as
   other improvements are made. An increase in compensation
   will require action by the newly created compensation commission.

8. EXPENSE ALLOWANCES. Members of the legislature should be
   allowed an expense reimbursement covering their travel and
   living costs while engaged in carrying out their legislative duties.
   The same allowance should obtain during the interim for days in
   attendance at interim committee meetings or other official and
   authorized legislative business. These allowances should be
   provided by statute.

   Specifically, for Maryland the same allowances should obtain
   during the interim for days in attendance at interim committee
   meetings or other official legislative business as are paid for
   days in attendance during the regular sessions.

9. INDIVIDUAL OFFICES. Provide private, individual offices for
   every member of the legislature, with nearby space for their
   assistants. The quality and amount of office space should not
   differ substantially between majority and minority party members.

10. PROVIDE SINGLE-MEMBER DISTRICTS. Legislative districts
    in both houses should be single-member.

11. STRENGTHEN MINORITY PARTY ROLE. Internal accountability,
    as well as the capacity of all legislators to represent their con-
    stituents effectively, depends upon the opportunity of minority
    party members to have an effective part in internal legislative
    affairs.

    MINORITY REPRESENTATION ON COMMITTEE ON RULES.
    Minority representation on the Committee on Rules should approx-
    imate the minority party proportion of the membership of the
    appropriate house.

    MINORITY PARTY MEMBERS ON COMMITTEE. Minority party
    members should be assigned to committees by the minority leader
    in consultation with the minority caucus.

12. REDUCE THE OVERALL SIZE OF THE LEGISLATURE. Although
    size reduction in a legislative body is extremely difficult to

achieve, it has been done in some states - such as in Vermont and
Iowa - and needs to be accomplished in others (New Hampshire,
Massachusetts, Georgia, and Pennsylvania). Where reduction in
size has occurred, it has most often required a constitutional
convention to accomplish it. In a few cases it has been done by
legislatively adopted constitutional amendment (Iowa, in 1968,
which becomes effective in November, 1971) ratified by the voters.
There should be 100 or fewer members in the house. The combined
size of both houses should be between 100 and 150.

The size of the House should be reduced to no more than 100
members. Change in the size of the legislature will require a
constitutional amendment.

13. OPEN COMMITTEES. The rules of each house should prohibit
    secret meetings except in matters affecting the security of the
    state, or which could unnecessarily damage the reputation of
    individuals in personnel matters. Such exceptions should be
    sparingly and responsibly employed.

14. ACT ON ALL BILLS. Committees should be required to report
    on all bills assigned to them, recommending for passage by the
    parent body those bills which enjoy the support of a majority of
    the members of the committee and killing all others.

15. COMMITTEE JURISDICTION. A description of the jurisdiction
    of committees should be contained in the rules of both houses
    and assignment of bills should be made in accord with the juris-
    diction of committees as described in the rules.

16. UNIFORM COMMITTEE RULES. There should be uniform pub-
    lished rules of committee procedure in both chambers.

17. JOINT RULES. There should be joint rules governing the relation-
    ship and the flow of legislation between the two houses of the
    legislature.

18. PUBLISH COMMITTEE ROLL CALLS. The committee report of
    action on bills to the respective houses should include those roll
    calls which are taken, showing how each member voted. These
    committee reports should be available to the press and public.
    Published roll calls should apply to those bills recommended for
    approval as well as those killed.

19. NOTICE OF MEETINGS. The rules should require a minimum
    notice of five legislative days for committee meetings and hearings,
    with widely disseminated announcement of schedule, location,
    agenda, and availability of public participation.

20. MANAGEMENT COMMITTEES. There should be an executive or management committee created in each house. Its membership should include the leaders of each party in each house, and the minority party should have representation on the committee in proportion to its numbers in the body as a whole. The Senate/ House management committees should combine as a joint management committee. The purpose of these committees should be to assume responsibility for the administrative management (housekeeping) functions relating to personnel, facilities, the research bureaus, budgets, and expenditures of their respective houses. The joint management committee should deal with matters of inter-house coordination.

21. WASHINGTON, D.C., OFFICE FOR THE LEGISLATURE. With the large and growing volume of activity generated by state-federal relationships, the legislature, beyond merely reacting to federal legislation, should be in a position to influence the development of new programs in accordance with the interests of the state. To do so, the legislature should have an office in the nation's capital to represent it and to be its most direct liaison with the Congress.

For small states, consideration might be given to joining with a number of sister states (either on a geographical or on a population basis) for the purpose of sharing the services of a Washington office. But in large states, the volume of inter-govermental traffic has reached a stage at which it would benefit the legislature greatly to have a full-time Washington office.

22. SPECIAL PROVISIONS. In additon to standard laws governing criminal behavior, there should be special provisions regulating legislative conflicts of interest.

PRACTICE BEFORE REGULATORY AGENCIES. Legislators or their firms should be prohibited from practicing before state regulatory agencies or in matters concerning state agencies for a fee.

PROHIBIT DOING BUSINESS WITH THE STATE. There should be a prohibition against legislators or the firms in which they own a major interest doing business with state agencies.

HOLDING OTHER PUBLIC OFFICE. Legislators should be prohibited from concurrently holding other continuing, paid public office.

FAMILY EMPLOYMENT. Members of a legislator's immediate family should be barred from employment by the legislature.

The House presently prohibits legislators or firms in which they own a major interest doing business with state agencies. This restriction should also apply to Senate members.

23. **DUAL COMMITTEE CONSIDERATION OF APPROPRIATION BILLS**
There should be a rule requiring dual committee consideration of legislation affecting significant sums of money. Such legislation, when considered and acted upon favorably by a substantive policy committee, should then automatically be referred to the Finance Committee for consideration of its fiscal impact.

24. **BILL DEADLINES.** The orderly flow of work through the legislature depends upon the existence of a series of deadlines at various critical stages throughout the legislative process. These deadlines should be adopted as part of the rules and should be consistently enforces.

The General Assembly has a deadline for bill introduction only. Approximately seventy percent of the bills passed in the last session were enacted in the final week of the session. Bill deadlines at critical stages in the legislative process should be adopted and enforced.

25. **CONSENT CALENDAR.** A consent calendar should be used in both houses.

26. **SUPPORT OF DISTRICT OFFICES.** District offices are vital to the effective representation by a legislator of his constituency. The legislature should make some contribution to the support of district offices for its members, and the amount of this contribution should be increased over time.

27. **IMPROVE PRESS FACILITIES.** Improved press facilities aid in the coverage of the work of the legislature. Committee rooms, and both chambers or galleries, should provide adequate space for the news media as well as lighting and electrical power connections for their equipment. Conference or interview rooms and office space should also be provided for the news media.

28. **FACILITIES FOR COMMITTEES.** Legislative effectiveness requires that committees have adequate physical facilities in which to do their work. This includes an adequate number of committee rooms and an adequate number of hearing rooms that will permit the seating of larger audiences.

Specifically, the Maryland General Assembly should provide an adequate number of committee hearing rooms to permit seating of larger audiences at hearings.

MASSACHUSETTS (29)

Functional, 32; Accountable, 35; Informed, 22; Independent, 21;
Representative, 23

GENERAL: The Massachusetts General Court meets in annual unlimited sessions. In the area of pre-session activity the legislature
is particularly strong: eighty percent to eighty-five percent of all
bills introduced are drafted, filed, printed, and assigned to committee
before the session begins.

The Legislative Reference Bureau, a small central research bureau
of nine professionals, is noted for the excellence of its studies. Its
small size, however, acts as a natural limitation upon the number of
assignments it can accept.

The fact that all substantive committees are joint committees allows
the provision of staff for all committees to be accomplished at a
substantial monetary savings over separate House and Senate staffs.
The Ways and Means Committee of each house already has a separate
professional staff. An important defect in the operation of committees,
however, is that they meet, as a regular practice, while both houses
are in session.

Massachusetts voters at the November, 1970, general election approved
a mandatory decennial census of every city and town for apportionment
purposes, beginning in 1971, which will be the basis for the division
of the state into single-member legislative districts.

These are the recommendations for the Massachusetts Legislature.

1. REDUCE THE OVERALL SIZE OF THE LEGISLATURE. Although
size reduction in a legislative body is extremely difficult to
achieve, it has been done in some states - such as in Vermont
and Iowa - and needs to be accomplished in others (New Hampshire,
Massachusetts, Georgia, and Pennsylvania). Where reduction in
size has occurred, it has most often required a constitutional
convention to accomplish it. In a few cases it has been done by
legislatively adopted constitutional amendment (Iowa, in 1968,
which becomes effective in November, 1971) ratified by the voters.
There should be 100 or fewer members in the house. The combined size of both houses should be between 100 and 150.

With 240 members, the House of the Massachusetts Legislature
is the second largest state legislative body in the United States.

2. INCREASE LEGISLATIVE COMPENSATION. No legislative sala-
    ries in the United States should be below the $10,000 a year level.
    Compensation of legislators in the larger states should be in the
    $20,000 to $30,000 range.

    Salaries of members of the legislature are far too low in com-
    parison with states of similar size and development. Current
    salaries are $11,400 per year plus $1,200 and a per diem rate
    for expenses. Compensation should be increased to the $20,000
    to $30,000 a year level.

3. COMMITTEE JURISDICTION. A description of the jurisdiction
    of committees should be contained in the rules of both houses,
    and assignment of bills should be made in accord with the juris-
    diction of committees as described in the rules.

    Precision in the assignment of bills to committee is of added
    importance in the case of Massachusetts, since all of its substan-
    tive committees are joint and bills are assigned by either house.

4. RECORD AND PUBLISH PROCEEDINGS OF COMMITTEES.
    Record and publish the record of committee hearings, proceedings,
    and votes.

    The practice of debating and voting on bills in executive sessions
    should be discontinued.

5. PUBLISH COMMITTEE ROLL CALLS. The committee report of
    action on bills to the respective houses should include those roll
    calls which are taken, showing how each member voted. These
    committee reports should be available to the press and public.
    Published roll calls should apply to those bills recommended for
    approval as well as those killed.

6. INTERIM COMMITTEES. When the legislature is not in session,
    the standing committees should become the interim committees
    for the purpose of conducting long-range studies of state policy
    issues. The Legislative Council or some similarly constituted,
    bi-partisan committee should serve as the supervising agency
    for interim committees and their studies, budgets, and personnel.
    The major committees should be staffed on a year-round basis.

    Although the General Court meets throughout the entire year,
    its standing committees cannot sit while it stands in recess
    unless expressly authorized to do so by a concurrent vote of each
    house. When the legislature is not in session, the standing com-
    mittees should be able to continue their activities without inter-
    ruption or the need for special approval.

7. INTERIM COMMITTEE REPORTING. Interim committees should be required to render formal reports concerning the topics they were charged with responsibility for investigating. These reports should cover the committee's recommendations, including drafts of proposed legislation where appropriate.

   The present practice of requiring only those committees and commissions specifically instructed to render reports should be discontinued. The reports of any interim group should be reproduced in sufficient number to meet public and legislative demand. Public access to any report should be guaranteed.

8. SUPPORT OF DISTRICT OFFICES. District offices are vital to the effective representation by a legislator of his constituency. The legislature should make some contribution to the support of district offices for its members, and the amount of this contribution should be increased over time.

   The Massachusetts Legislature should make a start toward meeting this objective by making a contribution toward the cost of district offices.

9. STRENGTHEN STAFF (RANK-AND-FILE MEMBERS). Rank-and-file members (majority and minority party on an equal basis) should be provided with individual staff assistance consisting of a minimum of an administrative assistant at the professional level and a secretary. Eventually, this should increase to the stated level of support both in the capital and in a district office.

10. STRENGTHEN STAFF SUPPORT. Legislative research, fiscal, legal, and planning agencies should be adequately staffed to full utility and at suitable salary levels for professional qualification. Professional staffing should be at a level to enable the legislature to conduct continuous, year-round examination of state resources and expenditures as well as program review and evaluation of state agencies. This staff should also prepare fiscal notes accompanying all appropriation bills, evaluating their fiscal impact over the short and long term. Staff agencies should be upgraded to the level at which competent and timely service can be provided to every member of the legislature.

    The Legislative Research Bureau is a competent, but highly understaffed, research arm of the legislature. Its staff should be enlarged, and as the Research Bureau's staff is increased, the need to upgrade their present physical quarters will be further emphasized.

11. COMMITTEE STAFFING. Standing committees should be staffed on a permanent, year-round basis.

12. **STRENGTHEN MINORITY PARTY ROLE.** Internal accountability, as well as the capacity of all legislators to represent their constituents effectively, depends upon the opportunity of minority party members to have an effective part in internal legislative affairs.

13. **STATEMENT OF INTENT BY AUTHOR OF A BILL.** The form in which a bill is introduced should include a statement by the author describing, in laymen's language, what the bill is intended to accomplish.

14. **BILL SUMMARY BY BILL-DRAFTING SERVICE.** The form in which bills are introduced should include a more extensive summar of the provisions of the bill prepared by the bill-drafting service.

15. **REQUIRE ROLL CALL ON PASSAGE OF BILLS.** A recorded roll call should be required on final passage of any legislative measure, and it should require a constitutional majority to pass any bill on final action by either house.

16. **REPRINT AMENDED BILLS.** When a bill is amended substantially, it should be reprinted and returned to the legislature with no more than an overnight delay. The reprint should show clearly the original text of the bill as well as the change created by the amendment.

17. **WASHINGTON, D.C., OFFICE FOR THE LEGISLATURE.** With the large and growing volume of activity generated by state-federal relationships, the legislature, beyond merely reacting to federal legislation, should be 'in a position to influence the development of new programs in accordance with the interests of the state. To do so, the legislature should have an office in the nation's capital to represent it and to be its most direct liaison with the Congress.

    For small states, consideration might be given to joining with a number of sister states (either on a geographical or on a population basis) for the purpose of sharing the services of a Washington office. But in large states, the volume of inter-governmental traffic has reached a stage at which it would benefit the legislature greatly to have a full-time Washington office.

18. **INDIVIDUAL OFFICES.** Provide private, individual offices for every member of the legislature, with nearby space for their assistants. The quality and amount of office space should not differ substantially between majority and minority party members.

Within the last biennium, every member of the General Court received, for the first time, some kind of office space. For Senators, that meant an office shared with one and sometimes two other Senators, but for Representatives it meant a desk in a large room housing ten or more other members of the House. Neither situation is adequate from the standpoint of privacy, storage space for records, books, and documents, or adjacent space for secretarial or professional assistants.

19. IMPROVE PRESS FACILITIES. Improved press facilities aid in the coverage of the work of the legislature. Committee rooms, and both chambers or galleries, should provide adequate space for the news media as well as lighting and electrical power connections for their equipment. Conference or interview rooms and office space should also be provided for the news media.

20. PRACTICE BEFORE REGULATORY AGENCIES. Legislators or their firms should be prohibited from practicing before state regulatory agencies or in matters concerning state agencies for a fee.

PROHIBIT APPOINTMENT TO STATE OFFICE. There should be a prohibition against a legislator accepting appointment to other state office during the term for which he is elected or within two years of the termination of the service as a member of the legislature.

HOLDING OTHER PUBLIC OFFICE. Legislators should be prohibited from concurrently holding other continuing, paid public office.

FAMILY EMPLOYMENT. Members of a legislator's immediate family should be barred from employment by the legislature.

21. SERVICE AGENCY FACILITIES. Space for service agencies should provide adequate working space for professional and clerical staff as well as library, files, and other storage requirements.

MICHIGAN (8)

Functional, 15; Accountable, 22; Informed, 9; Independent, 12; Representative, 3

GENERAL: The eighth-ranked Michigan Legislature displays a mixture of good and bad features of legislative structure, organization, procedure, and availability of decision-making resources.

Those features which contribute to the strengths of the Michigan Legislature include an extensive range of professional staff services;

the ability to maintain a continuous review of state expenditures and resources as well as the capacity to conduct program review and evaluation of state agencies; the provision of fiscal notes prepared by legislative staff, evaluating the financial impact of proposed legislation; annual unlimited sessions; single-member districts; and pre-session orientation of members.

Legislative salaries are $17,000 per year (increased from $15,000 on January 1, 1971, by action of the State Officers' Compensation Commission) plus expense allowance of $3,000 per year.

A record of committee roll call votes is publicly available; there is live radio and television coverage of House and Senate sessions and committee hearings; and there is an information officer for each party in each house.

Regulation of conflict of interest includes prohibiting legislators or their firms from practicing before state regulatory agencies (except adversary proceedings) or in matters concerning state agencies for a fee, or from doing business with state agencies; and it includes prohibitions against legislators holding other paid public office or accepting appointment to such office during the term for which they were elected.

At the time information was gathered for this report, physical facilities such as member offices, press facilities, and staff space ranged from barely adequate to inadequate. Since that time, however, a major renovation of the capital has been completed, resulting in a considerabl upgrading of these physical facilities.

There are a number of areas in which improvements can be made in the Michigan Legislature. The following are specific recommendations toward those ends.

1.   REDUCE THE NUMBER OF COMMITTEES. Ideally, there should be from ten to fifteen committees in each house, parallel in jurisdiction. This would reduce the general complexity of the legislature and would permit reducing the number of committee assignments per member.

At present there are thirty-two committees in the House and fifteen in the Senate. The House should reduce the number of its committees to fifteen, as in the Senate, making them parallel in jurisdiction. Adoption of this recommendation would permit a reduction in the number of committee assignments per member of the House. At present, thirty-six percent of the House members serve on more than three committees.

REDUCE THE NUMBER OF COMMITTEE ASSIGNMENTS. In order to make it possible for members to concentrate their attention and contribute effectively, there should be no more than three committee assignments for each member of the lower house and four committee assignments for each member of the Senate.

The multiplicity of assignments introduces problems of scheduling, strains the focus of attention on the part of members, and creates an inordinately heavy workload for members if committees are as active as they should be.

2.   COMMITTEE JURISDICTION. A description of the jurisdiction of committees should be contained in the rules of both house, and assignment of bills should be made in accord with the jurisdiction of committees as described in the rules.

3.   JOINT RULES. There should be joint rules governing the relationship and the flow of legislation between the two houses of the legislature.

In the past, the Michigan Legislature has adopted joint rules governing the flow of legislation between the two houses. During the past biennium, no joint rules were adopted. It is important that the joint rules be adopted on the first day of the session or during the first week of the session at the very latest.

4.   UNIFORM PUBLISHED RULES. There should be uniform, orderly, and reasonable published rules of procedure in each house.

The House rules give only minimal reference to committee rules. The House rules should be amended to spell out the rules of committee procedure, as is done in the Senate.

5.   RECORD AND PUBLISH PROCEEDINGS OF COMMITTEES. Record and publish the record of committee hearings, proceedings, and votes.

At present, only the roll calls are published from committee proceedings.

6.   COMMITTEE BILL REPORTS. Require committees to issue reports describing and explaining the committee's action on bills recommended for passage at the time the bill moves from the committee to the floor.

7.   LEGISLATIVE POWER TO CALL SPECIAL SESSIONS. Amend the constitution to permit the legislature to convene special

sessions either by petition of a majority of the members of both houses or the call of the presiding officer of each house.

8. POWER TO EXPAND SPECIAL SESSION AGENDA. Amend the constitution to permit the legislature to broaden the subject matter of a governor's call of a special session by a majority vote in each house, or prohibit the restriction of the agenda by the governor.

9. STRENGTHEN MINORITY PARTY ROLE. Internal accountability, as well as the capacity of all legislators to represent their constituents effectively, depends upon the opportunity of minority party members to have an effective part in internal legislative affairs.

   Minority representation on the Committee on Rules and/or Management Committee of the respective houses should approximate the proportion of minority representation in each house. Minority party members on committees should be appointed by the minority leader in each house. Although this has been done occasionally in the past as a matter of practice, the requirement should be incorporated in the rules in Michigan.

10. WASHINGTON, D.C., OFFICE FOR THE LEGISLATURE. With the large and growing volume of activity generated by state-federal relationships, the legislature, beyond merely reacting to federal legislation, should be in a position to influence the development of new programs in accordance with the interests of the state. To do so, the legislature should have an office in the nation's capital to represent it and to be its most direct liaison with the Congress.

    For small states, consideration might be given to joining with a number of sister states (either on a geographical or on a population basis) for the purpose of sharing the services of a Washington office. But in large states, the volume of inter-governmental traffic has reached a stage at which it would benefit the legislature greatly to have a full-time Washington office.

11. SUPPORT OF DISTRICT OFFICES. District offices are vital to the effective representation by a legislator of his constituency. The legislature should make some contribution to the support of district offices for its members, and the amount of this contribution should be increased over time.

12. STRENGTHEN STAFF (RANK-AND-FILE MEMBERS). Rank-and-file members (majority and minority party on an equal basis)

should be provided with individual staff assistance consisting of a minimum of an administrative assistant at the professional level and a secretary. Eventually, this should increase to the stated level of support both in the capital and in a district office.

13. INTERIM COMMITTEE REPORTING. Interim committees should be required to render formal reports concerning the topics they were charged with responsibility for investigating. These reports should cover the committee's recommendations, including drafts of proposed legislation where appropriate.

   Although the rules in Michigan's Legislature presently require interim committee reports, too often the practice fails to conform. This requirement should be enforced, and committees which fail to file reports should not be provided budgets for further investigations.

14. IMPROVED PHYSICAL FACILITIES. Although the renovation of the Michigan capital building has resulted in improved physical facilities, it will not be long before these facilities become inadequate due to pressures of growth. Plans for a new capital building have long been under consideration. Because the proposed building would require a number of years to complete, it is important that these or similar plans be implemented and that construction begin as soon as possible.

15. BILL DEADLINES. The orderly flow of work through the legislature depends upon the existence of a series of deadlines at various critical stages throughout the legislative process. These deadlines should be adopted as part of the rules and should be consistently enforced.

   These deadlines have been used in the past, but the rules have fallen into disuse. They should be re-established and observed.

16. ELECTRIC ROLL CALL RECORDER. An electric roll call recorder should be installed in the Senate, as in the House. This is recommended not simply because it would speed up the proceedings (worthwhile as this may be), but because it is an efficient method of producing an error-free record of roll call votes.

17. STATEMENT OF INTENT BY AUTHOR OF A BILL. The form in which a bill is introduced should include a statement by the author describing, in laymen's language, what the bill is intended to accomplish.

MINNESOTA (10)

Functional, 27; Accountable, 7; Informed, 13; Independent, 23;
Representative, 12

GENERAL: The Minnesota Legislature ranks 10th in its overall
characteristics. Its outstanding feature is the general openness and
accessibility of its processes and activities as shown by its relatively
high position (7) on the scale which measures accountability.

Constitutional session limitations, low salaries, and limited supporting
services for members (staff, information resources, etc.) account for
some of the weaknesses of the Minnesota Legislature.

Areas of potential improvement are spelled out in the following
recommendations.

1.   REDUCE THE OVERALL SIZE OF THE LEGISLATURE. Although
     size reduction in a legislative body is extremely difficult to
     achieve, it has been done in some states - such as in Vermont and
     Iowa - and needs to be accomplished in others (New Hampshire,
     Massachusetts, Georgia, and Pennsylvania). Where reduction
     in size has occurred, it has most often required a constitutional
     convention to accomplish it. In a few cases it has been done by
     legislatively adopted constitutional amendment (Iowa, in 1968,
     which becomes effective in November, 1971) ratified by the voters.
     There should be 100 or fewer members in the house. The combine
     size of both houses should be betwen 100 and 150.

     With 135 members of the House and sixty-seven members of the
     Senate, for a total number of 202, Minnesota has the largest
     Senate and the eighth largest legislature in the United States
     (New Hampshire, 424; Massachusetts, 280; Pennsylvania, 253;
     Georgia, 251; Illinois, 235; Connecticut, 213; New York, 207).
     The size of either one or both of the houses should be reduced
     to a combined number between 100 and 150.

2.   REDUCE THE NUMBER OF COMMITTEES. Ideally, there should
     be from ten to fifteen committees in each house parallel in
     jurisdiction. This would reduce the general complexity of the
     legislature and would permit reducing the number of committee
     assignments per member.

     There are twenty-eight committees in the House and eighteen in
     the Senate. Ideally, there should be from ten to fifteen committees
     in each house, parallel in jurisdiction.

3.   REDUCE THE NUMBER OF COMMITTEE ASSIGNMENTS. In
     order to make it possible for members to concentrate their at-
     tention and contribute effectively, there should be no more than
     three committee assignments for each member of the lower house
     and four committee assignments for each member of the Senate.
     The multiplicity of assignments introduces problems of scheduling,
     strains the focus of attention on the part of members, and creates
     an inordinately heavy workload for members if committees are
     as active as they should be.

4.   REMOVE CONSTITUTIONAL RESTRICTIONS ON SESSION AND
     INTERIM TIME. The legislature should have authority to function
     throughout a two-year term; ideally, this authority should provide
     a flexible biennial session pattern that permits the legislature
     to convene, recess, and reconvene as it deems desirable. The
     legislature should be able to meet in general session or conduct
     interim work as it deems necessary at any time throughout the
     period.

     A more modest but significant improvement could be achieved
     by amending the constitution to provide that the current limitation
     of 120 legislative days may be distributed throughout the biennial
     period rather than just the odd years.

5.   PRE-SESSION ORGANIZATIONAL MEETING. Amend the con-
     stitution to provide a pre-session organizing session following
     a general election. Some states make advantageous use of such
     a session during November or December of a general election
     year for the purpose of electing leaders, appointing committee
     chairmen, assigning members to committees, referring pre-filed
     bills to committee, holding committee organizational meetings,
     and conducting orientation conferences for new, as well as re-
     turning members, of the legislature. Through such pre-session
     meetings the committees can begin their work before the regular
     session convenes. This makes it possible to delay the start of
     the regular session until legislation is ready for floor action.

     PRE-SESSION ORIENTATION CONFERENCE. The legislature
     should hold an orientation conference for new legislators, pre-
     ferably after each general election. Orientation conferences
     enable members to speed the process of becoming more effective
     representatives, and they provide an opportunity for legislators
     to examine large policy areas apart from the pressure of the
     regular session.

6.   INCREASE LEGISLATIVE COMPENSATION. No legislative
     salaries in the United States should be below the $10,000 a year

level. Compensation of legislators in the larger states should
be in the $20,000 to $30,000 range.

Salaries of members of the legislature are far too low in comparison with states of similar size and development. Current
salaries of $4,800 should be doubled immediately and increased
again within the next few years as other improvements in the
legislature are made.

7. STRENGTHEN MINORITY PARTY ROLE. Internal accountability,
as well as the capacity of all legislators to represent their constituents effectively, depends upon the opportunity of minority
party members to have an effective part in internal legislative
affairs.

MINORITY REPRESENTATION ON COMMITTEE ON RULES.
Minority representation on the Committee on Rules should approximate the minority party proportion of the membership of
the appropriate house.

8. MINORITY PARTY MEMBERS ON COMMITTEE. Minority
party members in the Senate should be formally appointed to
committees by the minority leader in consultation with the minority caucus, as is done in the House.

9. COMMITTEE BILL REPORTS. Require committees to issue
reports describing and explaining the committee's action on bills
recommended for passage at the time the bill moves from the
committee to the floor.

10. INTERIM COMMITTEES. When the legislature is not in session,
the standing committees should become the interim committees
for the purpose of conducting long-range studies of state policy
issues. The Legislative Council or some similarly constituted,
bi-partisan committee should serve as the supervising agency
for interim committees and their studies, budgets, and personnel.
The major committees should be staffed on a year-round basis.

Presently twenty-one of the twenty-eight House standing committees have interim status. In the Senate, committees must request
interim status. All standing committees should automatically
become interim committees at the end of the session.

11. STRENGTHEN STAFF SUPPORT (LEADERS). Staff assistance
should be provided to all leaders of both the majority and minority parties. Such assistance should include a secretary and
an administrative assistant at the professional level, with space

to work reasonably adjacent to the offices of members and
leaders.

STRENGTHEN STAFF (RANK-AND-FILE MEMBERS). Rank-
and-file members (majority and minority party on an equal basis)
should be provided with individual staff assistance consisting of
a minimum of an administrative assistant at the professional
level and a secretary. Eventually, this should increase to the
stated level of support both in the capital and in a district office.

12. TRAVEL EXPENSES. Members of the legislature should be reimbursed for travel expenses incurred while carrying out their
legislative duties.

13. INDIVIDUAL OFFICES. Provide private, individual offices for
every member of the legislature, with nearby space for their
assistants. The quality and amount of office space should not
differ substantially between majority and minority party members.

14. WASHINGTON, D.C., OFFICE FOR THE LEGISLATURE. With
the large and growing volume of activity generated by state-federal
relationships, the legislature, beyond merely reacting to federal
legislation, should be in a position to influence the development
of new programs in accordance with the interests of the state.
To do so, the legislature should have an office in the nation's
capital to represent it and to be its most direct liaison with the
Congress.

For small states, consideration might be given to joining with
a number of sister states (either on a geographical or on a population basis) for the purpose of sharing the services of a Washington office. But in large states, the volume of inter-governmental
traffic has reached a stage at which it would benefit the legislature
greatly to have a full-time Washington office.

MISSISSIPPI (42)

Functional, 46; Accountable, 43; Informed, 45; Independent, 20; Representative, 28

GENERAL: The Mississippi Legislature recently employed the
Eagleton Institute of Politics to review in depth its internal operations
and procedures and to make recommendations for their improvement.
Eagleton's final report has been submitted to the legislature, which
is considering implementation of the various recommendations.

In June, 1968, voters approved a constitutional amendment providing for annual sessions of 125 days of the first year of the legislature's four year term and of ninety days for the second, third, and fourth years of that term (both Representatives and Senators serve four-year terms in Mississippi).

During the 1970 session the House created a House Management Committee that has the authority to schedule, upon request, interim meeting of the standing committees and to also provide staff for the standing committee during the session as well as the interim. The additional duties of the Management Committee relate to internal housekeeping tasks. The committee has its own staff of four professionals.

The House, in 1970, also created a House Post-Audit Department, but at this time it has not been possible to determine the full range and extent of its duties.

These advances foretell what could be accomplished by implementing some or all of the following recommendations.

1. REDUCE THE NUMBER OF COMMITTEES. Ideally, there should be from ten to fifteen committees in each house, parallel in jurisdiction. This would reduce the general complexity of the legislature and would permit reducing the number of committee assignments per member.

    Mississippi, with thirty-eight standing committees in the House and forty-two in the Senate, has the largest number of standing committees among the fifty state legislatures. There are clearly far more committees than should be necessary for the effective organization of work.

2. REDUCE THE NUMBER OF COMMITTEE ASSIGNMENTS. In order to make it possible for members to concentrate their attention and contribute effectively, there should be no more than three committee assignments for each member of the lower house and four committee assignments for each member of the Senate. The multiplicity of assignments introduces problems of scheduling, strains the focus of attention on the part of members, and creates an inordinately heavy workload for members if committees are as active as they should be.

    Of the House members, 99 percent have more than three committee assignments, and 100 percent of the Senate membership has more than four assignments.

3. OPEN COMMITTEES. The rules of each house should prohibit secret meetings except in matters affecting the security of the

state, or which could unnecessarily damage the reputation of
individuals in personnel matters. Such exceptions should be
sparingly and responsibly employed.

4.   COMMITTEE JURISDICTION. A description of the jurisdiction
of committees should be contained in the rules of both houses,
and assignment of bills should be made in accord with the jurisdiction of committees as described in the rules.

5.   COMMITTEE HEARINGS. There is no justification for permitting
any major piece of legislation to become law without having been
subjected to extensive, thorough, well-planned, and well-prepared
public hearings, in which representatives of the public, civic
organizations, and interest groups are not only invited but encouraged to participate.

6.   ACT ON ALL BILLS. Committees should be required to report
on all bills assigned to them, recommending for passage by the
parent body those bills which enjoy the support of a majority of
the members of the committee and killing all others.

7.   NOTICE OF MEETINGS. The rules should require a minimum
notice of five legislative days for committee meetings and hearings, with widely disseminated announcement of schedule, location,
agenda, and availability of public participation.

8.   RECORD AND PUBLISH PROCEEDINGS OF COMMITTEES.
Record and publish the record of committee hearings, proceedings,
and votes.

9.   PUBLISH COMMITTEE ROLL CALLS. The committee report of
action on bills to the respective houses should include those roll
calls which are taken, showing how each member voted. These
committee reports should be available to the press and public.
Published roll calls should apply to those bills recommended
for approval as well as those killed.

10.   DUAL COMMITTEE CONSIDERATION OF APPROPRIATION
BILLS. There should be a rule requiring dual committee consideration of legislation affecting significant sums of money.
Such legislation, when considered and acted upon favorably by
a substantive policy committee, should then automatically be
referred to the Finance Committee for consideration of its fiscal
impact.

11.   ESTABLISH AN AUTOMATIC CALENDAR OF BILLS. When a
bill is favorably reported out of committee to the floor, it should
go automatically onto the calendar in the order in which it was

reported out. It should require a vote of an extraordinary majority to move a bill from its position on calendar or to bypass it.
The rules committee should have no part in the scheduling of
bills. No session should adjourn until all bills on calendar have
been voted up or down or, by the vote of an extraordinary majority, have been moved from the calendar.

12. LEGISLATIVE POWER TO CALL SPECIAL SESSIONS. Amend
the constitution to permit the legislature to convene special sessions either by petition of a majority of the members of both
houses or the call of the presiding officer of each house.

13. POWER TO EXPAND SPECIAL SESSION AGENDA. Amend the
constitution to permit the legislature to broaden the subject matter of a governor's call of a special session by a majority vote
in each house, or prohibit the restriction of the agenda by the
governor.

14. INTERIM COMMITTEES. When the legislature is not in session,
the standing committees should become the interim committees
for the purpose of conducting long-range studies of state policy
issues. The Legislative Council or some similarly constituted,
bi-partisan committee should serve as the supervising agency
for interim committees and their studies, budgets, and personnel.
The major committees should be staffed on a year-round basis.

INTERIM COMMITTEE REPORTING. Interim committees should
be required to render formal reports concerning the topics they
were charged with responsibility for investigating. These reports
should cover the committee's recommendations, including drafts
of proposed legislation where appropriate.

To the present, the legislature has not effectively organized
itself to carry out its responsibilities during the interim. The
General Legislative Investigating Committee, composed of three
members of each house, is empowered to meet year-round,
although the bulk of its activity takes place between sessions.
The newly created (1970 regular session) House Management
Committee is also empowered to meet year-round. It can, as
well, upon the request of the chairman of any House standing
committee, authorize any standing committee (or subcommittee
thereof) to meet during any period the legislature is not in session.
The Management Committee can also employ staff for interim
committees. All other interim work is done by ad hoc, temporary,
committees established by the leadership to study specifically
designated topics. We recommend that when the legislature is
not in session, the standing committees (reduced in number,

according to Mississippi recommendation no. 1) should become
the interim committees for the purpose of conducting long-range
studies and investigations of state policy issues. The General
Legislative Investigation Committee is required, as no other
legislative committee is, to keep full and complete minutes and
records of all its proceedings. We recommend that this procedure
be adopted by all interim committees and that interim committees
should be required to render formal and public reports concerning
the topics they were charged with responsibility for investigating.

15. STRENGTHEN STAFF SUPPORT. Legislative research, fiscal,
legal, and planning agencies should be adequately staffed to full
utility and at suitable salary levels for professional qualification.
Professional staffing should be at a level to enable the legislature
to conduct continous, year-round examination of state resources
and expenditures as well as program review and evaluation of
state agencies. This staff should also prepare fiscal notes accompanying all appropriation bills, evaluating their fiscal impact
over the short and long term. Staff agencies should be upgraded
to the level at which competent and timely service can be provided
to every member of the legislature.

The Mississippi Legislature does not employ any full-time professional staff people in any capacity. Three bill draftsmen are
employed during a legislative session. In addition, on a specific
request basis, the staff of the state library supplies some refer-
ence-type assistance. The House Management Committee (created
in the 1970 regular session) is authorized to supply professional
staff assistance to standing committees, upon the request of a
committee's chairman, (interim, too). The Senate has no comparable committee. As a beginning, a centralized staff bureau
to provide bill-drafting, fiscal, and basic research services
should be created and staffed.

16. COMMITTEE STAFFING. Standing committees should be staffed
on a permanent, year-round basis.

The major committees of both houses should be provided professional assistants immediately, and all committees (reduced
in number, as previously recommended) within the near future.

17. STRENGTHEN STAFF SUPPORT (LEADERS). Staff assistance
should be provided to all leaders of both the majority and the
minority parties. Such assistance should include a secretary
and an administrative assistant at the professional level, with
space to work reasonably adjacent to the offices of members
and leaders.

The speaker and president pro tem should be provided with assistants at a professional level, too. Clerical personnel should
be made immediately available: to leaders on an individual basis,
not exceeding the ratio of one secretarial person for every three
members.

18. **LEGISLATIVE SALARIES.** Legislative salaries should be set
by statute and paid in equal monthly installments throughout the
biennium, and all unvouchered expense allowances should be
incorporated into an annual salary. Actual and necessary expenses
incurred in the process of carrying out legislative duties should
be reimbursed upon submission and approval of properly vouchered
evidence of expenditures.

INCREASE LEGISLATIVE COMPENSATION. No legislative
salaries in the United States should be below the $10,000 a year
level. Compensation of legislators in the larger states should
be in the $20,000 to $30,000 range.

19. **BILL DEADLINES.** The orderly flow of work through the legislature depends upon the existence of a series of deadlines at
various critical stages throughout the legislative process. These
deadlines should be adopted as part of the rules and should be
consistently enforced.

20. **REPRINTED AMENDED BILLS.** When a bill is amended substantially, it should be reprinted and returned to the legislature
with no more than an overnight delay. The reprint should show
clearly the original text of the bill as well as the change created
by the amendment.

21. **STATEMENT OF INTENT BY AUTHOR OF A BILL.** The form
in which a bill is introduced should include a statement by the
author describing, in laymen's language, what the bill is intended
to accomplish.

22. **BILL SUMMARY BY BILL-DRAFTING SERVICE.** The form in
which bills are introduced should include a more extensive summary of the provisions of the bill prepared by the bill-drafting
service.

23. **INDIVIDUAL OFFICES.** Provide private, individual offices for
every member of the legislature, with nearby space for their
assistants. The quality and amount of office space should not
differ substantially between majority and minority party members.

FACILITIES FOR COMMITTEES. Legislative effectiveness
requires that committees have adequate physical facilities in

which to do their work. This includes an adequate number of
committee rooms and an adequate number of hearing rooms
that will permit the seating of larger audiences.

SERVICE AGENCY FACILITIES. Space for service agencies
should provide adequate working space for professional and
clerical staff as well as library, files, and other storage requirements.

IMPROVE PRESS FACILITIES. Improved press facilities aid
in the coverage of the work of the legislature. Committee rooms,
and both chambers or galleries, should provide adequate space
for the news media as well as lighting and electrical power connections for their equipment. Conference or interview rooms
and office space should also be provided for the news media.

The chambers of both houses lack adequate space for reporters
and electrical connections and lighting to facilitate coverage
by television stations. There are no committee rooms capable
of seating fifty or more spectators. Moreover, the number of
regular committee meeting rooms is small, especially so in
light of the large number of committees in both houses. The
quality of those committee rooms (four in the House, six in the
Senate) is inadequate for legislators, members of the press, and
any spectators. We recommend the legislature immediately secure space in the capital or some other adjacent office building to
provide its committees with working space more suitable to their
needs. Such rooms should have seating for the public and seating/
working space for press representatives as well as tables for
committee members. Only the speaker of the House and the
president of the Senate (lieutenant governor) currently have private office space--and that is inadequate. Their offices should
be improved to meet an acceptable standard, and the president
pro tem of the Senate should also be provided adequate office
space. As a start, rank-and-file members, who currently have
no office space in the capital save their desk on the floor of the
chamber, should be provided at least shared office accommodations. While desirable that all offices be located in the capital,
it may be necessary to locate offices for the general membership
outside the capital building. Space problems are so critical in
Mississippi that the legislature should give immediate attention
to alternative solutions, such as a new legislative building or
some realignment of other state offices (perhaps calling for a
new or expanded state office building).

24. PROVIDE SINGLE-.MEMBER DISTRICTS. Legislative districts
in both houses should be single-member.

MISSOURI (35)

Functional, 36; Accountable, 30; Informed, 40; Independent, 49; Representative, 5

GENERAL: The most significant improvement in the Missouri Legislature in recent years was the passage of a constitutional amendment in the 1970 general election. The amendment provides for annual sessions (6.5 months in odd year, four months during even year); bill carry-over from the first session of the biennium to the second; automatic legislative review of gubernatorial vetoes; and removal of all salary limitations from the constitution, thus allowing compensation to be set by law and making the current $10 per diem expense allowance payable for every day the General Assembly is in session. The unique section of the constitution limiting the number of employees for each house (125 in the House, seventy-five in the Senate) was retained, but the phrase "unless otherwise provided by law" was appended to that section.

All Missouri Senators and the major leadership positions in both houses have better-than-average working conditions. Each has individual offices of good quality with adjacent space for staff. In addition, the leadership has convenient conference rooms available. All Senators and the leadership of both houses have individual secretaries.

To encourage additional improvement and modernization of the General Assembly, Missouri citizens should form a citizens' commission to study the General Assembly and make recommendations, as has been done in other states. These proposed recommendations might serve as a guide for such a commission.

1.   LEGISLATIVE POWER TO CALL SPECIAL SESSIONS. Amend the constitution to permit the legislature to convene special sessions either by petition of a majority of the members of both houses or the call of the presiding officer of each house.

2.   POWER TO EXPAND SPECIAL SESSION AGENDA. Amend the constitution to permit the legislature to broaden the subject matter of a governor's call of a special session by a majority vote in each house, or prohibit the restriction of the agenda by the governor.

3.   PRE-SESSION ORGANIZATIONAL MEETING. Amend the constitution to provide a pre-session organizing session following a general election. Some states make advantageous use of such a session during November or December of a general election

year for the purpose of electing leaders, appointing committee chairmen, assigning members to committees, referring pre-filed bills to committee, holding committee organizational meetings, and conducting orientation conferences for new, as well as returning, members of the legislature. Through such pre-session meetings the committees can begin their work before the regular session convenes. This makes it possible to delay the start of the regular session until legislation is ready for floor action.

4. PRE-SESSION ORIENTATION CONFERENCE. The legislature should hold an orientation conference for new legislators, preferably after each general election. Orientation conferences enable members to speed the process of becoming more effective representatives, and they provide an opportunity for legislators to examine large policy areas apart from the pressure of the regular session.

5. REDUCE THE OVERALL SIZE OF THE LEGISLATURE. Although size reduction in a legislative body is extremely difficult to achieve, it has been done in some states--such as in Vermont and Iowa--and needs to be accomplished in others (New Hampshire, Massachusetts, Georgia, and Pennsylvania). Where reduction in size has occurred, it has most often required a constitutional convention to accomplish it. In a few cases it has been done by legislatively adopted constitutional amendment (Iowa, in 1968, which becomes effective in November, 1971) ratified by the voters. There should be 100 or fewer members in the house. The combined size of both houses should be between 100 and 150.

With 163 members, the House of the Missouri Legislative is the seventh largest state legislative body in the United States. It is recommended that the House be reduced in numbers from its present 163 to 100 or fewer.

6. REDUCE THE NUMBER OF COMMITTEES. Ideally, there should be from ten to fifteen committees in each house, parallel in jurisdiction. This would reduce the general complexity of the legislature and would permit reducing the number of committee assignments per member.

With forty committees in the House and thirty-one in the Senate, there are more committees than should be necessary for the effective organization of the work.

7. REDUCE THE NUMBER OF COMMITTEE ASSIGNMENTS. In order to make it possible for members to concentrate their

attention and contribute effectively, there should be no more than
three committee assignments for each member of the lower house
and four committee assignments for each member of the Senate.
The multiplicity of assignments introduces problems of scheduling,
strains the focus of attention on the part of members, and creates
an inordinately heavy workload for members if committees are
as active as they should be.

At present, 85 percent of the members of the Senate have more
than four committee assignments each.

8. OPEN COMMITTEES. The rules of each house should prohibit
   secret meetings except in matters affecting the security of the
   state, or which could unnecessarily damage the reputation of
   individuals in personnel matters. Such exceptions should be
   sparingly and responsibly employed.

9. NOTICE OF MEETINGS. The rules should require a minimum
   notice of five legislative days for committee meetings and hearings,
   with widely disseminated announcement of schedule, location,
   agenda, and availability of public participation.

10. ACT ON ALL BILLS. Committees should be required to report
    on all bills assigned to them, recommending for passage by the
    parent body those bills which enjoy the support of a majority of
    the members of the committee and killing all others.

11. COMMITTEE BILL REPORTS. Require committees to issue
    reports describing and explaining the committee's action on bills
    recommended for passage at the time the bill moves from the
    committee to the floor.

12. PUBLISH COMMITTEE ROLL CALLS. The committee report of
    action on bills to the respective houses should include those calls
    which are taken, showing how each member voted. These commit-
    tee reports should be available to the press and public. Published
    roll calls should apply to those bills recommended for approval
    as well as those killed.

13. DUAL COMMITTEE CONSIDERATION OF APPROPRIATION BILLS
    There should be a rule requiring dual committee consideration of
    legislation affecting significant sums of money. Such legislation,
    when considered and acted upon favorably by a substantive policy
    committee, should then automatically be referred to the Finance
    Committee for consideration of its fiscal impact.

14. MANAGEMENT COMMITTEES. There should be an executive or
    management committee created in each house. Its membership

should include the leaders of each party in each house, and the minority party should have representation on the committee in proportion to its numbers in the body as a whole. The Senate/House management committees should combine as a joint management committee. The purpose of these committees should be to assume responsibility for the administrative management (housekeeping) functions relating to personnel, facilities, the research bureaus, budgets, and expenditures of their respective houses. The joint management committee should deal with matters of interhouse coordination.

15. INTERIM COMMITTEES. When the legislature is not in session, the standing committees should become the interim committees for the purpose of conducting long-range studies of state policy issues. The Legislative Council or some similarly constituted, bi-partisan committee should serve as the supervising agency for interim committees and their studies, budgets, and personnel. The major committees should be staffed on a year-round basis.

INTERIM COMMITTEE REPORTING. Interim committees should be required to render formal reports concerning the topics they were charged with responsibility for investigating. These reports should cover the committee's recommendations, including drafts of proposed legislation where appropriate.

16. LEGISLATIVE SALARIES. Legislative salaries should be set by statute and paid in equal monthly installments throughout the biennium, and all unvouchered expense allowances should be incorporated into an annual salary. Actual and necessary expenses incurred in the process of carrying out legislative duties should be reimbursed upon submission and approval of properly vouchered evidence of expenditures.

INCREASE LEGISLATIVE COMPENSATION. No legislative salaries in the United States should be below the $10,000 a year level. Compensation of legislators in the larger states should be in the $20,000 to $30,000 range.

17. EXPENSE ALLOWANCES. Members of the legislature should be allowed an expense reimbursement covering their travel and living costs while engaged in carrying out their legislative duties. The same allowance should obtain during the interim for days in attendance at interim committee meetings or other official and authorized legislative business. These allowances should be provided by statute.

18. BILL DEADLINES. The orderly flow of work through the legislature depends upon the existence of a series of deadlines at

various critical stages throughout the legislative process. These deadlines should be adopted as part of the rules and should be consistently enforced.

19. ESTABLISH AN AUTOMATIC CALENDAR OF BILLS. When a bill is favorably reported out of committee to the floor, it should go automatically onto the calendar in the order in which it was reported out. It should require a vote of an extraordinary majority to move a bill from its position on calendar or to bypass it. The Rules Committee should have no part in the scheduling of bills. No session should adjourn until all bills on calendar have been voted up or down or, by the vote of an extraordinary majority, have been moved from the calendar.

20. REMOVE LEGISLATIVE POWERS FROM LIEUTENANT GOVERNO The exercise of legislative powers, including such pro forma powers as presiding, casting tie-breaking votes, and signing enacted legislation, by the lieutenant governor, whether the powers derive from the constitution or the rule book, would seem to be a particularly serious breach of the separation of powers and the independence of the legislature. The constitution and/or rule book should be amended to permit these legislative powers presently exercised by the lieutenant governor to be set as the responsibility of the office of the president pro tem of the Senate.

21. STRENGTHEN STAFF SUPPORT. Legislative research, fiscal, legal, and planning agencies should be adequately staffed to full utility and at suitable salary levels for professional qualification. Professional staffing should be at a level to enable the legislature to conduct continuous, year-round examination of state resources and expenditures as well as program review and evaluation of state agencies. This staff should also prepare fiscal notes accompanying all appropriation bills, evaluating their fiscal impact over the short and long term. Staff agencies should be upgraded to the level at which competent and timely service can be provided to every member of the legislature.

22. INDIVIDUAL OFFICES. Provide private, individual offices for every member of the legislature, with nearby space for their assistants. The quality and amount of office space should not differ substantially between majority and minority party members.

Missouri Senators now have individual offices of good quality. Individual offices should be provided for all Representatives, who now share offices, and especially to the minority party members.

23. IMPROVE PRESS FACILITIES. Improved press facilities aid in the coverage of the work of the legislature. Committee rooms, and both chambers of galleries, should provide adequate space for the news media as well as lighting and electrical power connections for their equipment. Conference or interview rooms and office space should also be provided for the news media.

24. STRENGTHEN MINORITY PARTY ROLE. Internal accountability, as well as the capacity of all legislators to represent their constituents effectively, depends upon the opportunity of minority party members to have an effective part in internal legislative affairs.

25. BILL SUMMARY BY BILL-DRAFTING SERVICE. The form in which bills are introduced should include a more extensive summary of the provisions of the bill prepared by the bill-drafting service.

26. SPECIAL PROVISIONS. In addition to standard laws governing criminal behavior, there should be special provisions regulating legislative conflicts of interest.

PRACTICE BEFORE REGULATORY AGENCIES. Legislators or their firms should be prohibited from practicing before state regulatory agencies or in matters concerning state agencies for a fee.

PROHIBIT DOING BUSINESS WITH THE STATE. There should be a prohibition against legislators or the firms in which they own a major interest doing business with state agenceis.

27. REGULATION OF LOBBYISTS. The independence of the legislature and public confidence in its processes require the regulation of special-interest advocates. Lobbyists should be required to register with an agency of the legislature, and should be required to disclose who employs them, on behalf of what objectives, how much they are paid, and how much they spend and on whom. This information should be available to the press and the public. There should be specific and automatic penalties for failure to comply with these requirements.

28. TRANSFER AUDIT FUNCTION TO THE LEGISLATURE. A significant part of the legislature's ability to exercise oversight of executive departments and administrative agencies depends upon the power and capacity to conduct audits (financial and functional) of these units of the state government. These functions and responsibilities should be removed from the duties and resources

of the Office of Auditor and be established under a legislative
auditor.

All legislative fiscal affairs should be the direct responsibility of
the legislature or a legislative service agency. This includes
preparation of fiscal notes and exclusive control of its operating
expenditures.

29. ESTABLISH CITIZENS' COMMISSION ON THE LEGISLATURE.
    As a means of cultivating generalized support for the legislature
    as an institution, a citizens' commission should be created by
    joint resolution of the legislature, to study its operations, facilities
    and needs, and to recommend improvements. The appointive power
    should be consigned to the speaker and the president pro tem on
    an equal basis and should include consultation with the minority
    leader of each house. The citizens' commission should conduct
    its review over a two-year period, resulting in recommendations
    to the legislature and the public concerning the role the legislature
    is expected to perform in development of a truly effective and
    responsive state government, and the measures required to reach
    that objective. A key function of the commission is to educate
    the citizenry to problems, opportunities, and needs of the legis-
    lature. This purpose is best served by doing much of its work
    through public hearings conducted in the population centers of
    the state. A commission composed of from twenty-five to thirty-
    five leading citizens, representing various fields of activity,
    interest groups, and areas of the state, can contribute much to
    the development of public support for a more dynamic legislature.

MONTANA (41)

Functional, 26; Accountable, 28; Informed, 31; Independent, 46;
Representative, 49

GENERAL: In December, 1968, the Montana Citizens' Committee on
the State Legislature submitted its second report to the Legislative
Assembly with recommendations for reduction in the size of the
Legislative Assembly; annual sessions; annual compensation; single-
member districts; more adequate staff and services; interim work of
the legislature; and citizens' participation. Few of these recommendations have been adopted to date, but the Citizens' Committee has con-
tinued its attempts to stimulate legislator and public interest in their
recommendations.

In November, 1970, Montana voters approved the calling of a constitutional convention. The following recommendations support and expand
the committee's report.

1. REMOVE CONSTITUTIONAL RESTRICTIONS ON SESSION AND INTERIM TIME. The legislature should have authority to function throughout a two-year term; ideally, this authority should provide a flexible biennial session pattern that permits the legislature to convene, recess, and reconvene as it deems desirable. The legislature should be able to meet in general session or conduct interim work as it deems necessary at any time throughout the period.

   Amend the constitution to permit annual general session, limited to no fewer than ninety legislative days. The legislature should be permitted to reconvene following the completion of bill signing by the governor in order to consider the possibility of overriding vetoes.

2. LEGISLATIVE POWER TO CALL SPECIAL SESSIONS. Amend the constitution to permit the legislature to convene special sessions either by petition of a majority of the members of both houses or the call of the presiding officer of each house.

3. INTERIM COMMITTEES. When the legislature is not in session, the standing committees should become the interim committees for the purpose of conducting long-range studies of state policy issues. The Legislative Council or some similarly constituted, bi-partisan committee should serve as the supervising agency for interim committees and their studies, budgets, and personnel. The major committees should be staffed on a year-roung basis.

4. PROVIDE SINGLE-MEMBER DISTRICTS. Legislative districts in both houses should be single-member.

   In the House twenty-seven of thirty-eight legislative districts are multi-member; in the Senate, eleven of thirty-one are multi-member.

5. STRENGTHEN STAFF SUPPORT. Legislative research, fiscal, legal, and planning agencies should be adequately staffed to full utility and at suitable salary levels for professional qualification. Professional staffing should be at a level to enable the legislature to conduct continuous, year-round examination of state resources and expenditures as well as program review and evaluation of state agencies. This staff should also prepare fiscal notes accompanying all appropriation bills, evaluating their fiscal impact over the short and long term. Staff agencies should be upgraded to the level at which competent and timely service can be provided to every member of the legislature.

   COMMITTEE STAFFING. Standing committees should be staffed on a permanent, year-round basis.

STRENGTHEN STAFF SUPPORT (LEADERS). Staff assistance
should be provided to all leaders of both the majority and minority
parties. Such assistance should include a secretary and an
administrative assistant at the professional level, with space to
work reasonably adjacent to the offices of members and leaders.

STRENGTHEN STAFF (RANK-AND-FILE MEMBERS). Rank-and-
file members (majority and minority party on an equal basis)
should be provided with individual staff assistance consisting of
a minimum of an administrative assistant at the professional
level and a secretary. Eventually, this should increase to the
stated level of support both in the capital and in a district office.

6. INDIVIDUAL OFFICES. Provide private, individual offices for
   every member of the legislature, with nearby space for their
   assistants. The quality and amount of office space should not
   differ substantially between majority and minority party members.

   At a minimum, leaders should have private offices for themselves
   with separate, nearby offices for their assistants. A beginning
   can be made toward providing offices for members by making
   space available for shared offices among small numbers of
   members at first, then gradually reducing the members who share
   space until a private office is provided for each member.

7. FACILITIES FOR COMMITTEES. Legislative effectiveness
   requires that committees have adequate physical facilities in
   which to do their work. This includes an adequate number of
   committee rooms and an adequate number of hearing rooms that
   will permit the seating of larger audiences.

8. LEGISLATIVE SALARIES. Legislative salaries should be set
   by statute and paid in equal monthly installments throughout the
   biennium, and all unvouchered expense allowances should be incorporated into an annual salary. Actual and necessary expenses
   incurred in the process of carrying out legislative duties should
   be reimbursed upon submission and approval of properly vouchered
   evidence of expenditures.

   INCREASE LEGISLATIVE COMPENSATION. No legislative
   salaries in the United States should be below the $10,000 a year
   level. Compensation of legislators in the larger states should
   be in the $20,000 to $30,000 range.

   Salaries of members of the legislature are far too low. Current
   salaries, which average $1,200 per biennium, should be doubled
   immediately and increased again within the next few years as
   other improvements are made.

9. COMMITTEE JURISDICTION. A description of the jurisdiction
   of committees should be contained in the rules of both houses,
   and assignment of bills should be made in accord with the jurisdiction of committees as described in the rules.

10. OPEN COMMITTEES. The rules of each house should prohibit
    secret meetings except in matters affecting the security of the
    state, or which could unnecessarily damage the reputation of
    individuals in personnel matters. Such exceptions should be
    sparingly and responsibly employed.

11. MINORITY PARTY MEMBERS ON COMMITTEE. Minority party
    members should be assigned to committees by the minority leader
    in consultation with the minority caucus.

12. REDUCE THE NUMBER OF COMMITTEES. Ideally, there should
    be from ten to fifteen committees in each house parallel in juris-
    diction. This would reduce the general complexity of the legislature
    and would permit reducing the number of committee assignments
    per member.

    With nineteen committees in the House and twenty-two in the
    Senate, there are more committees than should be necessary for
    the effective organization of the work.

13. REDUCE THE NUMBER OF COMMITTEE ASSIGNMENTS. In
    order to make it possible for members to concentrate their
    attention and contribute effectively, there should be no more
    than three committee assignments for each member of the lower
    house and four committee assignments for each member of the
    Senate. The multiplicity of assignments introduces problems of
    scheduling, strains the focus of attention on the part of members,
    and creates an inordinately heavy workload for members if
    committees are as active as they should be.

    At present sixteen percent of the members in the House have more
    than three committee assignments each, and seventy-seven of
    the Senate have more than four committee assignments each.

14. PUBLISH COMMITTEE ROLL CALLS. The committee report of
    action on bills to the respective houses should include those roll
    calls which are taken, showing how each member voted. These
    committee reports should be available to the press and public.
    Published roll calls should apply to those bills recommended for
    approval as well as those killed.

15. ELECTRIC ROLL CALL RECORDER. The Senate should install
    and use an electric roll call recorder, as in the House. This is

recommended not simply because it would speed up the proceedings (worthwhile as this may be), but because it is an efficient method of producing an error-free record of roll call votes.

16. MANAGEMENT COMMITTEES. There should be an executive or management committee created in each house. Its membership should include the leaders of each party in each house, and the minority party should have representation on the committee in proportion to its numbers in the body as a whole. The Senate/House management committees should combine as a joint management committee. The purpose of these committees should be to assume responsibility for the administrative management (housekeeping) functions relating to personnel, facilities, the research bureaus, budgets, and expenditures of their respective houses. The joint management committee should deal with matters of interhouse coordination.

17. PRACTICE BEFORE REGULATORY AGENCIES. Legislators or their firms should be prohibited from practicing before state regulatory agencies or in matters concerning state agencies for a fee.

PROHIBIT DOING BUSINESS WITH THE STATE. There should be a prohibition against legislators or the firms in which they own a major interest doing business with state agencies.

PROHIBIT APPOINTMENT TO STATE OFFICE. There should be a prohibition against a legislator accepting appointment to other state office during the term for which he is elected or within two years of the termination of his service as a member of the legislature.

HOLDING OTHER PUBLIC OFFICE. Legislators should be prohibited from concurrently holding other continuing, paid public office.

FAMILY EMPLOYMENT. Members of a legislator's immediate family should be barred from employment by the legislature.

18. REMOVE LEGISLATIVE POWERS FORM LIEUTENANT GOVERNOR. The exercise of legislative powers, including such pro forma powers as presiding, casting tie-breaking votes, and signing enacted legislation, by the lieutenant governor, whether the powers derive from the constitution or the rule book, would seem to be a particularly serious breach of the separation of powers and the independence of the legislature. The constitution and/or rule book should be amended to permit these legislative powers

presently exercised by the lieutenant governor to be set as the responsibility of the office of the president pro tem of the Senate.

19. PRINTED BILL DOCUMENT FORMAT. The bill document printing procedure should permit the clear identification of the text of the existing statute which is being amended as well as the material which the bill proposes to delete or add. This is usually accomplished through the use of varying type faces, such as "strikethrough," italics, underlining, or bracketing. It should not be necessary to compare the text of a bill with the text of the existing code in order to determine what the bill does.

Bills should be printed in a standard format upon introduction, in quantity at least twice the number of members.

20. REPRINT AMENDED BILLS. When a bill is amended substantially, it should be reprinted and returned to the legislature with no more than an overnight delay. The reprint should show clearly the original text of the bill as well as the change created by the amendment.

21. SUPPORT OF DISTRICT OFFICES. District offices are vital to the effective representation by a legislator of his constituency. The legislature should make some contribution to the support of district offices for its members, and the amount of this contribution should be increased over time.

22. SERVICE AGENCY FACILITIES. Space for service agencies should provide adequate working space for professional and clerical staff as well as library, files, and other storage requirements.

23. IMPROVE PRESS FACILITIES. Improved press faciliteis aid in the coverage of the work of the legislature. Committee rooms, and both chambers or galleries, should provide adequate space for the news media as well as lighting and electrical power connections for their equipment. Conference or interview rooms and office space should also be provided for the news media.

24. STATEMENT OF INTENT BY AUTHOR OF A BILL. The form in which a bill is introduced should include a statement by the author describing, in laymen's language, what the bill is intended to accomplish.

NEBRASKA (9)

Functional, 35; Accountable, 1; Informed, 16; Independent, 30; Representative, 18

GENERAL: Nebraska's unicameral legislature ranks ninth in this study in overall structure and organization. Many of the difficulties confronting all other legislatures are absent here. There are no problems in inter-house coordination, controlling or regulating conference committees, or management of joint committees. There is no need for joint rules.

Because of factors such as a single house, small size (forty-ninth), and single-member districts, the Nebraska Legislature is the least complex and one of the more comprehensible legislative systems in operation. It ranks first among the fifty state legislatures on the scale measuring attributes of accountability.

The following recommendations are addressed to eliminating the weaknesses of the Nebraska Unicameral. References to general recommendations may call for an improvement in "both Houses"; for Nebraska, they of course mean only the Unicameral.

1. DISCONTINUE ROTATING LEADERSHIP. The practice of limiting presiding officers to a single, two-year term in that position weakens the legislature in its capacity to confront other branches and levels of government as a partner of equal stature and diffuses and disrupts the continuity of leadership within the legislative bodies. Although it is extremely difficult to change a practice such as this, because of its profoundly adverse effects on many aspects of legislative performance, it should be discontinued.

2. REQUIRE PARTISAN IDENTIFICATION. One of the prime purposes served by a legislature is that of focusing public attention on major questions of resource allocation. Another primary legislative purpose is to protect the legitimacy and insure the existence of an opposition. These objectives would seem to be particularly difficult to achieve in the non-partisan Nebraska system. The constitution should be amended to provide for the partisan identification of candidates for seats in the state legislature, and the legislature should organize on the basis of a majority and a minority along partisan lines.

3. REMOVE LEGISLATIVE POWERS FROM LIEUTENANT GOVERNOR The exercise of legislative powers, including such pro forma powers as presiding, casting tie-breaking votes and signing enacted legislation, by the lieutenant governor, whether the powers derive from the constitution or the rule book, would seem to be a particularly serious breach of the separation of powers and the independence of the legislature. The constitution and/or rule book should be amended to permit these legislative powers presently exercised by the lieutenant governor to be set as the

responsibility of the office of the president pro tem of the Senate.

A constitutional amendment to remove the lieutenant governor as
presiding officer of the Unicameral was defeated by the voters
on November 3, 1970.

4. REMOVE CONSTITUTIONAL RESTRICTIONS ON SESSION AND
    INTERIM TIME. The legislature should have authority to function
    throughout a two-year term; ideally, this authority should provide
    a flexible biennial session pattern that permits the legislature
    to convene, recess, and reconvene as it deems desirable. The
    legislature should be able to meet in general session on conduct
    interim work as it deems necessary at any time throughout the
    period.

5. INCREASE LEGISLATIVE COMPENSATION. No legislative
    salaries in the United States should be below the $10,000 a year
    level. Compensation of legislators in the larger states should be
    in the $20,000 to $30,000 range.

    The current salary of Nebraska legislators of $4,800 per year
    should be increased to the $10,000 to $15,000 level. Consideration
    might be given to the establishment of a public commission to
    make appropriate recommendations on all governmental salaries.

6. PRE-SESSION ORGANIZATIONAL MEETING. Amend the consti-
    tution to provide a pre-session organizing session following a
    general election. Some states make advantageous use of such a
    session during November or December of a general election
    year for the purpose of electing leaders, appointing committee
    chairmen, assigning members to committees, referring pre-filed
    bills to committee, holding committee organizational meetings,
    and conducting orientation conferences for new, as well as
    returning, members of the legislature. Through such pre-session
    meetings the committees can begin their work before the regular
    session convenes. This makes it possible to delay the start of
    the regular session until legislation is ready for floor action.

7. COMMITTEE JURISDICTION. A description of the jurisdiction
    of committees should be contained in the rules of both houses,
    and assignment of bills should be made in accord with the juris-
    diction of committees as described in the rules.

8. DUAL COMMITTEE CONSIDERATION OF APPROPRIATION BILLS.
    There should be a rule requiring dual committee consideration
    of legislation affecting significant sums of money. Such legislation,
    when considered and acted upon favorably by a substantive policy

committee, should then automatically be referred to the Finance
Committee for consideration of its fiscal impact.

9. SKELETON BILLS. There should be an explicit rule barring
    introduction of skeleton or "spot" bills. This rule should be
    enforced by the assigning authority (the presiding Officer or
    Rules Committee) by refusal to assign bills so identified to
    committee.

10. PUBLISH COMMITTEE ROLL CALLS. The committee report
    of action on bills to the respective houses should include those
    roll calls which are taken, showing how each member voted.
    These committee reports should be available to the press and
    public. Published roll calls should apply to those bills recom-
    mended for approval as well as those killed.

11. REPRINT AMENDED BILLS. When a bill is amended substantially
    it should be reprinted and returned to the legislature with no
    more than an overnight delay. The reprint should show clearly
    the original text of the bill as well as the change created by the
    amendment.

12. IMPROVE PRESS FACILITIES. Improved press facilities aid
    in the coverage of the work of the legislature. Committee rooms,
    and both chambers or galleries, should provide adequate space
    for the news media as well as lighting and electrical power con-
    nections for their equipment. Conference or interview rooms
    and office space should also be provided for the news media.

    Specific improvements for the Nebraska Legislature include
    the provision of more adequate press office space, the installation
    of electronic media coverage facilities in the chamber, and
    provision for press conference or interview rooms.

13. SPECIAL PROVISIONS. In addition to standard laws governing
    criminal behavior, there should be special provisions regulating
    legislative conflicts of interest.

    PRACTICE BEFORE REGULATORY AGENCIES. Legislators
    or their firms should be prohibited from practicing before state
    regulatory agencies or in matters concerning state agencies for
    a fee.

    PROHIBIT DOING BUSINESS WITH THE STATE. There should
    be a prohibition against legislators or the firms in which they
    own a major interest doing business with state agencies.

HOLDING OTHER PUBLIC OFFICE. Legislators should be prohibited from concurrently holding other continuing, paid public office.

FAMILY EMPLOYMENT. Members of a legislator's immediate family should be barred from employment by the legislature.

14. INTERIM COMMITTEES. When the legislature is not in session, the standing committees should become the interim committees for the purpose of conducting long-range studies of state policy issues. The Legislative Council or some similarly constituted, bi-partisan committee should serve as the supervising agency for interim committees and their studies, budgets, and personnel. The major committees should be staffed on a year-round basis.

15. EXPENSE ALLOWANCES. Members of the legislature should be allowed an expense reimbursement covering their travel and living costs while engaged in carrying out their legislative duties. The same allowance should obtain during the interim for days in attendance at interim committee meetings or other official and authorized legislative business. These allowances should be provided by statute.

16. STRENGTHEN STAFF SUPPORT. Legislative research, fiscal, legal, and planning agencies should be adequately staffed to full utility and at suitable salary levels for professional qualification. Professional staffing should be at a level to enable the legislature to conduct continuous, year-round examination of state resources and expenditures as well as program review and evaluation of state agencies. This staff should also prepare fiscal notes accompanying all appropriation bills, evaluating their fiscal impact over the short and long term. Staff agencies should be upgraded to the level at which competent and timely service can be provided to every member of the legislature.

17. INDIVIDUAL OFFICES. Provide private, individual offices for every member of the legislature, with nearby space for their assistants. The quality and amount of office space should not differ substantially between majority and minority party members.

NEVADA (13)

Functional, 13; Accountable, 10; Informed, 19; Independent, 14; Representative, 32

GENERAL: The Nevada Legislature, which ranks thirteenth in this study, has been fighting an uphill battle to improve its operations against a barrier of public apathy and resistance. The relatively high standing of the legislature of one of the smaller, less developed states testifies to the efforts of its members and staff to create an effective legislative system despite the lack of public support.

The recent history of the Nevada Legislature's efforts to install and maintain annual sessions points to this lack of support. From 1867 to 1957, general sessions of the legislature were restricted to odd-numbered years. In 1958 a constitutional amendment was adopted to provide for annual sessions. However, in the 1960 election voters approved an initiative returning the legislature to biennial sessions; 1960 was the only regular annual session of the legislature.

During the late 1960's a number of other steps were taken in an effort to improve the operations of the legislature and to restore the confidence of the voters in its ability to manage its affairs (including time) competently.

Among the changes brought about were the construction of a new legislative building which provides superior chambers and committee rooms, generally superior offices for legislative leaders, and adequate offices for the news media representatives, though no offices for rank-and-file legislators; a statutory requirement for fiscal notes and a procedural outline to guide their preparation; the creation of a joint (the Assembly Ways and Means and Senate Finance Committees) interim committee to control contingency fund disbursement to state agencies whose spending will exceed the amount of money appropriated for their operations and programs; and an increase in the membership of the Legislative Commission of the Legislative Council Bureau.

In the 1969 general session, the legislature again proposed a constitutional amendment to create annual sessions. On November 3, 1970, this and another to drop the sixty-day limitation on compensation for legislators were defeated by an overwhelming margin after a campaign in which the opposition organized a committee in every county of the state to fight passage of the amendments. A number of intermediary steps can be taken to improve the working conditions of the legislature pending the more difficult implementation of annual sessions. Here are specific recommendations, including the sessions recommendation.

1.   REMOVE CONSTITUTIONAL RESTRICTIONS ON SESSION AND
      INTERIM TIME. The legislature should have authority to function
      throughout a two-year term; ideally, this authority should provide
      a flexible biennial session pattern that permits the legislature
      to convene, recess, and reconvene as it deems desirable. The

legislature should be able to meet in general session or conduct interim work as it deems necessary at any time throughout the period.

2. ESTABLISH CITIZENS' COMMISSION ON THE LEGISLATURE. As a means of cultivating generalized support for the legislature as an institution, a citizens' commission should be created by joint resolution of the legislature, to study its operations, facilities, and needs and to recommend improvements. The appointive power should be consigned to the speaker and the president pro tem on an equal basis and should include consultation with the minority leader of each house. The citizens' commission should conduct its review over a two-year period, resulting in recommendations to the legislature and the public concerning the role the legislature is expected to perform in development of a truly effective and responsive state government, and the measures required to reach that objective. A key function of the commission is to educate the citizenry to problems, opportunities, and needs of the legislature. This purpose is best served by doing much of its work through public hearings conducted in the population centers of the state. A commission composed of from twenty-five to thirty-five leading citizens, representing various fields of activity, interest groups, and areas of the state, can contribute much to the development of public support for a more dynamic legislature.

3. PRE-SESSION ORGANIZATIONAL MEETING. Amend the constitution to provide a pre-session organizing session following a general election. Some states make advantageous use of such a session during November or December of a general election year for the purpose of electing leaders, appointing committee chairmen, assigning members to committees, referring pre-filed bills to committee, holding committee organizational meetings, and conducting orientation conferences for new, as well as returning, members of the legislature. Through such pre-session meetings the committees can begin their work before the regular session convenes. This makes it possible to delay the start of the regular session until legislation is ready for floor action.

PRE-SESSION ORIENTATION CONFERENCE. The legislature should hold an orientation conference for new legislators, preferably after each general election. Orientation conferences enable members to speed the process of becoming more effective representatives, and they provide an opportunity for legislators to examine large policy areas apart from the pressure of the regular session.

4.   INTERIM COMMITTEES. When the legislature is not in session,
     the standing committees should become the interim committees
     for the purpose of conducting long-range studies of state policy
     issues. The Legislative Council or some similarly constituted,
     bi-partisan committee should serve as the supervising agency
     for interim committees and their studies, budgets, and personnel.
     The major committees should be staffed on a year-round basis.

5.   LEGISLATIVE SALARIES. Legislative salaries should be set by
     statute and paid in equal monthly installments throughout the
     biennium, and all unvouchered expense allowances should be in-
     corporated into an annual salary. Actual and necessary expenses
     incurred in the process of carrying out legislative duties should
     be reimbursed upon submission and approval of properly vouchered
     evidence of expenditures.

     The Nevada constitution limits the number of days legislators
     may be paid to sixty days during a regular session and twenty
     days during a special session, while the amount of compensation
     is established by statute. The constitution sh ould be amended
     to delete this restriction.

6.   PROVIDE SINGLE-MEMBER DISTRICTS. Legislative districts
     in both houses should be single-member.

7.   REGULATION OF LOBBYISTS. The independence of the legisla-
     ture and public confidence in its processes require the regulation
     of special interest advocates. Lobbyists should be required to
     register with an agency of the legislature, and should be required
     to disclose who employs them, on behalf of what objectives, how
     much they are paid, and how much they spend and on whom.
     This information should be available to the press and the public.
     There should be specific and automatic penalties for failure to
     comply with these requirements.

8.   SPECIAL PROVISIONS. In addition to standard laws governing
     criminal behavior, there should be special provisions regulating
     legislative conflicts of interest.

     PRACTICE BEFORE REGULATORY AGENCIES. Legislators
     or their firms should be prohibited from practicing before state
     regulatory agencies or in matters concerning state agencies
     for a fee.

     FAMILY EMPLOYMENT. Members of a legislator's immediate
     family should be barred from employment by the legislature.

9. BILL DEADLINES. The orderly flow of work through the legislature depends upon the existence of a series of deadlines at various critical stages throughout the legislative process. These deadlines should be adopted as part of the rules and should be consistently enforced.

10. CONSENT CALENDAR. A consent calendar should be used in both houses.

11. UNIFORM COMMITTEE RULES. There should be uniform published rules of committee procedure in both chambers.

12. COMMITTEE JURISDICTION. A description of the jurisdiction of committees should be contained in the rules of both houses, and assignment of bills should be made in accord with the jurisdiction of committees as described in the rules.

13. PUBLISH COMMITTEE ROLL CALLS. The committee report of action on bills to the respective houses should include those roll calls which are taken, showing how each member voted. These committee reports should be available to the press and public. Published roll calls should apply to those bills recommended for approval as well as those killed.

14. DUAL COMMITTEE CONSIDERATION OF APPROPRIATION BILLS. There should be a rule requiring dual committee consideration of legislation affecting significant sums of money. Such legislation, when considered and acted upon favorably by a substantive policy committee, should then automatically be referred to the Finance Committee for consideration of its fiscal impact.

15. LEGISLATIVE POWER TO CALL SPECIAL SESSIONS. Amend the constitution to permit the legislature to convene special sessions either by petition of a majority of the members of both houses or the call of the presiding officer of each house.

16. POWER TO EXPAND SPECIAL SESSION AGENDA. Amend the constitution to permit the legislature to broaden the subject matter of a governor's call of a special session by a majority vote in each house, or prohibit the restriction of the agenda by the governor.

17. INDIVIDUAL OFFICES. Provide private, individual offices for every member of the legislature, with nearby space for their assistants. The quality and amount of office space should not

differ substantially between majority and minority party members.

NEW HAMPSHIRE (39)

Functional, 34; Accountable, 33; Informed, 42; Independent, 36; Representative, 43

GENERAL: The New Hampshire General Court again came within a very close reach of legislative modernization in the 1970 general election. On the ballot were two proposals: one to establish a seven-member compensation commission and the other to provide annual general sessions of restricted time. Both failed, by a slight margin, to receive the two-thirds majority needed. The sessions measure failed by a slim 525 votes.

Passage of the compensation commission amendment would have removed the $100 per year salary restriction from the constitution, authorizing the seven-man commission to set salaries biennially.

Being limited to ninety legislative days per biennium, New Hampshire has developed an extremely effective deadline system. Almost every type of deadline suggested by this study is in effect in both houses of the General Court. As a result, only eleven percent of the total number of bills passed were passed in the final week of the session.

Almost every committee in both houses has its own permanently assigned meeting room. Space has also recently been increased for minority party members.

A blue ribbon legislative advisory committee has been studying the organization, facilities, function, and needs of the legislature and will soon issue its final report. It will then be incumbent upon the committee's members to educate the General Court and all of New Hampshire's citizens on the need to adopt the committee's recommendations. Recommendations to improve the New Hampshire General Court are the following.

1.   REDUCE THE OVERALL SIZE OF THE LEGISLATURE. Although size reduction in a legislative body is extremely difficult to achieve, it has been done in some states--such as in Vermont and Iowa--and needs to be accomplished in others (New Hampshire, Massachusetts, Georgia, and Pennsylvania). Where reduction in size has occurred, it has most often required a constitutional convention to accomplish it. In a few cases it has been done by legislatively adopted constitutional amendment (Iowa, in 1968, which becomes effective in November, 1971)

ratified by the voters. There should be 100 or fewer members
in the house. The combined size of both houses should be between
100 and 150.

With 400 members, the New Hampshire House is the largest
state legislative body in the United States. Despite the difficulty
of bringing about this reduction, and recognizing that a recent
constitutional convention bypassed this question, it is nevertheless
recommended that the House be reduced in numbers from its
present 400 to 100 or fewer.

2. LEGISLATIVE SALARIES. Legislative salaries should be set
by statute and paid in equal monthly installments throughout
the biennium, and all unvouchered expense allowances should
be incorporated into an annual salary. Actual and necessary
expenses incurred in the process of carrying out legislative
duties should be reimbursed upon submission and approval of
properly vouchered evidence of expenditures.

INCREASE LEGISLATIVE COMPENSATION. No legislative
salaries in the United States should be below the $10,000 a year
level. Compensation of legislators in the larger states should
be in the $20,000 to $30,000 range.

The constitution should be amended to permit the legislature to
establish legislative compensation by statute. With a biennial
compensation level of $200, New Hampshire legislators are the
worst-paid in the nation. There is no expense allowance, and
mileage for legislators ceases after the ninetieth legislative day.
A constitutional amendment which would remove compensation
for legislators from the constitution and allow the salaries to
be set by a compensation commission was defeated in the 1970
general election. Reasonable legislative salaries--at the $10,000
to $15,000 level-- will not be realized until the people of New
Hampshire reduce the size of the House. Until then, legislative
compensation will represent nothing more than a bare token payment for service. But such a meager payment also precludes
the development of a legislative body which represents a balanced
cross section of the state. Instead, as in the New Hampshire
House, those attracted to service are primarily the well-to-do,
the retired, and the self-employed.

3. REMOVE CONSTITUTIONAL RESTRICTIONS ON SESSION AND
INTERIM TIME. The legislature should have authority to function
throughout a two-year term; ideally, this authority should provide
a flexible biennial session pattern that permits the legislature to
convene, recess, and reconvene as it deems desirable. The

legislature should be able to meet in general session or conduct interim work as it deems necessary at any time throughout the period.

The only limitation on session length is the number of legislative days for which mileage will be paid. Since there is no per diem for expenses, legislators rely on their mileage allowances to pay expenses. When it ceases after the ninetieth legislative day, this becomes an indirect limitation on session length. In accordance with the two foregoing recommendations, the constitution should be amended to provide unlimited annual sessions.

4.   LEGISLATIVE POWER TO CALL SPECIAL SESSIONS. Amend the constitution to permit the legislature to convene special sessions either by petition of a majority of the members of both houses or the call of the presiding officer of each house.

The constitution should be so amended; although the General Court may call itself into special session, the majority of elected members required to accomplish this should be reduced from sixty-seven percent to fifty-one percent.

5.   PRE-SESSION ORGANIZATIONAL MEETING. Amend the constitution to provide a pre-session organizing session following a general election. Some states make advantageous use of such a session during November or December of a general election year for the purpose of electing leaders, appointing committee chairmen, assigning members of committees, referring pre-filed bills to committee, holding committee organizational meetings, and conducting orientation conferences for new, as well as returning, members of the legislature. Through such pre-session meetings the committees can begin their work before the regular session convenes. This makes it possible to delay the start of the regular session until legislation is ready for floor action.

The constitution should be amended to provide a pre-session.

6.   PRE-SESSION ORIENTATION CONFERENCE. The legislature should hold an orientation conference for new legislators, preferably after each general election. Orientation conferences enable members to speed the process of becoming more effective representatives, and they provide an opportunity for legislators to examine large policy areas apart from the pressure of the regular session.

The New Hampshire General Court should expand its present program, as suggested in the general recommendation.

7. REDUCE THE NUMBER OF COMMITTEES. Ideally, there should
    be from ten to fifteen committees in each house, parallel in juris-
    diction. This would reduce the general complexity of the legisla-
    ture and would permit reducing the number of committee assign-
    ments per member.

    At present there are twenty-three committees in the House and
    fourteen in the Senate. If the House were able to reduce and
    consolidate its committees to the number approximating those
    of the Senate, and if it were possible to make those committees
    parallel in jurisdiction, this would contribute much to the reduc-
    tion in the general complexity of the organization of the House.

8. UNIFROM COMMITTEE RULES. There should be uniform pub-
    lished rules of committee procedure in both chambers.

9. COMMITTEE JURISDICTION. A description of the jurisdiction
    of committees should be contained in the rules of both houses,
    and assignment of bills should be made in accord with the juris-
    diction of committees as described in the rules.

10. OPEN COMMITTEES. The rules of each house should prohibit
    s ecret meetings except in matters affecting the security of the
    state, or which could unnecessarily damage the reputation of
    individuals in personnel matters. Such exceptions should be
    sparingly and responsibly employed.

11. NOTICE OF MEETINGS. The rules should require a minimum
    notice of five legislative days for committee meetings and hear-
    ings, with widely disseminated announcement of schedule, location,
    agenda, and availability of public participation.

12. COMMITTEE BILL REPORTS. Require committees to issue
    reports describing and explaining the committee's action on bills
    recommended for passage at the time the bill moves from the
    committee to the floor.

13. PUBLISH COMMITTEE ROLL CALLS. The committee report
    of action on bills to the respective houses should include those
    roll calls which are taken, showing how each member voted.
    These committee reports should be available to the press and
    public. Published roll calls should apply to those bills recom-
    mended for approval as well as those killed.

14. MANAGEMENT COMMITTEES. There should be an executive
    or management committee created in each house. Its membership
    should include the leaders of each party in each house, and the

minority party should have representation on the committee in
proportion to its numbers in the body as a whole. The Senate/
House management committees should combine as a joint management committee. The purpose of these committees should be to
assume responsibility for the administrative management (housekeeping) functions relating to personnel, facilities, the research
bureaus, budgets, and expenditures of their respective houses.
The joint management committee should deal with matters of
inter-house coordination.

Although some attempt is made at having a housekeeping or
management committee, this recommendation would provide
guidelines for better coordination of such activities and would
widen the scope of present management capabilities.

15. INTERIM COMMITTEES. When the legislature is not in session,
the standing committees should become the interim committees
for the purpose of conducting long-range studies of state policy
issues. The Legislative Council or some similarly constituted,
bi-partisan committee should serve as the supervising agency
for interim committees and their studies, budgets and personnel.
The major committees should be staffed on a year-round basis.

16. INTERIM COMMITTEE REPORTING. Interim committees should
be required to render formal reports concerning the topics they
were charged with responsibility for investigating. These reports
should cover the committee's recommendations, including drafts
of proposed legislation where appropriate.

17. STRENGTHEN MINORITY PARTY ROLE. Internal accountability,
as well as the capacity of all legislators to represent their constituents effectively, depends upon the opportunity of minority
party members to have an effective part in internal legislative
affairs.

MINORITY REPRESENTATION ON COMMITTEE ON RULES.
Minority representation on the Committee on Rules should approximate the minority party proportion of the membership of
the appropriate house.

18. STRENGTHEN STAFF SUPPORT. Legislative research, fiscal,
legal, and planning agencies should be adequately staffed to full
utility and at suitable salary levels for professional qualification.
Professional staffing should be at a level to enable the legislature
to conduct continuous, year-round examination of state resources
and expenditures as well as program review and evaluation of
state agencies. This staff should also prepare fiscal notes

accompanying all appropriation bills, evaluating their fiscal impact over the short and long term. Staff agencies should be upgraded to the level at which competent and timely service can be provided to every member of the legislature.

COMMITTEE STAFFING. Standing committees should be staffed on a permanent, year-round basis.

Although most legislative services available are provided by legislative staff agencies, those agencies are spread entirely too thin, considering the amount of services they are expected to provide to 424 legislators.

19. STRENGTHEN STAFF SUPPORT (LEADERS). Staff assistance should be provided to all leaders of both the majority and minority parties. Such assistance should include a secretary and an administrative assistant at the professional level, with space to work reasonably adjacent to the offices of members and leaders.

20. STRENGTHEN STAFF (RANK-AND-FILE MEMBERS). Rank-and-file members (majority and minority party on an equal basis) should be provided with individual staff assistance consisting of a minimum of an administrative assistant at the professional level and a secretary. Eventually, this should increase to the stated level of support both in the capital and in a district office.

21. INDIVIDUAL OFFICES. Provide private, individual offices for every member of the legislature, with nearby space for their assistants. The quality and amount of office space should not differ substantially between majority and minority party members.

22. FACILITIES FOR COMMITTEES. Legislative effectiveness requires that committees have adequate physical facilities in which to do their work. This includes an adequate number of hearing rooms that will permit the seating of larger audiences.

23. IMPROVE PRESS FACILITIES. Improved press facilities aid in the coverage of the work of the legislature. Committee rooms, and both chambers or galleries, should provide adequate space for the news media as well as lighting and electrical power connections for their equipment. Conference or interview rooms and office space should also be provided for the news media.

Although legislative proceedings, both in committee and in the chamber, are accessible to the press, there is need for improved press facilities.

24. ELECTRIC ROLL CALL RECORDER. There should be an electric
     roll call recorder in each house. This is recommended not simply
     because it would speed up the proceedings (worthwhile as this may
     be), but because it is an efficient method of producing an error-
     free record of roll call votes.

     With 400 Representatives in the New Hampshire House, a roll
     call now takes a minimum of fifty-five minutes to complete.
     Immediate attention should be given to installation of an electric
     roll call device.

25. SPECIAL PROVISIONS. In addition to standard laws governing
     criminal behavior, there should be special provisions regulating
     legislative conflicts of interest.

     PRACTICE BEFORE REGULATORY AGENCIES. Legislators
     or their firms should be prohibited from practicing before state
     regulatory agencies or in matters concerning state agencies for
     a fee.

     PROHIBIT DOING BUSINESS WITH THE STATE. There should
     be a prohibition against legislators or the firms in which they
     own a major interest doing business with state agencies.

     PROHIBIT APPOINTMENT TO STATE OFFICE. There should
     be a prohibition against a legislator accepting appointment to
     other state office during the term for which he is elected or
     within two years of the termination of his service as a member
     of the legislature.

     FAMILY EMPLOYMENT. Members of a legislator's immediate
     family should be barred from employment by the legislature.

26. PROVIDE SINGLE-MEMBER DISTRICTS. Legislative districts
     in both houses should be single-member.

     Legislative districts in the House are multi-member.

27. STATEMENT OF INTENT BY AUTHOR OF A BILL. The form
     in which a bill is introduced should include a statement by the
     author describing, in laymen's language, what the bill is intended
     to accomplish.

28. BILL SUMMARY BY BILL-DRAFTING SERVICE. The form in
     which bills are introduced should include a more extensive
     summary of the provisions of the bill, prepared by the bill-draft-
     ing service.

29. REQUIRE ROLL CALL ON PASSAGE OF BILLS. A recorded
    roll call should be required on final passage of any legislative
    measure, and it should require a constitutional majority to pass
    any bill on final action by either house.

30. ADOPT BACK-UP RULES OF PROCEDURES IN BOTH HOUSES.
    There should be officially adopted back-up rules (such as Mason's
    Manual or Jefferson's Manual) which come into operation when
    the standing rules fail to cover the parliamentary problem at
    hand.

31. CONSENT CALENDAR. A consent calendar should be used in
    both houses.

32. REPRINT AMENDED BILLS. When a bill is amended substantially,
    it should be reprinted and returned to the legislature with no more
    than an overnight delay. The reprint should show clearly the
    original text of the bill as well as the change created by the
    amendment.

NEW JERSEY (32)

Functional, 14; Accountable, 42; Informed, 18; Independent, 31;
Representative, 35

GENERAL: Ranked thirty-second overall, New Jersey showed strength
in two particular areas: functionality, where it ranked fourteenth, and
its ability to secure information, ranked eighteenth. Without doubt,
however, New Jersey's greatest strength lies in the enormous potential
it possesses to achieve excellence. There are no constitutional en-
cumbrances upon the future development or current operation of the
legislature.

But New Jersey's strengths have not resulted in a superior legislature
because its capacity for excellance has not been maximized. The
legislature has already drawn upon the services of the nearby Eagleton
Institute of Politics, which made its first comprehensive survey of
a state legislature in its home state, but the recommendations Eagleton
offered as at least a preliminary blueprint for meeting higher levels
of effectiveness have not been adopted in a significant measure. In a
similar vein, the detailed plans for a new legislative building, authorized in 1967, have not yet been implemented. Thus, New Jersey's
greatest strength is also its greatest burden - a large but unrealized
potential.

The following recommendations attempt to set an agenda for future
improvement.

1.   DEVELOP A MORE EFFECTIVE PATTERN OF HOLDING SESSIONS
     The New Jersey Legislature can meet for an unlimited amount
     of time each year, but during the last biennium, by tradition, the
     legislature met only on Mondays, convening at 1:00 p.m. and
     adjourning before 6:00 p.m. It met for twenty-five such sessions
     during 1969 and perhaps a few more in 1970, when five minute
     pro forma sessions sometimes preceded committee meetings the
     leadership was attempting to organize on Thursdays. This manner
     of conducting legislative activity can only be described as tanta-
     mount to no activity whatsoever. We recommend the legislature,
     through its leadership, immediately undertake to plan and organize
     legislative activity into much more concentrated and lengthy periods
     of work.

2.   CREATE AN OPERATING SYSTEM OF STANDING COMMITTEES.
     Standing committees of the legislature seem to exist mostly on
     paper in New Jersey. Committees seldom meet or hold public
     hearings, except when a public issue is so volatile that not to do
     so would be inexpedient politically. Committees do not develop,
     review, or report legislation to their respective houses, nor do
     they carry on a systematic or thorough review of the programs of
     state agencies under their jurisdictions. Almost all committee
     activity is perfunctory in nature. More than ninety percent of all
     bills which spend money are declared to be "policy bills" and are
     remanded to the "conferences" (caucuses) for review. It is the
     majority conference (caucus) which then either kills the bill or
     recommends it for passage. For controversial, hard-to-handle
     issues, the legislature creates a commission often made up of
     only a few legislators and a majority of public members. Forty
     to fifty commissions are usually alive at any given time. Com-
     missions will often make recommendations to the legislature
     concerning the bill(s) in their custody. In 1970, a system of
     requiring "committee reports" was instituted in the House. The
     reports consisted of attendance sheets for each meeting and the
     numbers of the bills considered. There was mounting opposition
     to even this rudimentary requirement as the session progressed.
     In addition, the Thursday committee meeting day was launched in
     1970, and it too met much opposition.

     The following recommendations that relate to committees are
     predicated on actually activating the committee system and the
     need to open the committee system to public scrutiny, for it is
     only in this way that the citizenry can really safeguard their
     interest.

3.   REDUCE THE NUMBER OF COMMITTEES. Ideally, there should
     be from ten to fifteen committees in each house, parallel in

jurisdiction. This would reduce the general complexity of the legislature and would permit reducing the number of committee assignments per member.

With twenty-three committees in either house, there are more committees than should be necessary for the effective organization of work. Ideally, there should be from ten to fifteen committees in each house, remaining, as at present, parallel in jurisdiction.

4. REDUCE THE NUMBER OF COMMITTEE ASSIGNMENTS. In order to make it possible for members to concentrate their attention and contribute effectively, there should be no more than three committee assignments for each member of the lower house and four committee assignments for each member of the Senate. The multiplicity of assignments introduces problems of scheduling, strains the focus of attention on the part of members, and creates an inordinately heavy workload for members if committees are as active as they should be.

Recommendation no. 3, above, would facilitate reducing the number of committee assignments. At present ten percent of the members of the House have more than three assignments each and twelve percent of the Senators have more than four. The number of assignments should be reduced to a maximum of three per House member and four per Senator.

5. UNIFORM COMMITTEE RULES. There should be uniform published rules of committee procedure in both chambers.

6. COMMITTEE JURISDICTION. A description of the jurisdiction of committees should be contained in the rules of both houses, and assignment of bills should be made in accord with the jurisdiction of committees as described in the rules.

7. OPEN COMMITTEES. The rules of each house should prohibit secret meetings except in matters affecting the security of the state, or which could unnecessarily damage the reputation of individuals in personnel matters. Such exceptions should be sparingly and responsibly employed.

8. NOTICE OF MEETINGS. The rules should require a minimum notice of five legislative days for committee meetings and hearings, with widely disseminated announcement of schedule, location, agenda, and availability of public participation.

9. ACT ON ALL BILLS. Committees should be required to report on all bills assigned to them, recommending for passage by the

parent body those bills which enjoy the support of a majority of the members of the committee and killing all others.

10. COMMITTEE HEARINGS. There is no justification for permitting any major piece of legislation to become law without having been subjected to extensive, thorough, well-planned, and well-prepared public hearings, in which representatives of the public, civic organizations, and interest groups are not only invited but encouraged to participate.

11. COMMITTEE BILL REPORTS. Require committees to issue reports describing and explaining the committee's action on bills recommended for passage at the time the bill moves from the committee to the floor.

12. PUBLISH COMMITTEE ROLL CALLS. The committee report of action on bills to the respective houses should include those roll calls which are taken, showing how each member voted. These committee reports should be available to the press and public. Published roll calls should apply to those bills recommended for approval as well as those killed.

13. DUAL COMMITTEE CONSIDERATION OF APPROPRIATION BILLS. There should be a rule requiring dual committee consideration of legislation affecting significant sums of money. Such legislation, when considered and acted upon favorably by a substantive policy committee, should then automatically be referred to the Finance Committee for consideration of its fiscal impact.

14. MANAGEMENT COMMITTEES. There should be an executive or management committee created in each house. Its membership should include the leaders of each party in each house, and the minority party should have representation on the committee in proportion to its numbers in the body as a whole. The Senate/ House management committees should combine as a joint management committee. The purpose of these committees should be to assume responsibility for the administrative management (housekeeping) functions relating to personnel, facilities, the research bureaus, budgets, and expenditures of their respective houses. The joint management committee should deal with matters of inter-house coordination.

15. INTERIM COMMITTEES. When the legislature is not in session, the standing committees should become the interim committees for the purpose of conducting long-range studies of state policy issues. The Legislative Council or some similarly constituted, bi-partisan committee should serve as the supervising agency

for interim committees and their studies, budgets, and personnel.
The major committees should be staffed on a year-round basis.

16. INTERIM COMMITTEE REPORTING. Interim committees should
be required to render formal reports concerning the topics they
were charged with responsibility for investigating. These reports
should cover the committee's recommendations, including drafts
of proposed legislation where appropriate.

17. FACILITIES FOR COMMITTEES. Legislative effectiveness
requires that committees have adequate physical facilities in
which to do their work. This includes an adequate number of
committee rooms and an adequate number of hearing rooms that
will permit the seating of larger audiences.

Although there are twenty-three committees per house, there is
only one committee room per house. The number of rooms
available to committees or their subcommittees should be drastically increased, and such rooms should have space for spectators
and the working press (including lights and power connections, for
radio and television) as well. Presently, there is not one legislative
hearing room capable of seating at least fifty spectators and
witnesses. It is imperative that such hearing rooms be made
available immediately.

18. BILL DEADLINES. The orderly flow of work through the legislature depends upon the existence of a series of deadlines at
various critical stages throughout the legislative process. These
deadlines should be adopted as part of the rules and should be
consistently enforced.

19. ESTABLISH AN AUTOMATIC CALENDAR OF BILLS. When a
bill is favorably reported out of committee to the floor, it should
go automatically onto the calendar in the order in which it was
reported out. It should require a vote of an extraordinary majority
to move a bill from its position on calendar or to bypass it. The
Rules Committee should have no part in the scheduling of bills.
No session should adjourn until all bills on calendar have been
voted up or down or, by the vote of an extraordinary majority,
have been moved from the calendar.

20. DISCONTINUE ROTATING LEADERSHIP. The practice of limiting
presiding officers to a single, two-year term in that position
weakens the legislature in its capacity to confront other branches
and levels of government as a partner of equal stature and diffuses
and disrupts the continuity of leadership within the legislative
bodies. Although it is extremely difficult to change a practice

such as this, because of its profoundly adverse effects on many
aspects of legislative performance, it should be discontinued.

New Jersey is one of the remaining half dozen states which still
limit its speaker of the General. Assembly to a single, two-year
term in that position.

21. STRENGTHEN MINORITY PARTY ROLE. Internal accountability,
    as well as the capacity of all legislators to represent their con-
    stituents effectively, depends upon the opportunity of minority
    party members to have an effective part in internal legislative
    affairs.

    Minority representation on the Senate Committee on Rules should
    approximate the minority party proportion of the membership of
    the Senate.

22. REPRINT AMENDED BILLS. When a bill is amended substantially,
    it should be reprinted and returned to the legislature with no
    more than an overnight delay. The reprint should show clearly
    the original text of the bill as well as the change created by the
    amendment.

23. STATEMENT OF INTENT BY AUTHOR OF A BILL. The form
    in which a bill is introduced should include a statement by the
    author describing, in laymen's language, what the bill is intended
    to accomplish.

    This is a very optional requirement at the present time, but it
    should become mandatory for all bills introduced.

24. BILL SUMMARY BY BILL-DRAFTING SERCICE. The form in
    which bills are introduced should include a more extensive summary
    of the provisions of the bill, prepared by the bill-drafting service.

25. STRENGTHEN STAFF SUPPORT. Legislative research, fiscal,
    legal, and planning agencies should be adequately staffed to full
    utility and at suitable salary levels for professional qualification.
    Professional staffing should be at a level to enable the legislature
    to conduct continuous, year-round examination of state resources
    and expenditures as well as program review and evaluation of
    state agencies. This staff should also prepare fiscal notes
    accompanying all appropriation bills, evaluating their fiscal impact
    over the short and long term. Staff agencies should be upgraded
    to the level at which competent and timely service can be provided
    to every member of the legislature.

Other forms of legislative staffing, beyond the centralized bureaus, are needed.

26. STRENGTHEN STAFF SUPPORT (LEADERS). Staff assistance should be provided to all leaders of both the majority and minority parties. Such assistance should include a secretary and an ad-ministrative assistant at the professional level, with space to work reasonably adjacent to the offices of members and leaders.

At present, only the major officers (speaker, majority leader, minority leader) have full-time assistants.

27. COMMITTEE STAFFING. Standing committees should be staffed on a permanent, year-round basis.

A strong beginning should be made toward permanent, year-round committee staffing for all committees. Only the Appropriations Committees of both houses are now staffed (two men per com-mittee), and their inability to assist the legislature in a meaningful review of the governor's budget - to cite one example - is testimony enough to the need for professional and experienced assistance for all committees. With the advent of an operating committee system, professional staff will be invaluable in launching - through legislative standing committees - the continuous study of the state's resources and expenditures, and a system of program review and evaluation so central to the legislature's responsibility to insure that the programs it creates are achieving the desired goals.

28. STRENGTHEN STAFF (RANK-AND-FILE MEMBERS). Rank-and-file members (majority and minority party on an equal basis) should be provided with individual staff assistance consisting of a minimum of an administrative assistant at the professional level and a secretary. Eventually, this should increase to the stated level of support both in the capital and in a district office.

Some movement toward the staffing of individual members is also in order, through provision of administrative assistants, perhaps beginning on a shared basis, but ultimately for each member, majority and minority alike.

29. INDIVIDUAL OFFICES. Provide private, individual offices for every member of the legislature, with nearby space for their assistants. The quality and amount of office space should not differ substantially between majority and minority party members.

Because they meet for only one day a week, the need to provide
office space for individual members has not been felt too strongly.
In fact, the lack of office space has become perhaps a subconscious
part of the rationale not to meet more than one day a week.
Legislative effectiveness, however, requires that members - just
as committees - have adequate physical facilities in which to do
their work. Private, individual offices for every member of the
legislature should be provided.

30. IMPROVED FACILITIES. The need for a new legislative building
has long been recognized, and legislation has been signed authorizing the construction of a new building. Planning for the new
facility began in 1959, when the State Capitol Development Program
was created. In 1967, the State Capitol Development Commission
issued a feasibility and preliminary report on a legislative building.
The plans for the new building include shared office space for
rank-and-file members; office suites for the leadership; space
for committee chairmen within committee rooms; conference
rooms for the majority and minority in each house; a press
mezzanine for viewing action on the floor as well as office space
for reporters; a large public (committee) hearing room and
fourteen other committee rooms, some of which could be divided
by folding, soundproof partitions; large public galleries in the
chambers; and space for future expansion that would temporarily
be used by the governor.

We recommend this plan be implemented and the necessary funds
appropriated to complete construction. Since the 1967 report
estimated thirty months would be required to construct the
building, it is imperative that temporary accommodations be
made in the meantime to relieve the most pressing requirements.

NEW MEXICO (11)

Functional, 3; Accountable, 16; Informed, 28; Independent, 39;
Representative, 4

GENERAL: Ranked eleventh in overall capability, the New Mexico
Legislature shows rather uneven development. It ranks very high
on the scales measuring its general ability to function (3) and the
opportunity for its members to represent their constituents (4),
but it is relatively low on the other scales.

Contributing to the generally favorable rating of the New Mexico
Legislature are such assets as its relatively small overall size (House,
seventy; Senate, forty-two), few committees (House, fifteen; Senate,
eight), and a new building.

On the other side of the ledger, consideration must be given to the
sharply limited sessions (sixty calendar days in odd-numbered years
and thirty calendar days, restricted primarily to budget and appropriation, in the even-numbered years), constitutionally limited pay at a
very low level ($20 per day of session time or $1,800 for the biennium),
and a shortage of staff support services.

The following recommendations concern improvements which could be
made.

1. REMOVE CONSTITUTIONAL RESTRICTIONS ON SESSION AND
    INTERIM TIME. The legislature should have authority to function
    throughout a two-year term; ideally, this authority should provide
    a flexible biennial session pattern that permits the legislature to
    convene, recess, and reconvene as it deems desirable. The legis-
    lature should be able to meet in general session or conduct interim
    work as it deems necessary at any time throughout the period.

    A more modest but significant improvement could be achieved by
    amending the constitution to provide that the current limitation
    of sixty days in the odd-numbered year and thirty days in the
    even-numbered year applies to legislative rather than calendar
    days and may be distributed throughout the year.

2. INCREASE LEGISLATIVE COMPENSATION. No legislative
    salaries in the United States should be below the $10,000 a year
    level. Compensation of legislators in the larger states should
    be in the $20,000 to $30,000 range.

    New Mexico legislators receive no salary at all. They are paid
    a $20 a day expense allowance for each day of legislative session.
    This amounts to $1,800 for the two-year period, since sessions
    are limited to a total of ninety calendar days per biennium. Legis-
    lative salaries should be provided by statute at the $10,000 to
    $15,000 level on an annual basis.

3. UNIFORM COMMITTEE RULES. There should be uniform pub-
    lished rules of committee procedure in the Senate, as is currently
    done in the House.

4. COMMITTEE JURISDICTION. A description of the jurisdiction
    of committees should be contained in the rules of both houses,
    and assignment of bills should be made in accord with the jurisdic-
    tion of committees as described in the rules.

5. PUBLISH COMMITTEE ROLL CALLS. The committee report of
    action on bills to the respective houses should include those roll
    calls which are taken, showing how each member voted. These

committee reports should be available to the press and public.
Published roll calls should apply to those bills recommended for
approval as well as those killed.

6. PRINTED BILL DOCUMENT FORMAT. The bill document printing
   procedure should permit the clear identification of the text of
   the existing statute which is being amended as well as the material
   which the bill proposes to delete or add. This is usually accomplished through the use of varying type faces, such as "strike-
   through," italics, underlining, or bracketing. It should not be
   necessary to compare the text of a bill with the text of the existing
   code in order to determine what the bill does.

7. REPRINT AMENDED BILLS. When a bill is amended substantially
   it should be reprinted and returned to the legislature with no
   more than an overnight delay. The reprint should show clearly
   the original text of the bill as well as the change created by the
   amendment.

8. SKELETON BILLS. There should be an explicit rule barring
   introduction of skeleton or "spot" bills. This rule should be
   enforced by the assigning authority (the presiding officer or
   Rules Committee) by refusal to assign bills so identified to
   committee.

9. BILL SUMMARY BY BILL-DRAFTING SERVICE. The form in
   which bills are introduced should include a more extensive
   summary of the provisions of the bill, prepared by the bill-drafting
   service.

10. MINORITY PARTY MEMBERS ON COMMITTEE. Minority party
    members should be assigned to committees by the minority leader
    in consultation with the minority caucus.

    Minority leaders now have informal power over minority party
    nominations to committee. Minority members should be formally
    assigned to committees by the minority leader in consultation
    with the minority caucus.

11. STRENGTHEN STAFF SUPPORT. Legislative research, fiscal,
    legal, and planning agencies should be adequately staffed to full
    utility and at suitable salary levels for professional qualification.
    Professional staffing should be at a level to enable the legislature
    to conduct continuous, year-round examination of state resources
    and expenditures as well as program review and evaluation of
    state agencies. This staff should also prepare fiscal notes accom-
    panying all appropriation bills, evaluating their fiscal impact

over the short and long term. Staff agencies should be upgraded to the level at which competent and timely service can be provided to every member of the legislature.

The New Mexico Legislature has a small but competent staff (organized under the Legislative Council and the Legislative Finance Committee), which provides a number of necessary services, such as bill drafting, fiscal analysis, and legislative research. However, in order to allow the legislature to conduct effective oversight of executive operations, the range, volume, and level of these services are in need of expansion. This can be accomplished most directly by authorizing additional staff positions and by increasing salary levels and qualifications.

12. STRENGTHEN STAFF SUPPORT (LEADERS). Staff assistance should be provided to all leaders of both the majority and minority parties. Such assistance should include a secretary and an administrative assistant at the professional level, with space to work reasonably adjacent to the offices of members and leaders.

STRENGTHEN STAFF (RANK-AND-FILE MEMBERS). Rank-and-file members (majority and minority party on an equal basis) should be provided with individual staff assistance consisting of a minimum of an administrative assistant at the professional level and a secretary. Eventually, this should increase to the state level of support both in the capital and in a district office.

At a minimum, leaders should be provided with assistance at a professional level. Some movement toward the staffing of individual members is also in order, through the provision of administrative assistants, perhaps beginning on a shared basis, but ultimately for each member.

13. COMMITTEE STAFFING. A beginning toward permanent, year-round committee staffing should be made by staffing some of the major committees.

14. SPECIAL PROVISIONS. In addition to standard laws governing criminal behavior, there should be special provisions regulating legislative conflicts of interest.

PRACTICE BEFORE REGULATORY AGENCIES. Legislators or their firms should be prohibited from practicing before state regulatory agencies or in matters concerning state agencies for a fee.

PROHIBIT DOING BUSINESS WITH THE STATE. There should be a prohibition against legislators or the firms in which they

own a major interest doing business with state agencies.

15. EXPENSE ALLOWANCES. Members of the legislature should
be allowed an expense reimbursement covering their travel and
living costs while engaged in carrying out their legislative duties.
The same allowance should obtain during the interim for days in
attendance at interim committee meetings or other official and
authorized legislative business. These allowances should be
provided by statute.

Expense allowances should include both session and interim time
while legislators are engaged in carrying out their legislative
duties. The allowance for living expenses, now set by statute,
should be increased from $20 to $25 or more per day.

NEW YORK (2)

Functional, 4; Accountable, 13; Informed, 1; Independent, 8;
Representative, 1

GENERAL: The New York Legislature ranks second among the state
legislatures of the United States. It has a powerful resource base,
and on the individual scales which measure information resources and
the attributes of representativeness it ranks first. The strengths of
the New York Legislature are noted here, followed by a series of
recommendations designed to mobilize New York's high volume and
wide range of resources on behalf of what can become a truly outstandi
legislative system.

Factors that help New York rank second are annual unlimited sessions
control over its own resources: time, staff and funds, and the ability
to set legislative salaries by statute; a wide range of staff services,
including fiscal research, committee staffing, leadership staffing,
and a full array of technical support; uniform, published rules of
committee procedure; and committee roll call votes regularly taken
recorded and published.

Bills are printed in clear, readable format, permitting easy identification of original statute, deleted material, and additions. Significantly
amended bills are reprinted, and original bills as well as amended
bills are printed in quantity and available to legislators, press, and
public from a central distribution point. Skeleton or "spot" bills are
prohibited, and bills are limited to a single topic.

The level of professional staffing permits the continuous, year-round
examination of state resources and expenditures as well as program

review and evaluation of state agencies. This staff also prepares
fiscal notes accompanying all appropriation bills, and dual committee
(finance and policy) consideration is given to bills involving significant
sums.

Legislators must disclose any interest of $5,000 or more in any corpo-
ration doing business with an agency regulated by the state. The
appointment of minority party members to committees is made by
the minority leader.

Among the recommendations suggested from a detailed analysis of the
New York Legislature are the following.

1. REDUCE THE NUMBER OF COMMITTEES. Ideally, there should
    be from ten to fifteen committees in each house, parallel in juris-
    diction. This would reduce the general complexity of the legislature
    and would permit reducing the number of committee assignments
    per member.

    Ideally, there should be from ten to fifteen committees in each
    house, parallel in jurisdiction. The number of committees in
    the Senate (thirty-two) is particularly too high. The Assembly
    has twenty committees.

2. REDUCE THE NUMBER OF COMMITTEE ASSIGNMENTS. In
    order to make it possible for members to concentrate their atten-
    tion and contribute effectively, there should be no more than three
    committee assignments for each member of the lower house and
    four committee assignments for each member of the Senate. The
    multiplicity of assignments introduces problems of scheduling,
    strains the focus of attention on the part of members, and creates
    an inordinately heavy workload for members if committees are
    as active as they should be.

    There should be no more than three committee assignments for
    each member of the lower house and four committee assignments
    for each member of the Senate. The Assembly meets this standard,
    while ninety-three percent of the Senate members have more
    than four assignments.

3. REDUCE THE OVERALL SIZE OF THE LEGISLATURE. Although
    size reduction in a legislative body is extremely difficult to
    achieve, it has been done in some states - such as in Vermont
    and Iowa - and needs to be accomplished in others (New Hampshire,
    Massachusetts, Georgia, and Pennsylvania). Where reduction in
    size has occurred, it has most often required a constitutional
    convention to accomplish it. In a few cases it has been done by

legislatively adopted constitutional amendment (Iowa, in 1968, which becomes effective in November, 1971) ratified by the voters. There should be 100 or fewer members in the house. The combined size of both houses should be between 100 and 150.

4. ADOPT BACK-UP RULES OF PROCEDURES IN BOTH HOUSES. There should be officially adopted back-up rules (such as Mason' Manual or Jefferson's Manual) which come into operation when the standing rules fail to cover the parliamentary problem at hand.

5. COMMITTEE BILL REPORTS. Require committees to issue reports describing and explaining the committee's action on bills recommend for passage at the time the bill moves from the committee to the floor.

6. RECORD AND PUBLISH PROCEEDINGS OF COMMITTEES. Record and publish the record of committee hearings, proceeding and votes.

7. USE OF AVAILABLE TIME. Through the use of a greater amount of the available time for sessions (stepped-up meeting schedule early in the session and longer overall session), it should be possible to reduce or eliminate the long night sessions the crowded calendars, the frequent necessity to suspend the rules, and the circus atmosphere which attends the ending of annual sessions.

8. COMMITTEE HEARINGS. There is no justification for permittin any major piece of legislation to become law without having been subjected to extensive, thorough, well-planned, and well-prepare public hearings, in which representatives of the public, civic organizations, and interest groups are not only invited but encouraged to participate.

During the past two or three years there has been improvement in the number of issues which are submitted to public hearing by the standing committees during the session. By using more of available session time (and by the adoption of other recom- mendations listed here), this procedure could be further improve There is no justification for permitting any major piece of legislation to become law without having been subjected to extensive, thorough, well-planned, and well-prepared public hearings, in which representatives of the public, civic organiza- tions, and interest groups are not only invited but encouraged to participate.

9. LEGISLATIVE SALARIES. Legislative salaries should be set
    by statute and paid in equal monthly installments throughout
    the biennium, and all unvouchered expense allowances should be
    incorporated into an annual salary. Actual and necessary
    expenses incurred in the process of carrying out legislative
    duties should be reimbursed upon submission and approval of
    properly vouchered evidence of expenditures.

10. INCREASE LEGISLATIVE COMPENSATION. No legislative
    salaries in the United States should be below the $10,000 a year
    level. Compensation of legislators in the larger states should
    be in the $20,000 to $30,000 range.

    The annual salary for New York legislators should be increased
    to the $20,000 to $30,000 a year range.

11. IMPROVE PRESS FACILITIES. Improved press facilities aid
    in the coverage of the work of the legislature. Committee
    rooms, and both chambers or galleries, should provide adequate
    space for the news media as well as lighting and electrical power
    connections for their equipment. Conference or interview rooms
    and office space should also be provided for the news media.

    This, as with other recommendations concerning physical facili-
    ties, will undoubtedly require awaiting completion of the new
    legislative office building now under construction. Completion
    is scheduled for 1972.

12. LEGISLATIVE POWER TO CALL SPECIAL SESSIONS. Amend
    the constitution to permit the legislature to convene special ses-
    sions either by petition of a majority of the members of both
    houses or the call of the presiding officer of each house.

13. POWER TO EXPAND SPECIAL SESSION AGENDA. Amend the
    constitution to permit the legislature to broaden the subject
    matter of a governor's call of a special session by a majority
    vote in each house, or prohibit the restriction of the agenda by
    the governor.

14. WASHINGTON, D.C., OFFICE FOR THE LEGISLATURE. With
    the large and growing volume of activity generated by state-
    federal relationships, the legislature, beyond merely reacting
    to federal legislation, should be in a position to influence the
    development of new programs in accordance with the interests
    of the state. To do so, the legislature should have an office in
    the nation's capital to represent it and to be its most direct
    liaison with the Congress.

For small states, consideration might be given to joining with
a number of sister states (either on a geographical or on a population basis) for the purpose of sharing the services of a Washington office. But in large states, the volume of inter-governmental
traffic has reached a stage at which it would benefit the legislatur
greatly to have a full-time Washington office.

15.   STRENGTHEN STAFF (RANK-AND-FILE MEMBERS). Rank-and-
      file members (majority and minority party on an equal basis)
      should be provided with individual staff assistance consisting of
      a minimum of an administrative assistant at the professional
      level and a secretary. Eventually, this should increase to the
      stated level of support both in the capital and in a district office.

      Also, legislative staff agencies should be upgraded to the level
      at which competent and timely service can be provided to every
      member of the legislature.

16.   LIMIT JOINT LEGISLATIVE COMMITTEES. No joint legislative
      committee should be established in an area in which a functioning
      standing committee is operating.

17.   STAFF (PATRONAGE). Eliminate party patronage from all legis-
      lative staffing.

18.   PRACTICE BEFORE REGULATORY AGENCIES. Legislators
      or their firms should be prohibited from practicing before state
      regulatory agencies or in matters concerning state agencies for
      a fee.

      PROHIBIT APPOINTMENT TO STATE OFFICE. There should
      be a prohibition against a legislator accepting appointment to
      other state office during the term for which he is elected or
      within two years of the termination of his service as a member
      of the legislature.

      FAMILY EMPLOYMENT. Members of a legislator's immediate
      family should be barred from employment by the legislature.

      Also, members and their staffs, who occupy presumably full-time
      positions and are paid professional salaries, should be barred
      from accepting outside fees or from performing outside services.

19.   INDIVIDUAL OFFICES. Provide private, individual offices for
      every member of the legislature, with nearby space for their
      assistants. The quality and amount of office space should not
      differ substantially between majority and minority party members

Implementation of this recommendation will probably have to await completion of the new building.

20. STANDING COMMITTEES. Standing committees should remain active throughout the sessions. In New York the speaker of the Assembly has been extending the life of standing committees in recent sessions. They now operate up to the last two weeks of the session. The life of standing committees should be extended throughout the session, and they should become the interim committees when the legislature is not in session.

21. MESSAGE OF NECESSITY. Abolish the practice of allowing the governor's "Message of Necessity" to route bills directly to the floor, bypassing committee consideration. When an emergency exists, the legislature should be able to speed up the consideration of a bill through suspension of the rules by the vote of an extraordinary majority. The much-abused practice has, in recent years, contributed very substantially to the logjam in the closing seventy-two hours of the session.

22. CONSENT CALENDAR. A consent calendar should be used in both houses.

NORTH CAROLINA (47)

Functional, 24; Accountable, 37; Informed, 44; Independent, 47; Representative, 44

GENERAL: The North Carolina General Assembly, in recognition of its own shortcomings, has created a citizens' commission to study the legislature's operations and procedures in order to recommend specific improvements. The commission has assigned task forces according to subject matter to pursue independent courses of study. The commission intends to issue at least an interim, if not a final, report to the 1970 session of the General Assembly. While it can be expected that the caliber of the commission's recommendations will be of the highest order, it is unfortunate that they have not yet drawn more public awareness to their efforts.

The North Carolina General Assembly has one of the newest and in some ways most attractive state legislative buildings. The chambers of the Senate and House are superior in most regards. There are three auditorium hearing rooms, one for each house and a shared room which seats almost 300 people. There are numerous committee rooms for each house (eleven in the House, nine in the Senate and eight shared between the houses) of superior quality. All members have individual,

private offices. The only apparent limitation in the legislative building
is that there are no news conference rooms available for the news
media, and there is a lack of space for future expansion of staff assigne
to leaders and members.

In 1969, the statutory provision limiting the number of days legislators
could be paid during regular session (120 days) was removed. The
General Assembly is, therefore, less encumbered in the odd-year sessions each biennium. The most recent innovation in legislative operations occurred at the 1970 general election, when voters approved a
constitutional amendment to permit the General Assembly's presiding
officers to convene the legislature in special sessions when petitioned
by two-thirds of the number of each house.

These recommendations for the North Carolina Legislature remain.

1. REMOVE CONSTITUTIONAL RESTRICTIONS ON SESSION AND
   INTERIM TIME. The legislature should have authority to function
   throughout a two-year term; ideally, this authority should provide
   a flexible biennial session pattern that permits the legislature to
   convene, recess, and reconvene as it deems desirable. The legislature should be able to meet in general session or conduct interir
   work as it deems necessary at any time throughout the period.

   Permit annual general sessions, limited to no fewer than ninety
   legislative days.

2. REDUCE THE NUMBER OF COMMITTEES. Ideally, there should
   be from ten to fifteen committees in each house parallel in jurisdiction. This would reduce the general complexity of the legislature and would permit reducing the number of committee assignments per member.

   With thirty-seven committees in the House and thirty in the
   Senate, there are more committees than should be necessary
   for the effective organization of the work. This overage is more
   severe in relation to the House than it is to the Senate.

3. REDUCE THE NUMBER OF COMMITTEE ASSIGNMENTS. In
   order to make it possible for members to concentrate their attention and contribute effectively, there should be no more than
   three committee assignments for each member of the lower
   house and four committee assignments for each member of the
   Senate. The multiplicity of assignments introduces problems of
   scheduling, strains the focus of attention on the part of members,
   and creates an inordinately heavy workload for members if committees are as active as they should be.

At present, ninety-nine percent of the members of the House have more than three committee assignments each, and 100 percent of the members of the Senate have more than four committee assignments each.

4. COMMITTEE JURISDICTION. A description of the jurisdiction of committees should be contained in the rules of both houses, and assignment of bills should be made in accord with the jurisdiction of committees as described in the rules.

5. NOTICE OF MEETINGS. The rules should require a minimum notice of five legislative days for committee meetings and hearings, with widely disseminated announcement of schedule, location, agenda, and availability of public participation.

6. OPEN COMMITTEES. The rules of each house should prohibit secret meetings except in matters affecting the security of the state, or which could unnecessarily damage the reputation of individuals in personnel matters. Such exceptions should be sparingly and responsibly employed.

7. COMMITTEE HEARINGS. There is no justification for permitting any major piece of legislation to become law without having been subjected to extensive, thorough, well-planned, and well-prepared public hearings, in which representatives of the public, civic organizations, and interest groups are not only invited but encouraged to participate.

8. RECORD AND PUBLISH PROCEEDINGS OF COMMITTEES. Record and publish the record of committee hearings, proceedings, and votes.

9. PUBLISH COMMITTEE ROLL CALLS. The committee report of action on bills to the respective houses should include those roll calls which are taken, showing how each member voted. These committee reports should be available to the press and public. Published roll calls should apply to those bills recommended for approval as well as those killed.

10. INTERIM COMMITTEES. When the legislature is not in session, the standing committees should become the interim committees for the purpose of conducting long-range studies of state policy issues. The Legislative Council or some similarly constituted, bi-partisan committee should serve as the supervising agency for interim committees and their studies, budgets, and personnel. The major committees should be staffed on a year-round basis.

In the past, two kinds of activity have taken place during the
interim; studies commissioned or undertaken personally by the
Legislative Research Commission, and independent (interim)
study commissions. Recognizing the problems resulting from
such a discontinuous approach, a partial solution has been evolvin
due to the lack of coordination, planning, scheduling, budgeting,
reviewing, and evaluating of interim activity. The Legislative
Services Commission and the Legislative Research Commission
have been attempting to fill the void to the degree possible. While
these ad hoc efforts are admirable in intent, we recommend a
more rational approach.

11. STRENGTHEN STAFF SUPPORT. Legislative research, fiscal,
    legal, and planning agencies should be adequately staffed to full
    utility and at suitable salary levels for professional qualification.
    Professional staffing should be at a level to enable the legislature
    to conduct continuous, year-round examination of state resources
    and expenditures as well as program review and evaluation of
    state agencies. This staff should also prepare fiscal notes ac-
    companying all appropriation bills, evaluating their fiscal impact
    over the short and long term. Staff agencies should be upgraded
    to the level at which competent and timely service can be provide(
    to every member of the legislature.

    COMMITTEE STAFFING. Standing committees should be staffed
    on a permanent, year-round basis.

    The Institute of Government at the University of North Carolina
    has, in the past, provided research and bill-drafting services to
    the General Assembly. The Legislative Services Office is now
    in the process of taking over all of the duties performed by the
    institute and, in addition, plans an expansion of services — es-
    pecially to major committees. The General Assembly has been
    operating, in spite of this service, with a level of professional
    staff services below minimally acceptable standards. It appears
    the Legislative Services Office will fulfill the need for a central
    research bureau. It should be completely staffed with bill draft-
    ers, fiscal analysts, and subject matter (research) specialists.
    All committees (reduced in total number) should be assigned
    professional staff assistants. The major committees should be
    so equipped immediately, and all committees should have per-
    manent, full-time staff as soon as possible.

12. STRENGTHEN STAFF SUPPORT (LEADERS). Staff assistance
    should be provided to all leaders of both the majority and minor-
    ity parties. Such assistance should include a secretary and an
    administrative assistant at the professional level, with space to

work reasonably adjacent to the offices of members and leaders.

No legislative leader now has a professional staff assistant.
Every leader should be provided a professional staff member
immediately.

13. STRENGTHEN STAFF (RANK-AND-FILE MEMBERS). Rank-
and-file members (majority and minority party on an equal basis)
should be provided with individual staff assistance consisting of
a minimum of an administrative assistant at the professional
level and a secretary. Eventually, this should increase to the
stated level of support both in the capital and in a district office.

No professional staff assistance is available to rank-and-file
members either. For the short-term future, it would appear
their needs will continue to grow as even more basic requirements
are met. Ultimately, each legislator should be provided a professional-level staff assistant. For the immediate future, secretarial assistance should be provided during the interim for the
use of the general membership.

14. REQUIRE ROLL CALL ON PASSAGE OF BILLS. A recorded
roll call should be required on final passage of any legislative
measure, and it should require a constitutional majority to pass
any bill on final action by either house.

15. ELECTRIC ROLL CALL RECORDER. There should be an electric
roll call recorder in each house. This is recommended not simply
because it would speed up the proceedings (worthwhile as this
may be), but because it is an efficient method of producing an
error-free record of roll call votes.

16. STATEMENT OF INTENT BY AUTHOR OF A BILL. The form
in which a bill is introduced should include a statement by the
author describing, in laymen's language, what the bill is intended
to accomplish.

17. BILL SUMMARY BY BILL-DRAFTING SERVICE. The form in
which bills are introduced should include a more extensive summary of the provisions of the bill, prepared by the bill-drafting
service.

18. IMPROVE PRESS FACILITIES. Improved press facilities aid
in the coverage of the work of the legislature. Committee rooms,
and both chambers or galleries, should provide adequate space
for the news media as well as lighting and electrical power connections for their equipment. Conference or interview rooms

and office space should also be provided for the news media.

Although the chambers of North Carolina's new legislative buildin are generally superior, they do not provide the type of lighting and electrical power connections that facilitate coverage by the electronic media. That can be rectified immediately. No space has been designated as a news conference room for use by press and broadcast media representatives. Conference or interview rooms should be made available to the media.

19. JOINT RULES. There should be joint rules governing the relatior ship and the flow of legislation between the two houses of the legis lature.

20. REPRINT AMENDED BILLS. When a bill is amended substantiall it should be reprinted and returned to the legislature with no mor than an overnight delay. The reprint should show clearly the orig inal text of the bill as well as the change created by the amend-ment.

21. PROVIDE SINGLE-MEMBER DISTRICTS. Legislative districts in both houses should be single-member.

22. SPECIAL PROVISIONS. In addition to standard laws governing criminal behavior, there should be special provisions regulating legislative conflicts of interest.

PRACTICE BEFORE REGULATORY AGENCIES. Legislators or their firms should be prohibited from practicing before state regulatory agencies or in matters concerning state agencies for a fee.

PROHIBIT DOING BUSINESS WITH THE STATE. There should be a prohibition against legislators or the firms in which they own a major interest doing business with state agencies.

23. DISCONTINUE ROTATING LEADERSHIP. The practice of limitin presiding officers to a single, two-year term in that position weakens the legislature in its capacity to confront other branches and levels of government as a partner of equal stature and diffuse and disrupts the continuity of leadership within the legislative bodies. Although it is extremely difficult to change a practice such as this, because of its profoundly adverse effects on many aspects of legislative performance, it should be discontinued.

The speaker of the House should not be limited, by tradition, to serving no more than one term.

NORTH DAKOTA (22)

Functional, 22; Accountable, 18; Informed, 17; Independent, 37; Representative, 31

GENERAL: A constitutional amendment which provided the North Dakota Legislature with official pre-session orientation and organizational meetings was approved by the voters in 1968. These sessions, generally lasting three days, are used to organize the legislature, educate newly elected members in procedure and rules, and report on the last interim's activities. To further develop post-election time, rules have been adopted to permit pre-session bill drafting, filing, printing, and assignment to committee and scheduling of committee hearings. First utilized in 1969, one-fifth of the total number of bills introduced in that session were filed and drafted according to these new rules.

Strictly limited in actual session time, North Dakota legislators have developed a refined system of interim activities. All committees are joint, and the membership of these committees closely approximates the membership of similar subject-matter standing committees meeting during the session. Each house has a Legislative Research Resolutions Committee which begins to operate toward the end of the session. The committees screen the research studies to be conducted during the interim by the Legislative Council and its interim subcommittees. Scheduling, planning, budgeting, review, and evaluation are handled by the Legislative Council.

End-of-session logjams are largely prevented in both houses by implementation of a series of bill deadlines, another compensating factor for a state with severely limited sessions. One-fifth of all House bills and one-fourth of all Senate bills were passed during the last week of the session. These figures compare favorably with other states.

An amendment that would have authorized appointment of a compensation commission to set legislative salaries and expense allowances, in effect replacing the existing commission dealing with expenses only, was rejected by the North Dakota voters in the 1970 general election. Salaries are now $5 a day for sixty legislative days per biennium. Another setback for the legislature occurred in the September, 1970, primary election when the voters passed a controversial measure (initiated by the people) canceling plans for a new state office building that would have provided additional space for the legislature. However, at the same primary election a call for a constitutional convention was approved. North Dakota should be able to vote on a new legislative article by the general election of 1972.

These recommendations for improvement of the North Dakota Legislature should be considered.

1. REMOVE CONSTITUTIONAL RESTRICTIONS ON SESSION AND INTERIM TIME. The legislature should have authority to function throughout a two-year term; ideally, this authority should provide a flexible biennial session pattern that permits the legislature to convene, recess, and reconvene as it deems desirable. The legislature should be able to meet in general session or conduct interim work as it deems necessary at any time throughout the period.

   The North Dakota Legislature's most severe restriction is that of session time. Although it has developed a fairly good program for interim activities, sixty legislative days every biennium is far too limiting to effectively cope with legislative problems. The legislature should consider an amendment to provide for unlimited annual sessions or, as an interim step, annual sessions limited to no fewer than ninety legislative days. A minor but nevertheless significant alternative would be to permit the legislature to reconvene, following the completion of bill signing by the governor, to consider overriding vetoes.

2. LEGISLATIVE POWER TO CALL SPECIAL SESSIONS. Amend the constitution to permit the legislature to convene special sessions either by petition of a majority of the members of both houses or the call of the presiding officer of each house.

3. MANAGEMENT COMMITTEES. There should be an executive or management committee created in each house. Its membership should include the leaders of each party in each house, and the minority party should have representation on the committee in proportion to its numbers in the body as a whole. The Senate/House management committees should combine as a joint management committee. The purpose of these committees should be to assume responsibility for the administrative management (housekeeping) functions relating to personnel, facilities, the research bureaus, budgets, and expenditures of their respective houses. The joint management committee should deal with matters of interhouse coordination.

4. OPEN COMMITTEES. The rules of each house should prohibit secret meetings except in matters affecting the security of the state, or which could unnecessarily damage the reputation of individuals in personnel matters. Such exceptions should be sparingly and responsibly employed.

5. NOTICE OF MEETINGS. The rules should require a minimum notice of five legislative days for committee meetings and hearings, with widely disseminated announcement of schedule, location, agenda, and availability of public participation.

6. COMMITTEE BILL REPORTS. Require committees to issue reports describing and explaining the committee's action on bills recommended for passage at the time the bill moves from the committee to the floor.

7. PUBLISH COMMITTEE ROLL CALLS. The committee report of action on bills to the respective houses should include those roll calls which are taken, showing how each member voted. These committee reports should be available to the press and public. Published roll calls should apply to those bills recommended for approval as well as those killed.

8. INCREASE LEGISLATIVE COMPENSATION. No legislative salaries in the United States should be below the $10,000 a year level. Compensation of legislators in the larger states should be in the $20,000 to $30,000 range.

   Current salary for legislators in North Dakota is $5 per diem, for a total of $300 per biennium. The constitution should be amended to allow compensation to be established by statute.

9. SUPPORT OF DISTRICT OFFICES. District offices are vital to the effective representation by a legislator of his constituency. The legislature should make some contribution to the support of district offices for its members, and the amount of this contribution should be increased over time.

10. PRINTED BILL DOCUMENT FORMAT. The bill document printing procedure should permit the clear identification of the text of the existing statute which is being amended, as well as the material which the bill proposes to delete or add. This is usually accomplished through the use of varying type faces such as "strike-through," italics, underlining, or bracketing. It should not be necessary to compare the text of a bill with the text of the existing code to determine what the bill does.

11. REPRINT AMENDED BILLS. When a bill is amended substantially, it should be reprinted and returned to the legislature with no more than an overnight delay. The reprint should show clearly the original text of the bill as well as the change created by the amendment.

12. BILL SUMMARY BY BILL-DRAFTING SERVICE. The form in which bills are introduced should include a more extensive summary of the provisions of the bill, prepared by the bill-drafting service.

13. STATEMENT OF INTENT BY AUTHOR OF A BILL. The form in which a bill is introduced should include a statement by the author describing, in laymen's language, what the bill is intended to accomplish.

14. STRENGTHEN STAFF SUPPORT. Legislative research, fiscal, legal, and planning agencies should be adequately staffed to full utility and at suitable salary levels for professional qualification. Professional staffing should be at a level to enable the legislature to conduct continuous, year-round examination of state resources and expenditures as well as program review and evaluation of state agencies. This staff should also prepare fiscal notes accompanying all appropriation bills, evaluating their fiscal impact over the short and long term. Staff agencies should be upgraded to the level at which competent and timely service can be provided to every member of the legislature.

15. STRENGTHEN STAFF SUPPORT (LEADERS). Staff assistance should be provided to all leaders of both the majority and minority parties. Such assistance should include a secretary and an administrative assistant at the professional level, with space to work reasonably adjacent to the offices of members and leaders.

16. STRENGTHEN STAFF (RANK-AND-FILE MEMBERS). Rank-and-file members (majority and minority party on an equal basis) should be provided with individual staff assistance consisting of a minimum of an administrative assistant at the professional level and a secretary. Eventually, this should increase to the stated level of support both in the capital and in a district office.

17. COMMITTEE STAFFING. Standing committees should be staffed on a permanent, year-round basis.

18. WASHINGTON, D.C., OFFICE FOR THE LEGISLATURE. With the large and growing volume of activity generated by state-federal relationships, the legislature, beyond merely reacting to federal legislation, should be in a position to influence the development of new programs in accordance with the interests of the state. To do so, the legislature should have an office in the nation's capital to represent it and to be its most direct liaison with the Congress.

For small states, consideration might be given to joining with a number of sister states (either on a geographical or on a population basis) for the purpose of sharing the services of a Washington office. But in large states, the volume of inter-governmental traffic has reached a stage at which it would benefit the legislature greatly to have a full-time Washington office.

19. INDIVIDUAL OFFICES. Provide private, individual offices for every member of the legislature, with nearby space for their assistants. The quality and amount of office space should not differ substantially between majority and minority party members.

20. FACILITIES FOR COMMITTEES. Legislative effectiveness requires that committees have adequate physical facilities in which to do their work. This includes an adequate number of committee rooms and an adequate number of hearing rooms that will permit the seating of larger audiences.

21. SERVICE AGENCY FACILITIES. Space for service agencies should provide adequate working space for professional and clerical staff as well as library, files, and other storage requirements.

22. IMPROVE PRESS FACILITIES. Improved press facilities aid in the coverage of the work of the legislature. Committee rooms, and both chambers or galleries, should provide adequate space for the news media as well as lighting and electrical power connections for their equipment. Conference or interview rooms and office space should also be provided for the news media.

23. PRACTICE BEFORE REGULATORY AGENCIES. Legislators or their firms should be prohibited from practicing before state regulatory agencies or in matters concerning state agencies for a fee.

PROHIBIT DOING BUSINESS WITH THE STATE. There should be a prohibition against legislators or the firms in which they own a major interest doing business with state agencies.

FAMILY EMPLOYMENT. Members of a legislator's immediate family should be barred from employment by the legislature.

24. REGULATION OF LOBBYISTS. The independence of the legislature and public confidence in its processes require the regulation of special interest advocates. Lobbyists should be required to register with an agency of the legislature, and should be required to disclose who employs them, on behalf of what objectives, how

much they are paid, and how much they spend and on whom. This
information should be available to the press and the public.
There should be specific and automatic penalties for failure to
comply with these requirements.

25. PROVIDE SINGLE-MEMBER DISTRICTS. Legislative districts
    in both houses should be single-member.

26. DISCONTINUE ROTATING LEADERSHIP. The practice of limiting
    presiding officers to a single, two-year term in that position
    weakens the legislature in its capacity to confront other branches
    and levels of government as a partner of equal stature and diffuses
    and disrupts the continuity of leadership within the legislative
    bodies. Although it is extremely difficult to change a practice
    such as this, because of its profoundly adverse effects on many
    aspects of legislative performance, it should be discontinued.

    Although neither speaker of the House nor president pro tem of
    the Senate is considered a powerful leadership position, the
    customary two-year limitation on those offices should be discon-
    tinued.

27. REMOVE LEGISLATIVE POWERS FROM LIEUTENANT GOVERNO
    The exercise of legislative powers, including such pro forma
    powers as presiding, casting tie-breaking votes, and signing
    enacted legislation, by the lieutenant governor, whether the powers
    derive from the constitution or the rule book, would seem to be a
    particularly serious breach of the separation of powers and the
    independence of the legislature. The constitution and/or rule
    book should be amended to permit these legislative powers pres-
    ently exercised by the lieutenant governor to be set as the respon-
    sibility of the office of the president pro tem of the Senate.

OHIO (16)

Functional, 18; Accountable, 24; Informed, 7; Independent, 40;
Representative, 9

GENERAL: The Ohio Legislature meets many of the structural
requirements of an effectively organized legislature. Its major
deficiencies appear to stem from inadequate resources, such as physical space and the number of types of staff support. Ohio has begun to
correct the problem of space shortage by the construction of a new
office building, not yet completed. Very few of the weaknesses are
the product of constitutional restrictions, with the exception of the
limitation on expense reimbursement of members. This would suggest

that any of the improvements which can be made are within the reach of the legislature itself. This should be particularly true since the Citizens' Commission on the Ohio Legislature has recently been appointed and will be in a position to make recommendations for improvement to the legislature.

The better features of the Ohio Legislature are flexible and unlimited biennial sessions, single-member districts, moderate size (House, ninety-nine; Senate, thirty-three), a small number of committees (House, fourteen; Senate, eight), a reasonable number of committee assignments per member (no member of the House has more than three assignments and no member of the Senate has more than four assignments). Legislative salaries are established by statute (but are currently on the low side at $12,750 a year).

The following recommendations are made for Ohio.

1. PRE-SESSION ORGANIZATIONAL MEETING. Amend the constitution to provide a pre-session organizing session following a general election. Some states make advantageous use of such a session during November or December of a general election year for the purpose of electing leaders, appointing committee chairmen, assigning members to committees, referring pre-filed bills to committee, holding committee organizational meetings, and conducting orientation conferences for new, as well as returning, members of the legislature. Through such pre-session meetings the committees can begin their work before the regular session convenes. This makes it possible to delay the start of the regular session until legislation is ready for floor action.

2. COMMITTEE JURISDICTION. A description of the jurisdiction of committees should be contained in the rules of both houses, and assignment of bills should be made in accord with the jurisdiction of committees as described in the rules.

3. OPEN COMMITTEES. The rules of each house should prohibit secret meetings except in matters affecting the security of the state, or which could unnecessarily damage the reputation of individuals in personnel matters. Such exceptions should be sparingly and responsibly employed.

    Although subject matter committees meet openly and conduct their business in public, the Rules Committees of the respective houses frequently meet in executive session.

4. NOTICE OF MEETINGS. The rules should require a minimum notice of five legislative days for committee meetings and hearings,

with widely disseminated announcement of schedule, location, agenda, and availability of public participation.

5. ACT ON ALL BILLS. Committees should be required to report on all bills assigned to them, recommending for passage by the parent body those bills which enjoy the support of a majority of the members of the committee and killing all others.

6. COMMITTEE BILL REPORTS. Require committees to issue reports describing and explaining the committee's action on bills recommended for passage at the time the bill moves from the committee to the floor.

7. DUAL COMMITTEE CONSIDERATION OF APPROPRIATION BILLS There should be a rule requiring dual committee consideration of legislation affecting significant sums of money. Such legislation, when considered and acted upon favorably by a substantive policy committee, should then automatically be referred to the Finance Committee for consideration of its fiscal impact.

This is presently done in the House but not in the Senate.

8. INTERIM COMMITTEES. When the legislature is not in session, the standing committees should become the interim committees for the purpose of conducting long-range studies of state policy issues. The Legislative Council or some similarly constituted, bi-partisan committee should serve as the supervising agency for interim committees and their studies, budgets, and personnel. The major committees should be staffed on a year-round basis.

9. INCREASE LEGISLATIVE COMPENSATION. No legislative salaries in the United states should be below the $10,000 a year level. Compensation of legislators in the larger states should be in the $20,000 to $30,000 range.

Salaries of members of the legislature are low in comparison with states of similar size and development. Current salaries of $12,750 should be raised to the $15,000 to $20,000 level.

10. EXPENSE ALLOWANCES. Members of the legislature should be allowed an expense reimbursement covering their travel and living costs while engaged in carrying out their legislative duties. The same allowance should obtain during the interim for days in attendance at interim committee meetings or other official and authorized legislative business. These allowances should be provided by statute.

11. SUPPORT OF DISTRICT OFFICES. District offices are vital to
    the effective representation by a legislator of his constituency.
    The legislature should make some contribution to the support of
    district offices for its members, and the amount of this contribution
    should be increased over time.

12. BILL DEADLINES. The orderly flow of work through the legislature
    depends upon the existence of a series of deadlines at various
    critical stages throughout the legislative process. These deadlines
    should be adopted as part of the rules and should be consistently
    enforced.

13. ESTABLISH AN AUTOMATIC CALENDAR OF BILLS. When a
    bill is favorably reported out of committee to the floor, it should
    go automatically onto the calendar in the order in which it was
    reported out. It should require a vote of an extraordinary majority
    to move a bill from its position on calendar or to bypass it. The
    rules committee should have no part in the scheduling of bills.
    No session should adjourn until all bills on calendar have been
    voted up or down or, by the vote of an extraordinary majority,
    have been moved from the calendar.

14. REPRINT AMENDED BILLS. When a bill is amended substantially,
    it should be reprinted and returned to the legislature with no
    more than an overnight delay. The reprint should show clearly
    the original text of the bill as well as the change created by the
    amendment.

    The Senate reprints only substitute bills; the House, some but not
    all amended bills. A copy of all substantially amended bills,
    regardless of the importance of the bill, should be available to
    every member of the legislature with no more than an overnight
    delay.

15. STRENGTHEN STAFF SUPPORT. Legislative research, fiscal,
    legal, and planning agencies should be adequately staffed to full
    utility and at suitable salary levels for professional qualification.
    Professional staffing should be at a level to enable the legislature
    to conduct continuous, year-round examination of state resources
    and expenditures as well as program review and evaluation of
    state agencies. This staff should also prepare fiscal notes
    accompanying all appropriation bills, evaluating their fiscal impact
    over the short and long term. Staff agencies should be upgraded
    to the level at which competent and timely service can be provided
    to every member of the legislature.

    The legislative agencies should be augmented by authorizing

additional staff positions to allow an increased level and volume
of services, such as budget review and analysis (which has recently
been improved), program review and evaluation, and long-range
fiscal forecasting.

16. STRENGTHEN STAFF SUPPORT (LEADERS). Staff assistance
should be provided to all leaders of both the majority and the
minority parties. Such assistance should include a secretary and
an administrative assistant at the professional level, with space
to work reasonably adjacent to the offices of members and leaders.

17. STRENGTHEN STAFF (RANK-AND-FILE MEMBERS). Rank-and-
file members (majority and minority party on an equal basis)
should be provided with individual staff assistance consisting of
a minimum of an administrative assistant at the professional
level and a secretary. Eventually, this should increase to the
stated level of support both in the capital and in a district office.

18. COMMITTEE STAFFING. Standing committees should be staffed
on a permanent, year-round basis.

Standing committees now have staff assistance from the Legislative
Service Commission at a ratio of about one professional staff
person per member. These staff people must nevertheless devote
time to both the working of the standing committees and the
Service Commission. The committees should be staffed on a
full-time, year-round basis.

19. WASHINGTON, D.C., OFFICE FOR THE LEGISLATURE. With
the large and growing volume of activity generated by state-federal
relationships, the legislature, beyond merely reacting to federal
legislation, should be in a position to influence the development
of new programs in accordance with the interests of the state.
To do so, the legislature should have an office in the nation's
capital to represent it and to be its most direct liaison with the
Congress.

For small states, consideration might be given to joining with a
number of sister states (either on a geographical or on a population basis) for the purpose of sharing the services of a Washington office. But in large states, the volume of inter-governmental
traffic has reached a stage at which it would benefit the legislature
greatly to have a full-time Washington office.

20. INDIVIDUAL OFFICES. Provide private, individual offices for
every member of the legislature, with nearby space for their
assistants. The quality and amount of office space should not

differ substantially between majority and minority party members.

The new office building should begin to alleviate the problem of lack of office space for members.

21. IMPROVE PRESS FACILITIES. Improved press facilities aid in the coverage of the work of the legislature. Committee rooms, and both chambers or galleries, should provide adequate space for news media as well as lighting and electrical power connections for their equipment. Conference or interview rooms and office space should also be provided for the news media.

Specifically, committee rooms should provide adequate space for the news media as well as lighting and electrical power connections for their equipment. Conference or interview rooms and office space should also be provided for the news media.

22. SPECIAL PROVISIONS. In addition to standard laws governing criminal behavior, there should be special provisions regulating legislative conflicts of interest.

PRACTICE BEFORE REGULATORY AGENCIES. Legislators or their firms should be prohibited from practicing before state regulatory agencies or in matters concerning state agencies for a fee.

PROHIBIT DOING BUSINESS WITH THE STATE. There should be a prohibition against legislators or the firms in which they own a major interest doing business with state agencies.

FAMILY EMPLOYMENT. Members of a legislator's immediate family should be barred from employment by the legislature.

23. TRANSFER AUDIT FUNCTION TO THE LEGISLATURE. A significant part of the legislature's ability to exercise oversight of executive departments and administrative agencies depends upon the power and capacity to conduct audits (financial and functional) of these units of the state government. These functions and responsibilities should be removed from the duties and resources of the Office of Auditor and be established under a legislative auditor.

OKALAHOMA (14)

Functional, 9; Accountable, 27; Informed, 24; Independent, 22; Representative, 8

GENERAL: The Oklahoma Legislature ranks fourteenth in overall capability. A rather uneven development is displayed by its varying position on scales measuring different facets of legislative capability. Oklahoma's high position on the representative (8) and on the functional (9) scales is offset by lower ranking on the informed (24) and independent (22) scales, indicating a mixture of good and bad features of organization, structure, and procedure.

Compensation of legislators is established by an independent, constitutional commission and is currently at $8,400 a year. This is below the minimum recommended in this study ($10,000 per year), but above the national average.

The legislature meets in annual, general sessions, limited to ninety legislative rather than calendar days, the usual requirement of states with constitutional session restrictions. Although the legislature does not use this amount of session time (1969, sixty-five days), end-of-session logjams appear not to be a problem. A study of four recent sessions shows that fewer than one percent of all bills passed were enacted during the last one-fifth of the session.

The fifteen committees of each house are parallel in scope and combine as joint interim committees when the legislature is not in session. No member of the Senate has more than four committee assignments, and only three members of the House have more than three.

Individual offices are provided for leaders in both houses, individual members in the Senate, and, on a shared basis, individual members in the House. Bills reported out of committee go automatically onto the bill calendar, and bills on which action is not completed carry over from the first to the second session of the term.

The small legislative staff provides a reasonably extensive number of services, but depends too heavily on part-time assistance and is not able to meet the volume of demands required to service all members adequately. Experimentation is underway on a number of electronic data-processing services, such as identifying the current status of bills, recording and tracing the history of actions on bills, bill drafting, and statutory retrieval.

From this study these major recommendations emerge.

1.   STRENGTHEN MINORITY PARTY ROLE. Internal accountability, as well as the capacity of all legislators to represent their constituents effectively, depends upon the opportunity of minority party members to have an effective part in internal legislative affairs.

     MINORITY REPRESENTATION ON COMMITTEE ON RULES.
     Minority representation on the Committee on Rules should

approximate the minority party proportion of the membership
of the appropriate house.

MINORITY PARTY MEMBERS ON COMMITTEE. Minority party
members should be assigned to committees by the minority leader
in consultation with the minority caucus.

The minority party is under-represented on many committees,
particularly the Rules Committee. During the 1969 regular session party, ratios were about four to one both in the House and
the Senate, while the Rules Committee ratios were, respectively,
twenty-six to one and fourteen to one. Minority representation on
the Committee on Rules of the respective houses should approximate the minority party proportion of membership in each house.

2. UNIFORM COMMITTEE RULES. There should be uniform published
   rules of committee procedure in both chambers.

3. COMMITTEE JURISDICTION. A description of the jurisdiction
   of committees should be contained in the rules of both houses,
   and assignment of bills should be made in accord with the jurisdiction of committees as described in the rules.

4. PUBLISH COMMITTEE ROLL CALLS. The committee report of
   action on bills to the respective houses should include those roll
   calls which are taken, showing how each member voted. These
   committee reports should be available to the press and public.
   Published roll calls should apply to those bills recommended for
   approval as well as those killed.

5. COMMITTEE HEARINGS. There is no justification for permitting
   any major piece of legislation to become law without having been
   subjected to extensive, thorough, well-planned, and well-prepared
   public hearings, in which representatives of the public, civic
   organizations, and interest groups are not only invited but encouraged to participate.

6. OPEN COMMITTEES. The rules of each house should prohibit
   secret meetings except in matters affecting the security of the
   state, or which could unnecessarily damage the reputation of
   individuals in personnel matters. Such exceptions should be
   sparingly and responsibly employed.

7. NOTICE OF MEETINGS. The rules should require a minimum
   notice of five legislative days for committee meetings and hearings,
   with widely disseminated announcement of schedule, location,
   agenda, and availability of public participation.

8. ACT ON ALL BILLS. Committees should be required to report on all bills assigned to them, recommending for passage by the parent body those bills which enjoy the support of a majority of the members of the committee and killing all others.

9. BALANCED COMMITTEES. Committees, in their composition, should reflect as accurately as possible the makeup of the entire house of which they are a part. There should be no "killer," "graveyard," or "cinch" committees.

10. REMOVE CONSTITUTIONAL RESTRICTIONS ON SESSION AND INTERIM TIME. The legislature should have authority to function throughout a two-year term; ideally, this authority should provide a flexible biennial session pattern that permits the legislature to convene, recess, and reconvene as it deems desirable. The legislature should be able to meet in general session or conduct interim work as it deems necessary at any time throughout the period.

11. LEGISLATIVE POWER TO CALL SPECIAL SESSIONS. Amend the constitution to permit the legislature to convene special sessions either by petition of a majority of the members of both houses or the call of the presiding officer of each house.

12. POWER TO EXPAND SPECIAL SESSION AGENDA. Amend the constitution to permit the legislature to broaden the subject matter of a governor's call of a special session by a majority vote in each house, or prohibit the restriction of the agenda by the governor

13. PRE-SESSION ORGANIZATIONAL MEETING. Amend the constitution to provide a pre-session organizing session following a general election. Some states make advantageous use of such a session during November or December of a general election year for the purpose of electing leaders, appointing committee chairmen, assigning members to committees, referring pre-filed bills to committee, holding committee organizational meetings, and conducting orientation conferences for new, as well as returning, members of the legislature. Through such pre-session meetings the committees can begin their work before the regular session convenes. This makes it possible to delay the start of the regular session until legislation is ready for floor action.

14. CONSENT CALENDAR. A consent calendar should be used in both houses.

15. ELECTRIC ROLL CALL RECORDER. An electric roll call recorder should be installed in the House, as in the Senate. This

is recommended not simply because it would speed up the proceedings (worthwhile as this may be), but because it is an efficient method of producing an error-free record of roll call votes.

16. WASHINGTON, D.C., OFFICE FOR THE LEGISLATURE. With the large and growing volume of activity generated by state-federal relationships, the legislature, beyond merely reacting to federal legislation, should be in a position to influence the development of new programs in accordance with the interests of the state. To do so, the legislature should have an office in the nation's capital to represent it and to be its most direct liaison with the Congress.

For small states, consideration might be given to joining with a number of sister states (either on a geographical or on a population basis) for the purpose of sharing the services of a Washington office. But in large states, the volume of inter-governmental traffic has reached a stage at which it would benefit the legislature greatly to have a full-time Washington office.

17. TRANSFER AUDIT FUNCTION TO THE LEGISLATURE. A significant part of the legislature's ability to exercise oversight of executive departments and administrative agencies depends upon the power and capacity to conduct audits (financial and functional) of these units of the state government. These functions and responsibilities should be removed from the duties and resources of the Office of Auditor and be established under a legislative auditor.

18. STRENGTHEN STAFF SUPPORT. Legislative research, fiscal, legal, and planning agencies should be adequately staffed to full utility and at suitable salary levels for professional qualification. Professional staffing should be at a level to enable the legislature to conduct continuous, year-round examination of state resources and expenditures as well as program review and evaluation of state agencies. This staff should also prepare fiscal notes accompanying all appropriation bills, evaluating their fiscal impact over the short and long term. Staff agencies should be upgraded to the level at which competent and timely service can be provided to every member of the legislature.

19. STRENGTHEN STAFF SUPPORT (LEADERS). Staff assistance should be provided to all leaders of both the majority and minority parties. Such assistance should include a secretary and an administrative assistant at the professional level, with space to work reasonably adjacent to the offices of members and leaders.

20. STRENGTHEN STAFF (RANK-AND-FILE MEMBERS). Rank-and-

file members (majority and minority party on an equal basis)
should be provided with individual staff assistance consisting of
a minimum of an administrative assistant at the professional
level and a secretary. Eventually, this should increase to the
stated level of support both in the capital and in a district office.

21. COMMITTEE STAFFING. Standing committees should be staffed
on a permanent, year-round basis.

22. INDIVIDUAL OFFICES. Provide private, individual offices for
every member of the legislature, with nearby space for their
assistants. The quality and amount of office space should not
differ substantially between majority and minority party members.

23. EXPENSE ALLOWANCES. Members of the legislature should be
allowed an expense reimbursement covering their travel and living
costs while engaged in carrying out their legislative duties. The
same allowance should obtain during the interim for days in
attendance at interim committee meetings or other official and
authorized legislative business. These allowances should be
provided by statute.

24. IMPROVE PRESS FACILITIES. Improved press facilities aid in
the coverage of the work of the legislature. Committee rooms,
and both chambers or galleries, should provide adequate space
for the news media as well as lighting and electrical power connections for their equipment. Conference or interview rooms and
office space should also be provided for the news media.

Specifically Oklahoma's practice of charging rent based on the
number of desks occupied in the press room should be discontinued.
Offices and equipment storage space should be provided for the
news media at public expense. Good media coverage of the legislative proceedings is critically important to an informed public.
Oklahoma is the only state which charges for the "privilege" of
occupying facilities for this purpose.

25. SUPPORT OF DISTRICT OFFICES. District offices are vital to
the effective representation by a legislator of his constituency.
The legislature should make some contribution to the support of
district offices for its members, and the amount of this contribution
should be increased over time.

OREGON (27)

Functional, 28; Accountable, 14; Informed, 35; Independent, 35;
Representative, 19

GENERAL: The Oregon Legislature embarked upon a program of reform several years age with the formation of the Advisory Committee on the Oregon Legislature. That citizens' group made a thorough study of the legislature and formulated a rather complete list of recommendations for legislative modernization that was then presented to the legislature. Some of those recommendations required constitutional amendments to implement, others did not.

Several constitutional amendments passed by the 1969 session of the legislature would have updated conditions in several key areas of legislative activity: the legislature would have been empowered to call an even-year session; the legislature would have been defined as a continuous body; secret sessions would have been unequivocally forbidden; and the size of the House would have been increased from sixty to sixty-five members, the Senate from thirty to thirty-five members. However, voters rejected their opportunities to adopt these changes and others at the May, 1970, primary and November, 1970, general election.

The legislature should continue to examine and consider all of the Citizens' Commissions's recommendations that it has not already adopted, as well as utilizing that report to educate public opinion to the legislature's needs and how they might best be met.

The legislature currently sponsors a one-week pre-session orientation conference for all new members. Special attention is given to a thorough discussion of budgetary matters. Oregonians interested in attending legislative committee meetings are given adequate notice of the time, place, and agenda, and roll calls on all final committee actions are recorded in the committee's minutes.

Following are additional recommendations for the modernization of the Oregon Legislature.

1. REMOVE CONSTITUTIONAL RESTRICTIONS ON SESSION AND INTERIM TIME. The legislature should have authority to function throughout a two-year term; ideally, this authority should provide a flexible biennial session pattern that permits the legislature to convene, recess, and reconvene as it deems desirable. The legislature should be able to meet in general session or conduct interim work as it deems necessary at any time throughout the period.

   Amend the constitution to permit annual general sessions, limited to no fewer than ninety legislative days. The constitution should also be amended to define the legislature as a continuous legal entity when it is not in sesssion, thereby allowing the legislature to conduct a full program of interim activities.

2. LEGISLATIVE POWER TO CALL SPECIAL SESSIONS. Amend
    the constitution to permit the legislature to convene special
    sessions either by petition of a majority of the members of both
    houses or the call of the presiding officer of each house.

3. PRE-SESSION ORGANIZATIONAL MEETING. Amend the consti-
    tution to provide a pre-session organizing session following a
    general election. Some states make advantageous use of such a
    session during November or December of a general election year
    for the purpose of electing leaders, appointing committee chairmen,
    assigning members to committees, referring pre-filed bills to
    committee, holding committee organizational meetings, and con-
    ducting orientation conferences for new, as well as returning,
    members of the legislature. Through such pre-session meetings
    the committees can begin their work before the regular session
    convenes. This makes it possible to delay the start of the regular
    session until legislation is ready for floor action.

4. INTERIM COMMITTEES. When the legislature is not in session,
    the standing committees should become the interim committees
    for the purpose of conducting long-range studies of state policy
    issues. The Legislative Council or some similarly constituted,
    bi-partisan committee should serve as the supervising agency for
    interim committees and their studies, budgets, and personnel.
    The major committees should be staffed on a year-round basis.

    When the legislature is not in session, the standing committees
    should become the interim committees for the purpose of conducting
    long-range studies of state policy issues.

5. STRENGTHEN STAFF SUPPORT. Legislative research, fiscal,
    legal, and planning agencies should be adequately staffed to full
    utility and at suitable salary levels for professional qualification.
    Professional staffing should be at a level to enable the legislature
    to conduct continuous, year-round examination of state resources
    and expenditures as well as program review and evaluation of
    state agencies. This staff should also prepare fiscal notes
    accompanying all appropriation bills, evaluating their fiscal impact
    over the short and long term. Staff agencies should be upgraded
    to the level at which competent and timely service can be provided
    to every member of the legislature.

    Professional legislative staffing should be augmented in order to
    provide such services as spot research, in-depth studies and
    program design, and public information services.

6. STRENGTHEN STAFF SUPPORT (LEADERS). Staff assistance
    should be provided to all leaders of both the majority and minority

parties. Such assistance should include a secretary and an administrative assistant at the professional level, with space to work reasonably adjacent to the offices of members and leaders.

All leaders, majority and minority, should be provided with assistants at a professional level.

7. STRENGTHEN STAFF (RANK-AND-FILE MEMBERS). Rank-and-file members (majority and minority party on equal basis) should be provided with individual staff assistance consisting of a minimum of an administrative assistant at the professional level and a secretary. Eventually, this should increase to the stated level of support both in the capital and in a district office.

Movement toward the staffing of individual members is also in order, through the provision of professional assistants, perhaps beginning on a shared basis, but ultimately for each member. The number of permanent, year-round committee staff members should also be increased.

8. TRANSFER AUDIT FUNCTION TO THE LEGISLATURE. A significant part of the legislature's ability to exercise oversight of executive departments and administrative agencies depends upon the power and capacity to conduct audits (financial and functional) of these units of the state government. These functions and responsibilities should be removed from the duties and resources of the Office of Auditor and be established under a legislative auditor.

9. INDIVIDUAL OFFICES. Provide private, individual offices for every member of the legislature, with nearby space for their assistants. The quality and amount of office space should not differ substantially between majority and minority party members.

Individual offices should be provided for members of the House, as already provided for members of the Senate, with reasonably adjacent space for staff. A beginning can be made toward providing offices for members by making space available for shared offices among small numbers of members at first, then gradually reducing the number who share space until a private office is provided for each member.

10. FACILITIES FOR COMMITTEES. Legislative effectiveness requires that committees have adequate physical facilities in which to do their work. This includes an adequate number of committee rooms and an adequate number of hearing rooms that will permit the seating of larger audiences.

More adequate committee rooms, spacious enough for visitors
and press, accessible, and with audiovisual and recording equipmen
are needed.

11. LEGISLATIVE SALARIES. Legislative salaries should be set by
statute and paid in equal monthly installments throughout the
biennium, and all unvouchered expense allowances should be
incorporated into an annual salary. Actual and necessary expenses
incurred in the process of carrying out legislative duties should
be reimbursed upon submission and approval of properly vouchered
evidence of expenditures.

INCREASE LEGISLATIVE COMPENSATION. No legislative
salaries in the United States should be below the $10,000 a year
level. Compensation of legislators in the larger states should
be in the $20,000 to $30,000 range.

Salaries of members of the legislature are far too low. Current
salaries, which average $3,000 a year, should be doubled immedi-
ately and increased again within the next few years as other
improvements are made.

12. PROVIDE SINGLE-MEMBER DISTRICTS. Legislative districts
in both houses should be single-member.

13. STRENGTHEN MINORITY PARTY ROLE. Internal accountability,
as well as the capacity of all legislators to represent their
constituents effectively, depends upon the opportunity of minority
party members to have an effective part in internal legislative
affairs.

MINORITY REPRESENTATION ON COMMITTEE ON RULES.
Minority representation on the Committee on Rules should
approximate the minority party proportion of the membership of
the appropriate house.

MINORITY PARTY MEMBERS ON COMMITTEE. Minority
party members should be assigned to committees by the minority
leader in consultation with the minority caucus.

14. ACT ON ALL BILLS. Committees should be required to report
on all bills assigned to them, recommending for passage by the
parent body those bills which enjoy the support of a majority of
the members of the committee and killing all others.

15. REDUCE THE NUMBER OF COMMITTEES. Ideally, there should
be from ten to fifteen committees in each house, parallel in

jurisdiction. This would reduce the general complexity of the legislature and would permit reducing the number of committee assignments per member.

16. REDUCE THE NUMBER OF COMMITTEE ASSIGNMENTS. In order to make it possible for members to concentrate their attention and contribute effectively, there should be no more than three committee assignments for each member of the lower house and four committee assignments for each member of the Senate. The multiplicity of assignments introduces problems of scheduling, strains the focus of attention on the part of members, and creates an inordinately heavy workload for members if committees are as active as they should be.

At present, thirteen percent of the members of the House have more than three committee assignments each, and twenty-three percent of the members of the Senate have more than four committee assignments each.

17. OPEN COMMITTEES. The rules of each house should prohibit secret meetings except in matters affecting the security of the state, or which could unnecessarily damage the reputation of individuals in personnel matters. Such exceptions should be sparingly and responsibly employed.

18. UNIFORM COMMITTEE RULES. There should be uniform published rules of committee procedure in the Senate as in the House.

19. JOINT RULES. There should be joint rules governing the relationship and the flow of legislation between the two houses of the legislature.

20. ELECTRIC ROLL CALL RECORDER. There should be an electric roll call recorder in the House and in the Senate. This is recommended not simply because it would speed up the proceedings (worthwhile as this may be), but because it is an efficient method of producing an error-free record of roll call votes.

21. MANAGEMENT COMMITTEES. There should be an executive or management committee created in each house. Its membership should include the leaders of each party in each house, and the minority party should have representation on the commitee in proportion to its numbers in the body as a whole. The Senate/ House management committees should combine as a joint management committee. The purpose of these committees should be to assume responsibility for the administrative management (housekeeping) functions relating to personnel, facilities, the research

bureaus, budgets, and expenditures of their respective houses.
The joint management committee should deal with matters of
interhouse coordination.

The new Joint Commission on Legislative Administration could
serve in the capacity of the management committee.

22. PRACTICE BEFORE REGULATORY AGENCIES. Legislators or
their firms should be prohibited from practicing before state
regulatory agencies or in matters concerning state agencies for
a fee.

PROHIBIT APPOINTMENT TO STATE OFFICE. There should be
a prohibition against a legislator accepting appointment to other
state office during the term for which he is elected or within two
years of the termination of his service as a member of the
legislature.

FAMILY EMPLOYMENT. Members of a legislator's immediate
family should be barred from employment by the legislature.

23. DUAL COMMITTEE CONSIDERATION OF APPROPRIATION BILLS
There should be a rule requiring dual committee consideration
of legislation affecting significant sums of money. Such legislation
when considered and acted upon favorably by a substantive policy
committee, should then automatically be referred to the Finance
Committee for consideration of its fiscal impact.

24. SUPPORT OF DISTRICT OFFICES. District offices are vital to
the effective representation by a legislator of his constituency.
The legislature should make some contribution to the support of
district offices for its members, and the amount of this contribution
should be increased over time.

25. BILL DEADLINES. The orderly flow of work through the legislature
depends upon the existence of a series of deadlines at various
critical stages throughout the legislative process. These deadlines
should be adopted as part of the rules and should be consistently
enforced.

Although there is a deadline for bill filing and introduction,
approximately forty-four percent of the bills passed by the legislature in the last session were enacted in the last twelve days of
the session. Additional deadlines are needed.

26. IMPROVE PRESS FACILITIES. Improved press facilities aid in
the coverage of the work of the legislature. Committee rooms,

and both chambers or galleries, should provide adequate space
for the news media as well as lighting and electrical power connections for their equipment. Conference or interview rooms and
office space should also be provided for the news media.

27. SERVICE AGENCY FACILITIES. Space for service agencies
should provide adequate working space for professional and
clerical staff as well as library, files, and other storage requirements.

28. AMENDING THE RULES. A due regard for the rights of the
minority, one of the means of insuring internal accountability,
requires stable rules of procedure. Although it is consistent with
majority rule to permit the adoption of rules of procedure at the
beginning of a term by a majority vote, once adopted, the requirement to change the rules should be by a two-thirds vote, as is
the case in most legislatures.

This procedure is observed in the House, but not in the Senate.

29. STATEMENT OF INTENT BY AUTHOR OF A BILL. The form
in which a bill is introduced should include a statement by the
author describing, in laymen's language, what the bill is intended
to accomplish.

30. CONSENT CALENDAR. A consent calendar should be used in
both houses.

PENNSYLVANIA (21)

Functional, 37; Accountable, 23; Informed, 23; Independent, 5;
Representative, 36

GENERAL: The 1968 constitutional convention in Pennsylvania,
followed by voter ratification of its proposals, succeeded in eliminating
a few of the remaining constitutional impediments to better legislative
operations. Creating single-member districts, eliminating the
requirement that bills be read at length on three separate legislative
days, clearing the way for flexible, biennial sessions, and insuring
the legislature's right to convene in special session were among the
changes introduced by the revised constitution.

One of the more severe problems of the Pennsylvania Legislature -
the inordinately large size of the House (203 members) - was not
improved; it was made worse. The pre-1968 constitution did not
specify a size limit, but the membership of the House had grown to

203 over the years. Although a number of proposals were offered in the convention to reduce that number, they were all defeated and the number was frozen at 203.

Anyone who has attended a session of the House must sympathize with the problems of members in trying to find out what is going on and with the problems of leaders in maintaining decorum and organizing a majority for the movement of legislation.

The size of the House remains one of the really pressing problems of the Pennsylvania Legislature.

The legislature has substantial control over its time, facilities, and other resources, contributing to a relatively high degree of independence. It has the resource base to become one of the outstanding legislatures in the country.

In 1968, the General Assembly created a commission for legislative modernization on which a number of distinguished Pennsylvanians served under the co-chairmanship of author James A. Michener and the president of the A. W. Mellon Educational and Charitable Trust, Theodore L. Hazelett, Jr. The report of this commission, "Toward Tomorrow's Legislature" (January, 1969), contained fifty-eight recommendations for improvement. A number of these recommendations have been implemented by the legislature, others have been implemented only in part, and some still await action.

The recommendations which follow are addressed to the areas in which improvements can be made. Although some of the recommendations made by the Pennsylvania Commission for Legislative Modernization are repeated, many go beyond their report.

1. REDUCE THE OVERALL SIZE OF THE LEGISLATURE. Although size reduction in a legislative body is extremely difficult to achieve, it has been done in some states--such as in Vermont and Iowa--and needs to be accomplished in others (New Hampshire, Massachusetts, Georgia, and Pennsylvania). Where reduction in size has occurred, it has most often required a constitutional convention to accomplish it. In a few cases it has been done by legislatively adopted constitutional amendment (Iowa, in 1968, which becomes effective in November, 1971) ratified by the voters. There should be 100 or fewer members in the house. The combined size of both houses should be between 100 and 150.

With 203 members, the House of the Pennsylvania Legislature is the third largest state legislative body in the United States. Despite the difficulty of bringing about reduction, and recognizing that a recent constitutional convention decided against it, it is nevertheless recommended that the House be reduced in numbers from its present 203 to no more than 100 members.

2.   REDUCE THE NUMBER OF COMMITTEES. Ideally, there should be from ten to fifteen committees in each house, parallel in jurisdiction. This would reduce the general complexity of the legislature and would permit reducing the number of committee assignments per member.

There are now twenty-three committees in the House and twenty-one in the Senate. The number should be reduced to from ten to fifteen committees in each house, parallel in jurisdiction.

The Commission for Legislative Modernization recommended the committees of both houses be reduced to thirteen (recommendation no. 12 in their report). During the 1969 session, Speaker Herbert Fineman reduced the number of House standing committees from thirty-two to twenty-three. A statement issued by the Democratic House leadership on June 11, 1969, recommended a further reduction (to approximately fifteen) be made in 1971.

3.   REDUCE THE NUMBER OF COMMITTEE ASSIGNMENTS. In order to make it possible for members to concentrate their attention and contribute effectively, there should be no more than three committee assignments for each member of the lower house and four committee assignments for each member of the Senate. The multiplicity of assignments introduces problems of scheduling, strains the focus of attention on the part of members, and creates an inordinately heavy workload for members if committees are as active as they should be.

At present, only two percent of the members of the House have more than three committee assignments each, but ninty-six percent of the members of the Senate have more than four committee assignments each. Reduction in the number of Senate committees would contribute to a more reasonable workload for Senators.

4.   OPEN COMMITTEES. The rules of each house should prohibit secret meetings except in matters affecting the security of the state, or which could unnecessarily damage the reputation of individuals in personnel matters. Such exceptions should be sparingly and responsibly employed.

5.   NOTICE OF MEETINGS. The rules should require a minimum notice of five legislative days for committee meetings and hearings, with widely disseminated announcement of schedule, location, agenda, and availability of public participation.

6. ACT ON ALL BILLS. Committees should be required to report on all bills assigned to them, recommending for passage by the parent body those bills which enjoy the support of a majority of the members of the committee and killing all others.

7. BALANCED COMMITTEES. Committees, in their composition, should reflect as accurately as possible the makeup of the entire house of which they are a part. There should be no "killer," "graveyard," or "cinch" committees.

8. COMMITTEE BILL REPORTS. Require committees to issue reports describing and explaining the committee's action on bills recommended for passage at the time the bill moves from the committee to the floor.

9. PUBLISH COMMITTEE ROLL CALLS. The committee report of action on bills to the respective houses should include those roll calls which are taken, showing how each member voted. These committee reports should be available to the press and public. Published roll calls should apply to those bills recommended for approval as well as those killed.

10. MANAGEMENT COMMITTEES. There should be an executive or management committee created in each house. Its membership should include the leaders of each party in each house, and the minority party should have representation on the committee in proportion to its numbers in the body as a whole. The Senate/ House management committees should combine as a joint management committee. The purpose of these committees should be to assume responsibility for the administrative management (housekeeping) functions relating to personnel, facilities, the research bureaus, budgets, and expenditures of their respective houses. The joint management committee should deal with matters of inter-house coordination.

11. JOINT RULES. There should be joint rules governing the relationship and the flow of legislation between the two houses of the legislature.

12. BILL DEADLINES. The orderly flow of work through the legislature depends upon the existence of a series of deadlines at various critical stages throughout the legislative process. These deadlines should be adopted as part of the rules and should be consistently enforced.

Deadlines are particularly needed in states with constitutionally restricted sessions, to enable them to get through a large volume of work in a limited amount of time. The Pennsylvania Legislature does not have the problem of limited session length; in fact, the converse may be true. Sessions take up so much of the year that there is virtually no interim during which committees can study the longer-range problems of the state in an atmosphere removed from the pressures of the session. The establishment of a sound system of deadlines would contribute to the completion of most session work in a six- or seven-month period, which has been the goal of the current leadership. (See Committee for Legislative Modernization, recommendation no. 46, and statement, June 4, 1969, commenting favorably.)

13. INTERIM COMMITTEES. When the legislature is not in session, the standing committees should become the interim committees for the purpose of conducting long-range studies of state policy issues. The Legislative Council or some similarly constituted, bi-partisan committee should serve as the supervising agency for interim committees and their studies, budgets, and personnel. The major committees should be staffed on a year-round basis.

In Pennsylvania, management committees of each house or a joint management committee should serve as the supervising agency for interim committees and their studies, budgets, and personnel.

14. INCREASE LEGISLATIVE COMPENSATION. No legislative salaries in the United States should be below the $10,000 a year level. Compensation of legislators in the larger states should be in the $20,000 to $30,000 range.

Legislative salaries are far too low in comparison with states of similar size and development. Current salaries ($7,200 per year plus $4,800 in expenses, for a total of $12,000, of which a part must be considered expense reimbursement) should be increased to the $20,000 to $30,000 level.

15. SUPPORT OF DISTRICT OFFICES. District offices are vital to the effective representation by a legislator of his constituency. The legislature should make some contribution to the support of district offices for its members, and the amount of this contribution should be increased over time.

16. CONSENT CALENDAR. A consent calendar should be used in both houses.

17. ELECTRIC ROLL CALL RECORDER. The Senate should install and use an electric roll call recorder. This is recommended

not simply because it would speed up the proceedings (worthwhile as this may be), but because it is an efficient method of producing an error-free record of roll call votes.

18. ESTABLISH AN AUTOMATIC CALENDAR OF BILLS. When a bill is favorably reported out of committee to the floor, it should go automatically onto the calendar in the order in which it was reported out. It should require a vote of an extraordinary majority to move a bill from its position on calendar or to bypass it. The Rules Committee should have no part in the scheduling of bills. No session should adjourn until all bills on calendar have been voted up or down or, by the vote of an extraordinary majority, have been moved from the calendar.

19. STRENGTHEN STAFF (RANK-AND-FILE MEMBERS). Rank-and-file members (majority and minority party on an equal basis) should be provided with individual staff assistance consisting of a minimum of an administrative assistant at the professional level and a secretary. Eventually, this should increase to the stated level of support both in the capital and in a district office.

20. CONSOLIDATE STAFF AGENCIES. Legislative research, fiscal, and planning staffs and agencies should be consolidated, professionalized, and augmented under more systematic management and supervision. This consolidated central staffing should be placed under the supervision of a joint legislative management committee or management committees of the respective houses. Party and member patronage should be eliminated from all legislative staffing.

21. WASHINGTON, D.C., OFFICE FOR THE LEGISLATURE. With the large and growing volume of activity generated by state-federal relationships, the legislature, beyond merely reacting to federal legislation, should be in a position to influence the development of new programs in accordance with the interests of the state. To do so, the legislature should have an office in the nation's capital to represent it and to be its most direct liaison with the Congress.

For small states, consideration might be given to joining with a number of sister states (either on a geographical or on a population basis) for the purpose of sharing the services of a Washington office. But in large states, the volume of inter-governmental traffic has reached a stage at which it would benefit the legislature greatly to have a full-time Washington office.

22. INDIVIDUAL OFFICES. Provide private, individual offices for
     every member of the legislature, with nearby space for their
     assistants. The quality and amount of office space should not
     differ substantially between majority and minority party members.

     The remaining four or five Senators who share office space
     should be provided with private offices. In the House, all rank-
     and-file members share offices. Members should be provided
     individual offices as soon as possible. Reduction in the size of
     the House would make accomplishment of this goal more prac-
     ticable.

23. FACILITIES FOR COMMITTEES. Legislative effectiveness re-
     quires that committees have adequate physical facilities in which
     to do their work. This includes an adequate number of committee
     rooms and an adequate number of hearing rooms that will permit
     the seating of larger audiences.

     Committee meeting rooms should be improved in quality and
     should not serve as offices for committee chairmen; chairmen
     should have individual offices. The number of hearing rooms
     should be increased to permit seating of larger audiences at
     hearings.

24. TRANSFER AUDIT FUNCTION TO THE LEGISLATURE. A sig-
     nificant part of the legislature's ability to exercise oversight of
     executive departments and administrative agencies depends
     upon the power and capacity to conduct audits (financial and
     functional) of these units of the state government. These functions
     and responsibilities should be removed from the duties and re-
     sources of the Office of Auditor and be established under a
     legislative auditor.

     Although post-auditing is now done by the legislature, this
     capability is in need of expansion to insure adequate oversight
     of state programs and expenditures.

25. IMPROVE PRESS FACILITIES. Improved press facilities aid
     in the coverage of the work of the legislature. Committee rooms,
     and both chambers or galleries, should provide adequate space
     for the news media as well as lighting and electrical power con-
     nections for their equipment. Conference or interview rooms
     and office space should also be provided for the news media.

     Specially for Pennsylvania, committee rooms should provide
     adequate space for the news media as well as lighting and

electrical power connections for their equipment. Conference
or interview rooms should also be provided for the news media.

RHODE ISLAND (36)

Functional, 33; Accountable, 46; Informed, 30; Independent, 41; Representative, 11

GENERAL: The Rhode Island General Assembly was studied by the
Eagleton Institute of Politics, Rutgers University, in 1968. Although
some of Eagleton's recommendations for improvement have been
adopted (e.g., reduction in number of committees and improved professional staffing), the legislature remains weak in a number of areas.

A small state with 100 single-member legislative districts, Rhode
Island ranked best in representative. In spite of that, the legislature
scored its worst in accountability, lending support to a frequently
heard charge of secretiveness in the Assembly.

One of the most serious handicaps against legislative improvement in
Rhode Island is the constitutional provision that limits pay to $5 per
diem for sixty legislative days a session. There has been a long
precedent in the state to defeat pay increases for the legislature ; the
most recently defeated provision, in November, 1970, would have
increased the per diem to $50 while retaining the sixty-day limitation
on compensation.

The legislature is currently in the process of building a stronger
staff: a Legislative Council staff with about fifteen professional members during sessions; a Legislative Press Bureau with two professional
writers; a Fiscal Advisory Staff which provides post-auditing, program
review, and evaluation, and a continuous study of state resources
and expenditures. However, the patronage system continues to be
used, particularly in committees, which are understaffed at best. In
1969 the General Assembly employed fifty-four doorkeepers to guard
a total of six chamber doors.

The committees (six in each house) have parallel jurisdiction, certainly
an ideal situation, but the legislature may be trying to operate with
too few committees to provide a balanced study of the issues. (Before
the number of committees was reduced, the Eagleton study had shown
that six of the former fifteen House committees had handled ninety-
three percent of legislation introduced; and six of seventeen in the
Senate, ninety-eight percent.)

Recommendations for Rhode Island are the following.

1. LEGISLATIVE SALARIES. Legislative salaries should be set
    by statute and paid in equal monthly installments throughout the
    biennium, and all unvouchered expense allowances should be in-
    corporated into an annual salary. Actual and necessary expenses
    incurred in the process of carrying out legislative duties should
    be reimbursed upon submission and approval of properly vouchered
    evidence of expenditures.

    INCREASE LEGISLATIVE COMPENSATION. No legislative
    salaries in the United States should be below the $10,000 a year
    level. Compensation of legislators in the larger states should
    be in the $20,000 to $30,000 range.

    Salaries of members of the legislature are far too low (only New
    Hampshire has lower compensation). The constitution should be
    amended to permit the legislature to set an annual salary for
    legislators by statute.

2. EXPENSE ALLOWANCES. Members of the legislature should
    be allowed an expense reimbursement covering their travel and
    living costs while engaged in carrying out their legislative duties.
    The same allowance should obtain during the interim for days
    in attendance at interim committee meetings or other official
    and authorized legislative business. These allowances should
    be provided by statute.

    The Rhode Island constitution limits expense allowances to eight
    cents a mile for travel to and from the General Assembly, not
    to exceed sixty legislative days.

3. LEGISLATIVE POWER TO CALL SPECIAL SESSIONS. Amend
    the constitution to permit the legislature to convene special
    sessions either by petition of a majority of the members of
    both houses or the call of the presiding officer of each house.

    Although the legislature can avoid adjourning sine die to retain
    the option of returning into the session, the legal power to convene
    in emergencies should be granted.

4. PRE-SESSION ORGANIZATIONAL MEETING. Amend the consti-
    tution to provide a pre-session organizing session following a
    general election. Some states make advantageous use of such
    a session during November or December of a general election
    year for the purpose of electing leaders, appointing committee
    chairmen, assigning members to committees, referring pre-filed
    bills to committee, holding committee organizational meetings,
    and conducting orientation conferences for new, as well as

returning members of the legislature. Through such pre-session meetings the committees can begin their work before the regular session convenes. This makes it possible to delay the start of the regular session until legislation is ready for floor action.

5. PRE-SESSION ORIENTATION CONFERENCE. The legislature should hold an orientation conference for new legislators, preferably after each general election. Orientation conferences enable members to speed the process of becoming more effective representatives, and they provide an opportunity for legislators to examine large policy areas apart from the pressure of the regular session.

6. INTERIM COMMITTEES. When the legislature is not in session, the standing committees should become the interim committees for the purpose of conducting long-range studies of state policy issues. The Legislative Council or some similarly constituted, bi-partisan committee should serve as the supervising agency for interim committees and their studies, budgets, and personnel. The major committees should be staffed on a year-round basis.

    Interim activities are also seriously hampered by the sixty-day limitation on compensation.

7. UNIFORM COMMITTEE RULES. There should be uniform published rules of committee procedure in both chambers.

8. JOINT RULES. There should be joint rules governing the relationship and the flow of legislation between the two houses of the legislature.

9. STRENGTHEN STAFF (RANK-AND-FILE MEMBERS). Rank-and-file members (majority and minority party on an equal basis) should be provided with individual staff assistance consisting of a minimum of an administrative assistant at the professional level and a secretary. Eventually, this should increase to the stated level of support in the capital and in a district office.

10. STRENGTHEN STAFF SUPPORT. Legislative research, fiscal, legal, and planning agencies should be adequately staffed to full utility and at suitable salary levels for professional qualification. Professional staffing should be at a level to enable the legislature to conduct continuous, year-round examination of state resources and expenditures as well as program review and evaluation of state agencies. This staff should also prepare fiscal notes accompanying all appropriation bills, evaluating their fiscal impact over the short and long term. Staff agencies should be

upgraded to the level at which competent and timely service can be provided to every member of the legislature.

Legislative staff should prepare fiscal notes accompanying all appropriation bills, evaluating their fiscal impact over the short and long term.

11. COMMITTEE STAFFING. Standing committees should be staffed on a permanent, year-round basis.

The professional quality of present committee staffing is too uneven and should be generally upgraded.

12. STAFF (PATRONAGE). Eliminate party patronage from all legislative staffing.

13. INDIVIDUAL OFFICES. Provide private, individual offices for every member of the legislature, with nearby space for their assistants. The quality and amount of office space should not differ substantially between majority and minority party members.

The capitol building has little space for expansion to allow for individual offices for all legislators, even if most of the executive offices were relocated. Therefore, consideration should be given to the construction of an adjacent legislative office building.

14. FACILITIES FOR COMMITTEES. Legislative effectiveness requires that committees have adequate physical facilities in which to do their work. This includes an adequate number of committee rooms and an adequate number of hearing rooms that will permit the seating of larger audiences.

15. IMPROVE PRESS FACILITIES. Improved press facilities aid in the coverage of the work of the legislature. Committee rooms, and both chambers or galleries, should provide adequate space for the news media as well as lighting and electrical power connections for their equipment. Conference or interview rooms and office space should also be provided for the news media.

16. PRACTICE BEFORE REGULATORY AGENCIES. Legislators or their firms should be probibited from practicing before state regulatory agencies or in matters concerning state agencies for a fee.

PROHIBIT DOING BUSINESS WITH THE STATE. There should be a prohibition against legislators or the firms in which they own a major interest doing business with state agencies.

PROHIBIT APPOINTMENT TO STATE OFFICE. There should be a prohibition against a legislator accepting appointment to other state office during the term for which he is elected or within two years of the termination of his service as a member of the legislature.

FAMILY EMPLOYMENT. Members of a legislator's immediate family should be barred from employment by the legislature.

17. OPEN COMMITTEES. The rules of each house should prohibit secret meetings except in matters affecting the security of the state, or which could unnecessarily damage the reputation of individuals in personnel matters. Such exceptions should be sparingly and responsibly employed.

18. NOTICE OF MEETINGS. The rules should require a minimum notice of five legislative days for committee meetings and hearings with widely disseminated announcement of schedule, location, agenda, and availability of public participation.

19. ACT ON ALL BILLS. Committees should be required to report on all bills assigned to them, recommending for passage by the parent body those bills which enjoy the support of a majority of the members of the committee and killing all others.

20. RECORD AND PUBLISH PROCEEDINGS OF COMMITTEES. Record and publish the record of committee hearings, proceedings and votes.

21. REQUIRE ROLL CALL ON PASSAGE OF BILLS. A recorded roll call should be required on final passage of any legislative measure, and it should require a constitutional majority to pass any bill on final action by either house.

22. ELECTRIC ROLL CALL RECORDER. There should be an electric roll call recorder in each house. This is recommended not simply because it would speed up the proceedings (worthwhile as this may be), but because it is an efficient method of producing an error-free record of roll call votes.

23. DUAL COMMITTEE CONSIDERATION OF APPROPRIATION BILL There should be a rule requiring dual committee consideration of legislation affecting significant sums of money. Such legislation when considered and acted upon favorably by a substantive policy committee, should then automatically be referred to the Finance Committee for consideration of its fiscal impact.

24. CONSENT CALENDAR. A consent calendar should be used in both houses.

25. BILL DEADLINES. The orderly flow of work through the legislature depends upon the existence of a series of deadlines at various critical stages throughout the legislative process. Thse deadlines should be adopted as part of the rules and should be consistently enforced.

   No bill may be introduced in the Rhode Island Legislature after the fiftieth legislative day. However, since skeleton bills are permitted, there is often a rash of bills just before the fiftieth day. Deadlines are also needed for committee and floor action.

26. SKELETON BILLS. There should be an explicit rule barring introduction of skeleton or "spot" bills. This rule should be enforced by the assigning authority (the presiding officer or Rules Committee) by refusal to assign bills so identified to committee.

27. REPRINT AMENDED BILLS. When a bill is amended substantially, it should be reprinted and returned to the legislature with no more than an overnight delay. The reprint should show clearly the original text of the bill as well as the change created by the amendment.

   Bills are now seldom reprinted after introduction to the legislature, unless the bill is of particular public interest. Law requires that amendments in the bill under consideration, as well as changes in existing statute that the bill would effect, be clearly identified.

28. BILL SUMMARY BY BILL-DRAFTING SERVICE. The form in which bills are introduced should include a more extensive summary of the provisions of the bill, prepared by the bill-drafting service.

29. REMOVE LEGISLATIVE POWERS FROM LIEUTENANT GOVERNOR. The exercise of legislative powers, including such pro forma powers as presiding, casting tie-breaking votes, and signing enacted legislation, by the lieutenant governor, whether the powers derive from the constitution or the rule book, would seem to be a particularly serious breach of the separation of powers and and the independence of the legislature. The constitution and/or rule book should be amended to permit these legislative powers presently exercised by the lieutenant governor to be set as the responsibility of the office of the president pro tem of the Senate.

Although most leadership power is in the hands of the Senate majority leader, the lieutenant governor, as president of the Senate, exercises some legislative powers. The constitution provides that he preside over the Senate and cast tie-breaking votes. He also assigns bills to committee. The constitution and the Senate rules should be amended to remove these legislative powers and place them in the office of a legislatively selected presiding officer.

SOUTH CAROLINA (44)

Functional, 50; Accountable, 45; Informed, 39; Independent, 10; Representative, 46

GENERAL: The South Carolina Legislature scored relatively well on the independence criteria (10). Contributing to that score were unlimited annual sessions, the ability of the legislature to expand the agenda of special sessions called by the governor, control by the legislature of its operating expenditures, and compensation set by statute.

Across the remainder of the FAIIR criteria, the South Carolina ranks were in the lowest twenty percent, which accounts for its general ranking of forty-four.

Recommendations which would raise this level include the following.

1. LEGISLATIVE POWER TO CALL SPECIAL SESSIONS. Amend the constitution to permit the legislature to convene special sessions either by petition of a majority of the members of both houses or the call of the presiding officer of each house.

    Although South Carolina currently meets in annual unrestricted sessions, the General Assembly does not have the power to call itself into special session, and compensation for special sessions ceases after forty legislative days.

2. POWER TO EXPAND SPECIAL SESSION AGENDA. Amend the constitution to permit the legislature to broaden the subject matter of a governor's call of a special session by a majority vote in each house, or prohibit the restriction of the agenda by the governor.

    Although a speaker's ruling determined that the House could expand the agenda of special session, no such rule exists in the Senate; this privilege should be granted in the constitution.

3. VETO REVIEW. No veto session is provided if the General
    Assembly has adjourned sine die.

4. PRE-SESSION ORGANIZATIONAL MEETING. Amend the consti-
    tution to provide a pre-session organizing session following a
    general election. Some states make advantageous use of such a
    session during November or December of a general election
    year for the purpose of electing leaders, appointing committee
    chairmen, assigning members to committees, referring pre-filed
    bills to committee, holding committee organizational meetings,
    and conducting orientation conferences for new, as well as
    returning, members of the legislature. Through such pre-session
    meetings the committees can begin their work before the regular
    session convenes. This makes it possible to delay the start of
    the regular session until legislation is ready for floor action.

5. PRE-SESSION ORIENTATION CONFERENCE. The legislature
    should hold an orientation conference for new legislators, prefer-
    ably after each general election. Orientation conferences enable
    members to speed the process of becoming more effective repre-
    sentatives, and they provide an opportunity for legislators to
    examine large policy areas apart from the pressure of the regular
    session.

6. REDUCE THE NUMBER OF COMMITTEES. Ideally, there should
    be from ten to fifteen committees in each house, parallel in
    jurisdiction. This would reduce the general complexity of the
    legislature and would permit reducing the number of committee
    assignments per member.

    REDUCE THE NUMBER OF COMMITTEE ASSIGNMENTS. In
    order to make it possible for members to concentrate their
    attention and contribute effectively, there should be no more than
    three committee assignments for each member of the lower house
    and four committee assignments for each member of the Senate.
    The multiplicity of assignments introduces problems of scheduling,
    strains the focus of attention on the part of members, and creates
    an inordinately heavy workload for members if committees are
    as active as they should be.

    There are eight standing committees in the House and twenty-six
    in the Senate. Both houses should consider revising their com-
    mittee structures as suggested. This would increase the number
    of House committees and decrease the number of Senate committees.
    When such a change is implemented, caution should be observed
    so that no House member has more than three committee

assignments and no Senate members has more than four. At
present, although the House conforms to this standard, 100 percent
of the Senate members have more than four committee assignments

7. UNIFORM COMMITTEE RULES. There should be uniform published rules of committee procedure in the Senate, as there are
in the Assembly.

8. COMMITTEE JURISDICTION. A description of the jurisdiction
of committees should be contained in the rules of both houses,
and assignment of bills should be made in accord with the jurisdiction of committees as described in the rules.

9. OPEN COMMITTEES. The rules of each house should prohibit
secret meetings except in matters affecting the security of the
state, or which could unnecessarily damage the reputation of
individuals in personnel matters. Such exceptions should be
sparingly and responsibly employed.

10. NOTICE OF MEETINGS. The rules should require a minimum
notice of five legislative days for committee meetings and hearings
with widely disseminated announcement of schedule, location,
agenda, and availability of public participation.

11. ACT ON ALL BILLS. Committees should be required to report
on all bills assigned to them, recommending for passage by the
parent body those bills which enjoy the support of a majority of
the members of the committee and killing all others.

12. COMMITTEE HEARINGS. There is no justification for permitting
any major piece of legislation to become law without having been
subjected to extensive, thorough, well-planned, and well-prepared
public hearings, in which representatives of the public, civic
organizations, and interest groups are not only invited but encouraged to participate.

13. COMMITTEE BILL REPORTS. Require committees to issue
reports describing and explaining the committee's action on bills
recommended for passage at the time the bill moves from the
committee to the floor.

14. DUAL COMMITTEE CONSIDERATION OF APPROPRIATION BILL
There should be a rule requiring dual committee consideration
of legislation affecting significant sums of money. Such legislation
when considered and acted upon favorably by a substantive policy
committee, should then automatically be referred to the Finance
Committee for consideration of its fiscal impact.

15. MANAGEMENT COMMITTEES. There should be an executive or management committee created in each house. Its membership should include the leaders of each party in each house, and the minority party should have representation on the committee in proportion to its numbers in the body as a whole. The Senate/ House management committees should combine as a joint management committee. The purpose of these committees should be to assume responsibility for the administrative management (housekeeping) functions relating to personnel, facilities, the research bureaus, budgets, and expenditures of their respective houses. The joint management committee should deal with matters of inter-house coordination.

16. INTERIM COMMITTEES. When the legislature is not in session, the standing committees should become the interim committees for the purpose of conducting long-range studies of state policy issues. The Legislative Council or some similarly constituted, bi-partisan committee should serve as the supervising agency for interim committees and their studies, budgets, and personnel. The major committees should be staffed on a year-round basis.

17. INTERIM COMMITTEE REPORTING. Interim committees should be required to render formal reports concerning the topics they were charged with responsibility for investigating. These reports should cover the committee's recommendations, including drafts of proposed legislation where appropriate.

18. LEGISLATIVE SALARIES. Legislative salaries should be set by statute and paid in equal monthly installments throughout the biennium, and all unvouchered expense allowances should be incorporated into an annual salary. Actual and necessary expenses incurred in the process of carrying out legislative duties should be reimbursed upon submission and approval of properly vouchered evidence of expenditures.

INCREASE LEGISLATIVE COMPENSATION. No legislative salaries in the United States should be below the $10,000 a year level. Compensation of legislators in the larger states should be in the $20,000 to $30,000 range.

Salaries of members of the legislature are far too low in comparison with states of similar size and development. Current salaries of $4,000 should be doubled immediately and increased again within the next few years as other improvements in the legislature are made.

19. PROVIDE SINGLE-MEMBER DISTRICTS. Legislative districts in both houses should be single-member.

Legislative districts in the House and the Senate are multi-member
They should be single-member. Accomplishing this requires an
amendment to the state constitution.

20. BILL DEADLINES. The orderly flow of work through the legislatur
    depends upon the existence of a series of deadlines at various
    critical stages throughout the legislative process. These deadlines
    should be adopted as part of the rules and should be consistently
    enforced.

21. ESTABLISH AN AUTOMATIC CALENDAR OF BILLS. When a
    bill is favorably reported out of committee to the floor, it should
    go automatically onto the calendar in the order in which it was
    reported out. It should require a vote of an extraordinary majority
    to move a bill from its position on calendar or to bypass it. The
    Rules Committee should have no part in the scheduling of bills.
    No session should adjourn until all bills on calendar have been
    voted up or down or, by the vote of an extraordinary majority,
    have been moved from the calendar.

22. REPRINT AMENDED BILLS. When a bill is amended substantially,
    it should be reprinted and returned to the legislature with no
    more than an overnight delay. The reprint should show clearly
    the original text of the bill as well as the change created by the
    amendment.

23. SKELETON BILLS. There should be an explicit rule barring
    introduction of skeleton or "spot" bills. This rule should be
    enforced by the assigning authority (the presiding officer or Rules
    Committee) by refusal to assign bills so identified to committee.

24. STATEMENT OF INTENT BY AUTHOR OF A BILL. The form
    in which a bill is introduced should include a statement by the
    author describing, in laymen's language, what the bill is intended
    to accomplish.

25. BILL SUMMARY BY BILL-DRAFTING SERVICE. The form in
    which bills are introduced should include a more extensive
    summary of the provisions of the bill, prepared by the bill-drafting
    service.

26. REQUIRE ROLL CALL ON PASSAGE OF BILLS. A recorded
    roll call should be required on final passage of any legislative
    measure, and it should require a constitutional majority to pass
    any bill on final action by either house.

27. STRENGTHEN STAFF SUPPORT. Legislative research, fiscal,
    legal, and planning agencies should be adequately staffed to full

utility and at suitable salary levels for professional qualification. Professional staffing should be at a level to enable the legislature to conduct continuous, year-round examination of state resources and expenditures as well as program review and evaluation of state agencies. This staff should also prepare fiscal notes accompanying all appropriation bills, evaluating their fiscal impact over the short and long term. Staff agencies should be upgraded to the level at which competent and timely service can be provided to every member of the legislature.

It is especially important for the South Carolina General Assembly to immediately move away from reliance on executive agencies for needed services and to develop its own staffing capability. The Legislative Council should be staffed on a year-round basis, with a staffing complement large enough to provide all needed services without being overextended.

28. STRENGTHEN STAFF SUPPORT (LEADERS). Staff assistance should be provided to all leaders of both the majority and minority parties. Such assistance should include a secretary and an administrative assistant at the professional level, with space to work reasonably adjacent to the offices of members and leaders.

29. STRENGTHEN STAFF (RANK-AND-FILE MEMBERS). Rank-and-file members (majority and minority party on an equal basis) should be provided with individual staff assistance consisting of a minimum of an administrative assistant at the professional level and a secretary. Eventually, this should increase to the stated level of support both in the capital and in a district office.

30. TRANSFER AUDIT FUNCTION TO THE LEGISLATURE. A significant part of the legislature's ability to exercise oversight of executive departments and administrative agencies depends upon the power and capacity to conduct audits (financial and functional) of these units of the state government. These functions and responsibilities should be removed from the duties and resources of the Office of Auditor and be established under a legislative auditor.

31. FACILITIES FOR COMMITTEES. Legislative effectiveness requires that committees have adequate physical facilities in which to do their work. This includes an adequate number of committee rooms and an adequate number of hearing rooms that will permit the seating of larger audiences.

32. INDIVIDUAL OFFICES. Provide private, individual offices for every member of the legislature, with nearby space for their assistants. The quality and amount of office space should not

differ substantially between majority and minority party members.

33. IMPROVE PRESS FACILITIES. Improved press facilities aid in
    the coverage of the work of the legislature. Committee rooms,
    and both chambers or galleries, should provide adequate space
    for the news media as well as lighting and electrical power
    connections for their equipment. Conference or interview rooms
    and office space should also be provided for the news media.

34. SPECIAL PROVISIONS. In addition to standard laws governing
    criminal behavior, there should be special provisions regulating
    legislative conflicts of interest.

    PRACTICE BEFORE REGULATORY AGENCIES. Legislators or
    their firms should be prohibited from practicing before state
    regulatory agencies or in matters concerning state agencies for
    a fee.

    PROHIBIT APPOINTMENT TO STATE OFFICE. There should be
    a prohibition against a legislator accepting appointment to other
    state office during the term for which he is elected or within two
    years of the termination of his service as a member of the
    legislature.

    FAMILY EMPLOYMENT. Members of a legislator's immediate
    family should be barred from employment by the legislature.

SOUTH DAKOTA (17)

Functional, 23; Accountable, 12; Informed, 15; Independent, 16;
Representative, 37

GENERAL: Constitutional restrictions and a low level of supporting
services and facilities combine to weaken the South Dakota Legislature
and interfere with its ability to do a more effective job. The foundation
is present for an improved legislature. In its favor are an effective
series of bill deadlines, the automatic calendaring of bills for floor
action as they are reported out of committee, the reasonable size of
the legislature (House, seventy-five; Senate, thirty-five), the existence
of a legislative audit capability, and the beginning of the use of electronic data processing for tracking legislation for indexing.

The barriers to more effective performance which remain stem from
restricted sessions (odd year, forty-five legislative days; even year,
thirty legislative days), low pay ($3,000, odd year; $2,000, even year),
no expense reimbursement of members, no ability on the part of the

legislature to call a special session or extend the agenda of a special session called by the governor, no pre-session activities, and no individual staff assistance for leaders or members. These and other conditions suggest improvements included in the recommendations for South Dakota.

1. REDUCE THE NUMBER OF COMMITTEES. Ideally, there should be from ten to fifteen committees in each house, parallel in jurisdiction. This would reduce the general complexity of the legislature and would permit reducing the number of committee assignments per member.

    At present there are twenty-five committees in the House and sixteen in the Senate. The House should reduce the number of its committees to a number similar to that of the Senate, making them parallel in jurisdiction.

2. PRE-SESSION ORIENTATION CONFERENCE. The legislature should hold an orientation conference for new legislators, preferably after each general election. Orientation conferences enable members to speed the process of becoming more effective representatives, and they provide an opportunity for legislators to examine large policy areas apart from the pressure of the regular session.

    Reduction in the number of House committees would permit fewer committee assignments per member in the House. At present, eighty-two percent of the members of the House serve on more than three committees.

3. COMMITTEE JURISDICTION. A description of the jurisdiction of committees should be contained in the rules of both houses, and assignment of bills should be made in accord with the jurisdiction of committees as described in the rules.

4. OPEN COMMITTEES. The rules of each house should prohibit secret meetings except in matters affecting the security of the state, or which could unnecessarily damage the reputation of individuals in personnel matters. Such exceptions should be sparingly and responsibly employed.

5. BALANCED COMMITTEES. Committees, in their composition, should reflect as accurately as possible the makeup of the entire house of which they are a part. There should be no "killer," "graveyard," or "cinch" committees.

6. INTERIM COMMITTEES. When the legislature is not in session,

the standing committees should become the interim committees
for the purpose of conducting long-range studies of state policy
issues. The Legislative Council or some similarly constituted,
bi-partisan committee should serve as the supervising agency
for interim committees and their studies, budgets, and personnel.
The major committees should be staffed on a year-round basis.

7. PROVIDE SINGLE-MEMBER DISTRICTS. Legislative districts
in both houses should be single-member.

8. INCREASE LEGISLATIVE COMPENSATION. No legislative salaries in the United States should be below the $10,000 a year level.
Compensation of legislators in the larger states should be in the
$20,000 to $30,000 range.

Current salaries of $5,000 per biennium should be doubled
immediately and increased again within the next few years.

9. EXPENSE ALLOWANCES. Members of the legislature should be
allowed an expense reimbursement covering their travel and
living costs while engaged in carrying out their legislative duties.
The same allowance should obtain during the interim for days in
attendance at interim committee meetings or other official and
authorized legislative business. These allowances should be
provided by statute.

10. REMOVE CONSTITUTIONAL RESTRICTIONS ON SESSION AND
INTERIM TIME. The legislature should have authority to function
throughout a two-year term; ideally, this authority should provide
a flexible biennial session pattern that permits the legislature to
convene, recess, and reconvene as it deems desirable. The legislature should be able to meet in general session or conduct interim
work as it deems necessary at any time throughout the period.

An intermediate step toward unlimited annual sessions would be
to amend the constitution to permit sessions limited to no fewer
than ninety legislative days. Another measure would be an
amendment to permit the legislature to reconvene following
completion of bill signing by the governor, in order to consider
the possibility of overriding vetoes.

11. LEGISLATIVE POWER TO CALL SPECIAL SESSIONS. Amend
the constitution to permit the legislature to convene special
sessions either by petition of a majority of the members of both
houses or the call of the presiding officer of each house.

12. POWER TO EXPAND SPECIAL SESSION AGENDA. Amend the
constitution to permit the legislature to broaden the subject

matter of a governor's call of a special session by a majority
vote in each house, or prohibit the restriction of the agenda by
the governor.

13. BILL CARRY-OVER. Amend the constitution to permit the carry-
over of bills from one session to the next within the same term.

14. PRE-SESSION ORGANIZATIONAL MEETING. Amend the constitution to provide a pre-session organizing session following a
general election. Some states make advantageous use of such a
session during November or December of a general election year
for the purpose of electing leaders, appointing committee chairmen,
assigning members to committees, referring pre-filed bills to
committee, holding committee organizational meetings, and
conducting orientation conferences for new, as well as returning,
members of the legislature. Through such pre-session meetings
the committees can begin their work before the regular session
convenes. This makes it possible to delay the start of the regular
session until legislation is ready for floor action.

15. STRENGTHEN MINORITY PARTY ROLE. Internal accountability,
as well as the capacity of all legislators to represent their
constituents effectively, depends upon the opportunity of minority
party members to have an effective part in internal legislative
affairs.

MINORITY REPRESENTATION ON COMMITTEE ON RULES.
Minority representation on the Committee on Rules should approximate the minority party proportion of the membership of the
appropriate house.

MINORITY PARTY MEMBERS ON COMMITTEE. Minority party
members should be assigned to committees by the minority
leader in consultation with the minority caucus.

16. ELECTRIC ROLL CALL RECORDER. There should be an electric
roll call recorder in each house. This recommended not simply
because it would speed up the proceedings (worthwhile as this
may be), but because it is an efficient method of producing an
error-free record of roll call votes.

17. STRENGTHEN STAFF SUPPORT. Legislative research, fiscal,
legal, and planning agencies should be adequately staffed to full
utility and at suitable salary levels for professional qualification.
Professional staffing should be at a level to enable the legislature
to conduct continuous, year-round examination of state resources
and expenditures as well as program review and evaluation of
state agencies. This staff should also prepare fiscal notes

accompanying all appropriation bills, evaluating their fiscal
impact over the short and long term. Staff agencies should be
upgraded to the level at which competent and timely service can
be provided to every member of the legislature.

18. STRENGTHEN STAFF SUPPORT (LEADERS). Staff assistance
should be provided to all leaders of both the majority and minority
parties. Such assistance should include a secretary and an
administrative assistant at the professional level, with space to
work reasonably adjacent to the offices of members and leaders.

19. STRENGTHEN STAFF (RANK-AND-FILE MEMBERS). Rank-and-
file members (majority and minority party on an equal basis)
should be provided with individual staff assistance consisting of
a minimum of an administrative assistant at the professional
level and a secretary. Eventually, this should increase to the
stated level of support both in the capital and in a district office.

20. COMMITTEE STAFFING. Standing committees should be staffed
on a permanent, year-round basis.

21. INDIVIDUAL OFFICES. Provide private, individual offices for
every member of the legislature, with nearby space for their
assistants. The quality and amount of office space should not
differ substantially between majority and minority party members.

A beginning can be made toward providing offices by sharing
offices among small numbers of members at first and then
gradually reducing the members who share space until every
member has a private office.

22. SERVICE AGENCY FACILITIES. Space for service agencies
should provide adequate working space for professional and
clerical staff as well as library, files, and other storage requirements.

23. FACILITIES FOR COMMITTEES. Legislative effectiveness
requires that committees have adequate physical facilities in
which to do their work. This includes an adequate number of
committee rooms and an adequate number of hearing rooms
that will permit the seating of larger audiences.

24. REMOVE LEGISLATIVE POWERS FROM LIEUTENANT GOVERNOR.
The exercise of legislative powers, including such pro forma
powers as presiding, casting tie-breaking votes, and signing
enacted legislation, by the lieutenant governor, whether the
powers derive from the constitution or the rule book, would seem

to be a particularly serious breach of the separation of powers and the independence of the legislature. The constitution and/or rule book should be amended to permit these legislative powers presently exercised by the lieutenant governor to be set as the responsibility of the office of the president pro tem of the Senate.

TENNESSEE (26)

Functional, 30; Accountable, 44; Informed, 11; Independent, 9; Representative, 26

GENERAL: The Tennessee General Assembly has a moderate size (House, ninety-nine; Senate, thirty-three); single-member districts in the Senate; and a nearly parallel structure of committees (the House has one more committee than the Senate).

Compensation is set by statute at $3,600. In odd years after the general election the legislature holds a pre-session organizational session of fifteen calendar days.

Since 1967, the Tennessee legislature meets in annual sessions by adjourning the odd-year session to a date certain in the even year.

New legislative facilities will be available during the next year. Planned at a total cost of $6,000,000, each legislator will have a separate office (ready in early 1971), new committee rooms will be ready early in 1972, and offices to house legislative staff will become available in mid-1972. The development of these facilities will immeasurably enhance the legislature's ability to go about its work. Recommendations for Tennessees's General Assembly include the following.

1. EXPENSE ALLOWANCES. Members of the legislature should be allowed an expense reimbursement covering their travel and living costs while engaged in carrying out their legislative duties. The same allowance should obtain during the interim for days in attendance at interim committee meetings or other official and authorized legislative business. These allowances should be provided by statute.

   The Tennessee constitution limits the number of days expenses can be paid to fifteen calendar days for an organizational session (in odd years), ninety legislative days of regular session per biennium, and thirty legislative days for any special session. Although the amount of the allowance is determined by statute, and the number of days can be exceeded for interim committee meetings, this provision has the effect of limiting the amount of time spent in session. It will require a change in the constitution to remove this indirect limitation on session time.

2. LEGISLATIVE POWER TO CALL SPECIAL SESSIONS. Amend the constitution to permit the legislature to convene special sessions either by petition of a majority of the members of both houses or the call of the presiding officer of each house.

The Tennessee constitution requires a written request of two-thirds of the members of each house to call the legislature into special session. This requirement is particularly prohibitive in a state such as Tennessee, which has a fairly evenly balanced party system. The constitution should be amended to permit the legislature to convene special sessions either by petition of a majority of the members of both houses or a call of the speaker of each house.

3. PROVIDE SINGLE-MEMBER DISTRICTS. Legislative districts in both houses should be single-member.

In the House, thirteen of ninety-three districts are multi-member. They should be single-member. Accomplishing this will not require amending the constitution.

4. STRENGTHEN STAFF SUPPORT. Legislative research, fiscal, legal, and planning agencies should be adequately staffed to full utility and at suitable salary levels for professional qualification. Professional staffing should be at a level to enable the legislature to conduct continuous, year-round examination of state resources and expenditures as well as program review and evaluation of state agencies. This staff should also prepare fiscal notes accompanying all appropriation bills, evaluating their fiscal impact over the short and long term. Staff agencies should be upgraded to the level at which competent and timely service can be provided to every member of the legislature.

A number of the services to the legislature are provided by or in conjunction with the executive branch. Post-auditing is done by the comptroller of the treasury; statute and code revision by the executive Law Revision Commission; fiscal notes and long-range economic forecasting by the Department of Finance and Administration. The legislature also relies in part on executive departments and agencies for information on federal subventions and federal legislation, reference and bibliography and spot research services, budget review and analysis, study of state resources and expenditures, and program review and evaluation.

To increase the effective capacity of the legislature to oversee executive operations, the volume and range of services provided by legislative staff need to be expanded. This can be accomplished most directly by enlarging the size of the present staff and creating an auditing office responsible directly to the legislature rather than to both the governor and the legislature.

5. COMMITTEE STAFFING. A beginning should be made toward permanent, year-round committee staffing for some of the major committees.

6. STRENGTHEN STAFF SUPPORT (LEADERS). Staff assistance should be provided to all leaders of both the majority and minority parties. Such assistance should include a secretary and an administrative assistant at the professional level, with space to work reasonably adjacent to the offices of members and leaders.

7. STRENGTHEN STAFF (RANK-AND-FILE MEMBERS). Rank-and-file members (majority and minority party on an equal basis) should be provided with individual staff assistance consisting of a minimum of an administrative assistant at the professional level and a secretary. Eventually, this should increase to the stated level of support both in the capital and in a district office.

All members of the legislature, perhaps beginning on a shared basis, majority and minority alike, should be provided full-time professional assistants.

8. LEGISLATIVE SALARIES. Legislative salaries should be set by statute and paid in equal monthly installments throughout the biennium, and all unvouchered expense allowances should be incorporated into an annual salary. Actual and necessary expenses incurred in the process of carrying out legislative duties should be reimbursed upon submission and approval of properly vouchered evidence of expenditures.

INCREASE LEGISLATIVE COMPENSATION. No legislative salaries in the United States should be below the $10,000 a year level. Compensation of legislators in the larger states should be in the $20,000 to $30,000 range.

Salaries of members of the legislature are far too low in comparison with states of similar size and development. Current salaries of $3,600 should be doubled immediately and increased again within the next few years as other improvements in the legislature are made.

9. UNIFORM COMMITTEE RULES. There should be uniform
    published rules of committee procedure in both chambers.

    Committees of the General Assembly usually adopt the rules of
    the parent house informally, but each house should have uniform
    published rules of committee procedure.

10. JOINT RULES. There should be joint rules governing the relation-
    ship and the flow of legislation between the two houses of the
    legislature.

11. MINORITY PARTY MEMBERS ON COMMITTEE. Minority party
    members should be assigned to committees by the minority
    leader in consultation with the minority caucus.

12. OPEN COMMITTEES. The rules of each house should prohibit
    secret meetings except in matters affecting the security of the
    state, or which could unnecessarily damage the reputation of
    individuals in personnel matters. Such exceptions should be
    sparingly and responsibly employed.

13. NOTICE OF MEETINGS. The rules should require a minimum
    notice of five legislative days for committee meetings and hearings
    with widely disseminated announcement of schedule, location,
    agenda, and availability of public participation.

14. COMMITTEE BILL REPORTS. Require committees to issue
    reports describing and explaining the committee's action on bills
    recommended for passage at the time the bill moves from the
    committee to the floor.

15. BILL DEADLINES. The orderly flow of work through the legis-
    lature depends upon the existence of a series of deadlines at
    various critical stages throughout the legislative process. These
    deadlines should be adopted as part of the rules and should be
    consistently enforced.

16. ESTABLISH AN AUTOMATIC CALENDAR OF BILLS. When a
    bill is favorably reported out of committee to the floor, it should
    go automatically onto the calendar in the order in which it was
    reported out. It should require a vote of an extraordinary
    majority to move a bill from its position on calendar or to bypass
    it. The Rules Committee should have no part in the scheduling
    of bills. No session should adjourn until all bills on calendar
    have been voted up or down or, by the vote of an extraordinary
    majority, have been moved from the calendar.

17. DUAL COMMITTEE CONSIDERATION OF APPROPRIATION
    BILLS. There should be a rule requiring dual committee con-
    sideration of legislation affecting significant sums of money.
    Such legislation, when considered and acted upon favorably by a
    substantive policy committee, should then automatically be re-
    ferred to the Finance Committee for consideration of its fiscal
    impact.

    The House should have a rule requiring dual committee considera-
    tion of legislation affecting significant sums of money. Such a rule
    exists in the Senate.

18. MANAGEMENT COMMITTEES. There should be an executive
    or management committee created in each house. Its membership
    should include the leaders of each party in each house, and the
    minority party should have representation on the committee in
    proportion to its numbers in the body as a whole. The Senate/
    House management committees should combine as a joint manage-
    ment committee. The purpose of these committees should be to
    assume responsibility for the administrative management (house-
    keeping) functions relating to personnel, facilities, the research
    bureaus, budgets, and expenditures of their respective houses.
    The joint management committee should deal with matters of
    inter-house coordination.

19. WASHINGTON, D.C., OFFICE FOR THE LEGISLATURE. With
    the large and growing volume of activity generated by state-
    federal relationships, the legislature, beyond merely reacting
    to federal legislation, should be in a position to influence the
    development of new programs in accordance with the interests
    of the state. To do so, the legislature should have an office in
    the nation's capital to represent it and to be its most direct
    liaison with the Congress.

    For small states, consideration might be given to joining with a
    number of sister states (either on a geographical or on a popula-
    tion basis) for the purpose of sharing the services of a Washing-
    ton office. But in large states, the volume of inter-governmental
    traffic has reached a stage at which it would benefit the legislature
    greatly to have a full-time Washington office.

20. PRACTICE BEFORE REGULATORY AGENCIES. Legislators
    or their firms should be prohibited from practicing before state
    regulatory agencies or in matters concerning state agencies for
    a fee.

PROHIBIT APPOINTMENT TO STATE OFFICE. There should be a prohibition against a legislator accepting appointment to other state office during the term for which he is elected or within two years of the termination of his service as a member of the legislature.

FAMILY EMPLOYMENT. Members of a legislator's immediate family should be barred from employment by the legislature.

21. BILL SUMMARY BY BILL-DRAFTING SERVICE. The form in which bills are introduced should include a more extensive summary of the provisions of the bill, prepared by the bill-drafting service.

22. SKELETON BILLS. There should be an explicit rule barring introduction of skeleton or "spot" bills. This rule should be enforced by the assigning authority (the presiding officer or Rules Committee) by refusal to assign bills so identified to committee.

23. REPRINT AMENDED BILLS. When a bill is amended substantially it should be reprinted and returned to the legislature with no more than an overnight delay. The reprint should show clearly the original text of the bill as well as the change created by the amendment.

24. PRINTED BILL DOCUMENT FORMAT. The bill document printing procedure should permit the clear identification of the text of the existing statute which is being amended as well as the material which the bill proposes to delete or add. This is usually accomplished through the use of varying type faces, such as "strike-through," italics, underlining, or bracketing. It should not be necessary to compare the text of a bill with the text of the existing code in order to determine what the bill does.

25. REDUCE THE NUMBER OF COMMITTEE ASSIGNMENTS. In order to make it possible for members to concentrate their attention and contribute effectively, there should be no more than three committee assignments for each member of the lower house and four committee assignments for each member of the Senate. The multiplicity of assignments introduces problems of scheduling, strains the focus of attention on the part of members, and creates an inordinately heavy workload for members if committees are as active as they should be.

At present thirteen percent of the members of the House have more than three committee assignments each, and thirty percent

of the members of the Senate have more than four committee
assignments each.

26. SUPPORT OF DISTRICT OFFICES. District offices are vital to
the effective representation by a legislator of his constituency.
The legislature should make some contribution to the support of
district offices for its members, and the amount of this contribution should be increased over time.

District offices are vital to the effective representation by a
legislator of his constituency. In 1970, twenty-four Representatives and eight Senators had some provision for an office in their
represented district. This support should be increased and extended to all members of the legislature.

27. IMPROVE PRESS FACILITIES. Improved press facilities aid
in the coverage of the work of the legislature. Committee rooms,
and both chambers or galleries, should provide adequate space
for the news media as well as lighting and electrical power
connections for their equipment. Conference or interview rooms
and office space should also be provided for the news media.

There is need for improved press facilities to aid in the coverage
of the work of the legislature. New committee rooms, which will
be available in planned new facilities in 1972, should provide
adequate space for the news media as well as lighting and electrical power connections for their equipment. In addition, live
radio and television coverage of committee hearings should be
permitted. Conference or interview rooms not far removed
from legislative activity should be available to the press.

                         TEXAS (38)

Functional, 45; Accountable, 36; Informed, 43; Independent, 4; Representative, 17

GENERAL: The speaker of the Texas House created a 1970 interim
committee, the Speaker's Committee of 100, to study the operations
and procedures of the House and to make recommendations in the
following areas: research and information service, bill drafting, the
House committee system, compensation for Representatives, standards
of legislative conduct, legislative facilities, and internal security
measures in the capital complex.

In addition to this promised advance, the thirty-eighth-ranked Texas
Legislature has a number of strengths which are considered in the

study: the legislature has the advantage of a thorough and informative pre-session orientation program; legislators receive an interim expense allowance, $1,700 a month for Senators and $825 a month for Representatives, that may be used for home district offices; all members of the legislature have individual private offices; committees are required to record and publish roll call votes on final committee action. House committees must also prepare a summary for each bill that they report out. The summary must include background information on the proposal, what the bill proposes to do, a section-by-section analysis of the content, and a summary of the committee hearing.

Among the recommendations proposed for the Texas Legislature are the following.

1. REMOVE CONSTITUTIONAL RESTRICTIONS ON SESSION AND INTERIM TIME. The legislature should have authority to function throughout a two-year term; ideally, this authority should provide a flexible biennial session pattern that permits the legislature to convene, recess, and reconvene as it deems desirable. The legislature should be able to meet in general session or conduct interim work as it deems necessary at any time throughout the period.

2. LEGISLATIVE POWER TO CALL SPECIAL SESSIONS. Amend the constitution to permit the legislature to convene special sessions either by petition of a majority of the members of both houses or the call of the presiding officer of each house.

3. POWER TO EXPAND SPECIAL SESSION AGENDA. Amend the constitution to permit the legislature to broaden the subject matter of a governor's call of a special session by a majority vote in each house, or prohibit the restriction of the agenda by the governor.

4. INTERIM COMMITTEES. When the legislature is not in session, the standing committees should become the interim committees for the purpose of conducting long-range studies of state policy issues. The Legislative Council or some similarly constituted, bi-partisan committee should serve as the supervising agency for interim committees and their studies, budgets, and personnel. The major committees should be staffed on a year-round basis.

   INTERIM COMMITTEE REPORTING. Interim committees should be required to render formal reports concerning the topics they were charged with responsibility for investigating. These reports should cover the committee's recommendations, including drafts of proposed legislation where appropriate.

In a few cases the standing committees continue their operations
during the interim, but the bulk of interim work is done by the
Legislative Council. In addition, the speaker of the House traditionally appoints speaker's committees to study and investigate
particular topics. When the legislature is not in session, the
standing committees should become the interim committees for
the purpose of conducting long-range studies of state policy issues.
The Legislative Council or some similarly constituted, bipartisan
committee should serve as the supervising agency for interim
committees and their studies, budgets, and personnel. Interim
committee reports are presently filed only seventy-five percent
of the time. This requirement should be enforced, and committees
which fail to file reports should not be provided budgets for
further investigation.

5.   REDUCE THE OVERALL SIZE OF THE LEGISLATURE. Although
size reduction in a legislative body is extremely difficult to
achieve, it has been done in some states--such as in Vermont
and Iowa--and needs to be accomplished in others (New Hampshire, Massachusetts, Georgia, and Pennsylvania). Where reduction in size has occurred, it has most often required a constitutional convention to accomplish it. In a few cases it has
been done by legislatively adopted constitutional amendment
(Iowa, in 1968, which becomes effective in November, 1971)
ratified by the voters. There should be 100 or fewer members
in the house. The combined size of both houses should be between
100 and 150.

Reduce the size of the House to no more than 100 members.

6.   REDUCE THE NUMBER OF COMMITTEES. Ideally, there
should be from ten to fifteen committees in each house, parallel
in jurisdiction. This would reduce the general complexity of
the legislature and would permit reducing the number of committee assignments per member.

With forty-five committees in the House and twenty-seven in the
Senate, there are more committees than should be necessary
for the effective organization of the work. This surplus is more
severe in the House than it is in the Senate.

7.   REDUCE THE NUMBER OF COMMITTEE ASSIGNMENTS. In
order to make it possible for members to concentrate their attention and contribute effectively, there should be no more than
three committee assignments for each member of the lower
house and four committee assignments for each member of the
Senate. The multiplicity of assignments introduces problems
of scheduling, strains the focus of attention on the part of

members, and creates an inordinately heavy workload for member
if committees are as active as they should be.

At present, ninety-nine percent of the members of the House have
more than three committee assignments each, and 100 percent
of the members of the Senate have more than four committee
assignments each.

8.   UNIFORM COMMITTEE RULES. There should be uniform published rules of committee procedure in both chambers.

9.   COMMITTEE JURISDICTION. A description of the jurisdiction
of committees should be contained in the rules of the Senate.
The House rules already prescribe the jurisdiction of committees
and bill assignments are made solely on the basis of those guidelines.

10.   NOTICE OF MEETINGS. The rules should require a minimum
notice of five legislative days for committee meetings and hearings, with widely disseminated announcement of schedule, location
agenda, and availability of public participation.

11.   ACT ON ALL BILLS. Committees should required to report on
all bills assigned to them, recommending for passage by the
parent body those bills which enjoy the support of a majority of
the members of the committee and killing all others.

12.   COMMITTEE BILL REPORTS. Require committees to issue
reports describing and explaining the committee's action on
bills recommended for passage at the time the bill moves from
the committee to the floor.

Committees of the House, which do take minutes, should record
the committee's deliberation. In the Senate more than one-half
of the committees tape-record their meetings.

13.   DUAL COMMITTEE CONSIDERATION OF APPROPRIATION
BILLS. There should be a rule requiring dual committee consideration of legislation affecting significant sums of money.
Such legislation, when considered and acted upon favorably by a
substantive policy committee, should then automatically be referred to the Finance Committee for consideration of its fiscal
impact.

14.   BILL DEADLINES. The orderly flow of work through the legislature depends upon the existence of a series of deadlines at
various critical stages throughout the legislative process. These

deadlines should be adopted as part of the rules and should be consistently enforced.

15.   ESTABLISH AN AUTOMATIC CALENDAR OF BILLS. When a bill is favorably reported out of committee to the floor, it should go automatically onto the calendar in the order in which it was reported out. It should require a vote of an extraordinary majority to move a bill from its position on calendar or to bypass it. The Rules Committee should have no part in the scheduling of bills. No session should adjourn until all bills on calendar have been voted up or down or, by the vote of an extraordinary majority, have been moved from the calendar.

16.   STATEMENT OF INTENT BY AUTHOR OF A BILL. The form in which a bill is introduced should include a statement by the author describing, in laymen's language, what the bill is intended to accomplish.

17.   REQUIRE ROLL CALL ON PASSAGE OF BILLS. A recorded roll call should be required on final passage of any legislative measure, and it should require a constitutional majority to pass any bill on final action by either house.

18.   REMOVE LEGISLATIVE POWERS FROM LIEUTENANT GOV-ERNOR. The exercise of legislative powers, including such pro forma powers as presiding, casting tie-breaking votes, and signing enacted legislation, by the lieutenant governor, whether the powers derive from the constitution or the rule book, would seem to be a particularly serious breach of the separation of powers and the independence of the legislature. The constitution and/or rule book should be amended to permit these legislative powers presently exercised by the lieutenant governor to be set as the responsibility of the office of the president pro tem of the Senate.

The lieutenant governor exercises a great many legislative powers. By the constitution, he is designated as president of the Senate and casts the tie-breaking vote. In addition, the rules provide that he act as leader of the Senate, with power to appoint committee chairmen, assign bills to committee, and appoint committee membership. Although the present lieutenant governor has considerable legislative experience (having served as a member of the House for six years, and having occupied the position of speaker of the House for four of those years), were the people of Texas to elect a lieutenant governor with no legislative experience, the exercise of these legislative powers by the lieutenant governor would be particularly awkward. In any

case, this requirement prevents the Senate from developing
leadership of its own choosing from among its own members.
The constitution should be amended to permit the reposing of
those legislative powers presently exercised by the lieutenant
governor in the office of president pro tem of the Senate.

19. LEGISLATIVE SALARIES. Legislative salaries should be set
by statute and paid in equal monthly installments throughout the
biennium, and all unvouchered expense allowances should be
incorporated into an annual salary. Actual and necessary expenses
incurred in the process of carrying out legislative duties should
be reimbursed upon submission and approval of properly vouchered
evidence of expenditures.

INCREASE LEGISLATIVE COMPENSATION. No legislative
salaries in the United States should be below the $10,000 a year
level. Compensation of legislators in the larger states should
be in the $20,000 to $30,000 range.

Legislative salaries should be provided by statute at the $15,000
level on an annual basis.

20. STRENGTHEN STAFF SUPPORT. Legislative research, fiscal,
legal, and planning agencies should be adequately staffed to full
utility and at suitable salary levels for professional qualification.
Professional staffing should be at a level to enable the legislature
to conduct continuous, year-round examination of state resources
and expenditures as well as program review and evaluation of
state agencies. This staff should also prepare fiscal notes accompanying all appropriation bills, evaluating their fiscal impact over
the short and long term. Staff agencies should be upgraded to the
level at which competent and timely service can be provided to
every member of the legislature.

21. STRENGTHEN STAFF (RANK-AND-FILE MEMBERS). Rank-
and-file members (majority and minority party on an equal basis)
should be provided with individual staff assistance consisting of
a minimum of an administrative assistant at the professional
level and a secretary. Eventually, this should increase to the
stated level of support both in the capital and in a district office.

22. COMMITTEE STAFFING. Standing committees should be staffed
on a permanent, year-round basis.

23. PRACTICE BEFORE REGULATORY AGENCIES. Legislators
or their firms should be prohibited from practicing before state
regulatory agencies or in matters concerning state agencies for
a fee.

PROHIBIT DOING BUSINESS WITH THE STATE. There should be a prohibition against legislators or the firms in which they own a major interest doing business with state agencies.

24. PROVIDE SINGLE-MEMBER DISTRICTS. Legislative districts in both houses should be single-member.

25. FACILITIES FOR COMMITTEES. Legislative effectiveness requires that committees have adequate physical facilities in which to do their work. This includes an adequate number of committee rooms and an adequate number of hearing rooms that will permit the seating of larger audiences.

Within the past year some additional space has become available in the capital as executive departments have been moved into separate office buildings, but until more new space becomes available, the legislature and its service agencies will be ill-housed. There is only one hearing room available to the legislature which seats over fifty spectators (the old supreme court chamber). Both houses therefore utilize their chambers extensively for public hearings. Long conference tables are located in the wide main aisle of the chamber and committee members sit there, with spectators occupying the desks of members. Several more hearing rooms should be provided. The number of committee rooms available to each house should be increased. The present rooms tend to be too small and lack space for spectators and news media.

26. SERVICE AGENCY FACILITIES. Space for service agencies should provide adequate working space for professional and clerical staff as well as library, files, and other storage requirements.

The facilities of both the Legislative Council staff and the Budget Board staff need to be expanded and upgraded.

27. JOINT RULES. There should be joint rules governing the relationship and the flow of legislation between the two houses of the legislature.

The Texas Legislature has adopted joint rules governing the flow of legislation between the two houses in the past. During the past biennium, no joint rules were adopted. It is important that the joint rules be adopted on the first day of the session at the very latest.

UTAH (15)

Functional, 38; Accountable, 5; Informed, 8; Independent, 29;
Representative, 24

GENERAL: The fact that the Utah Legislature ranks fifteenth in this
study is attributed to the members of the legislature who have literally
carved this position out of the rock of resistance presented by a highly
restrictive constitution, public reluctance to change the constitution,
and a state supreme court which tends toward strict construction of
the constitution, at times compounding these restrictions on the
legislature.

Until 1968, the constitution restricted the session of the legislature
to sixty calendar days every two years. At that time (after an
unsuccessful attempt in 1966) an amendment was ratified adding
twenty calendar days of budget session in the even-numbered year.

Until 1968, the constitution limited legislative compensation to a
salary of $500 per year plus expense allowance of $5 per day of
session, for a total biennial compensation of $1,300. In 1968, an
amendment was ratified increasing the salary, but changing it to a
per diem payment of $25 per day of session, and increasing the
expense allowance to $15 per day of session. These changes produced
a total biennial compensation of $3,200.

In two recent cases, the state supreme court has diminished the
ability of the legislature to perform its duties effectively and in the
most direct manner. In the first case, decided in July, 1967, the
court, citing Article XXIV, Section 12, of the state constitution,
declared that the legislature's Joint Legal Services Committee could
not retain legal counsel for the legislature. The court ruled that
legislators were "state officers," and as such the state attorney
general was their sole legal adviser. Therefore, only the attorney
general (the office, not necessarily the office holder) can provide
legal counsel to the legislature or any of its committees.

The second case came after two separate lower court decisions
involving the statutory payment to legislators of per diem expense
allowances for attendance at interim committee meetings of the
Legislative Council and the Joint Budget and Audit Committee: the
Legislative Council won its case, while the Budget and Audit Committee
lost. The Legislative Council decision was appealed for the state
by the attorney general, and the supreme court, after hearing the
pleas, ruled (in a unanimous decision) that the payments violated
Article VI, Section 7, of the state constitution. Section 7 prohibits the

appointment of any member of the legislature to any "civil office of profit" created (or the emoluments thereof increased) during the term for which he was elected. Thus the court ruled that legislators could not be reimbursed for expenses incurred while serving on an interim body of the legislature unless such expenses were provided by amending the constitution.

There are two very serious and deleterious effects of these decisions, and it would appear that the court's construction of the constitution is so narrow it not only preserves constitutional safeguards but also turns them into punitive restrictions upon recognized, accepted, and necessary practices of American legislative institutions. The Legislative Council case certainly inhibits the range, volume, and extent of studies, investigations, and meetings that legislative committees can undertake between regular sessions.

It seems clear that legislators will be forced to make one of two sacrifices, either of which is in the end result injurious to someone. The first choice is to undertake a full program of interim activities and thereby insure the complete discharge of their duties and responsibilities as legislators. In so doing they will sacrifice the development of their personal careers, business, and activities outside of the legislature because we cannot ignore the meager $3,200 paid legislators for their two years of service. The alternative sacrifice is to curtail legislative activity during the interim, at great peril to the state, because as in any state with session time so severely limited, salvation lies solely in being able to thoroughly accomplish vital work between sessions.

The Legislative Services Committee case strikes at another matter - the ability of the legislature to choose its own advisers. As it stands, the legislature must call on the attorney general, the chief legal officer of the state, a member of the executive branch, to give it legal advice. In practice the Legislative Services Committee has been allowed to select an attorney who is then deputized by the attorney general. What is pernicious is that the court has failed to recognize the inherent obligation of the legislature, in a system of checks and balances, to freely choose its own staff and advisers.

Some of the better features of the Utah Legislature, making up its strengths, are its size (House, sixty-nine; Senate, twenty-eight), single-member districts, a full schedule of session deadlines to expedite the flow of legialtion, uniform rules of committee procedure, a constitutional prohibition against secret sessions, a publicly available record of committee deliberations and actions, and the availability of a significant number of staff services provided by a small but effective fiscal and research agencies.

In a more hopeful turn of events, at the November, 1970, general election, Utah voters ratified a constitutional amendment (called the gateway amendment) allowing revision of an entire article rather than one section at a time. The Constitutional Revision Commission has indicated it will give the legislative article first priority, perhaps resulting in submission of a new article to the voters by the 1972 general election.

These recommendations would serve to improve Utah's Legislature.

1. REMOVE CONSTITUTIONAL RESTRICTIONS ON SESSION AND INTERIM TIME. The legislature should have authority to function throughout a two-year term; ideally, this authority should provide a flexible biennial session pattern that permits the legislature to convene, recess, and reconvene as it deems desirable. The legislature should be able to meet in general session or conduct interim work as it deems necessary at any time throughout the period.

   An intermediate step toward unlimited annual sessions would be to amend the constitution to permit annual sessions, limited to no fewer than ninety legislative days and unlimited by topic. A better alternative would be to change the present limitation from calendar days to legislative days, or to permit the legislature to extend the limited annual session, the amount of time needed, by a majority vote of the membership of both houses.

2. LEGISLATIVE POWER TO CALL SPECIAL SESSIONS. Amend the constitution to permit the legislature to convene special sessions either by petition of a majority of the members of both houses or the call of the presiding officer of each house.

3. POWER TO EXPAND SPECIAL SESSION AGENDA. Amend the constitution to permit the legislature to broaden the subject matter of a governor's call of a special session by a majority vote in each house, or prohibit the restriction of the agenda by the governor.

4. PRE-SESSION ORGANIZATIONAL MEETING. Amend the constitution to provide a pre-session organizing session following a general election. Some states make advantageous use of such a session during November or December of a general election year for the purpose of electing leaders, appointing committee chairmen, assigning members to committees, referring pre-filed bills to committee, holding committee organizational meetings, and conducting orientation conferences for new, as well as returning, members of the legislature. Through such pre-session

meetings the committees can begin their work before the regular
session convenes. This makes it possible to delay the start of
the regular session until legislation is ready for floor action.

5.   BILL CARRY-OVER. Amend the constitution to permit the carry-
over of bills from one session to the next within the same term.

6.   REDUCE THE NUMBER OF COMMITTEES. Ideally, there should
be from ten to fifteen committees in each house, parallel in
jurisdiction. This would reduce the general complexity of the
legislature and would permit reducing the number of committee
assignments per member.

For a legislature as small as Utah's (House, sixty-nine; Senate,
twenty-eight), there are too many committees (House, eighteen;
Senate, thirteen). The number of House committees should be
reduced to a number similar to that of the Senate, making them,
to the extent possible, parallel in jurisdiction.

7.   REDUCE THE NUMBER OF COMMITTEE ASSIGNMENTS. In
order to make it possible for members to concentrate their
attention and contribute effectively, there should be no more than
three committee assignments for each member of the lower house
and four committee assignments for each member of the Senate.
The multiplicity of assignments introduces problems of scheduling,
strains the focus of attention on the part of members, and creates
an inordinately heavy workload for members if committees are
as active as they should be.

At present twenty-nine percent of the members of the House have
more than three assignments each and twenty-five percent of the
Senators have more than four. The number of assignments should
be reduced to a maximum of three per House member and four
per Senator.

8.   COMMITTEE JURISDICTION. A description of the jurisdiction
of committees should be contained in the rules of both houses,
and assignment of bills should be made in accord with the jurisdiction of committees as described in the rules.

9.   PUBLISH COMMITTEE ROLL CALLS. The committee report
of action on bills to the respective houses should include those
roll calls which are taken, showing how each member voted.
These committee reports should be available to the press and
public. Published roll calls should apply to those bills recommended for approval as well as those killed.

10. INTERIM COMMITTEES. When the legislature is not in session, the standing committees should become the interim committees for the purpose of conducting long-range studies of state policy issues. The Legislative Council or some similarly constituted, bi-partisan committee should serve as the supervising agency for interim committees and their studies, budgets, and personnel. The major committees should be staffed on a year-round basis.

11. REPRINT AMENDED BILLS. When a bill is amended substantially, it should be reprinted and returned to the legislature with no more than an overnight delay. The reprint should show clearly the original text of the bill as well as the change created by the amendment.

12. INCREASE LEGISLATIVE COMPENSATION. No legislative salaries in the United States should be below the $10,000 a year level. Compensation of legislators in the larger states should be in the $20,000 to $30,000 range.

Legislative salaries should be provided by statute at the $10,000 to $15,000 level on an annual basis. Consideration might be given to the establishment of a public commission to make appropriate recommendations on all governmental salaries.

13. REGULATION OF LOBBYISTS. The independence of the legislature and public confidence in its processes require the regulation of special-interest advocates. Lobbyists should be required to register with an agency of the legislature, and should be required to disclose who employs them, on behalf of what objectives, how much they are paid, and how much they spend and on whom. This information should be available to the press and the public. There should be specific and automatic penalties for failure to comply with these requirements.

14. MANAGEMENT COMMITTEES. There should be an executive or management committee created in each house. Its membership should include the leaders of each party in each house, and the minority party should have representation on the committee in proportion to its numbers in the body as a whole. The Senate/ House management committees should combine as a joint management committees should combine as a joint management committee. The purpose of these committees should be to assume responsibility for the administrative management (housekeeping) functions relating to personnel, facilities, the research bureaus, budgets, and expenditures of their respective houses. The joint management committee should deal with matters of inter-house coordination.

15. INDIVIDUAL OFFICES. Provide private, individual offices for every member of the legislature, with nearby space for their

assistants. The quality and amount of office space should not differ substantially between majority and minority party members.

16. **STRENGTHEN STAFF SUPPORT.** Legislative research, fiscal, legal, and planning agencies should be adequately staffed to full utility and at suitable salary levels for professional qualification. Professional staffing should be at a level to enable the legislature to conduct continuous, year-round examination of state resources and expenditures as well as program review and evaluation of state agencies. This staff should also prepare fiscal notes accompanying all appropriation bills, evaluating their fiscal impact over the short and long term. Staff agencies should be upgraded to the level at which competent and timely service can be provided to every member of the legislature.

Also, the constitution, should be amended to clarify the authority of the legislature to retain its own legal counsel.

17. **STRENGTHEN STAFF SUPPORT (LEADERS).** Staff assistance should be provided to all leaders of both the majority and minority parties. Such assistance should include a secretary and an administrative assistant at the professional level; with space to work reasonably adjacent to the offices of members and leaders.

18. **STRENGTHEN STAFF (RANK-AND-FILE-MEMBERS).** Rank-and-file members (majority and minority party on an equal basis) should be provided with individual staff assistance consisting of a minimum of an administrative assistant at the professional level and a secretary. Eventually, this should increase to the stated level of support both in the capital and in a district office.

Some movement toward the staffing of individual members can be made through the provision of administrative assistants on the professional level, perhaps beginning on a shared basis, but ultimately for each member.

19. **COMMITTEE STAFFING.** A beginning should be made toward permanent committee staffing for some of the major committees.

20. **SKELETON BILLS.** There should be an explicit rule barring introduction of skeleton or "spot" bills. This rule should be enforced by the assigning authority (the presiding officer or Rules Committee) by refusal to assign bills so identified to committee.

21. **CONSENT CALENDAR.** A consent calendar should be used in both houses.

22. DISCONTINUE ROTATING LEADERSHIP. The practice of limiting presiding officers to a single, two-year term in that position weakens the legislature in its capacity to confront other branches and levels of government as a partner of equal stature and diffuses and disrupts the continuity of leadership within the legislative bodies. Although it is extremely difficult to change a practice such as this, because of its profoundly adverse effects on many aspects of legislative performance, it should be discontinued.

Utah still limits its speaker of the House, by custom, to a single two-year term in that position. In the 1971 session, Senator Haven Barlow was re-elected president pro tem of the Senate. Because of the change of party control in the House at the same time, the question of continuing leadership has not yet been tested. The practice of rotating leadership weakens the legislature and should be discontinued.

23. IMPROVE PRESS FACILITIES. Improved press facilities aid in the coverage of the work of the legislature. Committee rooms, and both chambers or galleries, should provide adequate space for the news media as well as lighting and electrical power connections for their equipment. Conference or interview rooms and office space should also be provided for the news media.

Specifically, committee rooms should provide adequate space for the news media as well as lighting and electrical power connections for their equipment. Conference or interview rooms and office space for the news media should also be provided.

24. FACILITIES FOR COMMITTEES. Legislative effectiveness requires that committees have adequate physical facilities in which to do their work. This includes an adequate number of committee rooms and an adequate number of hearing rooms that will permit the seating of larger audiences.

The number of committee hearing rooms should be increased to permit the seating of larger audiences.

25. STRENGTHEN MINORITY PARTY ROLE. Internal accountability as well as the capacity of all legislators to represent their constituents effectively, depends upon the opportunity of minority party members to have an effective part in internal legislative affairs.

MINORITY REPRESENTATION ON COMMITTEE ON RULES. Minority representation on the Committee on Rules should approximate the minority party proportion of the membership of the appropriate house.

MINORITY PARTY MEMBERS ON COMMITTEE. Minority party
members should be assigned to committees by the minority
leader in consultation with the minority caucus.

26. TRANSFER AUDIT FUNCTION TO THE LEGISLATURE. A signif-
    icant part of the legislature's ability to exercise oversight of
    executive departments and administrative agencies depends upon
    the power and capacity to conduct audits (financial and functional)
    of these units of the state government. These functions and
    responsibilities should be removed from the duties and resources
    of the Office of Auditor and be established under a legislative
    auditor.

27. BILL READING. Remove constitutional requirement that bills
    must be read in full on three separate legislative days. Rules
    should be uniform in requiring that bills be read by title only
    (so long as a printed copy is provided each member in advance)
    on three separate legislative days.

VERMONT (37)

Functional, 19; Accountable, 20; Informed, 34; Independent, 42;
Representative, 47

GENERAL: Some of the better features of the Vermont General
Assembly are the use of annual sessions (the legislature circumvents
the constitutional requirement of one regular session per biennium
by adjourning to a day certain rather than sine die), a small number
of committees (House, fifteen; Senate, thirteen), and salaries that
are set by statute. Its weaknesses range from inadequate compensation
to a critical lack of office space. Few of the weaknesses of the
legislature are the result of constitutional restrictions; the legislative
article of the Vermont constitution is notable in its use of broad
rather than restrictive guidelines. This would suggest that the legislative has within its immediate power the capability of implementing
broad reforms. A starting point for improvement might be the final
report of the Vermont Legislative Improvement Study Committee,
which has recently submitted its recommendations to the Legislative
Council.

Recommendations for the Vermont Legislature include the following.

1. LEGISLATIVE SALARIES. Legislative salaries should be set by
   statute and paid in equal monthly installments throughout the
   biennium, and all unvouchered expense allowances should be
   incorporated into an annual salary. Actual and necessary expenses

incurred in the process of carrying out legislative duties should
be reimbursed upon submission and approval of properly vouchered
evidence of expenditures.

INCREASE LEGISLATIVE COMPENSATION. No legislative
salaries in the United States should be below the $10,000 a year
level. Compensation of legislators in the larger states should
be in the $20,000 to $30,000 range.

By statute Vermont limits maximum pay to $4,500 per biennium.
Salary is set at $150 per week during regular or special session;
therefore, pay ceases after thirty weeks. This has the effect of
limiting the length of sessions in Vermont, where no limitations
would otherwise exist. The legislature should provide for an
annual salary for legislators of at least $10,000 per year.

2.   POWER TO EXPAND SPECIAL SESSION AGENDA. Amend the
     constitution to permit the legislature to broaden the subject
     matter of a governor's call of a special session by a majority
     vote in each house, or prohibit the restriction of the agenda by
     the governor.

3.   PRE-SESSION ORGANIZATIONAL MEETING. Amend the con-
     stitution to provide a pre-session organizing session following a
     general election. Some states make advantageous use of such a
     session during November or December of a general election
     year for the purpose of electing leaders, appointing committee
     chairmen, assigning members to committees, referring pre-
     filed bills to committee, holding committee organizational meeting
     and conducting orientation conferences for new, as well as
     returning, members of the legislature. Through such pre-session
     meetings the committees can begin their work before the regular
     session convenes. This makes it possible to delay the start of
     the regular session until legislation is ready for floor action.

4.   INTERIM COMMITTEES. When the legislature is not in session,
     the standing committees should become the interim committees
     for the purpose of conducting long-range studies of state policy
     issues. The Legislative Council or some similarly constituted,
     bi-partisan committee should serve as the supervising agency
     for interim committees and their studies, budgets, and personnel.
     The major committees should be staffed on a year-round basis.

5.   PROVIDE SINGLE-MEMBER DISTRICTS. Legislative districts
     in both houses should be single-member.

     In the House, thirty-six of seventy-two legislative districts are
     multi-member; and in the Senate, ten of twelve. They should be
     single-member.

6. STRENGTHEN STAFF SUPPORT. Legislative research, fiscal, legal, and planning agencies should be adequately staffed to full utility and at suitable salary levels for professional qualification. Professional staffing should be at a level to enable the legislature to conduct continuous, year-round examination of state resources and expenditures as well as program review and evaluation of state agencies. This staff should also prepare fiscal notes accompanying all appropriation bills, evaluating their fiscal impact over the short and long term. Staff agencies should be upgraded to the level at which competent and timely service can be provided to every member of the legislature.

7. INDIVIDUAL OFFICES. Provide private, individual offices for every member of the legislature, with nearby space for their assistants. The quality and amount of office space should not differ substantially between majority and minority party members.

At a minimum, leaders should have, immediately, private offices for themselves, with separate, nearby offices for their assistants. A beginning should be made toward providing offices for all members by making space available for shared offices among small numbers of members at first, than gradually reducing the number who share space until a private office is provided for each member.

8. FACILITIES FOR COMMITTEES. Legislative effectiveness requires that committees have adequate physical facilities in which to do their work. This includes an adequate number of committee rooms and an adequate number of hearing rooms that will permit the seating of larger audiences.

Vermont has no committee hearing rooms. The number of committee meeting rooms is adequate, but they are too small for even regular committee use. The legislature should provide at least two hearing rooms per house that permit the seating of larger audiences, as well as enlarging and renovating its present complement of committee rooms.

9. IMPROVE PRESS FACILITIES. Improved press facilities aid in the coverage of the work of the legislature. Committee rooms, and both chambers or galleries, should provide adequate space for the news media as well as lighting and electrical power connections for their equipment. Conference or interview rooms and office space should also be provided for the news media.

10. UNIFORM COMMITTEE RULES. There should be uniform published rules of committee procedure in both chambers.

11. STRENGTHEN MINORITY PARTY ROLE. Internal accountability, as well as the capacity of all legislators to represent their constituents effectively, depends upon the opportunity of minority party members to have an effective part in internal legislative affairs.

12. REMOVE LEGISLATIVE POWERS FROM LIEUTENANT GOVERNO The exercise of legislative powers, including such pro forma powers as presiding, casting tie-breaking votes, and signing enacted legislation, by the lieutenant governor, whether the powers derive from the constitution or the rule book, would seem to be a particularly serious breach of the separation of powers and the independence of the legislature. The constitution and/or rule book should be amended to permit these legislative powers presently exercised by the lieutenant governor to be set as the responsibility of the office of the president pro tem of the Senate.

13. REDUCE THE OVERALL SIZE OF THE LEGISLATURE. Although size reduction in a legislative body is extremely difficult to achieve, it has been done in some states - such as in Vermont and Iowa - and needs to be accomplished in others (New Hampshire, Massachusetts, Georgia, and Pennsylvania). Where reduction in size has occurred, it has most often required a constitutional convention to accomplish it. In a few cases it has been done by legislatively adopted constitutional amendment (Iowa, in 1968, which becomes effective in November, 1971) ratified by the voters. There should be 100 or fewer members in the house. The combine size of both houses should be between 100 and 150.

Although Vermont has a largely rural population of low density, the House of the legislature is the ninth largest legislative body (tied with New York and Texas at 150 members each) in the United States. Vermont is to be commended for having reduced the size of the House from 246 members during the reapportionme of 1965; however, further efforts should be made to reduce the size of the House to no more than 100 members.

14. MANAGEMENT COMMITTEES. There should be an executive or management committee created in each house. Its membership should include the leaders of each party in each house, and the minority party should have representation on the committee in proportion to its numbers in the body as a whole. The Senate/House management committees should combine as a joint management committee. The purpose of these committees should be to assume responsibility for the administrative management (housekeeping) functions relating to personnel, facilities, the research bureaus, budgets, and expenditures of their respective houses. The joint management committee should deal with matters of inter-house coordination.

15. TRANSFER AUDIT FUNCTION TO THE LEGISLATURE. A signif-
    icant part of the legislature's ability to exercise oversight of
    executive departments and administrative agencies depends upon
    the power and capacity to conduct audits (financial and functional)
    of these units of the state government. These functions and
    responsibilities should be removed from the duties and resources
    of the Office of Auditor and be established under a legislative
    auditor.

16. DUAL COMMITTEE CONSIDERATION OF APPROPRIATION BILLS.
    There should be a rule requiring dual committee consideration
    of legislation affecting significant sums of money. Such legislation,
    when considered and acted upon favorably by a substantive policy
    committee, should then automatically be referred to the Finance
    Committee for consideration of its fiscal impact.

17. REQUIRE ROLL CALL ON PASSAGE OF BILLS. A recorded
    roll call should be required on final passage of any legislative
    measure, and it should require a constitutional majority to pass
    any bill on final action by either house.

    Although five Representatives in the House or one Senator can
    request a roll call vote in their respective houses, roll call votes
    on final passage should be automatic. It should require a consti-
    tutional majority to pass any bill by either house. An electric
    roll call recorder should be installed.

18. ELECTRIC ROLL CALL RECORDER. There should be an electric
    roll call recorder in each house. This is recommended not
    simply because it would speed up the proceedings (worthwhile
    as this may be), but because it is an efficient method of producing
    an error-free record of roll call votes.

19. NOTICE OF MEETINGS. The rules should require a minimum
    notice of five legislative days for committee meetings and hearings,
    with widely disseminated announcement of schedule, location,
    agenda, and availability of public participation.

20. COMMITTEE BILL REPORTS. Require committees to issue
    reports describing and explaining the committee's action on bills
    recommended for passage at the time the bill moves from the
    committee to the floor.

21. PUBLISH COMMITTEE ROLL CALLS. The committee report of
    action on bills to the respective houses should include those roll
    calls which are taken, showing how each member voted. These
    committee reports should be available to the press and public.
    Published roll calls should apply to those bills recommended for
    approval as well as those killed.

22. BILL DEADLINES. The orderly flow of work through the legislature depends upon the existence of a series of deadlines at
various critical stages throughout the legislative process. These
deadlines should be adopted as part of the rules and should be
consistently enforced.

Vermont now has deadlines for bill filing, bill introduction, and
committee reports on referred legislation. The orderly flow of
work could be aided by the establishment of similar deadlines on
floor action, conference committee reports, and action by the
other house.

23. CONSENT CALENDAR. A consent calendar should be used in
both houses.

24. PRACTICE BEFORE REGULATORY AGENCIES. Legislators
or their firms should be prohibited from practicing before state
regulatory agencies or in matters concerning state agencies for
a fee.

PROBIBIT DOING BUSINESS WITH THE STATE. There should
be a prohibition against legislators or the firms in which they
own a major interest doing business with state agencies.

PROHIBIT APPOINTMENT TO STATE OFFICE. There should
be a prohibition against a legislator accepting appointment to
other state office during the term for which he is elected or
within two years of the termination of his service as a member
of the legislature.

FAMILY EMPLOYMENT. Members of a legislator's immediate
family should be barred from employment by the legislature.

VIRGINIA (34)

Functional, 25; Accountable, 19; Informed, 27; Independent, 26;
Representative, 48

GENERAL: A major victory for legislative improvement in Virginia
was scored in the 1970 general election with the passage of a new
constitution. Previously limited to a sixty-day biennial session in
even-numbered years, the General Assembly may now meet in odd-
numbered years for an additional thirty days. Either session may
be extended thirty days by a two-thirds vote of elected members of
both houses. Both houses may jointly provide for interim activities.
The previous restriction on compensation of sixty days in regular

session and thirty days in special session has been removed. With this change, legislators may be paid for session time if an extension is authorized, and may be paid for any interim work.

These new provisions lay the groundwork for further legislative modernization, as suggested in the following recommendations.

1. INTERIM COMMITTEES. When the legislature is not in session, the standing committees should become the interim committees for the purpose of conducting long-range studies of state policy issues. The Legislative Council or some similarly constituted, bi-partisan committee should serve as the supervising agency for interim committees and their studies, budgets, and personnel. The major committees should be staffed on a year-round basis.

2. PROVIDE SINGLE-MEMBER DISTRICTS. Legislative districts in both houses should be single-member.

    In the House, twenty of the sixty-three legislative districts are multi-member; in the Senate, five of thirty-three. They should be single-member.

3. STRENGTHEN STAFF SUPPORT. Legislative research, fiscal, legal, and planning agencies should be adequately staffed to full utility and at suitable salary levels for professional qualification. Professional staffing should be at a level to enable the legislature to conduct continuous, year-round examination of state resources and expenditures as well as program review and evaluation of state agencies. This staff should also prepare fiscal notes accompanying all appropriation bills, evaluating their fiscal impact over the short and long term. Staff agencies should be upgraded to the level at which competent and timely service can be provided to every member of the legislature.

    The following important services are not now provided to the legislature: continuous study of state resources and expenditures, budget review and analysis, program review and evaluation, and long-range fiscal forecasting.

4. UNIFORM COMMITTEE RULES. There should be uniform published rules of committee procedure in both chambers.

5. COMMITTEE JURISDICTION. A description of the jurisdiction of committees should be contained in the rules of both houses, and assignment of bills should be made in accord with the jurisdiction of committees as described in the rules.

This is presently done in the Senate but not in the House.

6. JOINT RULES. There should be joint rules governing the relationship and the flow of legislation between the two houses of the legislature.

7. STRENGTHEN MINORITY PARTY ROLE. Internal accountability, as well as the capacity of all legislators to represent their constituents effectively, depends upon the opportunity of minority party members to have an effective part in internal legislative affairs.

8. REDUCE THE NUMBER OF COMMITTEES. Ideally, there should be from ten to fifteen committees in each house parallel in jurisdiction. This would reduce the general complexity of the legislature and would permit reducing the number of committee assignments per member.

9. REDUCE THE NUMBER OF COMMITTEE ASSIGNMENTS. In order to make it possible for members to concentrate their attention and contribute effectively, there should be no more than three committee assignments for each member of the lower house and four committee assignments for each member of the Senate. The multiplicity of assignments introduces problems of scheduling, strains the focus of attention on the part of members, and creates an inordinately heavy workload for members if committees are as active as they should be.

At present, fifty percent of the members of the House have more than three committee assignments each, and sixty-five percent of the members of the Senate have more than four committee assignments each.

10. INCREASE LEGISLATIVE COMPENSATION. No legislative salaries in the United States should be below the $10,000 a year level. Compensation of legislators in the larger states should be in the $20,000 to $30,000 range.

EXPENSE ALLOWANCES. Members of the legislature should be allowed an expense reimbursement covering their travel and living costs while engaged in carrying out their legislative duties. The same allowance should obtain during the interim for days in attendance at interim committee meetings or other official and authorized legislative business. These allowances should be provided by statute.

11. UNIFORM PUBLISHED RULES. There should be uniform, orderly, and reasonable published rules of procedure in each house.

12. DUAL COMMITTEE CONSIDERATION OF APPROPRIATION BILLS. There should be a rule requiring dual committee consideration of legislation affecting significant sums of money. Such legislation, when considered and acted upon favorably by a substantive policy committee, should then automatically be referred to the Finance Committee for consideration of its fiscal impact.

13. PRACTICE BEFORE REGULATORY AGENCIES. Legislators or their firms should be prohibited from practicing before state regulatory agencies or in matters concerning state agencies for a fee.

PROHIBIT DOING BUSINESS WITH THE STATE. There should be a prohibition against legislators or the firms in which they own a major interest doing business with state agencies.

FAMILY EMPLOYMENT. Members of a legislator's immediate family should be barred from employment by the legislature.

14. COMMITTEE BILL REPORTS. Require committees to issue reports describing and explaining the committee's action on bills recommended for passage at the time the bill moves from the committee to the floor.

15. OPEN COMMITTEES. The rules of each house should prohibit secret meetings except in matters affecting the security of the state, or which could unnecessarily damage the reputation of individuals in personnel matters. Such exceptions should be sparingly and responsibly employed.

16. ACT ON ALL BILLS. Committees should be required to report on all bills assigned to them, recommending for passage by the parent body those bills which enjoy the support of a majority of the members of the committee and killing all others.

17. REMOVE LEGISLATIVE POWERS FROM LIEUTENANT GOVERNOR. The exercise of legislative powers, including such pro forma powers as presiding, casting tie-breaking votes, and signing enacted legislation, by the lieutenant governor, whether the powers derive from the constitution or the rule book, would seem to be a particularly serious breach of the separation of powers and the independence of the legislature. The constitution and/or rule book should be amended to permit these legislative powers presently exercised by the lieutenant governor to be set as the responsibility of the office of the president pro tem of the Senate.

The lieutenant governor, as president of the Senate in Virginia, also is chairman of the Rules Committee.

18. MANAGEMENT COMMITTEES. There should be an executive
or management committee created in each house. Its membership
should include the leaders of each party in each house, and the
minority party should have representation on the committee in
proportion to its numbers in the body as a whole. The Senate/
House management committees should combine as a joint management committee. The purpose of these committees should be to
assume responsibility for the administrative management (housekeeping) functions relating to personnel, facilities, the research
bureaus, budgets, and expenditures of their respective houses.
The joint management committee should deal with matters of
inter-house coordination.

19. SERVICE AGENCY FACILITIES. Space for service agencies
should provide adequate working space for professional and
clerical staff as well as library, files, and other storage requirements.

20. REPRINT AMENDED BILLS. When a bill is amended substantially,
it should be reprinted and returned to the legislature with no
more than an overnight delay. The reprint should show clearly
the original text of the bill as well as the change created by the
amendment.

21. BILL DEADLINES. The orderly flow of work through the legislature
depends upon the existence of a series of deadlines at various
critical stages throughout the legislative process. These deadlines
should be adopted as part of the rules and should be consistently
enforced.

Although some bill deadlines exist, sixty-six percent of the bills
passed by the legislature last session were enacted in the final
week of the session. A more regular and orderly flow of bill
processing could be established by the adoption of additional
deadlines.

WASHINGTON (19)

Functional, 12; Accountable, 17; Informed, 25; Independent, 19;
Representative, 39

GENERAL: Washington scored at approximately the same level on
four of the major criteria of FAIIR, indicating only a few major
barriers to legislative improvement as a whole.

Some of the advantages of the Washington legislature are its moderate
size (House, ninety-nine; Senate, forty-nine), control of its own

operating expenditures, compensation set by statute, data-processing equipment available to both houses, and a requirement that roll call votes be published on final committee actions.

Recommendations for the Washington Legislature include the following.

1. REMOVE CONSTITUTIONAL RESTRICTIONS ON SESSION AND INTERIM TIME. The legislature should have authority to function throughout a two-year term; ideally, this authority should provide a flexible biennial session pattern that permits the legislature to convene, recess, and reconvene as it deems desirable. The legislature should be able to meet in general session or conduct interim work as it deems necessary at any time throughout the period.

    An interim step to the achievement of annual, unlimited sessions would be to amend the constitution to permit the legislature to convene, recess, and reconvene as necessary over the two-year period of its term. Another alternative would be to remove the limit on length of sessions, or permit the legislature to extend its session for the amount of time needed by a vote of a majority of the members of each house. Where session time is strictly limited by the constitution, another valuable device would be to allow the legislature to reconvene after the governor's signing of bills, to consider overriding vetoes.

2. LEGISLATIVE POWER TO CALL SPECIAL SESSIONS. Amend the constitution to permit the legislature to convene special sessions either by petition of a majority of the members of both houses or the call of the presiding officer of each house.

3. PRE-SESSION ORGANIZATIONAL MEETING. Amend the constitution to provide a pre-session organizing session following a general election. Some states make advantageous use of such a session during November or December of a general election year for the purpose of electing leaders, appointing committee chairmen, assigning members to committees, referring pre-filed bills to committee, holding committee organizational meetings, and conducting orientation conferences for new, as well as returning, members of the legislature. Through such pre-session meetings the committees can begin their work before the regular session convenes. This makes it possible to delay the start of the regular session until legislation is ready for floor action.

4. INCREASE LEGISLATIVE COMPENSATION. No legislative salaries in the United States should be below the $10,000 a year level. Compensation of legislators in the larger states should be in the $20,000 to $30,000 range.

Current salaries, which average $3,600 a year, should be doubled immediately and increased again with the next few years as other improvements are made.

5. STRENGTHEN STAFF SUPPORT. Legislative research, fiscal, legal, and planning agencies should be adequately staffed to full utility and at suitable salary levels for professional qualification. Professional staffing should be at a level to enable the legislature to conduct continuous, year-round examination of state resources and expenditures as well as program review and evaluation of state agencies. This staff should also prepare fiscal notes accompanying all appropriation bills, evaluating their fiscal impact over the short and long term. Staff agencies should be upgraded to the level at which competent and timely service can be provided to every member of the legislature.

6. STRENGTHEN STAFF SUPPORT (LEADERS). Staff assistance should be provided to all leaders of both the majority and minority parties. Such assistance should include a secretary and an administrative assistant at the professional level, with space to work reasonably adjacent to the offices of members and leaders.

7. STRENGTHEN STAFF (RANK-AND-FILE MEMBERS). Rank-and-file members (majority and minority party on an equal basis) should be provided with individual staff assistance consisting of a minimum of an administrative assistant at the professional level and a secretary. Eventually, this should increase to the stated level of support both in the capital and in a district office.

8. COMMITTEE STAFFING. Standing committees should be staffed on a permanent, year-round basis.

9. INDIVIDUAL OFFICES. Provide private, individual offices for every member of the legislature, with nearby space for their assistants. The quality and amount of office space should not differ substantially between majority and minority party members.

10. INTERIM COMMITTEES. When the legislature is not in session, the standing committees should become the interim committees for the purpose of conducting long-range studies of state policy issues. The Legislative Council or some similarly constituted, bi-partisan committee should serve as the supervising agency for interim committees and their studies, budgets, and personnel. The major committees should be staffed on a year-round basis.

11. PROVIDE SINGLE-MEMBER DISTRICTS. Legislative districts in both houses should be single-member.

12. MINORITY PARTY MEMBERS ON COMMITTEE. Minority party members should be assigned to committees by the minority leader in consultation with the minority caucus.

13. REDUCE THE NUMBER OF COMMITTEE ASSIGNMENTS. In order to make it possible for members to concentrate their attention and contribute effectively, there should be no more than three committee assignments for each member of the lower house and four committee assignments for each member of the Senate. The multiplicity of assignments introduces problems of scheduling, strains the focus of attention on the part of members, and creates an inordinately heavy workload for members if committees are as active as they should be.

    At present fifteen percent of the members of the House have more than three committee assignments each, and eighty-eight percent of the members of the Senate have more than four committee assignments each. A reduction in the number of committees in both houses (House, sixteen; Senate, eighteen) would help reduce the number of committee assignments per member.

14. ACT ON ALL BILLS. Committees should be required to report on all bills assigned to them, recommending for passage by the parent body those bills which enjoy the support of a majority of the members of the committee and killing all others.

15. COMMITTEE HEARINGS. There is no justification for permitting any major piece of legislation to become law without having been subjected to extensive, thorough, well-planned, and well-prepared public hearings, in which representatives of the public, civic organizations, and interest groups are not only invited but encouraged to participate.

16. OPEN COMMITTEES. The rules of each house should prohibit secret meetings except in matters affecting the security of the state, or which could unnecessarily damage the reputation of individuals in personnel matters. Such exceptions should be sparingly and responsibly employed.

17. COMMITTEE JURISDICTION. A description of the jurisdiction of committees should be contained in the rules of both houses, and assignment of bills should be made in accord with the jurisdiction of committees as described in the rules.

18. TRANSFER AUDIT FUNCTION TO THE LEGISLATURE. A significant part of the legislature's ability to exercise oversight of executive departments and administrative agencies depends

upon the power and capacity to conduct audits (financial and
functional) of these units of the state government. These functions
and responsibilities should be removed from the duties and resources of the Office of Auditor and be established under a legislative auditor.

19.   MANAGEMENT COMMITTEES. There should be an executive
or management committee created in each house. Its membership
should include the leaders of each party in each house, and the
minority party should have representation on the committee in
proportion to its numbers in the body as a whole. The Senate/
House management committees should combine as a joint management committee. The purpose of these committees should be to
assume responsibility for the administrative management (housekeeping) functions relating to personnel, facilities, the research
bureaus, budgets, and expenditures of their respective houses.

The joint management committee should deal with matters of
inter-house coordination.

20.   WASHINGTON, D.C., OFFICE FOR THE LEGISLATURE. With
the large and growing volume of activity generated by state-federal
relationships, the legislature, beyond merely reacting to federal
legislation, should be in a position to influence the development
of new programs in accordance with the interests of the state. To
do so, the legislature should have an office in the nation's capital
to represent it and to be its most direct liaison with the Congress.

For small states, consideration might be given to joining with a
number of sister states (either on a geographical or on a population basis) for the purpose of sharing the services of a Washington office. But in large states, the volume of inter-governmental
traffic has reached a stage at which it would benefit the legislature
greatly to have a full-time Washington office.

21.   ELECTRIC ROLL CALL RECORDER. There should be an electric
roll call recorder in each house. This is recommended not simply
because it would speed up the proceedings (worthwhile as this
may be), but because it is an efficient method of producing an
error-free record of roll call votes.

22.   COMMITTEE BILL REPORTS. Require committees to issue
reports describing and explaining the committee's action on
bills recommended for passage at the time the bill moves from
the committee to the floor.

23.   ESTABLISH AN AUTOMATIC CALENDAR OF BILLS. When a
bill is favorably reported out of committee to the floor, it should

go automatically onto the calendar in the order in which it was reported out. It should require a vote of an extraordinary majority to move a bill from its position on calendar or to bypass it. The Rules Committee should have no part in the scheduling of bills. No session should adjourn until all bills on calendar have been voted up or down or, by the vote of an extraordinary majority, have been moved from the calendar.

24. SKELETON BILLS. There should be an explicit rule barring introduction of skeleton or "spot" bills. This rule should be enforced by the assigning authority (the presiding officer or Rules Committee) by refusal to assign bills so identified to committee.

25. DUAL COMMITTEE CONSIDERATION OF APPROPRIATION BILLS. There should be a rule requiring dual committee consideration of legislation affecting significant sums of money. Such legislation, when considered and acted upon favorably by a substantive policy committee, should then automatically be referred to the Finance Committee for consideration of its fiscal impact.

26. REMOVE LEGISLATIVE POWERS FROM LIEUTENANT GOVERNOR. The exercise of legislative powers, including such pro forma powers as presiding, casting tie-breaking votes, and signing enacted legislation, by the lieutenant governor, whether the powers derive from the constitution or the rule book, would seem to be a particularly serious breach of the separation of powers and the independence of the legislature. The constitution and/or rule book should be amended to permit these legislative powers presently exercised by the lieutenant governor to be set as the responsibility of the office of the president pro tem of the Senate.

In the state of Washington the lieutenant governor is also the chairman of the Senate Committee on Rules and Joint Rules. He may vote in all cases except final passage of a bill (unless there is a tie).

WEST VIRGINIA (25)

Functional, 10; Accountable, 32; Informed, 37; Independent, 24; Representative, 15

GENERAL: On November 3, 1970, a constitutional amendment approved by West Virginia voters made these changes in the legislative article: the sixty-calendar-day general session in odd-numbered years and thirty-calendar-day budget session in even-numbered years were altered to permit sixty-calendar-day general sessions each year; the

length of any general session can now be extended by a two-thirds
vote of members elected to each house; and, a seven-member Citizens'
Legislative Compensation Commission was established to replace the
provision setting annual legislative salaries at $1,500. Beginning in
1971, and every four years thereafter, the commission will be charged
with recommending salaries and expense allowances for legislators.
The legislature can decrease but not increase amounts suggested by
the commission.

West Virginia is in the process of expanding into two more office
buildings. As sub-administrative units of the executive branch move
out, there will be more space available in the capital for the legislature.

The legislature is also to be commended for the excellent pre-session
orientation conference it holds.

The following recommendations are proposed for West Virginia.

1. REMOVE CONSTITUTIONAL RESTRICTIONS ON SESSION AND
    INTERIM TIME. The legislature should have authority to function
    throughout a two-year term; ideally, this authority should provide
    a flexible biennial session pattern that permits the legislature
    to convene, recess, and reconvene as it deems desirable. The
    legislature should be able to meet in general session or conduct
    interim work as it deems necessary at any time throughout the
    period.

    Even though we applaud the session pattern just ratified by the
    voters in November, we feel that the legislature is still too con-
    strained in the amount of time available to it. For that reason
    we recommend that consideration be given in the near future to
    annual general sessions, limited to no fewer than ninety legisla-
    tive days. Above that the present limitation on calendar days
    should be changed to legislative days.

2. PRE-SESSION ORGANIZATIONAL MEETING. Amend the consti-
    tution to provide a pre-session organizing session following a
    general election. Some states make advantageous use of such
    a session during November or December of a general election
    year for the purpose of electing leaders, appointing committee
    chairmen, assigning members to committees, referring pre-filed
    bills to committee, holding committee organizational meetings,
    and conducting orientation conferences for new, as well as re-
    turning, members of the legislature. Through such pre-session
    meetings the committees can begin their work before the regular
    session convenes. This makes it possible to delay the start of
    the regular session until legislation is ready for floor action.

3.   INTERIM COMMITTEES. When the legislature is not in session, the standing committees should become the interim committees for the purpose of conducting long-range studies of state policy issues. The Legislative Council or some similarly constituted, bi-partisan committee should serve as the supervising agency for interim committees and their studies, budgets, and personnel. The major committees should be staffed on a year-round basis.

No provisions exist for standing committees to meet during the interim; expenses are allowed only for special interim committees created by resolution. There is, however, currently a movement underway to allow compensation for standing committee members meeting in the interim.

4.   PROVIDE SINGLE-MEMBER DISTRICTS. Legislative districts in both houses should be single-member.

All legislative districts in the Senate are multi-member; twenty-one out of forty-seven of the Representative districts are multi-member. They should be single-member.

5.   STRENGTHEN STAFF SUPPORT. Legislative research, fiscal, legal, and planning agencies should be adequately staffed to full utility and at suitable salary levels for professional qualification. Professional staffing should be at a level to enable the legislature to conduct continuous, year-round examination of state resources and expenditures as well as program review and evaluation of state agencies. This staff should also prepare fiscal notes accompanying all appropriation bills, evaluating their fiscal impact over the short and long term. Staff agencies should be upgraded to the level at which competent and timely service can be provided to every member of the legislature.

6.   STRENGTHEN STAFF SUPPORT (LEADERS). Staff assistance should be provided to all leaders of both the majority and minority parties. Such assistance should include a secretary and an administrative assistant at the professional level, with space to work reasonably adjacent to the offices of members and leaders.

Although a beginning has been made toward staffing of legislative leaders during sessions, such assistance should be provided year-round.

7.   STAFF (PATRONAGE). Member patronage should be eliminated from all legislative staffing.

8.   INDIVIDUAL OFFICES. Provide private, individual offices for

every member of the legislature, with nearby space for their
assistants. The quality and amount of office space should not
differ substantially between majority and minority party members.

At a minimum, leaders should have private offices with separate,
nearby offices for their assistants. A beginning can be made
toward providing offices for members by making space available
for shared offices among small numbers of members at first,
then gradually reducing the members who share space until a
private office is provided for each member.

9.   FACILITIES FOR COMMITTEES. Legislative effectiveness
     requires that committees have adequate physical facilities in
     which to do their work. This includes an adequate number of
     committee rooms and an adequate number of hearing rooms
     that will permit the seating of larger audiences.

10. UNIFORM COMMITTEE RULES. There should be uniform
     published rules of committee procedure in both chambers.

11. COMMITTEE JURISDICTION. A description of the jurisdiction
     of committees should be contained in the rules of both houses,
     and assignment of bills should be made in accord with the juris-
     diction of committees as described in the rules.

     This is presently done in the House but not in the Senate.

12. MINORITY PARTY MEMBERS ON COMMITTEE. Minority
     party members should be assigned to committees by the minority
     leader in consultation with the minority caucus.

     This is done as a matter of practice in the House, but should be
     compelled by the rules. It is not done at all in the Senate and
     should be.

13. INCREASE LEGISLATIVE COMPENSATION. No legislative
     salaries in the United States should be below the $10,000 a year
     level. Compensation of legislators in the larger states should
     be in the $20,000 to $30,000 range.

     Salaries of members of the legislature are far too low. Current
     salaries of $1,500 a year should be increased to at least $5,000
     a year immediately and then doubled at the next opportunity.
     This will require action by the newly created compensation
     commission.

     LEGISLATIVE SALARIES. Legislative salaries should be set
     by statute and paid in equal monthly installments throughout the

biennium, and all unvouchered expense allowances should be incorporated into an annual salary. Actual and necessary expenses incurred in the process of carrying out legislative duties should be reimbursed upon submission and approval of properly vouchered evidence of expenditures.

14. WASHINGTON, D.C., OFFICE FOR THE LEGISLATURE. With the large and growing volume of activity generated by state-federal relationships, the legislature, beyond merely reacting to federal legislation, should be in a position to influence the development of new programs in accordance with the interests of the state. To do so, the legislature should have an office in the nation's capital to represent it and to be its most direct liaison with the Congress.

For small states, consideration might be given to joining with a number of sister states (either on a geographical or on a population basis) for the purpose of sharing the services of a Washington office. But in large states, the volume of inter-governmental traffic has reached a stage at which it would benefit the legislature greatly to have a full-time Washington office.

15. DUAL COMMITTEE CONSIDERATION OF APPROPRIATION BILLS. There should be a rule requiring dual committee consideration of legislation affecting significant sums of money. Such legislation, when considered and acted upon favorably by a substantive policy committee, should then automatically be referred to the Finance Committee for consideration of its fiscal impact.

16. ELECTRIC ROLL CALL RECORDER. There should be an electric roll call recorder in the Senate, as there is in the House. This is recommended not only because it would speed up the proceedings (worthwhile as this may be), but because it is an efficient method of producing an error-free record of roll call votes.

17. REGULATION OF LOBBYISTS. The independence of the legislature and public confidence in its processes require the regulation of special-interest advocates. Lobbyists should be required to register with an agency of the legislature, and should be required to disclose who employs them, on behalf of what objectives, how much they spend and on whom. This information should be available to the press and the public. There should be specific and automatic penalties for failure to comply with these requirements.

18. SERVICE AGENCY FACILITIES. Space for service agencies should provide adequate working space for professional and clerical staff as well as library, files, and other storage requirements.

19. ACT ON ALL BILLS. Committees should be required to report on all bills assigned to them, recommending for passage by the parent body those bills which enjoy the support of a majority of the members of the committee and killing all others.

20. COMMITTEE BILL REPORTS. Require committees to issue reports describing and explaining the committee's action on bills recommended for passage at the time the bill moves from the committee to the floor.

21. OPEN COMMITTEES. The rules of each house should prohibit secret meetings except in matters affecting the security of the state, or which could unnecessarily damage the reputation of individuals in personnel matters. Such exceptions should be sparingly and responsibly employed.

22. NOTICE OF MEETINGS. The rules should require a minimum notice of five legislative days for committee meetings and hearings, with widely disseminated announcement of schedule, location, agenda, and availability of public participation.

23. COMMITTEE HEARINGS. There is no justification for permitting any major piece of legislation to become law without having been subjected to extensive, thorough, well-planned, and well-prepared public hearings, in which representatives of the public, civic organizations, and interest groups are not only invited but encouraged to participate.

24. REDUCE THE NUMBER OF COMMITTEE ASSIGNMENTS. In order to make it possible for members to concentrate their attention and contribute effectively, there should be no more than three committee assignments for each member of the lower house and four committee assignments for each member of the Senate. The multiplicity of assignments introduces problems of scheduling, strains the focus of attention on the part of members, and creates an inordinately heavy workload for members if committees are as active as they should be.

At present, twenty-six percent of the members of the House have more than three assignments each, and eighty-eight percent of the Senators have more than four. This can be attributed to the large size of committees. The average size of House committees is twenty-three to twenty-five members; Senate, nine to eighteen, two of the Senate committees having more than half the number of Senators as members. Another peculiarity of the legislative committee system is that some members have more than one committee chairmanship: in the House, one member has four chairmanships;

in the Senate, one member has three and one has four. No Representative or Senator should have more than one committee chairmanship.

25. IMPROVE PRESS FACILITIES. Improved press facilities aid in the coverage of the work of the legislature. Committee rooms, and both chambers or galleries, should provide adequate space for the news media as well as lighting and electrical power connections for their equipment. Conference or interview rooms and office space should also be provided for the news media.

26. PRINTED BILL DOCUMENT FORMAT. The bill document printing procedure should permit the clear identification of the text of the existing statute which is being amended as well as the material which the bill proposes to delete or add. This is usually accomplished through the use of varying type faces, such as "strike-through," italics, underlining, or bracketing. It should not be necessary to compare the text of a bill with the text of the existing code in order to determine what the bill does.

27. REPRINT AMENDED BILLS. When a bill is amended substantially, it should be reprinted and returned to the legislature with no more than an overnight delay. The reprint should show clearly the original text of the bill as well as the change created by the amendment.

The rules now require that bills be reprinted only once after the bill is reported out of committee.

28. BILL DEADLINES. The orderly flow of work through the legislature depends upon the existence of a series of deadlines at various critical stages throughout the legislative process. These deadlines should be adopted as part of the rules and should be consistently enforced.

Although deadlines exist for bill filing, introduction of bills, and referral to committee, approximately fifty percent of the bills passed in the last session were enacted in the final week of the session. Deadlines should also be adopted for committee and floor action.

WISCONSIN (5)

Functional, 7; Accountable, 21; Informed, 3; Independent, 4; Representative, 10

GENERAL: As the fifth-ranked legislature, Wisconsin displays a
fairly even development across the five scales measuring organization
and procedural effectiveness. It ranks near the top of each with the
exception of accountability. Weaknesses in this category are dealt
with in the recommendations.

In recent years, the Senate has improved steadily, but the Assembly
has fallen behind because of the lack of continuity which necessarily
accompanies frequent changes in party, and hence leadership and control. In the early decades of this century, Wisconsin's Legislature was
a national leader in producing innovations which were models for her
sister states as well as the federal government (viz., social insurance,
technical education, executive budgeting). A continuation of the momentum toward legislative improvement may restore this leadership
role.

The areas in which the Wisconsin Legislature shows strengths are
the following.

Legislators, press, and public have access to the work of the legislature
aided by the existence of regularly recorded and published roll calls
on final committee actions, the prohibition against skeleton bills, and
the provision of informative summaries contained in the format of
bill documents.

The legislative session in Wisconsin is unlimited as to length, frequency
or subject matter. This flexibility permits the Wisconsin Legislature
to meet periodically throughout the biennium. When floor action on
bills requires it, the legislature meets and then recesses when the
work calendar is completed. After committees have processed
additional legislation, the General Assembly reconvenes for whatever
period is required by the volume of work.

The variety of professional staff services permits the continuous,
year-round study of state resources and expenditures as well as
program review and evaluation of state agencies. Sessions of the
legislature are unlimited as to their length and subject matter, and
are flexible in their scheduling throughout the biennial period. The
legislature can expand the agenda of a special session because the
governor may not limit its subject matter.

Single-member districts, individual office space for most members,
and a full pre-session orientation conference contribute to the capacity
of individual members to represent their districts effectively. Legislators are prohibited from having an interest, direct or indirect, in
any firm which does business with the state.

There are a number of areas in which improvements can be made in the Wisconsin Legislature. These are specific recommendations toward that end.

1.   REDUCE THE NUMBER OF COMMITTEES. Ideally, there should be from ten to fifteen committees in each house, parallel in jurisdiction. This would reduce the general complexity of the legislature and would permit reducing the number of committee assignments per member.

   There are twenty-six committees in the Assembly and thirteen in the Senate. A considerable improvement could be achieved by reducing the number of Assembly committees to thirteen and by making them parallel in jurisdiction to those of the Senate.

2.   UNIFORM COMMITTEE RULES. There should be uniform published rules of committee procedure in the Senate, as there are in the Assembly.

3.   COMMITTEE JURISDICTION. A description of the jurisdiction of committees should be contained in the rules of both houses, and assignment of bills should be made in accord with the jurisdiction of committees as described in the rules.

4.   REPRINT AMENDED BILLS. When a bill is amended substantially, it should be reprinted and returned to the legislature with no more than an overnight delay. The reprint should show clearly the original text of the bill as well as the change created by the amendment.

5.   IMPROVE PRESS FACILITIES. Improved press facilities aid in the coverage of the work of the legislature. Committee rooms, and both chambers or galleries, should provide adequate space for the news media as well as lighting and electrical power connections for their equipment. Conference or interview rooms and office space should also be provided for the news media.

6.   STRENGTHEN MINORITY PARTY ROLE. Internal accountability, as well as the capacity of all legislators to represent their constituents effectively, depends upon the opportunity of minority party members to have an effective part in internal legislative affairs.

   MINORITY REPRESENTATION ON COMMITTEE ON RULES. Minority representation on the Committee on Rules should approximate the minority party proportion of the membership of the appropriate house.

MINORITY PARTY MEMBERS ON COMMITTEE. Minority party members in the House should be assigned to committee by the minority leader in consultation with the minority caucus. In the Senate minority committee members are now selected by the minority caucus.

7. REQUIRE ROLL CALL ON PASSAGE OF BILLS. A recorded roll call should be required on final passage of any legislative measure, and it should require a constitutional majority to pass any bill on final action by either house.

8. STATEMENT OF INTENT BY AUTHOR OF A BILL. The form in which a bill is introduced should include a statement by the author describing, in laymen's language, what the bill is intended to accomplish.

9. DUAL COMMITTEE CONSIDERATION OF APPROPRIATION BILLS. There should be a rule requiring dual committee consideration of legislation affecting significant sums of money. Such legislation, when considered and acted upon favorably by a substantive policy committee, should then automatically be referred to the Finance Committee for consideration of its fiscal impact.

10. COMMITTEE BILL REPORTS. Require committees to issue reports describing and explaining the committee's action on bills recommended for passage at the time the bill moves from the committee to the floor.

11. WASHINGTON, D.C., OFFICE FOR THE LEGISLATURE. With the large and growing volume of activity generated by state-federal relationships, the legislature, beyond merely reacting to federal legislation, should be in a position to influence the development of new programs in accordance with the interests of the state. To do so, the legislature should have an office in the nation's capital to represent it and to be its most direct liaison with the Congress.

For small states, consideration might be given to joining with a number of sister states (either on a geographical or on a population basis) for the purpose of sharing the services of a Washington office. But in large states, the volume of inter-governmental traffic has reached a stage at which it would benefit the legislature greatly to have a full-time Washington office.

12. SUPPORT OF DISTRICT OFFICES. District offices are vital to the effective representation by a legislator of his constituency. The legislature should make some contribution to the support

of district offices for its members, and the amount of this contribution should be increased over time.

13. STRENGTHEN STAFF SUPPORT (LEADERS). Staff assistance should be provided to all leaders of both the majority and minority parties. Such assistance should include a secretary and an administrative assistant at the professional level, with space to work reasonably adjacent to the offices of members and leaders.

STRENGTHEN STAFF (RANK-AND-FILE MEMBERS). Rank-and-file members (majority and minority party on an equal basis) should be provided with individual staff assistance consisting of a minimum of an administrative assistant at the professional level and a secretary. Eventually, this should increase to the stated level of support both in the capital and in a district office.

14. INCREASE LEGISLATIVE COMPENSATION. No legislative salaries in the United States should be below the $10,000 a year level. Compensation of legislators in the larger states should be in the $20,000 to $30,000 range.

Salaries of members of the legislature are rather low in comparison with states of similar size and development. Current salaries of $8,900 per annum should be increased to the $15,000 to $20,000 a year range.

15. SPECIAL PROVISIONS. In addition to standard laws governing criminal behavior, there should be special provisions regulating legislative conflicts of interest.

PRACTICE BEFORE REGULATORY AGENCIES. Legislators or their firms should be prohibited from practicing before state regulatory agencies or in matters concerning state agencies for a fee.

FAMILY EMPLOYMENT. Members of a legislator's immediate family should be barred from employment by the legislature.

16. ELECTRIC ROLL CALL RECORDER. An electric roll call recorder should be installed in the Senate, as in the House. This is recommended not simply because it would speed up the proceedings (worthwhile as this may be), but because it is an efficient method of producing an error-free record of roll call votes.

WYOMING (49)

Functional, 42; Accountable, 41; Informed, 50; Independent, 48; Representative, 42

GENERAL: Though it is ranked forty-ninth, Wyoming has an almost
ideal number of committees (eighteen in the House, fifteen in the Senate),
and the legislature has a joint rule which provides that corresponding
committees in each house may, by a majority vote in each house, act
together on the preparation, introduction, and consideration of bills.

The Wyoming committee system could be further streamlined by making
committees of both houses correspond exactly. This change would
be very useful if interim activities are extended beyond using the
House and Senate Ways and Means Committees as the sole standing
joint interim committee.

If the recommendation to provide the legislature with parallel standing
committees were implemented, each member of the House should
have no more than three committee assignments and each member
of the Senate should have no more than four committee assignments.
It is a credit to the Wyoming Legislature that this pattern is followed
at the present time. Recommendations proposed for Wyoming include
the following.

1.   REMOVE CONSTITUTIONAL RESTRICTIONS ON SESSION AND
     INTERIM TIME. The legislature should have authority to function
     throughout a two-year term; ideally, this authority should provide
     a flexible biennial session pattern that permits the legislature
     to convene, recess, and reconvene as it deems desirable. The
     legislature should be able to meet in general session or conduct
     interim work as it deems necessary at any time throughout the
     period.

     General sessions are constitutionally limited to forty calendar
     days per biennium; the constitution should be amended to permit
     annual general sessions limited to no fewer than ninety legislative
     days. If the latter alternative is chosen, new provisions should
     also permit the legislature to extend the limited annual session
     fifty percent by a majority vote of the membership of both
     houses.

2.   LEGISLATIVE POWER TO CALL SPECIAL SESSIONS. Amend
     the constitution to permit the legislature to convene special
     sessions either by petition of a majority of the members of both
     houses or the call of the presiding officer of each house.

3.   POWER TO EXPAND SPECIAL SESSION AGENDA. Amend the
     constitution to permit the legislature to broaden the subject
     matter of a governor's call of a special session by a majority
     vote in each house, or prohibit the restriction of the agenda by
     the governor.

4. PRE-SESSION ORGANIZATIONAL MEETING. Amend the constitution to provide a pre-session organizing session following a general election. Some states make advantageous use of such a session during November or December of a general election year for the purpose of electing leaders, appointing committee chairmen, assigning members to committees, referring pre-filed bills to committee, holding committee organizational meetings, and conducting orientation conferences for new, as well as returning, members of the legislature. Through such pre-session meetings the committees can begin their work before the regular session convenes. This makes it possible to delay the start of the regular session until legislation is ready for floor action.

5. PRE-SESSION ORIENTATION CONFERENCE. The legislature should hold an orientation conference for new legislators, preferably after each general election. Orientation conferences enable members to speed the process of becoming more effective representatives, and they provide an opportunity for legislators to examine large policy areas apart from the pressure of the regular session.

6. UNIFORM COMMITTEE RULES. There should be uniform published rules of committee procedure in both chambers.

7. COMMITTEE JURISDICTION. A description of the jurisdiction of committees should be contained in the rules of both houses, and assignment of bills should be made in accord with the jurisdiction of committees as described in the rules.

8. OPEN COMMITTEES. The rules of each house should prohibit secret meetings except in matters affecting the security of the state, or which could unnecessarily damage the reputation of individuals in personnel matters. Such exceptions should be sparingly and responsibly employed.

9. NOTICE OF MEETINGS. The rules should require a minimum notice of five legislative days for committee meetings and hearings, with widely disseminated announcement of schedule, location, agenda, and availability of public participation.

10. ACT ON ALL BILLS. Committees should be required to report on all bills assigned to them, recommending for passage by the parent body those bills which enjoy the support of a majority of the members of the committee and killing all others.

11. COMMITTEE HEARINGS. There is no justification for permitting any major piece of legislation to become law without having been

subjected to extensive, thorough, well-planned, and well-prepared
public hearings, in which representatives of the public, civic
organizations, and interest groups are not only invited but encouraged to participate.

12. COMMITTEE BILL REPORTS. Require committees to issue
reports describing and explaining the committee's action on bills
recommended for passage at the time the bill moves from the
committee to the floor.

13. RECORD AND PUBLISH PROCEEDINGS OF COMMITTEES.
Record and publish the record of committee hearings, proceedings,
and votes.

14. PUBLISH COMMITTEE ROLL CALLS. The committee report of
action on bills to the respective houses should include those
roll calls which are taken, showing how each member voted.
These committee reports should be available to the press and
public. Published roll calls should apply to those bills recommended for approval as well as those killed.

15. DUAL COMMITTEE CONSIDERATION OF APPROPRIATION BILLS.
There should be a rule requiring dual committee consideration
of legislation affecting significant sums of money. Such legislation,
when considered and acted upon favorably by a substantive policy
committee, should then automatically be referred to the Finance
Committee for consideration of its fiscal impact.

16. MANAGEMENT COMMITTEES. There should be an executive
or management committee created in each house. Its membership
should include the leaders of each party in each house, and the
minority party should have representation on the committee in
proportion to its numbers in the body as a whole. The Senate/
House management committee should combine as a joint management committee. The purpose of these committees should be to
assume responsibility for the administrative management
(housekeeping) functions relating to personnel, facilities, the
research bureaus, budgets, and expenditures of their respective
houses. The joint management committee should deal with matters
of inter-house coordination.

It is especially critical for a legislature limited to sessions of
such drastically short duration as is Wyoming to have a system
for facilitating "housekeeping" procedures in each house and
between the two houses.

17. INTERIM COMMITTEES. When the legislature is not in session,
the standing committees should become the interim committees

for the purpose of conducting long-range studies of state policy issues. The Legislative Council or some similarly constituted, bi-partisan committee should serve as the supervising agency for interim committees and their studies, budgets, and personnel. The major committees should be staffed on a year-round basis.

18. STRENGTHEN STAFF SUPPORT. Legislative research, fiscal, legal, and planning agencies should be adequately staffed to full utility and at suitable salary levels for professional qualification. Professional staffing should be at a level to enable the legislature to conduct continuous, year-round examination of state resources and expenditures as well as program review and evaluation of state agencies. This staff should also prepare fiscal notes accompanying all appropriation bills, evaluating their fiscal impact over the short and long term. Staff agencies should be upgraded to the level at which competent and timely service can be provided to every member of the legislature.

Each house of the Wyoming Legislature has two attorneys, a chief clerk, an assistant to the chief clerk, and a clerical pool. Legislative research, fiscal, legal, and planning agencies are nonexistent. The attorneys for both houses can provide only a minimum of bill drafting and review services. The legislature has no other independent capabilities and, therefore, must rely on state agencies to provide what services are needed. At present, the Wyoming Legislature has no provisions for code research, including reviews of judicial opinions, continuous study of resources and expenditures, budget review and analysis, legislative post-audit, program review and evaluation, fiscal notes, long-range planning, public information services, or in-depth studies and program design. It must also rely on outside help for reference work, spot research, bill summaries, and statute and code revision. Except for the forty calendar days per biennium when the legislature is in session, there is no staffing at all. As a first step toward creating an independent staff capability, the Wyoming Legislature should create a central staff bureau to provide research, bill drafting, fiscal analysis, bill summaries, spot research, and other generally needed services.

19. COMMITTEE STAFFING. Standing committees should be staffed on a permanent, year-round basis.

20. STRENGTHEN STAFF SUPPORT (LEADERS). Staff assistance should be provided to all leaders of both the majority and minority parties. Such assistance should include a secretary and an administrative assistant at the professional level, with space to work reasonably adjacent to the offices of members and leaders.

21. INDIVIDUAL OFFICES. Provide private, individual offices for every member of the legislature, with nearby space for their assistants. The quality and amount of office space should not differ substantially between majority and minority party members.

22. FACILITIES FOR COMMITTEES. Legislative effectiveness requires that committees have adequate physical facilities in which to do their work. This includes an adequate number of committee rooms and an adequate number of hearing rooms that will permit the seating of larger audiences.

Only the Ways and Means Committees of both houses have a designated place in which to meet. The other committees are shifted around to whatever space is available, not always in the legislature's area. In addition to greatly increasing the quantity and quality of committee rooms available, at least two rooms should be developed to serve as hearing rooms, to permit the seating of larger audiences.

23. IMPROVE PRESS FACILITIES. Improved press facilities aid in the coverage of the work of the legislature. Committee rooms, and both chambers or galleries, should provide adequate space for the news media as well as lighting and electrical power connections for their equipment. Conference or interview rooms and office space should also be provided for the news media.

24. PROVIDE SINGLE-MEMBER DISTRICTS. Legislative districts in both houses should be single-member.

Twelve of the twenty-three House districts and seven of the seventeen Senate districts are multi-member. They should be single-member. Accomplishing this requires an amendment to the state constitution.

25. LEGISLATIVE SALARIES. Legislative salaries should be set by statute and paid in equal monthly installments throughout the biennium, and all unvouchered expense allowances should be incorporated into an annual salary. Actual and necessary expenses incurred in the process of carrying out legislative duties should be reimbursed upon submission and approval of properly vouchered evidence of expenditures.

INCREASE LEGISLATIVE COMPENSATION. No legislative salaries in the United States should be below the $10,000 a year level. Compensation of legislators in the larger states should be in the $20,000 to $30,000 range.

Wyoming legislators receive $15 per diem in salary and $26 per diem for expenses for forty calendar days each biennium. The biennial total is $1,640. No legislative salaries in the United States should be below the $10,000 a year level. Current salaries, which average $1,640 per biennium, should be doubled immediately and increased again within the next few years as other improvements are made.

26. EXPENSE ALLOWANCES. Members of the legislature should be allowed an expense reimbursement covering their travel and living costs while engaged in carrying out their legislative duties. The same allowance should obtain during the interim for days in attendance at interim committee meetings or other official and authorized legislative business. These allowances should be provided by statute.

27. DISCONTINUE ROTATING LEADERSHIP. The practice of limiting presiding officers to a single, two-year term in that position weakens the legislature in its capacity to confront other branches and levels of government as a partner of equal stature and diffuses and disrupts the continuity of leadership within the legislative bodies. Although it is extremely difficult to change a practice such as this, because of its profoundly adverse effects on many aspects of legislative performance, it should be discontinued.

Wyoming is one of the remaining half dozen states which, by custom, still limits its speaker of the House and president of the Senate to a single, two-year term in that position. This practice weakens the legislature. Also detrimental to the legislative process is the custom of the presiding officer retiring from the legislature upon completion of his term as presiding officer.

28. SPECIAL PROVISIONS. In addition to standard laws governing criminal behavior, there should be special provisions regulating legislative conflicts of interest.

29. REGULATION OF LOBBYISTS. The independence of the legislature and public confidence in its processes require the regulation of special-interest advocates. Lobbyists should be required to register with an agency of the legislature, and should be required to disclose who employs them, on behalf of what objectives, how much they are paid, and how much they spend and on whom. This information should be available to the press and the public. There should be specific and automatic penalties for failure to comply with these requirements.

At present there are no laws or rules for regulation of lobbyists in the state of Wyoming.

30. CONSENT CALENDAR. A consent calendar should be used in both houses.

31. BILL DEADLINES. The orderly flow of work through the legislatur depends upon the existence of a series of deadlines at various critical stages throughout the legislative process. These deadlines should be adopted as part of the rules and should be consistently enforced.

32. REPRINT AMENDED BILLS. When a bill is amended substantially, it should be reprinted and returned to the legislature with no more than an overnight delay. The reprint should show clearly the original text of the bill as well as the change created by the amendment.

33. BILL SUMMARY BY BILL-DRAFTING SERVICE. The form in which bills are introduced should include a more extensive summary of the provisions of the bill, prepared by the bill-drafting service.

34. STATEMENT OF INTENT BY AUTHOR OF A BILL. The form in which a bill is introduced should include a statement by the author describing, in laymen's language, what the bill is intended to accomplish.

35. MINORITY PARTY MEMBERS ON COMMITTEE. Minority party members should be assigned to committees by the minority leader in consultation with the minority caucus.

Although this recommendation is followed by custom, it should be formalized in the rules. Minority party members should be assigned to committees by the minority leader in consultation with the minority caucus.

CONCLUSION

In presenting these recommendations our aim has been to provide an agenda for action which is long enough and weighty enough to represent significant movement in the direction of a more effectively organized and operating legislature. At the same time, we have wanted to avoid making a list so long and so far removed from current reality that it could not reasonably be implemented within the next few years--or ever.

We have tailored these recommendations to the shortcomings, as we have identified and documented them, for each state, and we have drawn on existing practice in some state or another for the content of a recommendation. This means that the recommendations are not the product of theoretical day dreams. They are currently operating practices or available resources in one or more of the American state legislatures.

If one were considering whether or not a particular recommendation were likely to produce the benefits advertised for it, he need only look at the legislature in which it exists, talk to the members, ask the other actors in and around the legislative arena how it works, what they think of it, and listen to them say, "I don't see how you get along without it."

We estimate that these recommendations could be implemented reasonably in a period of five or six years. As they are implemented there will, of course, be others to take their place: the legislature cannot remain static.

For ease in recording information, the questionnaire
was organized into the following nine categories: time,
staffing, facilities, committees, leadership, structure
and powers, rules and procedures, compensation, and
ethics. These classifications dealt with the means and
resources of state legislatures, rather than the ends
and objectives thereof. In order to evaluate the individual questions in relation to the overall legislative
procedure, the five major classifications--functional,
accountable, information, independent, and representa-
tive--were derived.

The questions numbered above 156 are continuations
of the original questions (numbers 1-156) which could
not be easily stored by the computer program handling
the data. In a few instances, these data were obtained
elsewhere than from the original questionnaire, e.g.,
the 1970 census preliminary population data. The
numbers appearing in parentheses after a question
number (1-156) are the continuation numbers (157-
199). Questions using continuation numbers include
question 21, which had two distinct parts and asked
for sixty-nine different responses.

Appendix A gives the answer(s) preferred to the questions in detail, ordered by conceptual schemes.

When "House and Senate" appear in parentheses after the question, it indicates that the question was asked for the House and Senate separately. Unless otherwise indicated, the scoring was the same for both houses.

When "Superior" is given as the preferred answer, the possible answers were "Superior," "Adequate," "Inadequate," and "Not Available."

No.	Question	Answer(s) in Order of Preference

Subcriterion No. 1: Amount and Distribution

| 3(178) | What are the types of limitations on session length, frequency, and permissible agenda? | Unlimited
Unlimited--pay ceases after a specified length of time
Annual--limited by time, with possible extensions or special sessions
Annual--limited by topic
Annual--limited by time, with no possible extensions or special sessions
Biennial--unlimited (session one year only)
Biennial--unlimited, but pay ceases after a specified length of time
Biennial--limited (session one year only) by time, with possible extensions or special sessions
Biennial--limited by time, with no possible extensions or special sessions |

Subcriterion No. 2: Management of Time Resources

11b (162)	Which of the following deadlines are used to regulate the flow of work? (House and Senate)	
	Bill filing	Deadline used
	Introduction of bills	Deadline used
	Referral to committees	Deadline used
	Committee reports on referred legislation	Deadline used
	Report out of second committee	Deadline used
	Floor action	Deadline used
	Report of committee(s) in other house	Deadline used
	Floor action in other house	Deadline used
	Conference committee	Deadline used
	Final floor action	Deadline used
	Action by governor	Deadline used
	Veto review action	Deadline used

| 111 | How often is there a time lag greater than overnight after amendment and before reprinting of revised bills? (Applicable only if the state prints bills after amendment) (House and Senate) | Never
Sometimes
Frequently
Always |

| 115 | Do more than two legislative days pass following the introduction of a bill before it is referred to committee? (House and Senate) | No |

Subcriterion No. 3: Use of Pre-Session, Post-Election Time

14(163) Which of the following pre-session
activities are authorized by statute
or rules? Which are actually practiced?
(House and Senate)

Pre-session bill drafting	Authorized and Practiced
Pre-session bill filing	Authorized and Practiced
Pre-session bill printing	Authorized and Practiced
Pre-session assignment of bills to committees	Authorized and Practiced
Pre-session assignment of members to committees	Authorized and Practiced
Pre-session post-election committee work	Authorized and Practiced

12 Is there an official organizational session   Yes
(excluding caucus activities) after the
elections but before the regular session
starts?

Criterion: Multi-Purpose Staff Support

Subcriterion No. 4: Assistants

26a1   Are there individual, full-time, pro-   Yes, for each individual
26a2   fessional assistants during the   category mentioned
session for the following?

House	Senate
Speaker	President pro tem
Speaker pro tem	Majority leader
Majority leader	Asst. majority leader
Asst. majority leader	Minority leader
Minority leader	Asst. minority leader
Asst. minority leader	Majority members
Majority members	Minority members
Minority members	

Criterion: Facilities

Subcriterion No. 5: Chambers

28ab   What is the general quality of the chambers?   Superior
(House and Senate)   Adequate
(The evaluation was based on the following--   Inadequate
not exclusive list.)

Adequacy of working space
Adequacy of circulation patterns
Ease of access
Heating
Lighting
Ventilation

30a,b   Is an electronic roll call recorder   Yes
Row 1   available? (House and Senate)

No.	Question	Answer (s) in Order of Preference
30a,b Row 6	What is the quality of the working area for the clerk, secretary and their staff?	Superior Adequate Inadequate Not available

Subcriterion No. 6: Offices for Leadership

31a,b	Is private office space available for the following leadership positions, and if so, what is its quality?	Superior
	Speaker Speaker pro tem President pro tem Minority leaders Majority leaders	Superior Superior Superior Superior Superior
30a,b Row 7	Is there convenient access between the chambers and the office of the presiding officer? (House and Senate)	Yes

Subcriterion No. 7: Committee Facilities

33b	What is the number of committee rooms available to the legislature?	Ranked in decreasing order of the actual number of rooms available to the whole legislature.
33a	What is the number of auditorium hearing rooms in each house? (An auditorium hearing room is defined as seating an audience of at least fifty people.)	This question was scored on the basis of the actual number of rooms available to the whole legislature (House, Senate, and shared).
33c	What is the quality of committee rooms? (House and Senate)	Superior
33d (174)	Do the committee rooms have audio-visual and recording equipment, and if so, what is the quality? (House and Senate)	Superior

Subcriterion No. 8: Service Agencies

37a	What is the quality of office space of the clerk of the House and secretary of the Senate and their associated employees?	Superior
30a,b Row 6	What is the quality of the working area for the clerk or secretary and their staff? (House and Senate)	Superior
37b	What is the quality of the office space for those service agencies serving the whole legislature? (House and Senate)	Superior

Subcriterion No. 9: Individual Members

32a	What is the distribution of office space among the members of the house? (House and Senate)	All single offices, with all members officed Mix of single and multiple offices, with all members officed More than two-thirds members officed somehow Between one-third and two-thirds members officed somehow Less than one-third members officed No offices except desks on floors for non-leaders

No.	Question	
32f	What is the quality of office space for members? (House and Senate)	Superior
32e	What is the percentage of members who have adjacent office space for staff? (House and Senate)	Ranked in decreasing order by percent and divided in four groups
36	What kind of parking facilities are available for legislators?	Reserved covered spaces Reserved lot only No special provisions
32g	Are there private lounges for members only, and if so, what is quality?	Superior

Subcriterion No. 10: House Size

No.	Question	
79	What is the actual size of the House? Since it was discovered that all Senate sizes fall into the optimum range, only the House was scored on this question. The House was scored on a continuous function basis, an extrapolation of which is in the "preferred answer" column.	

House Size	Percent
$\geq$ 203 members	0
203	10
200	15
180	40
160	57
140	78
120	93
100	98
$\leq$ 80	100

Subcriterion No. 11: Committee Structure

No.	Question	
38	What is the number of standing committees? (House and Senate) Each house was scored individually on a continuous function basis, an extrapolation of which appears in the "preferred answer" column.	

Number of Committees

House:	Percent
$\leq$ 8	0
10	68
15	99
17	100
20	94
25	57
$\geq$ 30	0
Senate:	
$\leq$ 4	0
5	20
10	94
12	100
15	99
20	76
$\geq$ 25	0

No.	Question	
45	What is the number of standing committees having interim status? (House and Senate)	Scoring for the House was based on the actual of committees divided by twenty, considered to be the optimum number of commitees having interim status for the House. Scoring for the Senate was based on the actual number of committees divided by sixteen, considered to be the optimum number of committees having interim status for the Senate. Scoring for joint committees was the same as that for the Senate.

378

No.	Question	Answer (s) in Order of Preference
42a	What is the number of committee assignments per number? (House and Senate)	Scoring for the House was based on the percentage of House members having more than three committee assignments.
		Scoring for the Senate was based on the percentage of Senate members having more than four committee assignments.
		A score of zero on this was best, and the states were ranked in increasing order of percent scored.

Criterion: Organizational and Procedural Features to Expedite Flow of Work

Subcriterion No. 12: Origin and Sponsorship of Bills

No.	Question	Answer
99	How often are committee bills used as a means of proposing legislation?	Sometimes Frequently Always Never
103	Is multiple or joint sponsorship of bills permitted? (House and Senate)	Yes
102	Must all bills be introduced by a legislator?	Yes
132	Is the origin of certain classes of bills (except impeachment) restricted to a particular house?	No

Subcriterion No. 13: Use of Joint Committees

No.	Question	Answer
40b	Are there provisions for and examples of occasional joint committee usage?	Yes
40c	If a "yes" answer is given to 40b, are joint committees used during sessions?	Sometimes Always Never
41	To whom do joint committees report?	Some special administrative unit Any administrative unit, but not to their respective houses To their respective houses

Subcriterion No. 14: Treatment of Committee Reports

No.	Question	Answer
57	Can a majority of house members (same majority as required to pass bills) withdraw bills from the committee's report for separate action? (House and Senate)	Yes
117	Are there specified requirements for bill readings? (House and Senate)	No
30a,b Row 1	Is an electric roll call recorder available? (House and Senate)	Yes
116a	Is use made of a consent calendar or some other procedure for expeditiously handling non-controversial legislation?	Yes

379

No.	Question	Answer(s) in Order of Preference

Subcriterion No. 15: Anti-Limbo Provisions

No.	Question	Answer(s) in Order of Preference
60a	Are bills favorably reported on by a committee required to be taken up on the floor? (House and Senate)	Yes
60b	If a "yes" answer to 60a, how are the bills taken up?	Taken up automatically Taken up by action of the leadership Taken up by action of Rules or Calendaring Committee
60c	If a "yes" answer to 60a, how often is the requirement observed?	Always Sometimes Rarely Never
53a	Must all bills be reported on? (House and Senate)	Yes
53b	If a "yes" answer to 53a, are there time limits for those reports, other than the last day?	Yes
65a	Is action required from each conference committee? (This includes requesting a new committee) (House and Senate)	Yes
100	Are there published rules describing the jurisdictions of committees? (House and Senate)	Yes
101	If a "yes" answer to 100, are bills assigned in keeping with these rules?	Frequently Always Sometimes Never
115	Do more than two legislative days pass following introduction of a bill before it is referred to a committee? (House and Senate)	No

Subcriterion No. 16: Emergency Procedure

No.	Question	Answer(s) in Order of Preference
125a	Can amendments be made from the floor?	Yes
125b	If a "yes" answer to 125a, what is the majority necessary to make the amendment?	Two-thirds majority required
105	Are exceptions to bill introduction deadlines permitted by action of an extraordinary majority? (House and Senate)	Yes
124	Are there provisions to limit debate? (House and Senate)	Yes

No.	Question	Answer(s) in Order of Preference

Subcriterion No. 17: Bill Carry-Over

| 114 | Is bill carry-over permitted? (This question is applicable only for states meeting annually) | Yes |

Criterion: Management and Coordination

Subcriterion No. 18: Powers and Continuity of Leadership

| 75b,d | May the presiding officer succeed himself without violation of statute or tradition? (House and Senate) | Yes |

76 Row 1-3	Does the presiding officer have the following powers? (House and Senate)	
	Appoint chairman of Rules Committee	Yes
	Appoint members of conference committees	Yes
	Control assignment and flow of legislation	Yes

Subcriterion No. 19: Inter-House Coordination

| 128 | Are there joint rules? | Yes |

| 69a | Is there an overlap between membership on the House Rules Committee and joint rules committees (where there are such committees)? | Yes |

| 69b | Is there a Leadership Committee with minority representation, responsible for the inter-house coordination of legislation? | Yes |

Criterion: Order, Decorum, Dignity of Office

Subcriterion No. 20: Order, Decorum, Dignity of Office

| 136 | Are legislative salaries based upon an annual rate? | Yes |

| 76 Row 6 | Is the presiding officer in fourth position or earlier to succeed to the governorship? | Yes |

| 130 | Are floor privileges restricted to legislators and staff? | Yes |

CONCEPTUAL SCHEME FOR ACCOUNTABILITY
Criterion: Comprehensibility

No.	Question	Answer(s) in Order of Preference

Subcriterion No 1: Districting

| 83 | What is the character of member districts? (House and Senate) | This question was scored as the ratio of the number of districts divided by the number of house seats. The optimum answer was 1, representing one representative per district. |

Subcriterion No. 2: Selection of Leaders

74a,b (195)	How is the presiding officer elected? (House and Senate)	Elected by full house Selected by caucus Selected by any other means
43 "Actual Column"	How are committee chairmen selected?	Appointment by Rules Committee or Committee on Committees Appointment by speaker or president of the Senate Appointment by president pro tem Elected by caucus Elected by seniority Elected by committee
66	Is there a stated, regular procedure for the selection of conference committee chairmen? (House and Senate)	Yes

Subcriterion No. 3: General Complexity

79 What is the actual size of the House?

Since it was discovered that all Senate sizes fall into the optimum range, only the House was scored on this question. The House was scored on a continuous function basis, an extrapolation of which is shown in the "preferred answer" column.

House Size	Percent
$\geq$ 203 members	0
203	10
200	15
180	40
160	57
140	78
120	93
100	98
$\leq$ 80	100

38 What is the number of standing committees? (House and Senate) Each house was scored individually on a continuous function basis, an extrapolation of which appears in the "preferred answer" column.

Number of Committees	
House	Percent
$\leq$ 8	0
10	68
15	99
17	100
20	94
25	57
$\geq$ 30	0
Senate	
$\leq$ 4	0
5	20
10	94
12	100
15	99
20	76
$\geq$ 25	0

No.	Question	Answer(s) in Order of Preference

Subcriterion No. 4: Explicit Rules and Procedures

No.	Question	Answer
52	Are there uniform committee rules? (House and Senate)	Yes
128	Are there joint rules?	Yes
127	Do the rules provide for a back-up, such as Jefferson's Manual or Mason's? (House and Senate)	Yes
100	Are there published rules describing the jurisdiction of committees? (House and Senate)	Yes
101	If a "yes" answer to 100, are bills assigned in keeping with these rules?	Frequently/Always Sometimes Never

Subcriterion No. 5: Anti-Limbo Provision

No.	Question	Answer
60a	Are bills favorably reported by a committee required to be taken up on the floor? (House and Senate)	Yes
53a	Must all bills be reported on? (House and Senate)	Yes
53b	If a "yes" answer to 53a, are there time limits for those reports, other than the last day?	Yes
65a	Is action required from each conference committee? (This includes requesting a new committee) (House and Senate)	Yes
115	Do more than two legislative days pass following introduction of a bill before it is referred to a committee? (House and Senate)	No

Subcriterion No. 6: Planning, Scheduling, Coordination, and Budgeting

No.	Question	Answer
11a (162)	Are provisions made for the formal regulation of the flow of work through the legislature? (House and Senate)	Yes
11b (162)	If a "yes" answer to 11a, which of the following deadlines are used to regulate the flow of work?	
	Bill filing	Deadline used
	Introduction of bills	Deadline used
	Referral to committees	Deadline used
	Committee reports on referred legislation	Deadline used
	Report out of second committee	Deadline used
	Floor action	Deadline used
	Report of committee(s) in other house	Deadline used
	Floor action in other house	Deadline used
	Conference committee	Deadline used
	Final floor action	Deadline used
	Action by governor	Deadline used
	Veto review action	Deadline used

No.	Question	

19a   Is there a central organization and body of procedures to schedule, plan, and budget for interim activities? (House and Senate)   Yes

19b   If a "yes" answer to 19a, what is the coverage of interim management?

       Planning   Yes
       Budgeting   Yes
       Scheduling   Yes
       Review/evaluation   Yes

91a   Are legislative operating expenditures based on a "sum certain" or "sum sufficient" basis?   Sum certain

Criterion: Adequacy of Information and Public Access to It

Subcriterion No. 7: Public Access to Legislative Activities

49a   Is notice regularly provided of committee meetings and agenda? (Under three legislative days or five calendar days is equivalent to no notice) (House and Senate)   Yes

49b   Is more than one week's notice provided? (House and Senate)   Yes

49c   Which of the following methods for announcing committee meetings are used? (House and Senate)   Scoring was based on the weighted sum of points for the various methods. Points are given in parentheses.

       Notice sent to people on mailing lists (5) Newspaper announcements (4) Regularly scheduled meetings (5) Notice placed on bulletin boards (2) Individual notices to members (2) Voice announcement on the floor (1)

46a   Are secret sessions prohibited in cases other than those dealing with personnel problems? (House and Senate)   Yes

47a   Is it mandatory that committee hearings be open to the public?   Yes

33a   What is the number of auditorium hearing rooms in each house? (An auditorium hearing room is defined as seating an audience of at least fifty people.)   This question was scored on the basis of the actual number of rooms available to the whole legislature. (House, Senate, and shared.)

30a,b Row 4   What is the quality of the visitors gallery? (House and Senate)   Superior

Subcriterion No. 8: Records of Voting and Deliberation

123a   Are roll call votes always required on final passage? (House and Senate)   Yes

384

No.	Question	Answer(s) in Order of Preference
123b	If a "no" answer to 123a, what is the percentage of members representing the minimum threshold to require a roll call vote of the body on final passage? (House and Senate)	Less than 9 percent Between 10-14 percent Between 15-19 percent Between 20-24 percent Over 25 percent
48a	Are committee votes regularly taken? (House and Senate)	Yes
48b	Are committee votes regularly recorded? (House and Senate)	Yes
48c	Are roll calls regularly taken and published on final committee actions? (House and Senate)	Yes
30a,b Row 1	Is an electric roll call recorder available? (House and Senate)	Yes
50a	Is a record of committee deliberation taken and available to the public? (House and Senate)	Yes
50b	Are the minutes and transcript taken and publicly available? (House and Senate)	Yes
70a	Are formal reports required of interim committees? (House, Senate, and joint)	Yes
	If a "yes" answer to 70a, with what frequency are reports required? (House, Senate, and joint)	Always Frequently Sometimes Never Equal credit is given for House and Senate answers, and/or joint answers
70b	Are the results of interim committee actions recorded and made public?	Yes

Subcriterion No. 9: Character and Quality of Bill Documents

No.	Question	Answer(s) in Order of Preference
92	Are printed bills regularly provided in standard format meeting printed standards of legibility?	Yes
94	Is the agency which drafts a bill required to prepare a bill summary for each piece of legislation?	Yes
93	Is a bill's author required to prepare a statement of legislative intent?	Yes
113	Must bills deal only with one subject?	Yes
104	Are skeleton bills permitted? (House and Senate)	No
107	Are bills printed in quantity upon introduction (i.e., at least two times the number of members)?	Yes

No.	Question	Answer(s) in Order of Preference
108	Are bills printed in quantity upon subsequent amendments? (i.e., at least two times the number of members)?	Yes
110	Is there a central distribution point for copies of bills and other legislative documents to the public?	Yes
111	How often is there a time lag greater than overnight after amendment and before reprinting of revised bills? (House and Senate)	Never
112	Do printing procedures permit the easy indentification of the following?	
	Original text	Yes
	Deletions	Yes
	Additions	Yes

Subcriterion No. 10: Access by Press and News Media

No.	Question	Answer(s)
47c	Is live radio and t.v. coverage of committee hearings permitted? (House and Senate)	Yes
33e (174)	Do the committee rooms have facilities for news media (such as space for newsmen and wiring for t.v. cameras), and if so, what is the quality? (House and Senate)	Superior Adequate Inadequate Not available
30a,b Row 5	Is there a press gallery and related facilities, and if so, what is the condition? (House and Senate)	Superior
129	Is coverage of floor action by radio and t.v. permitted? (House and Senate)	Yes
35c	Are electronic media coverage facilities available in the chamber? (House and Senate)	Yes
35b	Is office space available for reporters, and if so, what is their quality? (House and Senate)	Superior
35a	Are news conference rooms available and if so, what is their quality? (House and Senate)	Superior
21a Row 16 (188,189)	Is there a press officer for each house? (House and Senate)	Yes

Subcriterion No. 11: Information on Legislator's Interests

No.	Question	Answer(s)
147a	Does state law require mandatory public disclosures affecting legislative income?	Yes
147b	If a "yes" answer to 147a, to whom do the disclosure laws apply?	
	Individual Wife and minor children Partnerships and other constructive ownership	States were ranked by the number of "yes" answers to each of the twelve possible categories. Maximum score, twelve "yes" answers

No.	Question	Answer(s) in Order of Preference

For each of the above, which of the following
disclosures is required?

    Income
    Corporate security and holdings
    Land or other interest therein
    Campaign contributions

145   Is information conveniently available to the
public regarding each of the following
components of payment?

    Salary   Yes
    Expense allowance   Yes
    Retirement benefits   Yes
    Noncalculable benefits   Yes

Subcriterion No. 12: Information on Lobbyists

153   Is there regulation of lobbyists by statute,   Yes
and is the following information on lobbying
available to the public? (House and Senate)

    Asked for each of the following:

    Registration   Yes
    Disclosure of registration   Yes
    Disclosure of expenditures (on whom and
      amount)   Yes
    Disclosure of salaries   Yes

154   If a "yes" answer to any of 153, are there   Yes
specific penalties for failure to comply
with the regulations?

Subcriterion No. 13: Diffusion and Constraints on Leadership

74a,b   How is the presiding officer elected?   Elected by full house
Pt. I   (House and Senate)   Selected by caucus
(195)   Selected by any other means

74a,b   Are there at least the following three leadership   Yes
Pt. II   positions? (House and Senate)

    Speaker or president pro tem
    Majority leader
    Minority leader

43   How are committee chairmen selected?   Appointment by Rules Committee
This question was scored on both a "formal"   or Committee on Committees
(required) and "actual" (as done) basis.   Appointment by speaker or
        president of the Senate
    Appointment by president pro tem
    Elected by caucus
    Elected by seniority
    Elected by committee

44   How are committee members selected? (House   Appointed by caucus
and Senate)   Appointed by presiding officer
    Appointed by Rules Committee
        or Committee on Committees

No.	Question	Answer(s) in Order of Preference
60a	Are bills favorably reported on by a committee required to be taken up on the floor? (House and Senate)	Yes
60b (179)	If a "yes" answer to 60a, how are bills taken up?	Taken up automatically Taken up by action of the leadership Taken up by action of the Rules or Calendaring Committee
60c (179)	If a "yes" answer to 60a, how often is the requirement observed?	Always Sometimes Rarely Never
63	Are all conference committees equal to or larger than four members?	Yes
64	What restrictions are placed upon conference committees? (House and Senate)	Committees restricted to resolving differences Committees restricted to topic of bill No restrictions on conference committees
65a	Is action required from each conference committee? (House and Senate)	Yes
65b	Can a majority of members of both houses (the same majority as is required to pass bills) require the dissolution and reconstitution (with different members) of a conference committee? (House and Senate)	Yes
56a	Can house members report a bill out of committee? (House and Senate)	Yes
56b	If a "yes" answer to 56a, what is the majority needed?	Extraordinary majority Simple majority
57	Can a majority of house members (the same majority as is required to pass bills) withdraw bills from the committee's report for separate action? (House and Senate)	Yes
58	Can a majority of house members (the same majority as is required to pass bills) withdraw a bill from one committee and recommit it to another? (House and Senate)	Yes
54	Can a majority of committee members place a bill on the committee's agenda? (House and Senate)	Yes

No.	Question	Answer(s) in Order of Preference
55	Can a majority of committee members report a bill out without concurrence of the chairman? (House and Senate)	Yes

Subcriterion No. 14: Treatment of Minority

No.	Question	Answer(s) in Order of Preference
39, Col. 1, 2, 3 (196)	What is the frequency and magnitude of the departure from the "ideal" in terms of minority proportional membership on standing committees?	Scored as a percent, with 0.0 percent best. States ranked in increasing order of percent and divided into four groups.
77a,b	Do the Rules and Management Committees have members from the minority party who are elected by the minority party and whose proportion on that committee is not more than 49 percent and not less than the minority proportion of the house? (House and Senate)	
	Rules Committee	Yes
	Management Committee	Yes
78a,c	Does the minority leader appoint minority members of committees? (House and Senate)	Yes
78b,d	Does the minority leader have a position by right on the Management Committee? (House and Senate)	Yes

389

Criterion: Enough Time

No.	Question	Answer(s) in Order of Preference

Subcriterion No. 1: Session Time

3(178) — What are the types of limitations on session length, frequency, and permissible agenda?

Unlimited
Unlimited--pay ceases after a specified length of time
Annual--limited by time, with possible extensions or special sessions
Annual--limited by topic
Annual--limited by time, with no possible extensions or special sessions
Biennial--unlimited (session one year only)
Biennial--unlimited, but pay ceases after a specified length of time
Biennial--limited (session one year only) by time, with possible extensions or special sessions
Biennial--limited by time, with no possible extensions or special sessions

4 — How many days were spent in the last regular session?

$\geq$ 120 days
(Scored for number of days actually worked. Considered whether state met annually or biennially.)

Subcriterion No. 2: Pre-Session Activities

14a-f
(163) — Which of the following pre-session activities are authorized by statute or rules? Which are actually practiced? (House and Senate)

Pre-session bill drafting — Authorized and practiced
Pre-session bill filing — Authorized and practiced
Pre-session bill printing — Authorized and practiced
Pre-session assignment of bills to committees — Authorized and practiced
Pre-session assignment of members to committees — Authorized and practiced
Pre-session post-election committee work — Authorized and practiced

Criterion: Standing Committees (as Information-Processing and -Applying Units)

Subcriterion No. 3: Number of Committees

38   What is the number of standing committees? (House and Senate)

Answers were scored on a continuous function basis, an extrapolation of which appears in the "preferred answer" column.

Number of Committees	Percent
House: $\leq$ 8	0
10	68
15	99
17	100
20	94
25	57
$\geq$ 30	0
Senate: $\leq$ 4	0
5	20
10	94
12	100
15	99
20	76
$\geq$ 25	0

42a   What is the number of committee assignments per member? (House and Senate)

Scoring for the House was based on the percentage of House members having more than three committee assignments.

Scoring for the Senate was based on the percentage of Senate members having more than four committee assignments.

A score of zero on this was best, and the states were ranked in increasing order of percent scored.

Subcriterion No. 4: Testimony

49a   Is notice regularly provided of committee meetings and agenda? (Under three legislative days or five calendar days is equivalent to no notice.) (House and Senate)

Yes

49b   Is more than one week's notice provided? (House and Senate)

Yes

49c   Which of the following methods for announcing committee meetings are used? (House and Senate)

Scoring was based on the weighted sum of points for the various methods. Points are given in parentheses.

         Notice sent to people on mailing lists (5)
         Newspaper announcements (4)
         Regularly scheduled meetings (5)
         Notice placed on bulletin boards (2)
         Individual notices to members (2)
         Voice announcement on the floor (1)

47b   Is public testimony regularly solicited as a part of the decision-making process? (House and Senate)

Yes

No.	Question	Answer(s) in Order of Preference
47d	Are witnesses required to submit written testimony in advance? (House and Senate)	Frequently Always Sometimes Never
61	What subpoena power is available to committees?	Power in all committees Power in the house, needing special action for committee use No such power available

Subcriterion No. 5: Facilities

No.	Question	Answer(s) in Order of Preference
33b	What is the number of committee rooms available to the legislature?	Ranked in decreasing order of the actual number of rooms available to the entire legislature.
33a	What is the number of auditorium hearing rooms in each house? (An auditorium hearing room is defined as seating an audience of at least fifty people.)	This question was scored on the basis of the actual number of rooms available to the whole legislature. (House and Senate and shared.)
33c	What is the quality of the committee rooms?	Superior Adequate Inadequate Not Available
33d (174)	Do the committee rooms have audio-visual and recording equipment, and if so, what is the quality? (House and Senate)	Superior

Criterion: Interim Activities

Subcriterion No. 6: Interim Activities

No.	Question	Answer(s) in Order of Preference
17 (186)	What is the source of limitations on working days during the interim period?	No limitations Rules or procedural limitation Limitation by statute Limitations set in the constitution
19a	Is there a central organization and body of procedures to schedule, plan, and budget for interim activities? (House and Senate)	Yes
19b	If a "yes" answer to 19a, what is the coverage of interim management?	
	Planning Budgeting Scheduling Review/evaluation	Yes Yes Yes Yes
71	What is the subpoena power available to interim committees?	All interim committees have subpoena power Interim committees can get power by special application No interim committees have subpoena power

No.	Question	Answer(s) in Order of Preference

Subcriterion No. 7: Structure and Staffing

| 45 (185) | What is the number of standing committees having interim status? (House and Senate) | Scoring for the House was based on the actual of committees divided by twenty, considered to be the optimum number of committees having interim status for the House.

Scoring for the Senate was based on the actual number of committees divided by sixteen, considered to be the optimum number of committees having interim status for the Senate.

Scoring for joint committees was the same as that for the Senate. |

Subcriterion No. 8: Reporting and Records

70c	Must the reports of interim committees propose specific legislation or document adequacy of existing provision?	Yes
70a	Are formal reports required of interim committees (House, Senate, and joint)?	Yes
	If a "yes" answer to 70a, with what frequency are reports required? (House, Senate, and joint)	Always Frequently Sometimes Never Equal credit is given for House and Senate answers, and/or joint answers.
70b	Are the results of interim committee actions recorded and made public?	Yes

Criterion: Form and Character of Bills

Subcriterion No. 9: Bill Status and History

156a,b	Are the following services provided in an efficient manner?	
	Bill status	Yes
	Bill history	Yes
	Statute retrieval	Yes
	Journal indexing	Yes

Subcriterion No. 10: Bill Content and Summaries

| 92 | Are printed bills regularly provided in standard format meeting printed standards of legibility? | Yes |

No.	Question	Answer (s) in Order of Preference
94	Is the agency which drafts a bill required to prepare a bill summary for each piece of legislation?	Yes
93	Is a bill's author required to prepare a statement of legislative intent?	Yes
113	Must bills deal only with one subject?	Yes
104	Are skeleton bills permitted? (House and Senate)	No

Subcriterion No. 11: Quantity and Distribution

No.	Question	Answer
107	Are bills printed in quantity upon introduction (i.e., at least two times the number of members)?	Yes
108	Are bills printed in quantity upon subsequent amendments (i.e., at least two times the number of members)?	Yes
110	Is there a central distribution point for copies of bills and other legislative documents to the public?	Yes

Subcriterion No. 12: Timeliness and Quality

No.	Question	Answer
111	How often is there a time lag greater than overnight after amendment and before re-printing of revised bills? (House and Senate)	Never Sometimes Frequently Always
112	Do printing procedures permit the easy identification of the following?	
	Original text	Yes
	Deletions	Yes
	Additions	Yes

Criterion: Professional Staff Resources

Subcriterion No. 13: General Research Coverage

No.	Question	Answer
21a Row 10, 14, 15, 17-21 (188, 189, 190)	Is there a legislative agency which performs the following services? (House and Senate)	
	Program review and evaluation	Yes
	Reference and bibliography	Yes
	Spot research	Yes
	In-depth studies and program design	Yes
	Management of outside resources in in-depth studies and program design	Yes
	Reporting on federal legislation	Yes
	Information on federal subventions	Yes
24	Does the legislature maintain a Washington liaison office?	Yes

No.	Question	Answer (s) in Order of Preference

Subcriterion No. 14: Legal Staffing

21a Rows 1, 2, 3 (188, 189)	Is there a legislative agency which performs the following services? (House and Senate)	
	Bill drafting	Yes
	Review bills for legal form	Yes
	Bill summary	Yes

21a Rows 4, 5, 6 (188, 189)	Is there a legislative agency which performs the following services? (House and Senate)	
	Code research, including review of judicial opinion	Yes
	Statute and code revision	Yes
	Management of outside consultants in above fields	Yes

21b,c Rows 1, 2 (164, 165, 166)	If the services in 21a are available, to whom are they available?	
	Leaders	Yes
	Committees	Yes
	Members	Yes

Criterion: Fiscal Review Capabilities

Subcriterion No. 15: Fiscal Responsibility

89	Who develops the budget?	The governor The legislature and the governor jointly Only the legislature
62	Is there a formal requirement for dual committee consideration where significant sums are involved? (House and Senate)	Yes

Subcriterion No. 16: Staff Support for Fiscal Analysis and Review

21a Rows 7-13 (188, 189)	Is there a legislative agency which performs the following services? (House and Senate)	
	Continuous study of resources and expenditures	Yes
	Budget review and analysis	Yes
	Post-audit	Yes
	Program review and evaluation	Yes
	Fiscal notes	Yes
	Long-range forecasting	Yes
	Management of outside consultants in above fields	Yes

21b,c Row 3 (164, 165, 166)	Is staff assistance for budget review and and analysis available to the following? (House and Senate)	
	Leaders	Yes
	Committees	Yes
	Members	Yes

No.	Question	Answer(s) in Order of Preference

Subcriterion No 17: Fiscal Notes

| 96 | Are fiscal notes prepared by a legislative service agency? | Yes |
| 95 | Are fiscal notes required on bills having revenue or expenditure implications? | Yes |

CONCEPTUAL SCHEME FOR INDEPENDENCE

Criterion: Legislative Autonomy Regarding Legislative Procedures

No.	Question	Answer (s) in Order of Preference

Subcriterion No. 1: Time for Deliberation

No.	Question	Answer (s) in Order of Preference
3(178)	What are the types of limitations on session length, frequency, and permissible agenda?	Unlimited Unlimited--pay ceases after a specified length of time Annual--limited by time, with possible extensions or special sessions Annual--limited by topic Annual--limited by time, with no possible extensions or special sessions Biennial--unlimited (session one year only) Biennial--unlimited, but pay ceases after a specified length of time Biennial--limited (session one year only) by time, with possible extensions or special sessions Biennial--limited by time, with no possible extensions or special sessions
6a	Does the legislature have the power to call itself into special session?	Yes
6b	If a "yes" answer to 6a, indicate how the legislature may call itself into special session.	By call of presiding officers or by simple majority of each house Only by a simple majority of each house Only by the call of the presiding officers By a majority greater than 51 percent
15a	Can the legislature expand the agenda of a special session called by the governor?	Yes (If the agenda is unlimited in scope, then "not applicable" is an acceptable answer.)
15b	If a "yes" answer to 15a, what vote is needed?	Answer scored by percentage. A lower percent vote is preferred over a higher requirement.
17 (186)	What is the source of limitations on working days during the interim period?	No limitations Rules or procedural limitation Limitation by statute Limitations set in the constitution

Subcriterion No. 2: Expenditure Control and Compensation Reimbursement Powers

No.	Question	Answer (s) in Order of Preference
91b	Does the legislature have exclusive control over its operating expenditures (after appropriation)?	Yes
137 (191)	Are legislative salaries set by means other than statute or compensation commission?	No
141 (192)	Are legislative expense allowances set by means other than statute or compensation commission?	No
139 Row 4	What are the sources of limitations on the amount and/or rate of noncalculable benefits? (Scored only if the legislatures receive such noncalculable benefits such as an automobile, credit cards, etc.)	Statute Rules

No.	Question	Answer (s) in Order of Preference

Subcriterion No. 3: Reapportionment

| 84 | How does reapportionment take place? | By the legislature
By reapportionment commission
Any other method (examined to make sure it didn't fall into above categories) |

Subcriterion No. 4: Access to Information and Analysis

21a
(175)

Are the following services available?
(House and Senate)

Bill drafting	Yes
Review bills for legal form	Yes
Bill summary	Yes
Code research, including review of judicial opinion	Yes
Statute and code revision	Yes
Management of outside consultants in above fields	Yes
Continuous study of resources and expenditures	Yes
Budget review and analysis	Yes
Post-audit	Yes
Program review and evaluation	Yes
Fiscal notes	Yes
Long-range forecasting	Yes
Management of outside consultants in above fields	Yes
Reference and bibliography	Yes
Speech writing	Yes
Public information services	Yes
Spot research	Yes
In-depth studies and program design	Yes
Management of outside resources in in-depth studies and program design	Yes
Reporting on federal legislation	Yes
Information on federal subventions	

| 96 | Are fiscal notes prepared by a legislative service agency? | Yes |

| 24 | Does the legislature maintain a Washington liaison office? | Yes |

| 22a,b,c
(168, 160) | Professional staff (fiscal, research, and legal) per population | All three functions covered
Two functions covered
One function covered |

| 194 | Legislative expenditure per capita | Ranked in order of decreasing amount and divided into five groups |
| | Legislative expenditure as a percent of state budget | Ranked in order of decreasing percent and divided into five groups |

| 61 | What subpoena power is available to committees? | Power in all committees
Power in the house, needing special action for committee's use
No such power available |

No.	Question	Answer(s) in Order of Preference
71	What subpoena power is available to interim committees?	All interim committees have subpoena power Interim committees can get power by special application No interim committees have subpoena power

Subcriterion No. 5: Veto Relationships

90a	Are there types of vetoes which the legislature has no opportunity to override?	No
8a	Are veto sessions regularly provided by law?	Yes
8b	If veto sessions are not regularly provided for by law, can the legislature convene a veto session?	Yes

Subcriterion No. 6: Lt. Governor Problem

184	What is the role of the lt. governor as regards the legislature?	No real legislative role or legislative responsibility Presiding officer and able to vote in case of tie Any legislative role more pervasive than the above

Subcriterion No. 7: Budget Powers

89	Who develops the budget?	The governor The legislature and the governor jointly Only the legislature
7c	In the case of an executive budget, does legislative activity on the budget take place prior to its formal submission by the governor?	Yes
88a	Can the legislature raise budget items by a simple majority?	Yes

Subcriterion No. 8: Miscellaneous

102	Must all bills be introduced by a legislator?	Yes

Criterion: Capability for Effective Oversight of Executive Operations

Subcriterion No. 9: Oversight Capabilities

21a, Row 7 (188, 189)	Is there an agency which performs a continuous study of resources and expenditures? (House and Senate)	Yes
21a, Row 10 (188, 189)	Is there an agency which performs program review and evaluation? (House and Senate)	Yes

Subcriterion No. 10: Audit Capability

21a, Row 9 (188, 189)	Is there an agency which performs the post-audit function? (House and Senate)	Yes

Criterion: Interest Groups

Subcriterion No. 11: Lobbyists

153   Is there regulation of lobbyists by statute and is the following information on lobbying available to the public? (House and Senate)

Registration	Yes
Disclosure of registration	Yes
Disclosure of expenditures (on whom and amount)	Yes
Disclosure of salaries	Yes

154	If a "yes" answer to any of 153, are there specific penalties for failure to comply with the regulations?	Yes

Criterion: Conflicts and Dilution of Interest

Subcriterion No. 12: Dilution of Interest

146	In addition to standard laws governing criminal behavior, are there special provisions regulating conflicts of interest?	Yes
148	Are there prohibitions against legislators or their firms practicing before state regulatory agencies or in matters concerning state agencies for a fee?	Yes
149	Are there prohibitions against legislators or firms in which legislators own a major interest doing business with state agencies (except under open, public bidding procedures)?	Yes
150	Are there provisions against legislators concurrently holding other continuing (not ad hoc), paid public office (except paid military)?	Yes

152   Are legislators prohibited from accepting appointment to remunerative state office

(a) during the term for which they were elected		Yes
(b) within two years?		Yes

151	Are there prohibitions against the immediate family of legislators being employed by the legislature?	Yes

CONCEPTUAL SCHEME FOR REPRESENTATIVENESS

Criterion: Identification

No.	Question	Answer(s) in Order of Preference

Subcriterion No 1: Identification

| 83 | What is the character of member districts? | This question was scored as the ratio of the number of districts divided by the number of house seats. The optimum answer was 1, there being one representative per district. |
| 32b | What kind of contribution is made toward a home office? | District office provided
Cash contribution which can be used to support a district office
No district office provided, and no provision made for support of same |

Criterion: Diversity

Subcriterion No. 2: Qualifications

183 (86a)	What are the age minimum and residence requirements for legislators? (state and district requirements) (House and Senate)	It is preferred that there are no restrictions, or fewer rather than more, stringent restrictions on age and residency.
	Is United States citizenship required, and if so, how long?	It is preferred that citizenship be required at the time of election, but for no longer period.
	What is the difference between residency requested for voting and residency to be elected?	There should be no difference between the two requirements.

Subcriterion No. 3: Compensation

135	What is the biennial legislative salary, exclusive of expense allowances?	Biennial salary was divided by days worked to get daily pay rate. States were ranked in decreasing order of daily rate.
143	Are actual travel expenses reimbursed?	Yes
142	What provisions are made for legislative retirement benefits?	Better than other state employees The same as, or comparable with, other state employees Worse than other state employees No provisions for legislative retirement benefits

Subcriterion No. 4: Voting Requirements

| 51 | What are the quorum requirements for committees? (House and Senate) | Simple majority
Equal to or greater than 52 percent
No requirements or less than 50 percent |
| 63 | Are all conference committees equal to or larger than four members? | Yes |

No.	Question	Answer(s) in Order of Preference

Subcriterion No. 5: Size and Complexity of Legislative Body

79   What is the actual size of the House?

Since it was discovered that all Senate sizes fall into the optimum range, only the House was scored on this question. The House was scored on a continuous function basis, an extrapolation of which is in the "preferred answer" column.

Number of Committees

House Size	Percent
≤ 203 members	0
203	10
200	15
180	40
160	57
140	78
120	93
100	98
≥ 80	100

38   What is the number of standing committees? (House and Senate)

Each house was scored individually on a continuous function basis, an extrapolation of which appears in the "preferred answer" column.

Number of Committees

House	Percent
≤ 8	0
10	68
15	99
17	100
20	94
25	57
≥ 30	0

Senate	
≤ 4	0
5	20
10	94
12	100
15	99
20	76
≥ 25	0

Subcriterion No. 6: Diffusion and Constraints on Leadership

74ab
Part I
(195)
    How is the presiding officer elected? (House and Senate)

Elected by full house
Selected by caucus
Selected by any other means

74ab
Part II
    Are there at least the following three leadership positions? (House and Senate)

      Speaker or president pro tem
      Majority leader
      Minority leader

Yes

43   How are committee chairmen selected?

This question was scored on both a "formal" (required) and "actual" (as done) basis.

Appointment by Rules Committee or Committee on Committees
Appointment by speaker or president of the Senate
Appointment by president pro tem
Elected by caucus

No.	Question	Answer(s) in Order of Preference
		Elected by seniority Elected by committee
44	How are committee members selected? (House and Senate)	Appointment by caucus Appointment by presiding officer Appointment by Rules Committee or Committee on Committees
54	Can a majority of committee members place a bill on the committee's agenda? (House and Senate)?	Yes
55	Can a majority of committee members report a bill out without concurrence of the chairman? (House and Senate)	Yes
60a	Are bills favorably reported on by a committee required to be taken up on the floor? (House and Senate)	Yes
60b (179)	If a "yes" answer to 60a, how are the bills taken up?	Taken up automatically Taken up by action of the leadership Taken up by action of the Rules or Calendaring Committee
60c (179)	If a "yes: answer to 60a, how often is the requirement observed?	Always Sometimes Rarely Never
56a	Can house members report a bill out of committee? (House and Senate)	Yes
56b	If a "yes" answer to 56a, what is the majority needed?	Extraordinary majority Simple majority
57	Can a majority of house members (the same majority as is required to pass bills) withdraw bills from the committee's report for separate action? (House and Senate)	Yes
58	Can a majority of house members (the same majority as is required to pass bills) withdraw a bill from one committee and recommit it to another? (House and Senate)	Yes
64	What restrictions are placed upon conference committees? (House and Senate)	Committees restricted to resolving differences Committees restricted to topic of bill No restrictions on conference committees
65a	Is action required from each conference committee? (This includes requesting a new committee) (House and Senate)	Yes
65b	Can a majority of members of both houses (the same majority as is required to pass bills) require the dissolution and reconstitution (with different members) of a conference committee? (House and Senate)	Yes

Subcriterion No. 7: Access to Resources

26a1,2
(Last 2
rows)

Are there individual, full-time, professional
assistants during the session for the
following? (House and Senate)

        Majority members   Yes

        Minority members   Yes

21b,c
"Members
Column"
(166)

Which of the following staff services are
available to members? (House and Senate)

        Bill drafting   Available

        Code research, including review of   Available
            judicial opinion

        Budget review and analysis   Available

        Reference and bibliography   Available

        Spot research   Available

32a

What is the distribution of office space
among the members of the house? (House
and Senate)

All single offices, with all members
    officed

Mix of single and multiple offices,
    with all members officed

More than two-thirds members officed
    somehow

Between one-third and two-thirds
    members officed somehow

Less than one-third members officed

No offices except desks on floors
    for non-leaders

32e

How many members have adjacent office space
for staff? (House and Senate)

Ranked in decreasing order by percent
and divided into four groups.

Subcriterion No. 8: Treatment of Minority

39 (196)
Col. 1, 2, 3

What is the frequency and magnitude of the
departure from the "ideal" in terms of
minority proportional membership on
standing committees?

Scored as a percent with 0.0 percent
best. States ranked in increasing order
of percent and divided into four groups.

77a,b

Do the Rules and Management Committees
have members from the minority party who
are elected by the minority party and
whose proportion on that committee is not
more than 49 percent and not less than the
minority proportion of the house?
(House and Senate)

        Rules Committee   Yes

        Management Committee   Yes

32c

Does the minority receive the same treatment
in regard to office space as the majority?
(House and Senate)

Yes

78a,c

Does the minority leader appoint minority
members of committees? (House and Senate)

Yes

78b,d

Does the minority leader have a position
by right on the Management Committee?
(House and Senate)

Yes

No.	Question	Answer(s) in Order of Preference

Subcriterion No. 9: Known Rules

No.	Question	Answer(s)
126	Does each house have a body of published rules? (House and Senate)	Yes
128	Are there joint rules?	Yes
127	Do the rules provide for a back-up, such as Jefferson's Manual or Mason's? (House and Senate)	Yes
100	Are there published rules describing the jurisdictions of committees? (House and Senate)	Yes
101	If a "yes" answer to 100, are bills assigned in keeping with these rules?	Frequently/Always Sometimes Never
52	Are there uniform published committee rules? (House and Senate)	Yes
13a	During the period considered, was there a pre-session procedural orientation meeting? (House and Senate)	Yes
13b	If a "yes" answer to 13a, which of the following topics were covered?	
	Parliamentary procedures	Topic covered
	Legislative organization	Topic covered
	Organization of executive agencies	Topic covered
	Summary of last interim activities	Topic covered
	Any other activities (described individually by the states)	Topic covered
13c	What was the length of the orientation session, in half-days?	This question was scored on the actual length of the session, and ranked in order of decreasing number of half-days

Subcriterion No. 10: Bill Reading

No.	Question	Answer(s)
118	Is there a provision that requires a bill to be read (title only acceptable) on at least two separate days? (House and Senate)	Yes

Appendix B is an outline of the final conceptual schemes,
using short titles for the questions.

Criteria	Subcriteria	Question Number	Short Title
TIME AND ITS UTILIZATION	1. Amount and Distribution	3 (178)	Restrictions on Session Length
	2. Management of Time Resources	11b (162) 111 115	Scheduling Devices Printing Time Lag After Amendments Time Lag Between Introduction and Referral to Committee
	3. Use of Pre-Session, Post-election Time	14a-f (163) 12	Pre-Session, Post-Election Activities Organizational Session
MULTI-PURPOSE STAFF SUPPORT	4. Assistants	26a1 26a2	Personal Aide to Leaders and Members
FACILITIES	5. Chambers	28a,b 30a,b Rows 1,6	Quality of Chambers Special Equipment and Facilities
	6. Offices for Leadership	31a,b 30a,b Row 7	Leadership Offices Office Locations
	7. Committee Facilities	33b 33a 33c 33d (174)	Committee Rooms Auditorium Rooms Room Quality Special Equipment
	8. Service Agencies	37a 30a,b Row 6 37b	Clerks' and Secretaries' Offices Clerks' Work Areas Service Agencies-- Whole Body
	9. Individual Members	32a 32f 32e 36 32g	Office Space-- Quantity Office Space--Quality Personal Staff Offices Parking Lounges
STRUCTURAL CHARACTER-ISTICS RELATED TO MANAGEABILITY	10. House Size	79	Size of Houses
	11. Committee Structure	38 45 (185) 42a	Number of Standing Committees Standing Committees with Interim Status Standing Committee Assignments per Member
ORGANIZA-TIONAL AND PROCEDURAL FEATURES TO EXPEDITE FLOW OF WORK	12. Origin and Sponsorship of Bills	99 103 102 132	Use of Committee Bills Multiple and Joint Authorship Bills only by Legislators Restriction on House of Origin
	13. Use of Joint Committees	40b 40c 41	Provisions for Use Session Use Joint Committee Reportage

Criteria	Subcriteria	Question Number	Short Title
ORGANIZATIONAL AND PROCEDURAL FEATURES TO EXPEDITE FLOW OF WORK (cont.)	14. Treatment of Committee Reports	57	Withdrawal of Bills from Committee Reports
		117	Multiple Readings in Full
		30a,b	Electric Roll Call
		Row 1	
		116a	Consent Calendar
	15. Anti-Limbo Provisions	60a, b,c (179)	Treatment of Favorably Reported Bills
		53a,b	Required Action on Referred Bills
		65a	Conference Committee Action
		100	Committee Jurisdictions
		101	Referral Practices
		115	Time Lag on Referral
	16. Emergency Procedure	125a,b	Amendments from the Floor
		105	Exceptions to Bill Deadlines
		124a,b	Provisions to Limit Debate
	17. Bill Carry-Over	114	Bill Carry-Over
MANAGEMENT AND COORDI-NATION	18. Powers and Continuity of Leadership	75b,d	Self-Succession
		76 Rows 1-3	Powers of Presiding Officer
	19. Inter-House Coordination	128	Joint Rules
		69a	Overlapping Rules Committee Membership
		69b	Minority Participation in Inter-House Coordination.
ORDER, DECORUM, DIGNITY OF OFFICE	20. Order, Decorum and Dignity of Office	136	Annual Salary
		76	Speaker in Line for
		Row 6	Succession to Governorship
		130	Privileges of the Floor

Criteria	Subcriteria	Question Number	Short Title
COMPREHENSI-BILITY	1. Districting	83	Districting
	2. Selection of Leaders	74a,b (195)	Selection of Leaders
		43 "Actual" Column	Selection of Committee Chairmen
		66	Selection of Conference Committee Chairmen
	3. General Complexity	79	Size of House and Senate
		38	Number of Standing Committees
	4. Explicit Rules and Procedures		
	a. Rules of Procedure	52	Uniform Committee Rules
		128	Joint Rules
		127	Back-up Rules
	b. Rules of Jurisdiction	100	Committee Jurisdiction
		101	Referral Practice
	5. Anti-Limbo Provisions	60a	Floor Action on Bills "Do-Pass"-ed by Committee
		53a,b	Required Action on Referred Bills
		65a	Conference Committee Action
		115	Time Lag on Bill Referral
	6. Planning, Scheduling, Coordination, and Budgeting	11a,b (162)	Session Planning and Coordination
		19a,b	Interim Planning and Coordination
		91a	Sum Certain or Sum Sufficient Budget
ADEQUACY OF INFORMATION AND PUBLIC ACCESS TO IT	7. Public Access to Legislative Activities	49a,b c	Advance Notice of Meetings and Agendas
		46a	Secret Sessions--Meetings
		47a	Open Hearings
		33a	Auditorium Hearing Rooms
		30a,b Row 4	Visitors' Gallery
	8. Records of Voting and Deliberation	123a,b	Roll Call on Final Passage
		48a,b c	Committee Votes (Taken, Recorded, Published)
		30a,b Row 1	Electric Roll Call
		50a,b	Form of Committee Records
		70a,b	Interim Committee Records
	9. Character and Quality of Bill Documents		
	a. Content and Summary	92	Printed Bills
		94	Summary of Contents
		93	Statement of Legislative Intent
		113	One-Subject Bills
		104	Skeleton Bills

411

Criteria	Subcriteria	Question Number	Short Title
ADEQUACY OF INFORMATION AND PUBLIC ACCESS TO IT (cont.)	b. Quantity and Distribution	107	Quantity on Introduction
		108	Quantity after Amendment
		110	Central Distribution
	c. Timeliness and Quality	111	Printing Time After Amendment
		112	Identification of Textual Changes
	10. Access by Press and News Media		
	a. Committee and Hearing Rooms	47c	Permit Live Coverage--Committees
		33e	Press Equipment and Facilities in
		(174)	Committee Rooms
	b. Chambers	30a,b Row 5	Press Facilities in Chambers
		129	Permit Live Coverage--Floor
		35c	Technical Equipment and Facilities
	c. General Facilities	35b	Press Offices
		35a	News Conference Rooms
	d. Information Officer	21a Row 16 (188,189)	Press Officer
	11. Information on Legislators' Interests	147a,b	Mandatory Disclosures of Income
		145	Information on Compensation
	12. Information on Lobbyists	153	Public Information on Lobbyist Registration
		154	Penalties for Failure to Disclose
INTERNAL ACCOUNTABILITY	13. Diffusion and Constraints on Leadership		
	a. Leadership	74a,b Part 1 (195) Part 2	Leadership Selection Methods Breadth of Leadership
	b. Standing Committee Composition	43	Selection of Committee Chairmen
		44	Selection of Committee Members
	c. Calendaring	60a,b c (179)	Treatment of Favorably Reported Bills
	d. Conference Committees	63	Size of Conference Committees
		64	Powers of Conference Committees
		65a	Action by Conference Committees
		65b	Members' Powers over Dissolution of Conference Committees
	e. Standing Committee Reports	56a,b	Members' Control over Bills in Committee
		57	Members' Control over Items in Committee Reports
		58	Members' Power to Withdraw and Recommit
	f. Committee Members and Chairmen	54	Majority Power over Committee Agenda
		55	Majority Report Without Chairman

412

Criteria	Subcriteria	Question Number	Short Title
INTERNAL ACCOUNT- ABILITY (cont.)	14. Treatment of Minority a. Standing Committees	39/Cols. 1,2,3 (196) Part 1 Part 2	Minority Membership on Standing Committees Frequency of Departure from "Ideal" Magnitude of Departure from "Ideal"
	b. Rules and Management Committees	77a,b	Minority Membership on Management/ Rules Committees
	c. Minority Leader's Powers	78a,c 78b,d	Minority Leader's Powers Minority Leader on Management Committee

Criteria	Subcriteria	Question Number	Short Title
ENOUGH TIME	1. Session Time	3 (178) 4	Restrictions on Session Length Time Actually Used
	2. Pre-session Activities	14a-f (163)	Pre-Session, Post-election Activities
STANDING COMMITTEES (AS INFORMA-TION-PROCESS-ING AND -APPLY-ING UNITS)	3. Number of Committees	38 42a	Number of Standing Committees Committee Assignments per Member
	4. Testimony	49a,b,c 47b 47d 61	Notice of Meetings Solicitation of Public Testimony Advance Written Submission Subpoena Powers--Standing Committees
	5. Facilities	33b 33a 33c 33d (174)	Committee Rooms Auditorium Hearing Rooms Room Quality Special Facilities
INTERIM ACTIVITIES	6. Interim Activities	17 (186) 19a,b 71	Limitations Interim Planning and Coordination Subpoena Powers--Interim Committees
	7. Structure and Staffing	45 (185)	Standing Committees with Interim Status
	8. Reporting and Records	70c 70a 70b	Legislative Proposals Required Reports Committee Records
FORM AND CHARACTER OF BILLS	9. Bill Status and History	156a,b	Bill Status and History
	10. Bill Content and Summaries	92 94 93 113 104	Printing Standards Summary of Contents Statement of Legislative Intent One-Subject Bills Skeleton Bills
	11. Quantity and Distribution	107 108 110	Quantity Printing on Introduction Quantity Printing After Amendment Central Distribution
	12. Timeliness and Quality	111 112	Printing Delay After Amendment Identification of Textual Changes
PROFESSIONAL STAFF RESOURCES	13. General Research Coverage	21a Rows 10, 14,15,17, 18,19,20, 21 (188,189, 190) 24	Coverage of Staff-- Non-Legal, Non-Fiscal Washington Office

Criteria	Subcriteria	Question Number	Short Title
PROFESSIONAL STAFF RESOURCES (cont.)	14. Legal Staffing	21a Rows 1, 2,3 (188,189)	Technical Drafting Services
		21a Rows 4, 5,6 (188,189)	Code Research and Code Revision
		21b,c Rows 1,2 (164,165, 166)	Availability of Legal Staff Services
FISCAL REVIEW CAPABILITIES	15. Fiscal Responsi- bility	89 62	Budget Role Dual Committee Review
	16. Staff Support for Fiscal Analysis and Review a. Coverage	21a Rows 7,8, 9,10,11, 12,13 (188,189)	Coverage of Fiscal Staff Services
	b. Availabil- ity	21b,c Row 3 (164,165, 166)	Availability of Fiscal Analysis
	17. Fiscal Notes	96 95	Fiscal Notes by Legislative Agency Fiscal Notes Required

415

Criteria	Subcriteria	Question Number	Short Title
LEGISLATIVE AUTONOMY REGARDING LEGISLATIVE PROCEDURES	1. Time for Deliberation a. Frequency and Duration of Sessions	3 (178)	Restrictions on Session Length
	b. Special Sessions	6a	Legislative Power to Call Special Sessions
		6b	Methods to Call Special Sessions
		15a	Expansion of Special Session Agenda
		15b	Vote Requirements
	c. Interim Programs	17 (186)	Limitations on Interim Programs
	2. Expenditure Control and Compensation-Reimbursement Powers	91b	Legislative Control of Legislative Expenditures
		137 (191)	Method of Setting Legislative Salaries
		141 (192)	Method of Setting Expense Allowances
		139 Row 4	Source of Limitations on Non-Calculable Benefits
	3. Reapportionment	84	Reapportionment
LEGISLATIVE INDEPENDENCE FROM EXECUTIVE BRANCH	4. Access to Information and Analysis a. Coverage	21a (175)	Services Available
		96	Independent Legislative Fiscal Notes
		24	Washington Office
	b. Staff Size/Population and Distribution	22a,b,c (168, 160)	Professional Staff Size/Population
	c. Level of Legislative Support	New Element (194)	Legislative Expenditure (total) per Capita
		New Element (194)	Legislative Expenditure as Percent of State Budget
	d. Subpoena Powers	61	Subpoena Powers--Standing Committee
		71	Subpoena Powers--Interim Committee
	5. Veto Relationships a. Pocket Veto	90a,b	Pocket Veto (90b annotation reflected in 90a classification)
	b. Methods of Override	8a	Veto Sessions
		8b	Legislative Power to Convene Veto Sessions
	6. Lieutenant Governor Problem	New Element (184)	Role of Lieutenant Governor

Criteria	Subcriteria	Question Number	Short Title
LEGISLATIVE INDEPENDENCE FROM EXECUTIVE BRANCH (cont.)	7. Budget Powers	89	Budget Development Roles
		7c	Pre-Submission Analysis
		88a	Raise Budget Items
	8. Miscellaneous	102	Bills only by Legislators
CAPABILITY FOR EFFECTIVE OVERSIGHT OF EXECUTIVE OPERATIONS	9. Oversight Capabilities	21a Row 7 (188,189)	Study of Resources and Expenditures
		21a Row 10 (188,189)	Program Review and Evaluation
	10. Audit Capability	21a Row 9 (188,189)	Post-Audit Service Available
INTEREST GROUPS	11. Lobbyists	153	Lobby Registration
		154	Penalties for Failure to Disclose
CONFLICTS AND DILUTION OF INTEREST	12. Dilution of Interest	146	Conflict of Interest Laws
		148	Prohibition of Legal Practice
		149	Prohibition of Other Business Transaction
		150	Prohibition Against Dual Public Employment
		152	Accepting Appointments During Term of Office
		151	Employment of Legislators' Families

FINAL CONCEPTUAL SCHEME FOR EVALUATING STATE LEGISLATURES
ACCORDING TO THEIR DEGREE OF REPRESENTATIVENESS

Criteria	Subcriteria	Question Number	Short Title
IDENTIFICA-TION	1. Identification	83 32b	Districting District Offices
DIVERSITY	2. Qualifications	86a (183, 161)	Qualifications for Office
	3. Compensation a. Salary b. Expense c. Retirement	135 143 142	Salary Travel Reimbursement Retirement Provisions
	4. Voting Require- ments	51 63	Committee Quorum Requirements Size of Conference Committees
MEMBER EFFECTIVENESS	5. Size and Com- plexity of Leg- islative Body	79 38	Size of House and Senate Number of Standing Committees
	6. Diffusion and Constraints on Leadership a. Leadership	74a,b (195) a2,b2	Selection of Leadership Breadth of Leadership
	b. Standing Committee Composition	43 44	Selection of Committee Chairmen Selection of Committee Members
	c. Committee Members and Chairmen	54 55	Majority Power over Committee Agenda Majority Report Without Chairman
	d. Calendaring	60a,b,c (179)	Treatment of Favorably Reported Bills
	e. Standing Committee Reports	56a,b 57 58	Members' Control over Bills in Committee Members' Control over Items in Committee Reports Members' Powers to Withdraw and Recommit
	f. Conference Committees	64 65a 65b	Powers of Conference Committees Action by Conference Committees Members' Powers over Dissolution of Conference Committees
	7. Access to Resources a. Staff	26a,1,2 last 2 Rows 21b,c "Mem- bers" column (166)	Staff for Non-Leaders Availability of Staff Services to Members

Criteria	Subcriteria	Question Number	Short Title
MEMBER EFFECTIVENESS (cont.)	7. Access to Resources (cont.) b. Facilities	32a 32e	Members' Offices--Quantity Members' Staff Offices
	8. Treatment of Minority a. Standing Committees	39/Cols. 1,2,3 Part 1 (196) Part 2	Minority Membership on Standing Committees Frequency of Department from "Ideal" Magnitude of Departures from "Ideal"
	b. Rules and Management Committees	77a,b	Minority Membership on Management/ Rules Committees
	c. Officing	32c	Minority Officing
	d. Minority Leader's Powers	78a,c 78b,d	Minority Leader Appoints Minority Committee Members Minority Leader on Management Committee
	9. Known Rules a. House Rules	126 128 127	Published Rules Joint Rules Back-up Rules
	b. Committee Rules	100 101 52	Committee Jurisdictions Referral Practices Uniform Committee Rules
	c. Procedural Orientation	13a,b 13c	Procedural Orientation and Coverage Duration
	10. Bill Reading	118	Separate Day Reading by Title only

419

C

OUTLINE

OF

THE EVALUATIVE APPARATUS
AND SUBCRITERIA
WEIGHTINGS

Appendix C is an outline of the evaluative apparatus and subcriteria weightings, once again in order of the FAIIR conceptual schemes. It gives such information as the number of groups the states fell into and how consolidations among groupings were performed. Since weights were used in the final ranking apparatus, Appendix C also shows those weightings.

Question Number and Short Title	Procedure Used	Subcriteria and Weights	Criteria
178(3) Restrictions on Session Length	Form a nine-way ranking on the basis of type of session limitation:	1. Amount and Distribution (7)	Time and Its Utilization
11b, Scheduling 162 Devices	Combine House and Senate by number of scheduling devices used to form a fifteen-way ranking.	2. Management of Time Resources (8)	
111 Printing Time Lag After Amendments	Rank House and Senate in order of "never" better than "sometimes" better than "frequently" better than "always" better than "no reprint" to form two five-way rankings, and combine by sum of ranks to form a six-way ranking.		
115 Time Lag Between Introduction and Referral to Committee	Combine House and Senate by number of "no" answers to form a three-way ranking. Combine these three by a weighted sum of normalized rankings to form a thirty-three-way ranking.		
14 Pre-Session, Post-Election Activities Authorized	Combine House and Senate by number of "yes" answers, giving double weights to "yes" for bill drafting and bill printing, to form ten-way ranking.	3. Use of Pre-Session, Post-Election Time (5)	
163 Pre-Session, Post-(14) Election Activities Practiced	Combine House and Senate as above, but also include in number of "yeses" a "yes" answer to question 12, to form a sixteen-way ranking.		
12 Organizational Session	Combine these two by total number of (weighted) "yes" answers to form a nineteen-way ranking.		
26a Personal Aides to 1, 2 Leaders and Members	Combine House and Senate by number of "yes" answers to form an eleven-way ranking.	4. Assistants (4)	Multi-Purpose Staff Support
28a,b Quality of Chambers	Rank House and Senate in order of "superior," "adequate," "inadequate," and "no answer," forming four-way rankings, and combine by sum of ranks to form a six-way ranking.	5. Chambers (3)	Facilities
30a,b Electric (Row 1) Roll Call Recorder	Combine House and Senate by number of "available" answers to form a three-way ranking.		
30a,b Staff (Row 6) Working Area	Rank House and Senate in order of "superior," "adequate," "inadequate," and "not available," forming four-way rankings, and combine by sum of ranks to form a six-way ranking. combine these three by a weighted sum of normalized rankings to form an eighteen-way ranking.		

Question Number and Short Title	Procedure Used	Subcriteria and Weights	Criteria
31a,b Leadership Offices	Combine House and Senate by sum of scores to form an eleven-way ranking.	6. Offices for Leadership (2)	Facilities (cont.)
30a,b Office (Row 7) Location	Rank House and Senate in order of "superior," "adequate," "inadequate," and "not available," forming four-way rankings, and combine by sum of ranks to form a seven-way ranking.		
	Combine these two by a seven x eleven matrix, eleven-edge dominant, to form a forty-three way ranking.		
33b Committee Rooms	Rank by sum of number of House, Senate, and shared committee rooms, and consolidate into a three-way grouping.	7. Committee Facilities (7)	
33a Auditorium Hearing Rooms	Rank as above and consolidate into a four-way grouping. Combine these two by a four x three modified symmetric matrix to form a nine-way ranking for rooms.		
33c Quality of Committee Rooms	Rank House and Senate in order of "superior," "adequate," and "inadequate," forming three-way rankings, and combine by a three x three symmetric matrix to form a four-way ranking.		
174 Audio-Visual (33d) Equipment And Quality	Rank House and Senate in order of "superior," "adequate," "inadequate," and "not available," forming four-way rankings, and combine by sum of ranks to form a four-way ranking. Combine these two quality rankings by a four x four matrix, committee room quality edge-dominant, to form a twelve-way ranking for quality. Finally, combine the rooms and quality rankings by a nine x twelve special form matrix (see Matrix A) to form a thirty-three-way ranking.		
37a Clerks' And Secretaries' Offices	Rank House and Senate in order of "superior," "adequate," "inadequate," and "not applicable," forming four-way rankings, and combine by sum of ranks to form a five-way ranking.	8. Service Agencies (3)	
30a,b Staff (Row 6) Working Area	Rank as in subcriterion no.5 to form six-way ranking.		
37b Service Agencies' Office Quality	Rank in decreasing order of score, and consolidate into a four-way grouping.		
	Combine these three by the sum of normalized rankings to form a twenty-four-way ranking.		
32a Officing of Members	Rank House and Senate in order of "all singles," "mixed singles and doubles," "GT two-thirds," "from one-third to two-thirds," "LT one-third," and "no offices," forming (possible) six-way rankings. Combine by a six x six symmetric matrix to form an eight-way ranking.	9. Individual Members (4)	
32f Quality Of Members' Offices	Rank House and Senate in order of "superior," "adequate," "inadequate," and "not applicable," froming four-way rankings, and combine by a four x four symmetric matrix to form a seven-way ranking.		

Question Number and Short Title	Procedure Used	Subcriteria and Weights	Criteria
2e Adjacent Office Space for Staff	Rank House and Senate in order of "GT 67 percent," "33-67 percent," "LT 33 percent," and "not applicable," forming (possible) four-way rankings, and combine by a four x four symmetric matrix to form a four-way ranking.	9. Individual Members (4) (cont.)	Facilities (cont.)
6 Parking	Form three-way groupings on basis of type of parking available to members, and combine House and Senate by a three x three symmetric matrix to form a four-way ranking.		
2g Private Lounges for Members	Rank House and Senate in order of "superior," "adequate," "inadequate," and "not available," forming four-way rankings, and combine by a four x four symmetric matrix to form an eight-way ranking. Combine these five rankings by a weighted sum of normalized rankings to form a twenty-nine-way ranking.		
9 Size of House	Use graph to score House size by percent, and rank by decreasing score. Consolidate into a five-way grouping.	10. House Size (7)	Structural Characteristics Related to Manageability.
8 Number of Standing Committees	Use graph to assign percent score to House and Senate for number of standing committees. Combine House and Senate by the sum of squares of differences between 100 and percent scores to form a forty-one-way ranking.	11. Committee Structure (9)	
35 (45) Ratio of Number of Standing Committees with Interim Status to Number of Standing Committees	Sum ratios for House, Senate, and joint, and rank by decreasing score. Consolidate into a three-way grouping.		
2a Standing Committee Assignments per Member	Score House by percent of members with more than three committee assignments, and Senate by percent of members with more than four committee assignments. Combine House and Senate by sum of squares of percents to form a forty-two-way ranking. Combine these three by the sum of normalized rankings to form a fifty-way ranking.		
9 Use of Committee Bills	Rank in order of "sometimes," "frequently," "always," "never," and "not applicable/no answer," to form a four-way ranking.	12. Origin and Sponsorship of Bills (3)	Organizational and Procedural Features to Expedite Flow of Work
43 Multiple and Joint Authorship	Rank House and Senate by number of "yes" answers to form two three-way rankings, and combine by a three x three symmetric matrix to form a four-way ranking.		

Question Number and Short Title	Procedure Used	Subcriteria and Weights	Criteria
102 Bills Only by Legislators	Form two-way ranking by whether or not answer is "yes."	Origin and Sponsorship of Bills (cont.)	Organizational and Procedural Features to Expedite Flow of Work (cont.)
132 Restrictions on House of Origin	Form two-way ranking by whether or not answer is "no"(or "not applicable,"for Nebraska). Combine these four by a weighted sum of normalized rankings to form a ten-way ranking.		
40b Provisions for Use	Form two-way ranking by whether or not answer is "yes"(or "not applicable,"for Nebraska).	13. Use of Joint Committees (3)	
40c Session Use	Rank in order of "sometimes,""always,""never," and "not applicable,"to form a four-way ranking.		
41 Joint Committee Reports to	Rank in order of "reporting to administrative unit/not applicable,""reporting to other,"and "reporting to respective house/ no answer,"to form a three-way ranking. Combine these three by the sum of normalized rankings to form a ten-way ranking.		
57 Withdrawal of Bills from Committee Reports	Combine House and Senate into a three-way ranking by whether answers are both "yes," both "no,"or both "not applicable." (Some of the last are corrected for individual report to be placed in first, or "yes,"rank).	14. Treatment of Committee Reports (3)	
117 Multiple Readings in Full	Rank House and Senate by whether or not there are no full readings required, forming two-way rankings, and combine by sum of ranks to form a two-way ranking.		
30a,b Electric Roll (Row 1) Call Recorder	Combine House and Senate by number of "available"answers to form a three-way ranking.		
116a Consent Calendar	Combine House and Senate by number of "yes" answers as to whether a consent calendar is used to expedite non-controversial legislation, to form a three-way ranking. Combine these four by the sum of normalized rankings to form a fourteen-way ranking.		
60, 179 Treatment of Favorably Reported Bills	Score 60a "yes" better than "no"; 60b (179) "taken up automatically"better than"taken up by action of leadership"better than "taken up by action of Rules Committee or Calendaring Committee"; and 60c (179) "always"better than "sometimes"better than "rarely"or "never." Rank House and Senate by three-way algorithm on answers to 60a, 60b, and 60c (in order that) to form a four-way ranking for House and five-way ranking for Senate. Consolidate the latter into a four-way grouping (by equating last two ranks) and combine with House by a four x four symmetric matrix to form a six-way ranking.	15. Anti-Limbo Provisions (6)	

Question Number and Short Title	Procedure Used	Subcriteria and Weights	Criteria
3a,b Required Action on Referred Bills	Form two-way groupings by whether or not answer is "yes" to required action on referred bills, and within first (or "yes") group by whether or not there is a time limit on reports, forming three-way rankings for House and Senate. Combine these two by a three x three symmetric matrix to form a five-way ranking.	15. Anti-Limbo Provisions (6) (cont.)	Organizational and Procedural Features to Expedite Flow of Work (cont.)
5a Conference Committee Action	Combine House and Senate by number of "yes" answers to form a three-way ranking.		
00 Published Rules on Committee Jurisdiction 01 Referral Practices	Form two groups by whether answer to no.100 is "yes," and within the first (or "yes") group, rank by answer to no.101, with "always" better than "frequently" better than "sometimes" better than "never," to form four-way rankings for House and Senate. Combine these by a four x four symmetric matrix to form a six-way ranking.		
15 Time Lag on Referral	Combine House and Senate by the number of "no" answers to form a three-way ranking. Combine these five rankings by a weighted sum of normalized rankings to form a thirty-two-way ranking.		
25a,b Amendments from the Floor	Combine House and Senate by number of "yes" answers into three groups, and within first two groups rank in order of vote required to make amendment two-thirds better than simple majority) to form a four-way ranking.	16. Emergency Procedure (5)	
05 Exceptions to Bill Deadlines	Combine House and Senate by number of "yes" answers to form a three-way ranking (if no deadline exists, count as a "yes" answer).		
24a,b Provisions to Limit Debate	Rank House and Senate by the vote required to limit debate, with "simple majority" better than "extraordinary majority," or "N/A" better than "less than simple majority," to form three-way rankings. Combine these by a three x three symmetric matrix to form a four-way ranking. Combine these three by a weighted sum of normalized rankings to form a twelve-way ranking.		
14 Bill Carry-Over Permitted	Form two-way ranking in order of "yes" or "N/A" better than "no."	17. Bill Carry-Over (3)	
5b,d May Presiding Officer Succeed Himself?	Combine House and Senate by number of "yes" answers to form a three-way ranking.	18. Powers and Continuity of Leadership (8)	Management and Coordination
6 Powers of Presiding Officers	Combine House and Senate by number of "yes" answers, and consolidate into a three-way grouping.		
Rows -3)	Combine these two by a three x three symmetric matrix to form a six-way ranking.		

Question Number and Short Title	Procedure Used	Subcriteria and Weights	Criteria
128 Joint Rules	Form a two-way ranking by whether or not answer is "yes" (count Nebraska as a "yes").	19. Inter-House Coordina- tion (4)	Managem~ and Coor- dination (cont.)
69a Overlapping Rule Committee Membership	Form a two-way ranking by whether or not answer is "yes" (corrected for inter-house coordination).		
69b Minority Parti- cipation in Inter-House Coordination	Form a two-way ranking by whether or not answer is "yes" (count Nebraska as a "yes"). Combine these three by sum of ranks to form a four-way ranking.		
136 Annual Salary	Form a two-way ranking by whether or not salary is based on an annual rate.	20. Order, Decorum, and Dignity of Office (6)	Order, Decorum, Dignity of Office
76 (Row 6) Speaker in Line for Succession to Governorship	Form a two-way ranking by whether or not answer is "yes." Combine these two by sum of ranks to form a three-way ranking.		
130 Privileges of the Floor	Combine House and Senate by number of "yes" answers to form a three-way ranking, and combine with above by a three x three matrix, the annual salary/speaker succession edge- dominant, to form a nine-way ranking. Finally, combine all the subcriteria by a weighted sum of normalized rankings to form a fifty-one-way ranking for the functional schedule.		

Matrix A

Groups		1	2	3	4	5	6	7	8	9	10	11	12
	1	1	2	3	4	5	6	13	14	15	16	17	18
	2	7	8	9	10	11	12	25	26	27	28	29	30
	3	19	20	21	22	23	24	37	38	39	40	41	42
	4	31	32	33	34	35	36	49	50	51	52	53	54
	5	43	44	45	46	47	48	61	62	63	64	65	66
	6	57	58	59	60	61	62	73	74	75	76	77	78
	7	69	70	71	72	73	74	85	86	87	88	89	90
	8	81	82	83	84	85	86	97	98	99	100	101	102
	9	93	94	95	96	97	98	102	103	104	105	106	107

Question Number and Short Title	Procedure Used	Subcriteria and Weights	Criteria
83 Districting	Rank House and Senate by decreasing order of ratio of districts to seats, expressed as per- cents. Combine House and Senate by sum of squares of the difference between 100 and (ratio) percents to form a thirty-four-way ranking.	1. Districting (5)	Order, Decorum, and Dignity of Office (cont.)
195 Selection of (74a,b) Leaders	Rank House and Senate by whether selection is by full house, by caucus, or by other means, and combine House and Senate by a three x three special form matrix (see Matrix A) to form a five-way ranking.	2. Selection of Leaders (4)	
43 Selection of Committee Chairmen, "Actual" Column	Rank House and Senate by whether selection is by caucus, by speaker/pres. pro tem, by Rules Committee, or by other, and combine House and Senate by sum of ranks to form a six-way ranking.		
66 Selection of Conference Com- mittee Chairmen	Combine House and Senate by number of "yes" answers to form a three-way ranking. Consolidate six-way ranking to a five-way grouping by equating last two ranks, and combine with above five-way ranking by a five x five symmetric matrix (this would form a twelve-way ranking). Modify the scoring values by three points if there is at least one "yes" answer to question 66 (ranks 1 and 2), to form a thirteen-way ranking for this subcriterion.		
79a,b Size of House and Senate	Use graph to give percent score to size of House, and rank in decreasing order of score. Consolidate into a five-way grouping.	3. General Complexity (9)	Comprehen- sibility
38 Number of Stand- ing Committees	Rank House and Senate in decreasing order of percent score, and combine by the sum of the squares of the difference between 100 and the percent score. Consolidate into a five-way grouping. Combine these two five-way groupings by a five x five symmetric matrix to form a twelve-way ranking.		
52 Uniform Committee Rules	Combine House and Senate by number of "yes" answers to form a three-way ranking.	4. Explicit Rules and Procedures (10)	
128 Joint Rules	Form two-way ranking by whether answer is "yes" or "no" (put Nebraska in rank 1). Com- bine with above by a three x two matrix, three-edge dominant, to form a six-way ranking.	a. Rules of Procedure	
127 Back-up Rules	Combine House and Senate by number of "yes" answers to form a three-way ranking, and com- bine with above six-way ranking by a three x six matrix, six-edge dominant, to form a twelve-way ranking.		
100 Published Rules	Rank House and Senate by whether bill referral	b. Rules of	

Question Number and Short Title	Procedure Used	Subcriteria and Weights	Criteria
on Committee Jurisdiction 101 Bill Referral Practice	practice is "always," "frequent/sometimes," "never," or "N/A"--first three correspond to a "yes" answer on question 100, the last to a "no" answer--to form two three-way rankings, and combine by a three x three symmetric matrix to form a five-way ranking. Combine a and b by the sum of normalized rankings to form a twenty-way ranking.	Jurisdiction	Compreher sibility (cont.)
60a Floor Action on Bills "Do-Pass" by Committees	Combine House and Senate by number of "yes" answers to form a three-way ranking.	5. Anti-Limbo Provisions (8)	
53a,b Required Action on Referred Bills	Rank House and Senate by number of "yes" answers to the two parts to form two three-way rankings, and combine by a three x three symmetric matrix to form a five-way ranking. Combine these two by a three x five modified symmetric matrix to form a seven-way ranking.		
65a Conference Committee Action	Combine House and Senate by number of "yes" answers to form a three-way ranking.		
115 Time Lag on Bill Referral	Combine House and Senate by number of "no" answers to form a three-way ranking, and combine with above by a three x three symmetric matrix to form a five-way ranking. Combine above seven-way ranking with this five-way ranking by a five x seven matrix, seven-edge dominant, to form a sixteen-way ranking for anti-limbo provisions.		
11a,b,162 Session Planning and Co-ordination	Combine House and Senate by number of "yes" answers to types of work flow deadlines used to form a fifteen-way ranking.	6. Planning, Scheduling, Coordination, and Budgeting (2)	
19a,b, Interim Planning and Coordination	Combine House and Senate by number of "yes" answers to whether there are central organization and procedures for interim activities to form three groups, within each of which rank according to number of "yes" answers to types of coverage of interim management, to form a seven-way ranking.		
91a Sum Certain or Sum Sufficient Budget	Form two-way ranking by whether budget is sum certain or sum sufficient, and combine with above seven-way ranking by a two x seven special form matrix (see Matrix B) to form a ten-way ranking. Finally, combine the fifteen-way and ten-way rankings by a ten x fifteen modified symmetric matrix to form a twenty-way ranking.		
49a,b c Advance Notice of Meetings and Agenda	For House, form into three groups by number of "yes" answers to advance notice of committee meetings and agenda, and to more than one week's	7. Public Access to Legisla-tive Activi-	Adequacy of Infor-mation

Question Number and Short Title	Procedure Used	Subcriteria and Weights	Criteria
	notice; within each group rank according to score for announcing methods used, to form a twenty-three-way ranking. For Senate, rank similarly, forming a twenty-two-way ranking. Consolidate each into a four-way grouping, and combine by a four x four symmetric matrix into an eight-way ranking.	ties (8)	and Public Access to it
46a Secret Sessions Prohibited	Combine House and Senate by number of "yes" answers to form a three-way ranking.		
47a Open Hearings	Form a two-way ranking by whether answer is "yes" or "no," and combine with above by a two x three matrix, three-edge dominant, to form a six-way ranking.		
33a Auditorium Hearing Rooms	Rank in decreasing order of percent score to form a nine-way ranking, and consolidate into a six-way grouping.	Public Access to Legislative Activities (8) (cont.)	Adequacy of Information and Public Access to It (cont.)
30a,b Visitors' Row 4 Gallery	Rank House and Senate by whether gallery condition is "superior," "adequate." "inadequate." or "not available." forming two three-way rankings, and combine by sum of ranks to form a four-way ranking. Combine these last two by a four x six matrix, six-edge dominant, to form a seventeen-way ranking. Finally, combine the eight-way committee meeting ranking, the six-way secrecy/open hearing ranking, and the last seventeen-way ranking by a weighted sum of normalized ranking to form a forty-one-way ranking.		
123a,b, Roll Call on Final Passage	Form two groups by whether or not roll call vote is required, and within the "not required" group rank by increasing percent vote required to have roll call, forming two four-way rankings. Combine House and Senate by a four x four symmetric matrix to form a five-way ranking.	8. Records of Voting and Deliberation (11)	
48a,b,c Committee Votes (Taken, Recorded, Published)	Rank House and Senate separately by three-way algorithm to form two five-way rankings, and combine by a five x five symmetric matrix to form a seven-way ranking.		
30a,b Electric Roll Row 1 Call Recorder	Combine House and Senate by number of available answers to form a three-way ranking.		
50a,b Form of Committee Records	Form three groups by number of "yes" answers for House and Senate as to whether or not committee records are taken and publicly available. Within each group, rank as follows: score eight points if transcripts are taken and publicly available, three points if taken only, and zero if not taken; score six points if minutes are taken and publicly available, two points if taken		

Question Number and Short Title	Procedure Used	Subcriteria and Weights	Criteria
70a,b Interim Committee Records	only, and zero if not taken. Sum scores and rank in decreasing order of score sums. This forms a thirteen-way ranking. House and Senate-joint. Rank in following order: "yes/always" above "yes/frequently" above "yes/sometimes" above "yes/never" above "no." This forms a four-way ranking for "Interim Committee Report Required and Submitted" frequency. For "Interim Committee Action Publicly Recorded," form a two-way ranking by whether or not there is at least one "yes" answer. Combine these two by a two x four matrix, four-edge dominant, to form an eight-way ranking. Finally, combine these five questions by a weighted sum of normalized rankings to form a forty-eight-way ranking.	Records of Voting and Deliberation (11) (cont.)	Adequacy of Information and Public Access to It (cont.)
92 Printed Bills	Combine 92, 94, and 93, in this order, by three-way algorithm (on "yes" answers) to form a five-way ranking.	9. Character and Quality of Bill Documents (9)	
94 Summary of Contents			
93 Statement of Legislative Intent			
113 One-Subject Bills	Form two-way ranking by whether answer is "yes."		
104 Skeleton Bills	Combine House and Senate by number of "no" answers to form a three-way ranking, and combine with above by a two x three special-form matrix (see Matrix C) to form a five-way ranking. Combine these five-way rankings by a five x five symmetric matrix to form a ten-way ranking.	a. Content and Summary	
107 Quantity on Introduction	Combine 107, 108, and 110, in this order, by three-way algorithm (on "yes" answers) to form a six-way ranking.	b. Quantity and Distribution	
108 Quantity After Amendment			
110 Central Distribution			
111 Printing Time Lag After Amendment	Rank House and Senate separately on whether answer is "never," "frequently," "sometimes," "always," or "not printed," to form five-way rankings, and combine by a five x five symmetric matrix to form a six-way ranking.	c. Timeliness and Quality	
112 Identification of Textual Changes	Rank by number of "yes" answers to form a three-way ranking, and combine with above by sum of ranks to form an eight-way ranking. Finally, combine a, b, and c by sum of normalized rankings to form a thirty-four-way ranking.		

Question Number and Short Title	Procedure Used	Subcriteria and Weights	Criteria
47c Permit Live Coverage-- Committees	Combine House and Senate by number of "yes" answers to form a three-way ranking.	10. Access by Press and News Media (9)	Adequacy of Information and Public Access to It (cont.)
174 Press Equipment (33e) and Facilities in Committee Rooms	Rank House and Senate in order of "superior," "adequate," "inadequate," and "not available," and combine them by sum of ranks to form a five-way ranking. Combine these two by a five x three matrix, three-edge dominant, to form a seven-way ranking.	a. Committee and Hearing Rooms	
30a,b Press Facilities Row 5 in Chambers	Rank House and Senate in order of "superior," "adequate," "inadequate," and "not available," and combine them by sum of ranks to form a six-way ranking.	b. Chambers	
129 Permit Live Coverage--Floor	Combine House and Senate by number of "yes" answers to form a three-way ranking.		
35c Technical Equipment and Facilities	Combine House and Senate by number of "available" answers to form a three-way ranking. Combine these last two by a three x three special-form matrix (see Matrix D) to form a five-way ranking, and combine it with the six-way ranking by a five x six special-form matrix (see matrix E) to form an eleven-way ranking.		
35b Press Offices	Rank House and Senate in order of "superior," "adequate," "inadequate," and "not available," and combine by sum of ranks to form a four-way ranking.	c. General Facilities	
35a News Conference Rooms	Rank same as 35b to form a four-way ranking, and combine the two by a four x four symmetric matrix to form a ten-way ranking.		
188,189 Press Officer (21a,Row 16)	Combine House and Senate by number of "yes" answers to form a two-way ranking. Finally, combine a, b, c, and d by a weighted sum of normalized rankings to form a forty-four-way ranking.	d. Information Officer	
147a,b Mandatory Disclosures of Income	Form two groups on basis of whether or not answer is "yes," and within the first group (or "yes" group) rank by number of "yes" answers to types of incomes on which disclosure is required, to form an eight-way ranking, which is consolidated into a three-way grouping.	11. Information on Legislators' Interests (4)	
145 Information on Compensation	Form a two-way ranking by whether answer is "yes" or "no," and combine with above by a two x three matrix, three-edge dominant, to form a five-way ranking.		

Question Number and Short Title	Procedure Used	Subcriteria and Weights	Criteria
153 Regulation of Lobbyists	Rank House by number of "yes" answers to form a three-way ranking. Rank Senate similarly to form a four-way ranking, but equate last two ranks to consolidate into a three-way ranking, and combine with House by a three x three symmetric matrix to form a five-way ranking.	12. Information on Lobbyists (4)	Adequacy of Information and Public Acce to It (cont.)
154 Penalties for Failure to Dis- Close	Form a two-way ranking by whether or not answer is "yes," and combine with above by sum of ranks to form a six-way ranking.		
195 Selection of (74a,b Leadership Part I)	Rank House and Senate by whether selection is by full house, by caucus, or by other means, and combine these three-way rankings by a three x three special-form matrix (see Matrix F) to form a five-way ranking.	13. Diffusion and Constraints on Leadership (8)	Internal Account- ability
74a,b Breadth of Part II Leadership	Combine House and Senate by number of "yes" answers to form a three-way ranking, and combine with above by a three x five matrix, three-edge dominant to form a seven-way ranking.	a. Leadership	
43 Selection of Committee Chairmen	Rank House and Senate by whether selection is by caucus/Senate president pro tem/ speaker, by Rules Committee/Committee on Committees, or by seniority/other, and com- bine these three-way rankings by sum of ranks to form a four-way ranking.	b. Standing Committee Composition	
44 Selection of Committee Members	Rank House and Senate by whether selection is by caucus, by presiding officer, by Rules Committee, or by other and combine these by sum of ranks to form a five-way ranking. Combine these two by a four x five truncated symmetric matrix to form a nine-way ranking.		
60,179 Treatment of Favorably Re- ported Bills	Score 60a "yes" better than "no"; 60b (179) "automatically taken up" better than "taken up by leadership" better than "taken up by committee," and 60c (179) "always" better than "sometimes" better than "rarely/never." In order of 60a, 60b, and 60c, rank House by three-way algorithm to form a four-way ranking, which is consolidated into a three-way grouping by equating last two ranks. Similarly, rank Senate answers by three-way algorithm to form a five-way ranking, and consolidate into a three-way grouping by equating last three ranks. Then combine these three-way groupings by a three x three sym- metric matrix to form a four-way ranking.	c. Calendaring	
63 Size of Con- ference Committees	Form two-way ranking by whether or not conference committees have four or more members.	d. Conference Committees	

434

Question Number and Short Title	Procedure Used	Subcriteria and Weights	Criteria
64 Powers of Conference Committees	Rank House and Senate by whether committees are restricted to resolving differences, to bill topic, to no restrictions, or other answer, forming two four-way rankings, and combine by a four x four symmetric matrix to form a seven-way ranking.	Conference Committees (cont.)	Internal Accountability (cont.)
65a Action Required from Conference Committees	Combine House and Senate by number of "yes" answers to form a four-way ranking ("not applicable" forms last rank).		
65b Members' Powers over Dissolution of Conference Committees	Combine House and Senate by number of "yes" answers to form a four-way ranking ("not applicable" forms last rank). Finally, combine these four rankings by a weighted sum of normalized rankings to form a seventeen-way ranking.		
56a,b Members' Control over Bills in Committee	Form two-way grouping on whether or not members can report a bill out; within the "yes" group, rank by vote required in order of extraordinary majority, simple majority, or other, to form a four-way ranking. Combine House and Senate by a four x four symmetric matrix to form a seven-way ranking.	e. Standing Committee Reports	
57 Members' Control over Items in Committee Reports	Combine House and Senate by number of "yes" answers ("not applicable" forms last rank) to form a three-way ranking.		
58 Members' Powers to Withdraw and Recommit	Combine House and Senate by number of "yes" answers to form a three-way ranking. Finally, combine these three rankings by the sum of normalized rankings to form an eighteen-way ranking.		
54 Majority Power over Committee Agenda	Combine House and Senate by number of "yes" answers to form a three-way ranking.	f. Committee Members and Chairmen	
55 Majority Report Without Chairman	Combine House and Senate by number of "yes" answers to form a three-way ranking, and combine with above by a three x three symmetric matrix to form a five-way ranking. Finally, combine a, b, c, d, e, f by the sum of normalized rankings to form a fifty-way ranking.		
196 Magnitude and (39) Frequency of Departure from "Ideal" for Proportional Minority Membership on Standing Committees	Combine House and Senate by sum of squares of scores for percent of committees with negative departure (expressed as a decimal) and for average negative departure from ideal (expressed as a decimal), to form a thirty-one-way ranking, which is consolidated into a four-way grouping.	14. Treatment of Minority (9) a. Standing Committees	
77a,b Minority Pro-	Combine House and Senate by number of "yes"	b. Rules and	

435

Question Number and Short Title	Procedure Used	Subcriteria and Weights	Criteria
portional Membership on Rules Committee	answers into a three-way ranking.	Management Committees	Internal Accountability (cont.)
77a,b Minority Proportional Membership on Management Committee	Combine House and Senate by number of "yes" answers into a three-way ranking, and combine with above by a three x three symmetric matrix to form a six-way ranking.		
78a,c Minority Leader Appoints Minority Committee Members	Combine House and Senate by number of "yes" answers into a three-way ranking.	c. Minority Leader's Powers	
78b,d Minority Leader on Management Committee	Combine House and Senate by number of "yes" answers into a three-way ranking, and combine with above by a three x three symmetric matrix to form a five-way ranking. Finally, combine a, b, and c by a weighted sum of normalized rankings to form a twenty-three-way ranking. Lastly, combine all the subcriteria by a weighted sum of normalized rankings to form a fifty-one-way ranking.		

Matrix A

	F	C	O
Full	1	2	3
Caucus	2	4	5
Other	3	5	6

Matrix B

	1	2	3	4	5	6	7
1	1	2	3	7	8	11	11
2	4	5	6	9	10	12	12

Matrix C

	1	2	3
1	1	2	4
2	3	5	5

Matrix D

	1	2	3
1	1	2	7
2	3	4	7
3	5	6	7

Matrix E

	1	2	3	4	5	6
1	1	2	4	7	11	11
2	7	8	9	10	14	14
3	2	3	5	8	12	12
4	4	5	6	9	13	13
5	11	12	13	14	15	15

Matrix F

	F	C	O
Full House	1	2	3
Caucus	2	4	5
Other	3	5	6

Question Number and Short Title	Procedure Used	Subcriteria and Weights	Criteria
178 Patterns of (3) Restrictions on Session Length, Frequency, and Agenda	Identify nine session patterns ranging from "wholly unlimited" to "limited biennial session."	1. Session Time (9)	Enough Time
4 Time Actually Used in Recent General Session	For annual and biennial states, split into two groups, each based on actual number days work. Combine above two by nine x four matrix, nine-edge dominant, to form a fourteen-way ranking. Consolidate into a four-way grouping.		
14a,f Permissible and 163 Actual Pre-Session Post-Election Activities	Count number of "yes" answers for each of six activities (a) possible and (b) actually practiced in House and Senate. Consolidate resulting sixteen-way grouping into three groups.	2. Pre-Session Activities (5)	
38 Number of Standing Committees	Give percent score from chart for Senate and House. Combine score by sum of squares of difference from 100 percent, yielding a forty-one-way grouping.	3. Number of Committees (8)	Standing Committees
42a Number of Committee Assignments per Member	Score as a percent of members with more than three committee assignments in House, and more than four in Senate, and combine by sum of squares of percents, yielding a forty-two-way grouping. Combine two questions by sum of scores, yielding a fifty-way grouping.		
49 Public Notice of Committee Meetings	Count "yes" answers to parts a (regular notice) and b (one week's notice) for each house separately, yielding three-way grouping, within which rank by decreasing weighted score for part c (methods for announcements), yielding a twenty-three-way grouping for House, and a twenty-two-way grouping for Senate. Consolidate each house into a four-way grouping, combine by a four x four symmetric matrix, yielding an eight-way ranking for meeting notice.	4. Testimony (6)	
47b Is Public Testimony Regularly Solicited? d How Often Are Witnesses Required to Submit Written Testimony in Advance?	Combine House and Senate by number of "yes" answers to part b (regular solicitation of public testimony) to form a three-way ranking. Combine House and Senate answers to frequency of advance written testimony (part d) by a four x four special-form matrix (see Matrix A) to form a four-way ranking. These rankings for parts b and d were combined by a special-form four x three matrix (see Matrix B) to form a five-way ranking for testimony.		
61 Location of Subpoena Power	House and Senate answers combined by a special-form three x three matrix (see Matrix C) to form a four-way ranking for subpoena power.		

Question Number and Short Title	Procedure Used	Subcriteria and Weights	Criteria
	Combine subpoena power ranking with testimony ranking by a four x five matrix, four-edge dominant, to form a fourteen-way ranking.	Testimony (6) (cont.)	Standing Committees (cont.)
	Finally, combine last ranking with the meeting ranking by an eight x fourteen matrix, eight-edge dominant, to form a twenty-eight-way final ranking.		
33b Number of Committee Rooms	Sum the number of committee rooms for House, Senate, and shared, and consolidate scores into a three-way ranking.	5. Facilities (6)	
a Number of Auditorium Hearing Rooms	Sum the number of auditorium hearing rooms for House, Senate, and shared and consolidate scores into a four-way ranking.		
	Combine these two by a four x three modified symmetric matrix to form a nine-way ranking.		
c What Is Quality of Committee Rooms?	Rank House and Senate in order of "superior," "adequate," and "inadequate," forming three-way rankings, and combine by a three x three symmetric matrix to form a four-way ranking.		
174 Availability and (33d) Quality of Audio-Visual and Recording Equipment for Committee Rooms	Combine House and Senate scores by summing to form a four-way ranking.

Combine last two by a four x four matrix, committee room quality edge-dominant, to form a twelve-way ranking for quality of rooms.

Combine twelve-way ranking with the nine-way ranking for number of committee and hearing rooms by a special form nine x twelve matrix (see Matrix D) to form a thirty-three-way facilities final ranking. | | |
186 Source and Nature (17) of Limitations on Interim Activities	Rank states by source of limitations into a four-way grouping.	6. Interim Committee Activities (8)	Interim Activities
19a,b Is There a Central Organization and Body of Procedures to Schedule, Plan, and Budget for Interim Activities?	Combine House and Senate into three groups by number of "yes" answers, within each group of which rank states by extent of interim management (planning budget, scheduling, and review/evaluation), to form an eight-way ranking. Combine these two by a four x eight special matrix (see Matrix E) into a nine-way ranking.		
71 Interim Committee Subpoena Powers	Consolidate House, Senate, and joint committee subpoena power answers into four-way grouping. Finally, combine these last two by a nine x four matrix, four-edge dominant, to form a sixteen-way interim committee activities ranking.		

Question Number and Short Title	Procedure Used	Subcriteria and Weights	Criteria
185 (45) Ratio of Standing Committees with Interim Status to Number of Standing Committees	Sum House, Senate, and joint ratios, and then consolidate into a three-way grouping.	7. Structure and Staffing (8)	Interim Activities (cont.)
70c Must Interim Committee Reports Propose Specific Legislation?	Combine House, Senate and joint by number of "yes" answers into a two-way grouping (those states with at least one "yes" in first group).	8. Reporting and Recording (4)	
70a Are Formal Reports Required of Interim Committees? How Often Must They Be Submitted?	Combine House, Senate, and joint by number of "yes" answers, plus scoring for frequency, into a thirteen-way ranking.		
70b Are Results of Interim Committee Actions Recorded and Made Public?	Same as 70c. Combine 70b and c by two x two symmetric matrix into a three-way ranking. Finally, combine these two by a three x thirteen special matrix (see Matrix F) into an eight-way final reporting and records ranking.		
156a,b Are Efficient Services (e.g., EDP Equipment) Available for Bill Status, Bill History, and Journal Indexing?	Rank each house separately by three-way algorithm on basis of "yes" answers to form six-way rankings. Equate ranks 3, 4, and 5 to form four-way groupings, and combine House and Senate by four x four symmetric matrix into a four-way ranking.	9. Bill Status History and Index (7)	
92 Are Bills Regularly Provided in Standard Format? 94 In Practice, Is Agency Drafting Bill Required to Prepare a Summary? 93 Is Bill's Author Required to State Intent?	Combine 92, 94, and 93, in order given, by three-way algorithm on basis of "yes" answers to form a five-way ranking.	10. Bill Content and Summaries (4)	Form and Character of Bills
113 Must Bills Deal with Only One Subject?	Form two-way ranking by whether answer is "yes" or "no."		
104 Are Skeleton Bills Permitted?	Combine House and Senate by number of "no" answers to form a three-way ranking. Combine these two by a three x two matrix, two-edge dominant, to form a five-way ranking for bill topics. Finally, combine bill characteristics and topics by a five x five symmetric matrix to form an eleven-way final bill content and summaries ranking.		

Question Number and Short Title	Procedure Used	Subcriteria and Weights	Criteria
107 Are Bills Printed in Quantity upon Introduction?	Combine 107, 108, and 110, in that order, by three-way algorithm on basis of "yes" answers to form a six-way ranking for quantity and distribution.	11. Quantity and Distribution (1)	Form and Character of Bills (cont.)
108 Are Bills Printed in Quantity upon Subsequent (Main) Amendments?			
110 Is There a Central Distribution Point for Copies of Bills to the Public?			
111 How Often Is There a Time Lag Greater Than Overnight After Amendment and Before Reprinting of Revised Bills?	Rank House and Senate separately by (increasing) frequency of time lag or no reprinting at all into four-way rankings, and then combine by a four x four symmetric matrix into a five-way ranking.	12. Timeliness and Quality (6)	
112 Do Printing Procedures Permit Easy Identification of Original Text, Deletions, and Additions?	Rank by number of "yes" answers to form a five-way ranking. Finally, combine by a five x five special-form matrix (see Matrix G) to form a seven-way ranking for timeliness and quality.		
188-190 Availability (21a Rows of Staff 10,14,15, Service for 17-21) Various Listed Categories	Categories considered here were program review and evaluation, reference and bibliography, speech writing, spot research, in-depth studies and program design, management of outside resources, reporting on federal legislation, and information on federal subventions. Rank House and Senate separately on number of "yes" answers to above categories, both forming nine-way rankings.	13. General Research Coverage (4)	Professional Staff Resources
24 Does Legislature Maintain a Washington Liaison Office?	Two-way ranking on basis of "yes" answer or not. Finally, combine these three by sum of rankings into a twelve-way general research coverage ranking.		
188-189 Availability (21a) of Staff Rows 1,2,3, Service Rows 4,5,6 for Various Listed Categories	For technical drafting categories (bill drafting, review bills for legal form, and bill summary) combine House and Senate by number of "yes" answers to form a three-way ranking. For code categories (code research, including reviews of judicial opinion, statute and code revision, and management of outside consultants), combine House and Senate as above to form a three-way ranking. Combine these two by a three x three symmetric matrix to form a six-way ranking.	14. Legal Staffing (6)	

Question Number and Short Title	Procedure Used	Subcriteria and Weights	Criteria
164-166 Availability (21b,c of Legal Row 1 Staff Services, Row 2 Bill Drafting, Code Research, Including Reviews of Judicial Opinions	Rank the availability of legal staff services for bill drafting for House or Senate leaders, committees, and/or members by number of "yes" answers into a two-way ranking. Similarly, rank for code research, yielding a five-way ranking. Combine these two by a five x two matrix, two-edge dominant, to form a seven-way ranking. Consolidate this seven-way into a six-way grouping by equating last two ranks, and combine with above six-way ranking by a six x six symmetric matrix, forming a thirteen-way legal staffing ranking.	Legal Staffing (6) (cont.)	Professional Staff Resources (cont.)
89 Who Develops Budget, governor and/or legislature?	Form a two-way ranking on basis of whether governor develops budget, or must develop jointly with legislature.	15. Fiscal Responsibility (11)	Fiscal Review Capabilities
62 Is There a Formal Requirement for Dual Committee Consideration Where Significant Sums Are Involved?	Combine House and Senate by number of "yes" answers to form a three-way ranking. Finally, combine these by a two x three matrix, two-edge dominant, to form an eight-way fiscal responsibility ranking.		
188-189 Availability (21a) of Fiscal Rows 7-13 Staff for Various Categories	Categories considered here were continuous study of resources and expenditures, budget review and analysis, post-audit, program review and evaluation, fiscal notes, long-range forecasting, and management of outside consultants. Rank House and Senate separately on basis of number of "yes" answers to above categories, both forming eight-way rankings, and combine by sum of ranks into a nine-way ranking.	16. Staff Support for Fiscal Analysis and Review (6) a. Coverage	
164-166 Is Budget (21b,c) Review and Row 3 Analysis Service Available?	Rank availability of service for House or Senate leaders, committees, and/or members by number of "yes" answers into a five-way ranking, and combine with the above nine-way ranking by a five x nine matrix, nine-edge dominant, to form a nineteen-way final ranking.	b. Availability	
96 Are Fiscal Notes Prepared by a Legislative Service Agency?	Form three-way ranking by whether answer was "yes," "no," or "N/A."	17. Fiscal Notes (1)	
95 Are Fiscal Notes Required on Bills Having Revenue or Expenditure Implications?	Form three-way ranking by whether answer is "yes" to both, one, or no houses. Combine these two by summing scores to form a six-way ranking. Finally, combine all subcriteria by a weighted sum of normalized rankings to form a fifty-one-way final ranking for information.		

Question Number and Short Title	Procedure Used	Subcriteria and Weights	Criteria

Matrix A

Freq.	Always	Sometimes	Never
F.	1	2	4	6
A.	2	3	4	6
S.	4	4	5	6
N.	6	6	6	6

Matrix B

Groups	1	2	3
1	1	2	4
2	1	2	4
3	2	3	5
4	4	5	6

Matrix C

Senate	All Ctes.	In Hse.	No Power
All Ctes.	1	2	3
In Hse.	2	2	3
No Power	3	3	4

Matrix D

Groups	1	2	3	4	5	6	7	8	9	10	11	12
1	1	2	3	4	5	6	13	14	15	16	17	18
2	7	8	9	10	11	12	25	26	27	28	29	30
3	19	20	21	22	23	24	37	38	39	40	41	42
4	31	32	33	34	35	36	49	50	51	52	53	54
5	43	44	45	46	47	48	61	62	63	64	65	66
6	57	58	59	60	61	62	73	74	75	76	77	78
7	69	70	71	72	73	74	85	86	87	88	89	90
8	81	82	83	84	85	86	97	98	99	100	101	102
9	93	94	95	96	97	98	102	103	104	105	106	107

Matrix E

Groups	1	2	3	4	5	6	7	8
1	1	3	3	3	7	7	7	7
2	2	4	4	4	8	8	8	8
3	5	6	6	6	9	9	9	9
4	5	6	6	6	9	9	9	9

Matrix F

Groups	1	2	3	4	5	6	7	8	9	10	11	12	13
1	1	2	4	4	4	1	2	1	1	2	4	7	7
2	2	3	5	5	5	2	3	2	2	3	5	8	8
3	4	5	6	6	6	4	5	4	4	5	6	9	9

Matrix G

	1	2	3	4	5
1	1	2	3	4	5
2	2	3	4	5	6
3	3	4	5	6	7
4	2	3	4	5	6
5	3	4	5	6	7

Question Number and Short Title	Procedure Used	Subcriteria and Weights	Criteria
178(3) Limits on Session Length	Identify nine session patterns ranging from "wholly unlimited" to "limited--biennial session."	1. Time (16) a. Frequency and Duration of Sessions	Legislative Autonomy Regarding Legislative Procedures
6a,b Legislative Power to Call Special Sessions and Methods to Call Special Sessions	Rank by "yes" and "no" in part a and rank these according to the order in part b, of "simple majority only," "simple majority," "only 51+," and "N/A" to form a five-way ranking.	b. Special Sessions	
15a,b Expansion of Special Session Agenda and Vote Requirements	Rank by "yes" and "no" in part a and, within the "yes" group, rank by answer to part b, to form a four-way ranking. Combine and rank above two by a five x four special-form matrix (see Matrix A) to form six-way ranking.		
186 Limitations on (17) Interim Programs	Rank by whether no limit, rule/other, statutory limit, or constitutional limit to form a four-way ranking. Finally, combine a, b, and c by a weighted sum of normalized scores to form a twenty-four-way ranking.	c. Interim Programs	
91b Legislative Control of Legislative Expenditures	Rank by whether "yes" or "no" to form a two-way ranking.	2. Expenditure Control and Compensation Reimbursement Powers (12)	
191 Method of (137) Setting Legislative Salaries	Rank by statute, independent commission, and constitution to form a three-way ranking.		
192 Method of (141) Setting Expense Allowances	Rank according to whether it is by statute, independent commission, joint rules, constitution, or N/A, to form six-way ranking.		
139 Source of Row 4 Limitations on Non-Calcualable Benefits	Rank by "statute," "rules," or "N/A and no answer" to form three-way ranking. Combine these two by a three x six special-form matrix (see Matrix B) to form four-way ranking. Now combine this ranking with question 191 by sum of ranks to form a six-way ranking. Finally, combine this ranking with question 91b and rank by a sum of normalized scores to form a six-way ranking.		

Question Number and Short Title	Procedure Used	Subcriteria and Weights	Criteria
84 Reapportionment	Rank by legislature or other to form a two-way ranking.	3. Reapportion-ment (4)	
175 Distribution of (21a) Staff Services	Combine the number of House and Senate staff services to form a four-way ranking.	4. Access to Information and Analysis (14)	Legislative Indepen-dence from Executive Branch
96 Independent Legis-lative Fiscal Notes 24 Washington Office	Rank by "yes," "no," and "N/A" to form a three-way ranking. If not in first group, give states bonus to raise one position if "yes" answer to question 24. Combine these two by a three x four special-form matrix (see Matrix C) to form a seven-way ranking.	a. Coverage	
168 Legal, Fiscal, and (22a,b,c) General Research Staff	Rank by the number of "staff" answers to form a three-way ranking. Then combine with 160 (state population) to form staff size/population three-way ranking. Finally, combine above two rankings by a three x three symmetric matrix to form a six-way ranking.	b. Staff Size/ Population and Distri-bution	
194 Legislative Ex-penditure per Capita	Rank by legislative expenditure per capita and then consolidate to form a five-way grouping.	c. Level of Legislative Support	
194 Legislative Ex-penditure as Percent of State Budget	Rank by percent score and then consolidate to form a five-way grouping. Combine above two groupings by a five x five symmetric matrix to form a ten-way ranking.		
61 Subpoena Powers, Standing Committees	Combine House and Senate by a three x three special-form matrix (see Matrix D) to form a four-way ranking.	d. Supoena Powers	
71 Subpoena Powers, Interim Committees	Rank according to whether power in all House and Senate committees or joint committees, power in House, power in all committees in one house and no power in the other, or no power, to form a four-way ranking. Combine above two rankings by a four x four symmetric matrix to form an eight-way ranking. Finally, combine a, b, c, d by a weighted sum of normalized scores to form a forty-eight-way ranking.		
90a,b Pocket Veto	Form a two-way ranking on basis of whether answer is "no" or "yes," also reflecting 90b annotations in ranking.	5. Veto Relationship (8) a. Pocket Veto	

Question Number and Short Title	Procedure Used	Subcriteria and Weights	Criteria
8a,b Veto Sessions and Legislative Power to Convene Veto Sessions	Rank by whether legislature can convene a veto session, law provides for a veto session, or there is no veto session provision, to form a three-way ranking. Combine by two x three special-form matrix (see Matrix E) to form a three-way ranking.	b. Methods of Override	Legislative Independence from Executive Branch (cont.)
184 Role of Lt. Governor	Rank by whether lt. governor has no legislative role, has a presiding role only, or has a full legislative role, to form a three-way ranking.	6. Lt. Governor Problem (2)	
89 Budget Development Roles	Rank by whether budget developed by governor only or by governor and legislature, to form two-way ranking.	7. Budget Powers (6)	
7c Pre-Submission Analysis	Rank by whether answer is "yes" or "no" to form two-way ranking.		
88a Raise Budget Items	Rank by whether answer is "yes" or "no" to form two-way ranking. Combine above two rankings by a two x two matrix, 88-edge dominant, then combine with 89 by sum of ranks to form a four-way ranking.		
102 Bills Only by Legislators	Rank by whether answer is "yes" or "no" to form a two-way ranking.	8. Miscellaneous (1)	
188,189 Study of 21a Row 7) Resources and Expenditures	Combine House and Senate by number of "yes" answers to form a two-way ranking.	9. Oversight Capabilities (10)	Capability for Effective Oversight of Executive Operations
188,189 Program (21a Row 9) Review and Evaluation	Combine House and Senate by number of "yes" answers to form a three-way ranking. Combine above two rankings by number of "yes" answers to form a four-way ranking.		
188,189 Post-Audit (21a Row 10) Review Available	Combine House and Senate by number of "yes" answers to form a three-way ranking.	10. Audit Capability (8)	
153 Regulation of Lobbyists	Combine House and Senate by number of "yes" answers to form a seven-way ranking.	11. Lobbyists (8)	Interest Groups
154 Penalties for Failure to Disclose	Form a two-way grouping by whether answer is "yes" or "no," and combine with above by a seven x two matrix, seven-edge dominant, to form a ten-way ranking.		
146 Conflict-of-Interest Laws	Combine 146, 148, 149 by three-way rule on basis of "yes" answers to form a seven-way ranking.	12. Dilution of Interest (11)	Conflicts and Dilution of interest

Question Number and Short Title	Procedure Used	Subcriteria and Weights	Criteria
148 Prohibition of Legal Practice		Dilution of Interest (11) (cont.)	Conflicts and Dilution of Interest (cont.)
149 Prohibition of Other Business Transaction			
150 Prohibition Against Dual Public Employment	Combine 150, 152b, 152a by three-way rule on basis of "yes" answers, to form a six-way ranking.		
152 Accepting Appointments During Term of Office			
151 Employment of Legislators' Families	Rank by whether "yes" answer or not and then combine with above two by consolidating the seven-way grouping to a six-way grouping by equating ranks 4 and 5 and then combining with six-way ranking by a six x six symmetric matrix to form nineteen-way ranking. A "no" answer to question 151 reduces rank position by one, still resulting in a nineteen-way ranking. Finally, combine all subcriteria by a weighted sum of normalized scores to form a fifty-one way ranking of independence.		

Matrix A

	1	2	3	4	5
1	1	2	2	2	4
2	2	3	3	3	5
3	2	3	3	3	5
4	3	4	4	4	6

Matrix B

	1	2	3	4	5	6
1	1	1	2	3	4	2
2	3	3	4	5	6	4
3	1	1	2	3	4	2

Matrix C

	1	2	3	4
1	1	2	5	7
2	3	4	6	8
3	3	4	6	8

Matrix D

	5	3	1
5	1	2	4
3	2	2	5
1	4	5	6

Matrix E

	1	2	3
1	1	2	3
2	4	4	4

446

REPRESENTATIVE SCHEDULE

Question Number and Short Title	Procedure Used	Subcriteria and Weights	Criteria
83 What Is Character of House and Senate Districts?	Rank House and Senate separately by decreasing order of ratio of number of districts to number of seats, then combine by sum of squares of difference between ratio and 1 (expressed as percent) to form a thirty-four-way ranking.	1. Identification (18)	Identification
32b What Sort of Provision or Contribution Is Made for Home District Offices?	Rank House and Senate each in three groups, depending on whether there is provision, some contribution, or no provision, and combine by sum of ranks to form a four-way ranking. Instead of 1, 2, 3, and 4, weight this four-way ranking as 1, 3, 6, and 11, and combine with thirty-four-way ranking by sum of ranks to form a thirty-way ranking for identification.		
183 (86a) Row 1 What Is Difference Between Age Minimum to Be Elected to State Legislature and Voting Age?	Rank House and Senate together by sum of squares of (age differences) in increasing order to form a twelve-way ranking, and consolidate into a four-way grouping.	2. Qualifications (3)	
Row 2 What Is Difference Between Residency Requirements for Voting and to Be Elected?	Rank House and Senate together by sum of residency differences in increasing order to form a fourteen-way ranking, and consolidate into a three-way grouping. Combine these by a three x four matrix, four-edge dominant, to form an eleven-way ranking.		
161 (86a) Row 4 For How Long Is U.S. Citizenship Required to be Elected?	Rank House and Senate together by sum of citizenship lengths and consolidate into a four-way grouping. Finally, combine these last two by sum of rankings to form an eleven-way ranking for qualifications.		
135 Salary for Legislators	Divide biennial salary by days worked to get rate in dollars/day, and rank in decreasing order to get a forty-eight-way ranking.	3. Compensation (12) a. Salary	Diversity
143 Are Actual Travel Expenses Reimbursed?	Form two-way ranking by whether answer is "yes" or "no."	b. Expenses	
142 What Retirement Benefits Are Provided (Compared with Other State Employees)?	Rank in order of "better than," "same as," or "worse than" other state employees, or "none provided," to form a three-way ranking. Consolidate the forty-eight-way ranking into a four-way grouping, and combine with travel expense two-way ranking by a two x four special-form matrix (see Matrix A) to form an eight-way ranking. Combine this with retirement benefits three-way ranking by a three x eight special-form matrix (see Matrix B) to form a fourteen-way ranking for compensation.	c. Retirement	
51 What Are the Quorum Requirements for Committees?	Rank in order of simple majority, extraordinary majority, or no requirements, and combine House and Senate by sum of orders into a four-way ranking.	4. Voting Requirements (3)	

447

Question Number and Short Title	Procedure Used	Subcriteria and Weights	Criteria
63 Have All Conference Committees More Than Four Members?	Form three-way ranking by whether answer is "yes," "no," or "N/A." Consolidate into a two-way grouping by equating the "no" and "N/A" answers, and combine with above four-way ranking by a four x two matrix, four-edge dominant, to form a five-way ranking for voting requirements.	Voting Requirements (3) (cont.)	Diversity (cont.)
79 What Is Number of Seats in House (Senate)?	Use graph to assign percent score to House size, and rank in decreasing order of percent score. Consolidate into a five-way grouping.	5. Size and Complexity of Legislative Body (13)	
38 What Is Number of Standing Committees in House (Senate)?	Use graph to assign percent scores for House (Senate) standing committee size, and combine by sum of squares of differences between percents and 100 to form a forty-one-way ranking. Consolidate into a five-way grouping.

Finally, combine above two groupings by a five x five symmetric matrix to form an eleven-way ranking for this subcriterion. | | |
195 What Is Selection (74a,b) Method for Presiding Officers?	Rank in order of "full house," "caucus," and "other," and combine House and Senate by three x three symmetric matrix into a five-way ranking.	6. Diffusion and Constraints on Leadership (5)	
74a,b Breadth of Leadership	Combine House and Senate by sum of "yes" answers to form a three-way ranking, and combine with above ranking by a three x five matrix, five-edge dominant, to form a seven-way ranking.	a. Minimum Number and Coverage	
43 Selection of Committee Chairmen	Rank by "caucus/pres. pro tem pres. of Sen." above "Rules Committee/Committee on Committees" above "seniority/speaker/other," and combine House and Senate by a three x three symmetric matrix to form a six-way ranking.	b. Standing Committee Compensation	Member Effectiveness
44 Selection of Committee Members	Rank in order of "caucus," "presiding officer," "Rules Committee," and "other," and combine House and Senate by a four x four symmetric matrix to form a twelve-way ranking.		
54 Majority Power over Committee Agenda	Combine House and Senate by sum of "yes" answers to form a three-way ranking.	c. Committee Members and Chairmen	
55 Majority Report Without Chairman	Combine House and Senate by sum of "yes" answers to form a three-way ranking, and combine with above three-way ranking by a three x three symmetric matrix to form a five-way ranking.		
60, Treatment of 179 Favorably	Combine House answers by three-way rule to form a four-way ranking. Combine Senate answers by three-way rule to form a five-way ranking. Consolidate above into three-way groupings by equating last two ranks for House,	d. Calendaring	

Question Number and Short Title	Procedure Used	Subcriteria and Weights	Criteria
	and last three ranks for Senate, and combine by a three x three symmetric matrix into a four-way ranking.	Calendaring (cont.)	Member Effective-ness (cont.)
56a,b Members' Control over Bills in Committee	Combine House and Senate by a four x four symmetric matrix to form a seven-way ranking.	e. Standing Committee Reports	
57 Members' Control over Items in Committee Reports	Combine House and Senate by sum of "yes" answers into a three-way ranking. Consolidate into two-way ranking by equating "no" and "N/A" answers.		
58 Members' Powers to Withdraw and Recommit	Combine House and Senate by sum of "yes" answers into a three-way ranking. Combine these last three rankings by sum of rankings to form a nine-way ranking.		
64 Powers of Conference Committees	Combine House and Senate by a four x four symmetric matrix to form a seven-way ranking.	f. Conference Committees	
65a,b Action by Conference Committees, Members' Powers over Dissolution of Conference Committees	Combine House and Senate by a four x four symmetric matrix to form a six-way ranking. Combine above two groupings by a ten x ten symmetric matrix to form a fifteen-way ranking. Finally, combine a, b, c, d, e, and f by a weighted sum of normalized rankings into a fifty-way ranking.		
26a Staff for 1,2 Non-Leaders	House and Senate combined by number of "yes" answers to form a two-way ranking.	7. Access to Resources (15)	
166 Availability of (21b,c) Staff Services to Members ("Members" Column)	House and Senate combined by number of "yes" answers to form a six-way ranking. Combine above two groupings by a two x six special matrix (see Matrix C) into a nine-way ranking.	a. Staff	
32a Members' Offices	Combine House and Senate by a five x five symmetric matrix to form an eight-way ranking.	b. Facilities	
32e Members' Staff Offices	Combine House and Senate by a four x four symmetric matrix to form a five-way ranking. Combine above two groupings by a five x eight matrix, eight-edge dominant, into a fifteen-way ranking and consolidate into a nine-way grouping. Combine the two nine-way rankings by a nine x nine matrix with "Available Service and Professional Assistants"-edge dominant to form a twenty-two-way ranking.		

449

Question Number and Short Title	Procedure Used	Subcriteria and Weights	Criteria
39, Frequency and Magni- 196 tude of Departures from "Ideal"	Combine House and Senate by sum of squares in increasing order to form a thirty-five-way rank-ing, and consolidate into a four-way grouping	8. Treatment of Minority (14) a. Standing Committees	Member Effective- ness (cont.)
77a,b Minority Pro- portional Mem- bership on Management/ Rules Committees	Combine House and Senate by number of "yes" answers to form two three-way rankings, and combine these by a three x three symmetric matrix to form a six-way ranking.	b. Rules and Management Committees	
32c Minority Officing	Combine House and Senate by number of "yes" answers to form a three-way ranking.	c. Officing	
78a,c Minority Leader Appoints Minority Committee Members	Combine House and Senate by number of "yes" answers to form a three-way ranking.	d. Minority Leader's Powers	
78d,d Minority Leader Is on Management Committee	Combine House and Senate by number of "yes" answers to form a three-way ranking, and com-bine with the one just above by sum of rankings to form a five-way ranking. Combine Parts a, b, c, and d by weighted sum of normalized rankings to form a twenty-nine-way ranking.		
126 Published Rules	Combine House and Senate by sum of "yes" answers into a one-way ranking, and then combine 126, 128, 127 (in this order) by three-way rule to form a six-way ranking.	9. Known Rules (15) a. House Rules	
128 Joint Rules			
127 Back-up Rules			
100 Published Rules on Committee Jurisdictions	Combine House and Senate by sum of "yes" answers into a three-way ranking.	b. Committee Rules	
101 Referral Practices	Score "always" better than "frequently" better than "sometimes/never," and combine House and Senate by a three x three symmetric matrix to form a five-way ranking.		
52 Uniform Committee Rules	Combine House and Senate by sum of "yes" answers into a three-way ranking. Combine questions 100 and 101 by a three x five special-form matrix (see Matrix D) to form a five-way ranking, and combine with question 52 by a three x five modified symmetric matrix to form an eight-way ranking.		
13a,b Procedural Orientation and Coverage	Combine House and Senate on pre-session orientation by sum of "yes" answers to form a three-way grouping, and within these groups rank by number of "yes" answers to types of coverage to form an eight-way ranking.	c. Procedural Orientation	
13c Duration	Consolidate House and Senate into two four-way		

Question Number and Short Title	Procedure Used	Subcriteria and Weights	Criteria
	groupings and combine by a four x four symmetric matrix to form a five-way ranking. Combine these two by a five x eight special-form matrix (see Matrix E) to form an eight-way ranking. Finally, combine a, b, and c by a weighted sum of normalized rankings to obtain a thirty-eight-way ranking.	Procedural Orientation (cont.)	Member Effectiveness (cont.)
118 Separate Day Reading by Title Only	Combine House and Senate by sum of "yes" answers into a three-way ranking. Finally, combine all the subcriteria by a weighted sum of normalized rankings to form a fifty-one-way representative ranking.	10. Bill Reading (2)	

Matrix A

Groups	1	2	3	4
(Yes) 1	1	2	5	7
(No) 2	3	4	6	8

Matrix B

Groups	1	2	3	4	5	6	7	8
(Better) 1	1	2	3	4	13	14	19	19
(Same) 2	5	6	7	8	15	16	20	20
(None) 3	9	10	11	12	17	18	21	21

Matrix C

	1	2	3	4	5	6
1	1	2	4	7	11	16
2	2	3	5	8	12	17

Matrix D

	1	2	3	4	5
1	2	2	7	7	
	3	4	4	8	8
	5	6	6	9	9

Matrix E

	1	2	3	4	5	6	7	8
1	1	1	2	2	3	3	4	4
2	2	2	3	3	4	4	5	5
3	3	3	4	4	5	5	6	6
4	7	7	7	7	7	7	7	7
5	8	8	8	8	8	8	8	8

Appendix D is the documentation for the computer programs used to classify the data and to perform the
FAIIR rankings.

BM10X--CCSL LES PROJECT RANKED TABLES PROGRAM

The program BM10 is specifically designed to calculate tables ranked by state from the base data of the CCSL LES project questionnaire. Control cards are used to specify the combinations wanted from the base data.

Each question in the base data is a fifty-one-state vector containing twenty character columns of coded data for each state and one "test" state. A BM10X data vector is completely identified by the question number, the starting column number, and the number of columns in the base data.

Each ranked table may deal with up to eight such data vectors. For ranking purposes, each element of a data vector is assigned a numeric value. A numeric code may stand for itself as its own value, or an ID block may be specified to assign values to each possible code or to a range of numeric codes.

The ranking process combines a set of data vectors into a vector result which is sorted into ascending or descending order. Normally, this result is assigned rank numbers (1, 2, 3, . . .) where states of equal result value have the same rank.

The result vector of a table generation may be stored and referenced in a later table.

Input to BM10X consists of alternate records of ID blocks and table generation cards. The first two cards in each table generation record are taken as a title and subtitle.

ID Blocks

An ID block specifies a set of value assignments corresponding to a set of data codes and, further, assigns a ten-character label to each data code for printout purposes.

ID Block Header Card

Columns 1-2	Two-character block name (never blank-blank).
Column 3	One-digit, column-width specification (blank, or $\emptyset$ through 9, where blanks, $\emptyset$, and 1 all mean 1).
Column 13	Same as column 3 if column is blank.

Code-Label-Value Card

Columns 1-8	Data code. Up to eight columns, depending on width specified in the header.
Columns 9-18	Ten-character label for code.
Columns 19-20	Two-digit value associated with the specified code and label (-9 to 99). If field is blank, a value equal to the card position in the block is assigned (card 6 would have value 6).
Columns 21-80	Ignored.

ID Block Terminator Card

Columns 1-3	END.
Columns 4-10	Blank.
Columns 11-80	Ignored.

Up to seventy ID blocks may be specified in each record, each block with up to thirty code-label-value cards.

When the ID block is used, the data code is compared with each code in the block. If a match is found, the corresponding label and value are assigned. If no match is found, the last code-label-value specified in the block is used.

SAMPLE ID BLOCK

Card Column	1	9	19
Block Header Card	AB2		
	11	YES YES	
	Ø1	NO YES	Ø1
Code-Label-Value Cards	1Ø	YES NO	Ø2
	1-	YES N/A	Ø1
	ØØ	NO NO	Ø3
		NO ANSWER	99
		REJECT	99
Terminator Card	END		

This block specifies a two-character code set covering a pair of "yes/no" answers coded as 1/Ø, with one special case "yes-not applicable" coded as 1-, and the normal "no answer" and "*reject*" (if no match is found) cases. When the identifier, AA, is used on a data vector specification card, values and labels would be assigned according to the specified codes.

Table Generation Cards

The generation of a table result vector is effected by collecting various operation and specification cards up to a table command card.

Data Vector Card

A data vector card specifies the question number, the column number, and the character width which defines the data vector within the base data. It also gives an operator which specifies how the vector is to be combined with the result of previous data vector cards in building the current table result. If the data vector codes are not to be treated as numerics, a non-blank ID block name in the previous ID block record should be used to give values to the codes. Two twelve-character fields define a name or column header to identify the vector in the table printout.

Columns 1-3	Question number (ØØ1 to 199, leading zeros must be specified).
Column 4	Ignored.
Columns 5-6	Starting column number from the base data minus 10 (column 11 is Ø1). If this field is left blank or zero, the question number in columns 1-3 will be used as an internal vector storage address.
Column 7	Data code width in characters (Ø to 9, where Ø or blank means 1).
Column 8	Ignored.
Column 9	Operator character.
Column 10	Ignored.
Columns 11-12	ID block name.
Columns 14-25	Column header, part 1.
Columns 26-37	Column header, part 2.
Columns 38-80	Ignored.

456

Data Vector Card Operator Characters

A data vector may be added to, subtracted from, multiplied by, or divided into the accumulating table vector result. The blank operator is normally addition, but when no ID block is specified on the data vector card (code is numeric), it becomes a subtract (the anomaly forces descending rank for numbers where ascending rank is used). The arithmetic operators are ignored if a "way" or "distance" table is generated.

The period operator causes the data vector to be ignored in the table result. This is used to print a column in the table for information only.

The operator X causes the next two cards to be read as fifty-one two-digit values (-9 to 99) into the internal vector storage address specified by the question number field. All other fields are ignored. The data cards read start in column 3, with thirty-nine values on the first card and twelve on the second. The data vector card with an X operator is not counted in the table, nor is it printed.

The grouping operator (=) declares that the ID block specified defines a grouping of the data codes (numeric). All codes in the ID block are numeric with a decimal point coded.

The codes specified in the ID block are compared with the data code, and a match is found if the data code is numerically greater than the ID block code.

Hence

```
QQ6
  .ØØ5  GROUP 1   Ø1
- .ØØ1  GROUP 2   1Ø
        *REJECT*  99
END
```

will cause data vector element codes that are greater than Ø.ØØ5 to be labeled "GROUP 1" and valued at Ø1, whereas codes that are greater than -.ØØ1 but less than or equal to Ø.ØØ5 to be labeled "GROUP 2" and valued at 1Ø. Any codes less than or equal to -.ØØ1 will be labeled "*REJECT*."

Table Vector Result Initialization

Normally, the vector result is initialized to zero, but value initialization cards allow a non-zero initial vector to be collected.

| Column 1 | Operation code (+,-,*, or /). |
| Column 2-10 | Value with decimal point coded. |

Hence:

```
+1ØØ.Ø

/3

+1.
```

will initialize the data vector to 34 1/3.

Command Cards

Command cards cause some specific action. Most of the command cards cause generation of a table.

Column 1	Command letter (see below for range of possible letters).
Column 2	Command letter if column 1 is blank.
Column 3-4	If non-blank, a two-digit number (1 to 39) specifying the internal vector storage address where the table result vector is to be stored.

457

Columns 5-80   Ignored.

The command characters R, Q, V, U, and X cause combination of the data vectors as specified by the data vector cards.

R   Result is the ascending rank value.

Q   Result is the descending rank value.

V   Result is the result value (printed in ascending order).

U   Result is the result value (printed in descending order).

X   Result is the result value (not printed).

The command W causes combination of the data vectors by the "way" rule, where the data vectors are specified in decreasing order of importance. The result is formed from an ascending rank of the first vector, which ranks are subranked on the second vector, etc. The result is an ascending rank value.

The commands D, C, F, and E cause combination of the data vectors by the "distance rule." The resultant vector is the sum of the squares of the data vectors.

D   Sum of the squares of (100 minus the data vector), the result is the
           ascending rank values.

C   Sum of the squares of the data vector, the result is the descending rank
           values.

F   Sum of the squares of (100 minus the data vector), result is the sum
           value.

E   Sum of the squares of the data vector, the result is the sum value.

Miscellaneous Commands

P   Suppresses printing of the current table in progress.

T·   Causes the next card to be read as a new title.

S   Causes the next card to be read as a new subtitle card.

The Matrix Combination

Pairs of data vector cards may be re-evaluated by use of a matrix declaration.

Column 1   M or N,M reads the matrix as two-digit values (-9, 99);
                  N reads the matrix as four-digit values (-999, 9999).

Column 2   Same as column 1 if column 1 is blank.

Column 3-4   Column count of matrix (1 to 52).

Columns 5-6   Row count of matrix (1 to 52).

Following the matrix card, BM10X expects to read one dummy row and then the number of rows specified on the matrix card. Each row may require one, two, or three cards, depending on the number of columns specified. Each card starts in column 3. Columns 1-2 are ignored.

458

Hence

M Ø3Ø4
```
     1 2 3
 1   1 2 4
 2   2 3 5
 3   4 5 6
 4   7 8 9
```

specifies a three-column by four-row matrix with values from 1 to 9.

The matrix is filled with 100.0 outside the area specified (up to 52 x 52).

The matrix combination references the matrix, using the values of the two preceding data vector cards as indexes, the first for column and the second for row. The effect in the table result is as if the first data vector were zero and the second contained the appropriate values from the matrix.

Special Cases Involving Internal Vector Storage

Since table results are values and not codes, only a grouping (=) operator can assign labels and new values to data vectors taken from internal vector storage.

If the table result stored in an internal data vector is negative but wants to be treated as positive, the column width specified on the data vector card must be non-zero (otherwise it is normally blank). This applies only to tables generated by the "distance" rule and data vector cards evaluated using the grouping operator (=).

System Information

Files for BM10X

BM10X uses three files, INPUT, OUTPUT, and BWORK

PROGRAM BM10X (INPUT, OUTPUT, BWORK)

The file INPUT contains alternate logical records of ID block definitions and table specification cards. The file OUTPUT receives the printed table output.

The file BWORK is a condensed binary version of the base data tape. BWORK has fifty-one binary records of length 400. Each record contains the twenty data code characters for each of the 200 questions for that single state. The file BWORK is generated from the state order base data file by the program BM4.

PROGRAM BM4 (TAPE 1, BWORK)

Since BWORK is accessed repeatedly by BM10X, it should be disk-resident.

System Compatibilities

BM10X uses COMPASS assembly language routines, which use RUN Fortran subroutine calling structure. These are all CDC 6400 Scope 3.1 products.

The code and file structure are dependent on CDC 6400 word and character size and on SCOPE system files.

COMPUTER DATA STRUCTURE FOR THE CCSL LES PROJECT

Machine data for the CCSL LES Project was coded from state questionnaires consisting of 156 questions each. The fifty-first state was a "test" state.

The data were coded into eighty-column card images whose contents are described in the "green sheets" or master data-coding guide. The card structure was as follows.

Column 1-2	State Number	
	$\emptyset1 - 5\emptyset$	States listed alphabetically by state name.
	51	The "test" state.
Columns 3-5	Question Number	
	$\emptyset\emptyset1 - 199$	Question numbers.
	Above 156	Pseudo question numbers whose data is coded from annotations, continuations, and hand combinations of the original 156 questionnaire set.
Column 6	Annotation Code	
		No annotations.
	1	Annotation of additional information.
	2	Coding problem.
	3	Resolved coding problem.
	4	Coding problem needing reference to state.
	5	Coding problem resolved by reference to state.
Columns 7-10	Identification Code	Which part of the question the annotation refers to.
Columns 11-30	Question Data	
	Column location and codes for data are detailed in the "green sheets."	
Columns 31-79	Annotations	
	Natural language annotations and comments.	
Column 80	Annotation Continuation Code	
	A, B, C, $\cdots$, Z	Letter continuation code.

The master data tape has two files of card images (trailing blanks truncated) and is unlabeled, even parity, BCD at 556 BPI.

The first file contains the data card images sorted by state and subsorted by question. The second file contains the data card images sorted by question and subsorted by state.

The tape was written on a Control Data 604 tape drive by CAL SCOPE 3.1/2.5 X 96.81 (University of California at Berkeley) in October, 1970.

460

Appendix E is an index to the questions used, in numerical order and by appearance within the FAIIR criteria.

Question Number	Component	Short Title	Functional	Accountability	Information	Independence	Representativeness	Omitted
1		Years Used for Data						X
2		Session Patterns						X
3 (178)		Restrictions on Session Length	1		1	1a		
4		Actual Time Used			1			
5a		Limits on Compensable Days						X
b		Limits on Reimbursable Days						X
6a		Legislative Power to Call Special Sessions				1b		
b		Methods of Calling Special Sessions				1b		
7a,b		Time for Budget Review						X
c		Pre-Submitted Analysis				7		
8a		Veto Sessions				5b		
b		Legislative Power to Convene Veto Sessions				5b		
9a,b,c		Effective Dates of Statutes						X
d		Procedures for Emergency Timing						X
10a,b		Compactness						X
11a (162)		Work Flow Management	2	6				
b (162)		Scheduling Devices	2	6				
c		Logjam Indicator--Bills						X
d		Logjam Indicator-- Committees						X
12		Official Organizational Session	3					
13a,b		Procedural Orientation and Coverage					9c	
c		Duration					9c	
14a-f (163)		Pre-session Post-Election Activities	3		2			
g-h		Pre-session Post-Election Activities						X
15a		Expansion of Special Session Agenda				1b		

463

Question Number	Component	Short Title	Functional	Accountability	Information	Independence	Representativeness	Omitted
b		Vote Requirements				1b		
16		Interim Programs						X
17(186)		Limitations on Interim Program			6	1c		
18		Interim Meeting Days						X
19a,b		Interim Planning and Coordination		6	6			
20		Staffing						X
21a(175)		Services Available				4a		
(188-190)	Rows 1,2,3	Technical Drafting Services			14			
"	Rows 4,5,6	Code Research and Code Revision			-14	-		
"	Row 7	Study of Resources and Expenditures				9		
"	Row 9	Post-Audit Services Available				10		
"	Row 10	Program Review and Evaluation				9		
"	Row 16	Press Officer		10d				
"	Rows 7,8,9, 10,11,12,13	Coverage of Fiscal Staff Services			16a			
"	Rows 10,14, 15,17,18,19, 20,21	Coverage of Staff Services			13			
21b and c (166)	"Members Col."	Availability of Staff Services to Members					7a	
(164-166)	Rows 1,2	Availability of Legal Staff			14			
(164-166)	Row 3	Availability of Fiscal Analysis			16b			
(164-166)	Cols. 1,2 Rows 4,5,6	Availability of General Research Services						X
(167)	Col. 4 only	Availability of Services						X
22a,b,c (168,160)		Professional Staff Size/Population				4b		
23a,b		Characteristics of Staff						X
24		Washington Office			13	4a		
25a,b		Clerical Support						X

Question Number	Component	Short Title	Func-tional	Account-ability	Infor-mation	Indepen-dence	Repre-senta-tive-ness	Omitted
26a1,2		Personal Aides to Leaders and Members	4					
a1,2	Last 2 Rows	Staff for Non-Leaders				7a		
b		Compensations of Staff						X
27		Clerks' and Secretaries' Office						X
28a,b		Quality of Chambers	5					
29a,b		Sound Systems						X
30a,b	Rows 1,6	Special Facilities and Equipment	5					
	Row 1	Electric Roll Call	14	8				
	Row 2	Telephones						X
	Row 3	Audio-Visual Equipment						X
	Row 4	Visitors' Gallery		7				
	Row 5	Press Facilities in Chambers		10b				
	Row 6	Clerks' Work Area	8					
	Row 7	Office Location	6					
31a,b		Leadership Offices	6					
32a		Members' Offices--Quantity	9				7b	
b		District Offices					1	
c		Minority Officing					8c	
d		Minority Officing						X
e		Members' Staff Offices	9				7b	
f		Members' Offices--Quantity	9					
g		Lounges	9					
h		Dining Facilities						X
33a		Auditorium Room	7	7	5			
b		Committee Room	7		5			
c		Room Quality	7		5			
d(174)		Special Equipment	7		5			
e(174)		Press Equipment in Committee Rooms		10a				

Question Number	Component	Short Title	Functional	Accountability	Information	Independence	Representativeness	Omitted
34a		Caucus Facilities						X
b		Caucus Equipment						X
35a		News Conference Rooms		10c				
b		Press Offices		10c				
c		Technical Equipment and Data		10b				
36		Parking	9					
37a		Clerks' and Secretaries' Offices	8					
b		Service Agencies for Whole Body	8					
c,d		Service Agencies in Houses						X
38		Number of Standing Committees	11	3	3		5	
39		Interim Meeting Days of Standing Committees						X
39(196)	Col. 1,2,3	Minority Membership on Standing Committees		14a			8a	
	Part I	Frequency of Departure from "Ideal"		14a			8a	
	Part 2	Magnitude of Departure from "Ideal"		14a			8a	
40a		Number of Joint Committees						X
b		Provisions for Use	13					
c		Session Use	13					
d		Interim Use						X
41		Joint Committee Reportage	13					
42a		Committee Assignments/ Member	11		3			
b		List of Committee Chairmen						X
43		Selection of Committee Chairmen		13b			6b	
	"Actual" Col.	Selection of Committee Chairmen		2				
44		Selection of Committee Members		13b			6b	
45(185)		Standing Committees with Interim Status	11		7			

Question Number	Component	Short Title	Functional	Accountability	Information	Independence	Representativeness	Omitted
46a		Secret Sessions		7				
b		Automatic Kill						X
47a		Open Hearings		7				
b		Solicitation of Public Testimony			4			
c		Permit Live Coverage of Committees		10a~				
d		Advance Written Submission of Testimony			4			
48a,b,c		Committee Votes (Taken, Recorded, Published)		8				
49a,b,c		Advance Notice of Meetings and Agendas		7	4			
50a,b		Form of Committee Records		8				
51		Committee Quorum Requirements					4	
52		Uniform Committee Rules		4a			9b	
53a,b		Required Action on Referred Bills	15	5				
c		Required Action on Referred Bills						X
54		Majority Power on Committee Agenda		13f			6c	
55		Majority Report Without Chairmen		13f			6c	
56a,b		Member Control on Bills in Committee		13e			6e	
57		Member Control over Items in Committee Reports	14	13e			6e	
58		Member Power to Withdraw and Recommit		13e			6e	
59		Block Approval of Committee Recommendations						X
60a,b,c (179)		Treatment of Favorably Reported Bills	15	13c			6d	
a		Floor Action on Bills "Do Pass"-ed by Committees		5				
61		Subpoena Powers, Standing Committees			4	4d		
62		Dual Committee Review			15			

Question Number	Component	Short Title	Functional	Accountability	Information	Independence	Representativeness	Omitted
63		Size of Conference Committees		13d			4	
64		Powers of Conference Committees		13d			6f	
65a		Action by Conference Committees	15	5,13d			6f	
b		Members' Powers on Dissolution of Conference Committees		13d			6f	
66		Selection of Conference Committee Chairmen		2				
67		Role of Leadership on Management Committees						X
68		Powers of Management Committees						X
69a		Overlaying Rules Committee Membership	19					
b		Minority Participation in Inter-House Coordination	19					
70a,b		Interim Committee Reports		8	8			
c		Legislative Proposals			8			
71		Subpoena Powers, Interim Committees			6	4d		
72		Structure of Interim Activities						X
73		Number of Interim Committees						X
	Cols. 1,2,3	Minority Membership of Interim Committees						X
	Col. 5	Professional Staffing						X
	Col. 7	Interim Meeting Days--Interim Committee						X
74a,b (195)		Selection of Leadership		2,13a			6a	
a_2,b_2		Breadth of Leadership		13a			6a	
75a,c		Terms of Presiding Officers						X
b,d		Self-Succession	18					
76	Rows 1-3	Powers of Presiding Officers	18					
	Rows 4,5	Powers of Presiding Officers						X

Question Number	Component	Short Title	Functional	Accountability	Information	Independence	Representativeness	Omitted
	Row 6	Speaker in Line for Succession to Governorship	20					
77a		Minority Membership in Management and Rules Committees		14b			8b	
78a,c		Minority Leaders' Powers		14c			8d	
b,d		Minority Leader on Management Committee		14c			8d	
79		Size of House and Senate	10	3			5	
80		Range of House Membership						X
81		Source of Size Limitation						X
82		Nature of Limitations on House Size						X
83		Districting		1			1	
84		Reapportionment				3		
85		Staggered Terms						X
86a(183, 161)		Qualifications for Office					2	
b		Source of Qualification Requirements						X
87		Partisanship						X
88a		Raise Budget Items				7		
b		Lower Budget Items						X
c		Vote Requirements to Override Veto Appropriations						X
89		Budget Roles			15	7		
90a,b		Pocket Veto				5a		
c		Vote Requirement to Override Veto						X

469

Question Number	Component	Short Title	Functional	Accountability	Information	Independence	Representativeness	Omitted
91a		"Sum Certain" or "Sum Sufficient" Budget		6				
b		Legislative Control of Legislative Expenditures				2		
92		Printed Bills		9a	10			
93		Statement of Legislative Intent		9a	10			
94		Summary of Contents		9a	10			
95		Fiscal Notes Required			17			
96		Fiscal Notes by Legislative Agency			17	4a		
97		Fiscal Notes by Executive Agency							X
98		Long-Range Coverage of Fiscal Notes							X
99		Use of Committee Bills	12					
100		Committee Jurisdictions	15	4b			9b	
101		Referral Practice	15	4b			9b	
102		Bills Only by Legislators	12			8		
103		Multiple and Joint Authorship	12					
104		Skeleton Bills		9a	10			
105		Exceptions to Bill Deadlines	16					
106		Frequency of Deadline Exceptions						X
107		Quantity Printing on Introductions		9b	11			
108		Quantity Printing After Amendment		9b	11			
109		Oversize Runs						X
110		Central Distribution		9b	11			
111		Printing Delay After Amendment	2	9c	12			
112		Identification of Textual Changes		9c	12			
113		One-Subject Bills		9a	10			
114		Bill Carry-Over	17					

Question Number	Component	Short Title	Func-tional	Account-ability	Infor-mation	Indepen-dence	Repre-senta-tive-ness	Omitted
115		Time Lag on Bill Referral	2, 15	5				
116a		Consent Calendar	14					
b		Scheduling Devices						X
117		Multiple Readings in Full	14					
118		Separate Day Reading by Title only					10	
119		Frequency Rules Governing Reading and Calendaring Suspended						X
120		Vote Requirement on General Statutes						X
121		Vote Requirement on Tax Measures						X
122		Extraordinary Vote for Emergency Legislation						X
123		Roll Call on Final Passages		8				
124		Provisions to Limit Debate	16					
125a		Amendments from the Floor	16					
b		Requirements to Amend	16					
126		Published Rules					9a	
127		Back-up Rules		4a			9a	
128		Joint Rules	19	4a			9a	
129		Permit Live Floor Coverage		10b				
130		Floor Privileges	20					
131		Escape Clause in Restric-tions of Guests						X
132		Restriction on House of Origin	12					
133		Percentage Bills Vetoed for Technical Reasons						X
134		Percentage Bills Passed to Correct Earlier Bills						X
135		Salary					3a	
136		Base for Salaries	20					
137(191)		Method of Setting Legisla-tive Salaries				2		

Question Number	Component	Short Title	Functional	Accountability	Information	Independence	Representativeness	Omitted
138		Effective Date of Legislative Salary						X
139	Row 1	Source of Limitations on Salary						X
	Row 2	Source of Limitations on Expense Allowance						X
	Row 3	Source of Limitations on Retirement Benefits						X
	Row 4	Source of Limitations on Non-Calculable Benefits				2		
140		Maximum Expense Allowances						X
141(192)		Method of Setting Expense Allowances				2		
142		Retirement Provisions					3c	
143		Travel Reimbursements					3b	
144		Authorization of Leadership Differentials						X
145		Information on Compensation		11				
146		Conflict-of-Interest Laws				12		
147a,b		Mandatory Disclosure of Income		11				
c,d		Mandatory Disclosure of Income						X
148		Prohibition of Legal Practice				12		
149		Prohibition of Other Business				12		
150		Prohibition against Dual Public Empolyment				12		
151		Employment of Legislator's Families				12		
152		Accepting Appointments During Term of Office				12		
153		Lobby Registration		12		11		
154		Penalties for Failure to Disclose		12		11		
155		Advisory Body on Conflicts of Interest						X
156a,b		Bill Status and History			9			

Question Number	Component	Short Title	Func-tional	Account-ability	Infor-mation	Indepen-dence	Repre-senta-tive-ness	Omitted
New Element (184)		Role of Lieutenant Governor				6		
New Element (194)		Legislative Expenditure (Total per Capita)				4c		
New Element (194)		Legislative Expenditure as Percent of State Budget				4c		

BIBLOGRAPHY

Because of the availability of current bibliographies in the general area of comparative state governments, this bibliography deals only narrowly with literature linking legislative policies to demographic, social, economic, and other measurable variables. (A more general bibliography is CCSL, "Selected Bibliography on State Legislatures," June, 1968.)

Blalock, Herbert, Jr. Social Statistics. New York: McGraw-Hill, 1960.

_____. Casual Inferences in Nonexperimental Research. Chapel Hill: University of North Carolina Press, 1964.

Cnudde, Charles, and McCrone, Donald. "Party Competition and Welfare Policies in the American States," American Political Science Review, LXIII, 3 (September, 1969), 858-66.

Cowart, Andrew T. "Anti-Poverty Expenditures in the American States: A Comparative Analysis," Midwest Journal of Political Science, XIII, 2 (May, 1964), 219-36.

Crew, Robert E., Jr. "Dimensions of Public Policy: A Factor Analysis of State Expenditures," Social Science Quarterly, L, 2 (September, 1969), 381-88.

Crittenden, John. "Dimensions of Modernization in the American States," American Political Science Review, LXI, 4, 989-1001.

Dawson, Richard E. "Social Development, Party Competition, and Policy." American Party Systems. Edited by William N. Chambers and Walter Dean Burnham. New York: Oxford University Press, 1967.

_____, and James Robinson. "The Politics of Welfare." Politics in the American States. Edited by Herbert Jacob and Kenneth Vines. Boston: Little, Brown and Company, 1965.

Dye, Thomas. "Malapportionment and Public Policy in the States," Journal of Politics, XXVII, 3 (1965), 586-601.

_____. Politics, Economics, and the Public: Policy Outcomes in the American States. Chicago: Rand McNally & Co., 1966.

_____. "Income Inequality and American State Politics," American Political Science Review, LXIII (March, 1969), 157-62.

Elazar, Daniel J. _American Federalism: A View From the States_. New York: Thomas Y. Crowell, 1966.

Fenton, John H. _People and Parties in Politics_. Glenview, Ill.: Scott, Foresman & Co., 1966.

_____, and Donald Chamberlayne. "The Literature Dealing with the Relationships Between Political Processes, Socioeconomic Conditions and Public Policies in the American States: A Bibliographical Essay," _Polity_, I, 3 (Spring, 1969), 388-404.

Francis, Wayne A. _Legislative Issues in the Fifty States: A Comparative Analysis_. Chicago: Rand McNally & Co., 1967.

Fry, Brian R., and Richard F. Winters. "The Politics of Redistribution." A paper delivered at Sixty-fifth Annual Meeting, American Political Science Association, New York, 1969.

Grumm, John G. "Structural Determinants of Legislative Output." _Legislatures in Developmental Perspective_. Edited by Allan Kornberg and Lloyd D. Musolf. Durham, North Carolina: Duke University Press, 1970.

Hofferbert, Richard. "The Relation Between Public Policy and Some Structural and Evironmental Variables in the American States," _American Political Science Review_, LX, 1 (1966), 73-82.

_____. "Ecological Development and Policy Change in the American States," _Midwest Journal of Political Science_, X, 4 (November, 1966), 464-83.

_____. "Socioeconomic Dimensions of the American States: 1890-1960," _ibid_. XII, 3 (August, 1968), 401-18.

_____. "Elite Influence in State Policy Formation: A Model for Comparative Inquiry," _Polity_, II, 3 (1970), 316-44.

Jacob, Herbert. "The Consequences of Malapportionment: A Note of Caution," _Social Forces_, XLIII, 2 (1964), 256-61.

_____, and Michael Lipsky. "Outputs, Structure and Power: An Assessment of Changes in the Study of State and Local Politics," _Journal of Politics_, XXX, 2 (1968), 510-38.

_____, and Kenneth Vines, eds. _Politics in the American States_. Boston: Little, Brown & Co., 1965.

Lockard, Duane. "State Party Systems and Policy Outputs." Political Research and Political Theory. Edited by Oliver Garceau. Cambridge, Massachusetts.: Harvard University Press, 1968.

McCrone, Donald J., and Charles Cnudde. "On Measuring Public Policy." State Politics. Edited by R. E. Crew, Jr. Belmont, California.: Wadsworth Publishing Co., Inc., 1962.

Patterson, Samuel C. "The Political Cultures of the American States," Journal of Politics, XXX (February, 1968), 187-209.

Sharkansky, Ira. "Economic and Political Correlates of State Government Expenditures: General Tendencies and Deviant Cases," Midwest Journal of Political Science, XI, 2 (1967), 173-92.

_____. "Government Expenditures and Public Services in the American States," American Political Science Review, LXI, 4 (1967), 1066-77.

_____. "Some More Thoughts About the Determinants of Government Expenditures," National Tax Journal, XX, 3 (September, 1967), 171-79.

_____. Spending in the American States. Chicago: Rand-McNally & Co., 1968.

_____. "Economic Development, Regionalism and State Political Systems," Midwest Journal of Political Science, XII, 1 (February, 1968), 41-61.

_____. "Regionalism, Economic Status and the Public Policies of American States," Social Science Quarterly, XLIX, 1 (June, 1968), 9-26.

_____. "The Utility of Elazar's Political Culture: A Research Note," Polity, II, 1 (Fall, 1969), 66-83.

_____, ed. "Regionalism, Economic Status, and Public Policies." Policy Analysis in Political Science. Chicago: Markham Publishing Co., 1970.

_____, and Richard Hofferbert. "Dimensions of State Politics, Economics, and Public Policy," American Political Science Review, LXIII, 3 (September, 1969), 867-79.

Walker, Jack L. "The Diffusion of Innovations Among the American States," American Political Science Review, LXIII, 3 (September, 1969), 880-99.

Young, Ruth C., and José Moreno. "Economic Development and Social Rigidity: A Comparative Study of the Forty-Eight States," <u>Economic Development and Cultural Change</u>, XII, 4, Pt. I (July, 1965), 439-52.

The Citizens Conference on State Legislatures is a non-partisan, non-profit organization formed in 1965 by leaders from business, education, labor, agriculture and government, and is a part of a wider national effort to improve the effectiveness of state government. It began as a private sector response to requests for educational and service assistance to the modernization of state legislatures in order to elevate the competence and efficiency of the state legislative bodies.

The organization is supported by grants from private foundations and from contributions from business and labor. Substantial support has come from The Ford Foundation, The Carnegie Corporation of New York, Rockefeller Brothers Fund and The Sears Roebuck Foundation. The CCSL is directed by a national Board of Trustees headed by Salt Lake City publisher John W. Gallivan, and is advised by a national Program Development Committee, chaired by Horace Sheldon, Director of the Governmental Affairs Office for The Ford Motor Company. The President of the Citizens Conference is former Kansas Governor John Anderson, Jr. A staff of 25 is under the supervision of Larry Margolis, Executive Director.

The Conference has been successful in helping to identify problems in the various states. It has worked with successful programs in more than half of the states in the nation. The CCSL conducts its activities within the framework of the Tax Reform Act of 1969. It conducts non-partisan research and study and makes the resulting information available to the general public. Technical assistance is provided to governmental officials and agencies upon proper authorization. Contributions to the CCSL, a 501 (c) (3) organization, are tax deductible.